Lecture Notes in Computer Science 16040

Founding Editors

Gerhard Goos
Juris Hartmanis

The series Lecture Notes in Computer Science (LNCS), including its subseries Lecture Notes in Artificial Intelligence (LNAI) and Lecture Notes in Bioinformatics (LNBI), has established itself as a medium for the publication of new developments in computer science and information technology research, teaching, and education.

LNCS enjoys close cooperation with the computer science R & D community, the series counts many renowned academics among its volume editors and paper authors, and collaborates with prestigious societies. Its mission is to serve this international community by providing an invaluable service, mainly focused on the publication of conference and workshop proceedings and postproceedings. LNCS commenced publication in 1973.

Anne Remke · Bernhard Steffen
Editors

Formal Methods for Industrial Critical Systems

30th International Conference, FMICS 2025
Aarhus, Denmark, August 27–28, 2025
Proceedings

 Springer

Editors
Anne Remke 🆔
University of Münster
Münster, Germany

Bernhard Steffen 🆔
Technische Universität Dortmund
Dortmund, Germany

ISSN 0302-9743   ISSN 1611-3349 (electronic)
Lecture Notes in Computer Science
ISBN 978-3-032-00941-8   ISBN 978-3-032-00942-5 (eBook)
https://doi.org/10.1007/978-3-032-00942-5

This Springer imprint is published by the registered company Springer Nature Switzerland AG
The registered company address is: Gewerbestrasse 11, 6330 Cham, Switzerland

If disposing of this product, please recycle the paper.

Preface

As Program Chairs we would like to welcome the reader to the proceedings of FMICS 2025, the 30th International Conference on Formal Methods for Industrial Critical Systems, which took place in Aarhus, Denmark on August 27–28, 2025.

The aim of the FMICS conference series is to provide a forum for researchers and practitioners who are interested in the development and application of formal methods in industry. FMICS brings together scientists and engineers who are active in the area of formal methods and interested in exchanging their experiences in the industrial usage of these methods. The FMICS conference series also strives to promote research and development for the improvement of formal methods and tools for industrial applications.

FMICS is the ERCIM Working Group conference on Formal Methods for Industrial Critical Systems, and it is the key conference at the intersection of industrial applications and Formal Methods.

The program of FMICS 2025 consisted of 13 contributions selected from 24 submissions, complemented by two invited talks given by Ina Schieferdecker (TU Berlin) and Arnd Hartmanns (University of Twente).

FMICS 2025 was part of CONFEST 2025, an umbrella, hosting also the conferences CONCUR and QEST+FORMATS, as well as a number of pre- and post-conference workshops.

We were pleased to implement a single-blind review process of all submitted content, and we thank the members of the program committee and the reviewers for their effort in selecting the papers to be presented.

Moreover, we are grateful to Springer for being, as usual, a very reliable partner for the proceedings production, and to ERCIM for the continuous support. We hope all participants had lively scientific discussions at this edition of the event and also later, and we hope when reading these proceedings they find valuable new insights that support their research and its uptake.

June 2025

Anne Remke
Bernhard Steffen

Organization

Program Chairs

Anne Remke   University of Münster, Germany
Bernhard Steffen   TU Dortmund, Germany

Program Committee

Erika Ábrahám   RWTH Aachen University, Germany
Davide Basile   ISTI CNR Pisa, Italy
Pedro D'Argenio   Universidad Nacional de Córdoba, Argentina
Jennifer Davis   Collins Aerospace, USA
Luca Di Stefano   Technical University of Vienna, Austria
Hubert Garavel   Inria Grenoble Rhône-Alpes, France
Jan Friso Groote   Eindhoven University of Technology,
                                  The Netherlands
Matthias Güdemann   University of Applied Sciences Munich (HM),
                                  Germany
Paula Herber   University of Münster, Germany
Peter Hoefner   Australian National University, Australia
Jan Kretínsky   Masaryk University, Brno, Czech Republic
Tiziana Margaria   University of Limerick and Lero, Ireland
Mieke Massink   CNRS, ISTI, Pisa, Italy
Stephan Merz   Inria, Villers-lès-Nancy, France
Stefan Mitsch   DePaul University, USA
Rosemary Monahan   Maynooth University, Ireland
David Monniaux   CNRS, Verimag, Saint Martin d'Hères, France
Cristina Seceleanu   Mälardalen University, Sweden
Martina Seidl   Johannes Kepler University Linz, Austria
Monika Seisenberger   Swansea University, UK
Wendelin Serwe   Inria, Grenoble, France
Laura Titolo   Code Metal, USA
Virginie Wiels   ONERA, DTIS, Toulouse, France
Anton Wijs   Eindhoven University of Technology,
                                  The Netherlands
Zhen Zhang   Utah State University, Logan, USA
Petra van den Bos   University of Twente, Enschede, The Netherlands

Reviewers

Zachary Assoumani	Inria, France
Jore Booy	Eindhoven University of Technology, The Netherlands
Marie-Laure Potet	Grenoble-INP, VERIMAG, France
Maria Belen Rodriguez	University of Twente, The Netherlands
Jack Stodart	Australian National University, Australia
Landon Taylor	Utah State University, USA
Matthias Volk	Eindhoven University of Technology, The Netherlands

Contents

Cyber-Physical Systems

Embedded Systems

Invited Talks

Navigating the Growing Field of Research on AI for Software Testing – The Taxonomy for AI-Augmented Software Testing and an Ontology-Driven Literature Survey

Ina K. Schieferdecker$^{(\boxtimes)}$ (iD)

Technische Universität Berlin, Einsteinufer 25, 10587 Berlin, Germany
ina.schieferdecker@tu-berlin.de
https://www.tu-berlin.de

Abstract. In industry, software testing is the primary method to verify and validate the functionality, performance, security, usability, and so on, of software-based systems. Test automation has gained increasing attention in industry over the last decade, following decades of intense research into test automation and model-based testing. However, designing, developing, maintaining and evolving test automation is a considerable effort. Meanwhile, AI's breakthroughs in many engineering fields are opening up new perspectives for software testing, for both manual and automated testing. This paper reviews recent research on AI augmentation in software test automation, from no automation to full automation. It also discusses new forms of testing made possible by AI. Based on this, the newly developed taxonomy, *ai4st*, is presented and used to classify recent research and identify open research questions.

Keywords: Software Testing · Test Automation · Artificial Intelligence · *ai4st* · Software Engineering · Software Quality · Ontology · Semantic Web

1 Introduction

> "Testing with AI will take software test automation to the next level."

The integration of artificial intelligence (AI) within the fields of software engineering and software testing has become a prominent area of research. Various novel testing methods and tools are being discussed and presented, yet there is a lack of comprehensive reviews addressing the range of options for augmenting software testing with AI. The present paper aims to address this gap by providing an introductory overview of software testing, which forms the foundation for

A. Remke and B. Steffen (Eds.): FMICS 2025, LNCS 16040, pp. 3–20, 2025.
https://doi.org/10.1007/978-3-032-00942-5_1

elaborating novel testing methods enabled by AI and for developing a taxonomy on AI for software testing ($ai4st$):

Software testing is an essential part of the software development life cycle (SDLC) to ensure that software products are released with sufficient quality, reduced risks and minimized number of defects contained. Testing addresses both the verification of the software under test, i.e. whether the software is technically of high quality, and its validation, i.e. whether the software meets the requirements. Testing uses methods of code analysis, also known as static testing because the software is not being run, and execution analysis, also known as dynamic testing because the software is being run. Dynamic testing is conducted at different levels of software composition, for example, at component level for basic software components such as classes in object-oriented programming or functions in functional programming, at integration level for compositions of software components, and at system level where the complete software-based system is tested. Software testing can be performed manually for first impressions or when test automation is not cost-effective, and automatically when testing requires automation, for example for real-time testing, or when test repetition is more efficient with test automation. Test cases, executed manually or automatically, are designed and/or generated from software requirements, software designs, bug reports or other sources of information, collectively known as the test basis. Test cases can be defined abstractly, i.e. logically at a high level with abstract preconditions, inputs, expected outputs and expected postconditions, or concretely, i.e. at a lower level with detailed preconditions, inputs, expected outputs and expected postconditions. Test cases may also contain timing requirements or other actions and procedures to make them executable. Sets of test cases form test suites. Their execution is logged and analysed for missed preconditions or mismatches with expected outputs or postconditions. The evaluation of the test runs, including the mismatches, verifies the correctness of the test cases or reports failures of the software under test. Debugging is used to identify the root causes of these failures, i.e. the errors that lead to them.

Furthermore, effective monitoring and management of the overall testing process must be implemented to ensure or enhance the quality of the software produced. In close relation to the SDLC, the testing processes can vary in terms of size, phases, teams, and so forth. They can be sequential, iterative, agile, or they can follow the principles of the W-model [57]. However, they share the common phases of testing as defined by the fundamental testing process [58] being planning and control, analysis and design, implementation and execution, evaluation and reporting, and completion and teardown.

However, the utilisation of AI in testing is not fully realised when it is confined solely to these phases of the fundamental test process. While it is imperative to acknowledge that testing requires also more general approaches, such as project management or technical infrastructural management, which can also be improved with AI, it is necessary to delve further into the particularities of testing. And indeed, research publications on software testing with AI is steadily growing and so is the understanding of where and how to apply AI in testing is increasing. However, an overarching view relating AI support to the various testing activities and their processes is missing.

Taxonomies, and their formalisation as ontologies, are particularly useful for classifying and consolidating knowledge. They are powerful tools for organising, presenting and using knowledge effectively. They can act as a foundation for reasoning, interoperability and intelligent data usage. Ontologies are formalised, machine-readable representations of knowledge, extending and formalising taxonomies with additional semantics, constraints and logic. Unlike hierarchical taxonomies, ontologies enable richer querying, inference and relationship discovery.

Therefore, after reviewing taxonomies and ontologies on software testing in general and the use of AI for testing in particular in Sect. 2, an ontology dedicated to AI for software testing was developed and is presented in Sect. 3. Referred to as *ai4st*, this ontology can be used to classify contributions from research papers on using AI techniques to evolve and/or improve software testing activities and processes. Selected results are presented and discussed in Sect. 4. The paper concludes with an outline of future work in Sect. 5.

2   Related Work

According to [63], taxonomies have been proposed for every knowledge area of software engineering (SE) within the SE body of knowledge. These SE knowledge areas are defined in the SWEBOK [67] and include among others software testing fundamentals, test levels, test techniques, test-related measures, test process, software testing in the development processes and the application domains, testing of and testing through emerging technologies, and software testing tools.

However, although the highly detailed SWEBOK provides extensive descriptions of software engineering concepts, methods and techniques, including those for software testing, it does not define a comprehensive glossary or coherent taxonomy. This is somewhat surprising given the intensive discussion of the development of a SWEBOK ontology [2,55,68]. According to [63], no other overarching ontology besides SWEBOK has been proposed, except for numerous taxonomies specific to certain knowledge areas including software testing [14–16,46,64,65].

Taxonomies can be formally defined using first-order logic, the Web Ontology Language OWL [38] or the UML-based Ontology Modelling Language OntoUML [25]. OWL has attracted considerable interest, particularly due to its association with the Semantic Web and the support offered by the Protégé tool. Nevertheless, in most cases, there is no formally defined ontology available for taxonomies proposed in the literature that can be reused for classification purposes, e.g. for the classification of software test research contributions.

In addition, although numerous ontologies related to software testing (ST) exist [62], they are limited in their coverage of the research field, their ability to classify research contributions, and/or their relation to established glossaries and/or taxonomies: According to [7], ontologies for SE including ST are either generic, such as the software engineering ontology network SEON [5], or specific to a knowledge area, such as software testing like the Reference Ontology on Software Testing ROoST [56].

It is important to note that these two ontologies (and others, such as OntoTest [4] and TestTDO [61]) focus on the conceptual grounding of SE or ST concepts, respectively, with regard to their philosophical relations, rather than focusing on the established body of knowledge. A body of knowledge provides not just terms and relations, but also definitions, explanations, examples and/or best practices. Relevant bodies of knowledge for software testing include the SWEBOK [67], the SE terms by ISO, IEC and IEEE in [31], also known as SEVOCAB, and the ST terms by ISTQB in [32], also known as the ISTQB Glossary.

Furthermore, ROoST [56], being also part of SEON, OntoTest [4] or the ontology presented in [71] focus on dynamic testing only. Although TestTDO [61] includes static testing, it does not link to bodies of knowledge either.

It should also be noted that large-scale research taxonomies such as the Computer Science Ontology CSO [48] do not detail software testing. It categorises 'Testing and Debugging' as a research topic comprising 15 subtopics only. Similarly, the ACM Computing Classification System [47] only covers some aspects of software testing research.

In summary, and to the best of the author's knowledge, there is no software testing ontology that

- is formally defined, machine-processable, and downloadable as OWL (or in a comparable format),
- can be reused and extended for new application scenarios like software testing research classification,
- is closely linked to well-established and standardized bodies of knowledge, and
- covers the software testing knowledge area extensively.

The development of this ontology is described in the following section.

3   The Ontology for Artificial Intelligence in Software Testing – *ai4st*

In order to support the classification of research contributions in the area of using AI methods and techniques for the improvement of ST activities and processes, a dedicated taxonomy named *ai4st* has been developed by

- making primarily use of the terms defined by ISTQB [32][1],
- defining it in OWL [38] to support machine-processability,

---

[1] Where necessary, these terms are supplemented by SEVOCAB terms (see ISO 24765:2017). Where research exceeds the scope of standardised terminology, the author has provided the most accurate description possible.

– assigning the CC-BY-SA license [9] to support reuse, and
– providing it via GitHub [51] to enable contributions and/or the uptake by others.

Furthermore, the *ai4st* taxonomy is based on a four layer model consisting of

– the lightweight universal foundational ontology gUFO [3] for grounding,
– the software testing concept ontology stc [53],
– the AI for software engineering ontology *ai4se* [49], and
– the consolidated overarching *ai4st* ontology itself.

The ontology gUFO [3] is a simplified version of the Unified Foundational Ontology UFO, designed for easier integration with ontology-driven conceptual modelling, particularly in domains such as information systems. It supports objects (enduring entities) and qualities related to them, which are used to classify research papers into the dimensions of the *ai4st* taxonomy.

The *stc* ontology [53] represents a selection of terms in the ISTQB glossary. The glossary contains keywords from software testing syllabi, covering foundation, advanced, and expert-level concepts, methods, and techniques in the software testing profession. Currently under development using the Protégé tool, the *stc* ontology consists of over 200 classes representing software testing terms and 20 object properties representing their relations. Each term is described as being defined by ISTQB, SEVOCAB, or as proprietary. The development of *stc* began with the concept maps provided by ISTQB and has evolved beyond them, as these concept maps are informal and mainly represent top-level terms in software testing.

As a predecessor to *ai4st*, the *ai4se* taxonomy [49] was created to structure the emerging research field of applying AI to SE and to address its nuances. *ai4se* is structured along four dimensions:

– Purpose: The goal of using AI is to understand, generate or improve SE artefacts/processes. A new approach may address one, two, or all three of these purposes; for example, it may address both understanding and generation.
– Target: The SE activity being addressed in (1) development and (2) operations, as well as in the corresponding (3) processes. Whenever models are central to an approach, as they are in Model-Driven SE, this is denoted as well. An approach may target several SE activities. SE processes consist of SE activities and constitute activities themselves, allowing for a more detailed representation of an SE target.
– AI Type: The AI techniques being used by an approach, including Symbolic, Subsymbolic, Generative, Agentic, and General AI. One approach may use several types of AI.
– Level: The degree of automation is based on a five-level scale ranging from (0) no support to (4) full automation. The highest level achieved by an approach is indicated. Currently, level 3 (AI-assisted selection) is the most common.

When the *ai4se* taxonomy was used to classify a large set of research papers, it became clear that a tool-based approach, such as that offered by the Semantic

Web, was preferable to manual classification. Hence, the *ai4se* ontology was developed [50]. It also became apparent that, in order to address the specifics of using AI for software testing, a more specific taxonomy and machine-processable ontology for software testing research would be preferable. The resulting *ai4st* ontology [51] is shown in Fig. 1 with its (top-level) dimensions[2].

4 Classification of AI for Software Testing Research

The classification of AI for software testing research is an ongoing project. To check the validity of the *ai4st* ontology, an adapted, lightweight systematic literature review (SLR), as described in [59], was conducted to analyse related research. This SLR protocol was followed:

- **Review title**: Initial SLR on the application of the *ai4st* taxonomy.
- **Objectives of the review**:
  1. To test the validity of the *ai4st* taxonomy with an initial research selection.
  2. To determine a classification of this initial research selection.
- **Research questions**:
  - RQ1: Which standardized terms are being used in *ai4st* related research?
  - RQ2: Which alternative terms are being used in *ai4st* related research?
  - RQ3: Are the *ai4st* taxonomy dimensions useful to classify the pre-selected research?
- **Database**: Research papers from the conference proceedings of the latest International Conference on Software Engineering, ICSE 2025 in Ottawa, Canada and its co-located conferences and workshops; and referenced papers for backward snowballing the research. Forward snowballing was in this case unnecessary, as ICSE 2025 represented the most recent research publications at that time. A complementary search of the IEEE and ACM digital libraries has added further software testing and AI-related research papers published between 2020 and 2025.
- **Inclusion criteria**:
  - Peer-reviewed original research.
  - Online available.
  - Research on AI for ST.
- **Exclusion criteria**:
  - Meta-research such as evaluations, benchmarking, comparisons, surveys, taxonomies, roadmaps
  - Testing of software-based systems like IoT, cloud, vehicle, etc.
  - Research on ST for AI.
  - Posters and tutorials.

---

[2] For the *ai4st* classification, the classes of the software testing ontology *stc* have been reified/punned to individuals to represent the software testing terms. The hierarchical relationship between the concepts has been kept in a separate object property 'has parent'. These terms constitute the target classifiers in *ai4st*.

(a) The dimensions of the *ai4st* taxonomy: Research Topic, Solution Purpose, ST Target, AI Type, Automation Level.

(b) The classification of a sample paper about testing and debugging, aiming at understanding and improving the testing activities, using deep learning methods, and providing AI-assisted selections.

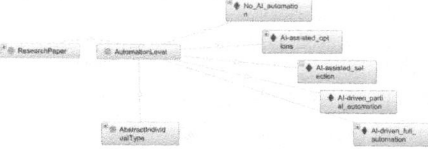

(c) The solution purpose classifiers to understand, generate, or improve ST artefacts

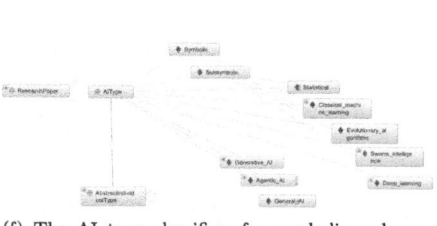

(d) The automation level classifiers consisting of no AI support, providing AI-assisted options or AI-assisted selections, or supporting AI-driven partial automation or AI-driven full automation.

(e) The target classifiers represent the ST techniques, activities, or processes to which an AI system is being applied[2]

(f) The AI type classifiers for sumbolic, subsymbolic, generative, agentic, or general AI. Subsymbolic AI is classified into statistical, classical machine learning, evolutionary algorithms, swarm intelligence, and deep learning AI.

Fig. 1. Research Paper Classification with *ai4st*

- **Selection process**:
  1. Title and abstract screening for the pre-selection of unique research candidates by use of
     (a) the concept map resulting from the *stc* ontology [53] to identify ST-related research, and
     (b) the concept map resulting from the *ai4st* dimensions 'AI type' to identify AI related research in the ST-related subset of research.
  2. Full text review and assessment of the research contributions for the final selection of unique research.

3. Tools:
- Online research libraries, including dblp, ACM DL, IEEE Xplore, and Google Scholar to identify related work; and
- Python for text analysis and post-processing of finally selected research, supported by MS Visual Studio, Google AI Studio, and LibreOffice.

- **Synthesis process**:
  - Review of the new and synonym candidate terms for inclusion into the *stc* ontology.
  - Classification of the selected research for inclusion into the *ai4st* ontology.

Alongside the analysis of recent AI for ST research, a new SLR approach has been developed. Rather than using simple search expressions, the pre-selection of papers uses more detailed concept maps that are derived from the relevant ontologies and also include synonyms, as shown in Fig. 2. Additionally, the SLR results are used to verify, improve and extend the ontologies further. Therefore, assessing the research texts also involves searching for new term and new synonym candidates. The potential for further refining this kind of ontology-based SLR, as well as SLR-based ontology refinement, depends on the features of digital library APIs that enable more powerful automated searches and research (meta-)data collections.

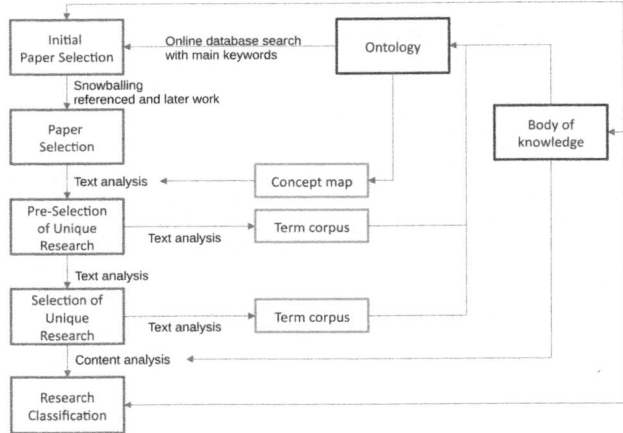

Fig. 2. Overview on the ontology-driven systematic literature review (SLR) combined with the SLR-driven ontology development

In result of the SLR and text (title and abstract) analysis, of the 1643 papers identified, 1150 referred to a term in the *stc* ontology in their abstracts and/or titles, but 735 of these referred to only one term, indicating that the paper merely references a fact about software testing. Another 1337 papers used variations of the terms in the *stc* ontology, such as 'unit test' instead of 'unit-level test'[3]. 460 papers referred to only one variation. Papers using two or more original or alternative terms, what makes them candidate papers for the *ai4st* taxonomy, form a body of 949 papers. Of these 949 papers, 656 contained terms from the *ai4st* ontology related to AI. Within the 656 papers, 38 relevant original research papers for *ai4st* were identified.

Furthermore, the text analysis revealed 40 new *stc* term candidates, 53 new *stc* synonym candidates and 26 terms that can be treated as either new term or synonym candidates. These new term candidates include terms such as 'test result' and 'fuzz testing', which are included in the ISTQB Glossary – a collection of over 600 terms – but are not yet included in the initial *stc* ontology, which contains over 200 terms. The new term candidates also include terms such as 'flaky test' and 'genetic testing', which are not included in the ISTQB Glossary but are extensively discussed in research. Another four new term candidates, such as 'test bot' and 'bias testing', and one new synonym candidate, 'AI-based', have been identified for the *ai4st* ontology. This is mainly because the SRL focused on ST rather than AI. In the next release of *ai4st*, the decision will be made as to which new term or synonym candidates, beyond those required for research classification in this paper (see below), will be added and whether distinguishing AI types in more detail would be useful.

Table 1. List of Research Papers

Ref	Title
[12]	A Method and Experiment to evaluate Deep Neural Networks as Test Oracles for Scientific Software
[40]	A new approach for automatic test case generation from use case diagram using LLMs and prompt engineering
[17]	Acceptance Test Generation with Large Language Models: An Industrial Case Study
[11]	AI in Service of Software Quality: How ChatGPT and Personas Are Transforming Exploratory Testing
[33]	AI-Assisted Test Script Generation for GUI Applications
[39]	AI-Based Enhancement of Test Models in an Industrial Model-Based Testing Tool
[36]	AI-Driven Acceptance Testing: first insights exploring the educational potential for test analysts
[29]	AI-Driven Testing: Unleashing Autonomous Systems for Superior Software Quality Using Generative AI
[37]	AI-driven web API testing

(continued)

---

[3] In a future version of the *stc* ontology, more synonym terms will be added to better cope with variations and synonyms of terms.

Table 1. (*continued*)

Ref	Title
[23]	AI-Powered Multi-Agent Framework for Automated Unit Test Case Generation: Enhancing Software Quality through LLMs
[26]	AIs Understanding of Software Test Architecture
[43]	An Agent-based Architecture for AI-Enhanced Automated Testing for XR Systems
[34]	An Approach To Extract Optimal Test Cases Using AI
[21]	An Approach to GUI Test Scenario Generation Using Machine Learning
[44]	AsserT5: Test Assertion Generation Using a Fine-Tuned Code Language Model
[41]	Automation of Test Skeletons Within Test-Driven Development Projects
[69]	BugBlitz-AI: An Intelligent QA Assistant
[20]	ClozeMaster: Fuzzing Rust Compiler by Harnessing LLMs for Infilling Masked Real Programs
[66]	Deep Multiple Assertions Generation
[6]	Development of Cloud and Artificial Intelligence based Software Testing Platform (ChArIoT)
[22]	Generative AI for Software Test Modelling with a focus on ERP Software
[60]	Ethical AI-Powered Regression Test Selection
[28]	Getting pwn.d by AI: Penetration Testing with Large Language Models
[72]	GUI-Based Software Testing: An Automated Approach Using GPT-4 and Selenium WebDriver
[8]	Leveraging Large Language Models for Usability Testing: a Preliminary Study
[18]	LLM-Based Labelling of Recorded Automated GUI-Based Test Cases
[70]	New Approaches to Automated Software Testing Based on Artificial Intelligence
[42]	On the Effectiveness of LLMs for Manual Test Verifications
[19]	Owl Eye: An AI-Driven Visual Testing Tool
[35]	Reducing Workload in Using AI-based API REST Test Generation
[10]	Reinforcing Penetration Testing Using AI
[24]	RIVER 2.0: an open-source testing framework using AI techniques
[1]	TCP-Net++: Test Case Prioritization Using End-to-End Deep Neural Networks Deployment Analysis and Enhancements
[30]	TOGLL: Correct and Strong Test Oracle Generation with LLMs
[54]	Using an agent-based approach for robust automated testing of computer games
[12]	Using Large Language Models to Generate Concise and Understandable Test Case Summaries
[45]	Visual Test Framework: Enhancing Software Test Automation with Visual Artificial Intelligence and Behavioral Driven Development
[27]	WIP: Assessing the Effectiveness of ChatGPT in Preparatory Testing Activities

Due to space limitations, the classification of the selected 38 papers given in Table 1 is not fully shown here. The complete results on pre-selected research and finally selected unique research, as well as the usage of terms and the assessment of new term and synonym candidates, are provided in [52].

The research questions RQ1, RQ2, and RQ3 of this SLR are answered briefly as follows: Classifying the unique research led to an extension of the *stc* ontology with:

- three new terms defined in the ISTQB Glossary: 'visual testing' [19,43,45], 'assertion' [44,66], and 'penetration testing' [10,28]
- eight new terms not in the ISTQB Glossary:
  - two test techniques: 'mutation testing' [6] and 'concolic testing' [24];
  - five test activities: 'test selection' [60], 'test generation' [20,22,70], 'test verification' [42], 'test prioritization' [1], and 'test documentation' [13];
  - one non-functional testing: 'penetration testing' [10,28]; and
  - one basic concept: 'ethics' [60]

Furthermore, the new synonym 'test architecture' [26] for 'test approach' was added. In response to RQ1 and RQ2, the software testing targets in the unique research papers were successfully classified by combining the new terms and synonyms with the terms in *stc*, and hence in *ai4st*.

Alongside this, RQ3 can also be answered positively. This small selection of unique research covers all potential purposes and levels of automation supported by AI. With regard to the types of AI, all but general AI (due to its non-existence) and evolutionary algorithms (which are currently not in focus) are represented. Additionally, 28 software testing targets are addressed, representing over 10% of the extended *stc* ontology.

In addition, *ai4st* can be used as a research knowledge base. One straightforward application is elaborating on the classified research corpus: As the classification can be queried like a database, it is easy to formulate queries about the research corpus, such as which software testing targets are addressed or which research supports AI-assisted option automation, see the listings below.

```
1 PREFIX rdf: <http://www.w3.org/1999/02/22-rdf-syntax-ns#>
2 PREFIX ai4st: <http://purl.org/ai4st/ontology#>
3 SELECT ?paper
4 WHERE {
5   ?paper ai4st:hasLevel ai4st:AI-assisted_options .
6 }
```

Listing 1.1. All papers on AI-assisted options automation.

```
1 PREFIX rdf: <http://www.w3.org/1999/02/22-rdf-syntax-ns#>
2 PREFIX ai4st: <http://purl.org/ai4st/ontology#>
3 SELECT DISTINCT ?target
4 WHERE {
5   ?paper rdf:type ai4st:ResearchPaper .
6   ?paper ai4st:hasTarget ?target .
7 }
```

Listing 1.2. All software testing targets addressed by research papers.

5   Outlook

This paper describes ongoing work on representing the exhaustive body of knowledge on software testing using an in-depth ontology. This ontology can also form the basis for exploring new research fields in software testing, such as the emerging area of using AI techniques and tools in software testing (ST). To this end, the paper presents the initial versions of

- the *stc* ontology on software testing concepts, which is mainly based on the ISTQB Glossary and completed with SEVOCAB and proprietary software testing vocabulary.
- the *ai4st* ontology that classifies AI for ST research according to the *purpose* of the AI-based solution, the software testing *target* being addressed, the *type* of AI being used, and the *level* of automation achieved.
- an exemplary SLR on AI for ST, revealing 38 original research papers classified in the *ai4st* ontology.

The research results including the ontologies *stc* and *ai4st* as well as the paper selections from the SLR are available online for reuse and further uptake. The *ai4st* can be used not only to understand the concepts in this research field better, but also to explore research related to a specific aspect, such as all papers on agentic AI for ST, using SPARQL queries.

The next step will be to extend *stc* to cover the remaining ISTQB terms, to further refine *ai4st* to cover more AI-related details, and carefully revise new term and synonym candidates stemming from SLRs for potential addition. This will form the basis for classifying further research results on the application of *ai4st* including *stc*.

Acknowledgement. The ideas presented in this paper were developed through constructive dialogue within the Testing, Analysis and Verification (TAV) section of the German Informatics Society (GI), the German Testing Board (GTB), and the International Software Testing Qualifications Board (ISTQB). While the author wrote this paper independently, she acknowledges that the writing process was aided by DeepL to fine-tune the wording. The author has no competing interests to declare that are relevant to the content of this article.

References

1. Abdelkarim, M., ElAdawi, R.: TCP-Net++: test case prioritization using end-to-end deep neural networks - deployment analysis and enhancements. In: 2023 IEEE International Conference on Artificial Intelligence Testing (AITest), Athens, Greece, pp. 99–106. IEEE (2023). https://doi.org/10.1109/AITest58265.2023.00024. https://ieeexplore.ieee.org/document/10229439/
2. Abran, A., Cuadrado, J.J., García-Barriocanal, E., Mendes, O., Sánchez-Alonso, S., Sicilia, M.A.: Engineering the ontology for the SWEBOK: issues and techniques. In: Ontologies for Software Engineering and Software Technology, pp. 103–121 (2006)

3. Almeida, J.P.A., Guizzardi, G., Falbo, R., Sales, T.P.: gUFO: a lightweight implementation of the unified foundational ontology (UFO) (2019). http://purl.org/nemo/doc/gufo

4. Barbosa, E.F., Nakagawa, E.Y., Maldonado, J.C.: Towards the establishment of an ontology of software testing. In: SEKE, vol. 6, pp. 522–525 (2006)

5. Borges Ruy, F., de Almeida Falbo, R., Perini Barcellos, M., Dornelas Costa, S., Guizzardi, G.: SEON: a software engineering ontology network. In: Blomqvist, E., Ciancarini, P., Poggi, F., Vitali, F. (eds.) EKAW 2016. LNCS (LNAI), vol. 10024, pp. 527–542. Springer, Cham (2016). https://doi.org/10.1007/978-3-319-49004-5_34

6. Caglar, O., Taskin, F., Baglum, C., Asik, S., Yayan, U.: Development of cloud and artificial intelligence based software testing platform (ChArIoT). In: 2023 Innovations in Intelligent Systems and Applications Conference (ASYU), Sivas, Turkiye, pp. 1–6. IEEE (2023). https://doi.org/10.1109/ASYU58738.2023.10296551. https://ieeexplore.ieee.org/document/10296551/

7. Calero, C., Ruiz, F., Piattini, M.: Ontologies for software engineering and software technology. Springer (2006)

8. Calvano, M., Curci, A., Lanzilotti, R., Piccinno, A., Ragone, A.: Leveraging large language models for usability testing: a preliminary study. In: Companion Proceedings of the 30th International Conference on Intelligent User Interfaces, Cagliari, Italy, pp. 78–81. ACM (2025). https://doi.org/10.1145/3708557.3716341. https://dl.acm.org/doi/10.1145/3708557.3716341

9. CC: CC BY-SA 4.0 license, attribution-sharealike 4.0 international, legal code (2025). https://creativecommons.org/licenses/by-sa/4.0/legalcode.en

10. Confido, A., Ntagiou, E.V., Wallum, M.: Reinforcing penetration testing using AI. In: 2022 IEEE Aerospace Conference (AERO), Big Sky, MT, USA, pp. 1–15. IEEE (2022). https://doi.org/10.1109/AERO53065.2022.9843459. https://ieeexplore.ieee.org/document/9843459/

11. De Almeida A., Collins, E., Oran, A.C.: AI in service of software quality: how ChatGPT and personas are transforming exploratory testing. In: Proceedings of the XXIII Brazilian Symposium on Software Quality, Salvador, Bahia, Brazil, pp. 179–188. ACM (2024). https://doi.org/10.1145/3701625.3701657. https://dl.acm.org/doi/10.1145/3701625.3701657

12. De Santiago Júnior, V.A.: A method and experiment to evaluate deep neural networks as test oracles for scientific software. In: Proceedings of the 3rd ACM/IEEE International Conference on Automation of Software Test, Pittsburgh, Pennsylvania, pp. 40–51. ACM (2022). https://doi.org/10.1145/3524481.3527232. https://dl.acm.org/doi/10.1145/3524481.3527232

13. Djajadi, N., Deljouyi, A., Zaidman, A.: Using large language models to generate concise and understandable test case summaries. In: Early Research Achievements (ERA). https://doi.org/10.1109/ICPC66645.2025.00040. https://azaidman.github.io/publications/djajadiICPC2025.pdf

14. Engström, E., Petersen, K., Ali, N.B., Bjarnason, E.: SERP-test: a taxonomy for supporting industry-academia communication. Softw. Qual. J. **25**, 1269–1305 (2017)

15. Felderer, M., Schieferdecker, I.: A taxonomy of risk-based testing. Int. J. Softw. Tools Technol. Transfer **16**(5), 559–568 (2014). https://doi.org/10.1007/s10009-014-0332-3

16. Felderer, M., Zech, P., Breu, R., Büchler, M., Pretschner, A.: Model-based security testing: a taxonomy and systematic classification. Softw. Test. Verif. Reliab. **26**(2), 119–148 (2016)

17. Ferreira, M., Viegas, L., Faria, J.P., Lima, B.: Acceptance Test Generation with Large Language Models: An Industrial Case Study (2025). https://doi.org/10.48550/arXiv.2504.07244. http://arxiv.org/abs/2504.07244. arXiv:2504.07244

18. Franzosi, D.B., Alégroth, E., Isaac, M.: LLM-based labelling of recorded automated GUI-based test cases. In: 2025 IEEE Conference on Software Testing, Verification and Validation (ICST), Napoli, Italy, pp. 453–463. IEEE (2025). https://doi.org/10.1109/ICST62969.2025.10988984. https://ieeexplore.ieee.org/document/10988984/

19. Gamal, A., Emad, R., Mohamed, T., Mohamed, O., Hamdy, A., Ali, S.: Owl eye: an AI-driven visual testing tool. In: 2023 5th Novel Intelligent and Leading Emerging Sciences Conference (NILES), Giza, Egypt, pp. 312–315. IEEE (2023). https://doi.org/10.1109/NILES59815.2023.10296575. https://ieeexplore.ieee.org/document/10296575/

20. Gao, H., Yang, Y., Sun, M., Wu, J., Zhou, Y., Xu, B.: ClozeMaster: Fuzzing Rust Compiler by Harnessing LLMs for Infilling Masked Real Programs, p. 712. IEEE Computer Society (2025). https://doi.org/10.1109/ICSE55347.2025.00175. https://www.computer.org/csdl/proceedings-article/icse/2025/056900a712/251mH1NLq1y. iSSN: 1558-1225

21. Gao, J., et al.: An approach to GUI test scenario generation using machine learning. In: 2022 IEEE International Conference on Artificial Intelligence Testing (AITest), Newark, CA, USA, pp. 79–86. IEEE (2022). https://doi.org/10.1109/AITest55621.2022.00020. https://ieeexplore.ieee.org/document/9898132/

22. Garg, A., Sharma, D.: Generative AI for software test modelling with a focus on ERP software. In: 2023 International Conference on Advances in Computation, Communication and Information Technology (ICAICCIT), Faridabad, India, pp. 187–193. IEEE (2023). https://doi.org/10.1109/ICAICCIT60255.2023.10466102. https://ieeexplore.ieee.org/document/10466102/

23. Garlapati, A., Satya Sai Muni Parmesh, M.N.V., Savitha, S, J.: AI-powered multi-agent framework for automated unit test case generation: enhancing software quality through LLM's. In: 2024 5th IEEE Global Conference for Advancement in Technology (GCAT), Bangalore, India, pp. 1–5. IEEE (2024). https://doi.org/10.1109/GCAT62922.2024.10923987. https://ieeexplore.ieee.org/document/10923987/

24. Ghimis, B., Paduraru, M., Stefanescu, A.: RIVER 2.0: an open-source testing framework using AI techniques. In: Proceedings of the 1st ACM SIGSOFT International Workshop on Languages and Tools for Next-Generation Testing, Virtual USA, pp. 13–18. ACM (2020). https://doi.org/10.1145/3416504.3424335. https://dl.acm.org/doi/10.1145/3416504.3424335

25. Guizzardi, G., Fonseca, C.M., Benevides, A.B., Almeida, J.P.A., Porello, D., Sales, T.P.: Endurant types in ontology-driven conceptual modeling: towards OntoUML 2.0. In: Trujillo, J.C., et al. (eds.) ER 2018. LNCS, vol. 11157, pp. 136–150. Springer, Cham (2018). https://doi.org/10.1007/978-3-030-00847-5_12

26. Hagar, J., Wissink, T.: AIs understanding of software test architecture. In: 2025 IEEE International Conference on Software Testing, Verification and Validation Workshops (ICSTW), Naples, Italy, pp. 194–199. IEEE (2025). https://doi.org/10.1109/ICSTW64639.2025.10962517. https://ieeexplore.ieee.org/document/10962517/

27. Haldar, S., Pierce, M., Capretz, L.F.: WIP: assessing the effectiveness of ChatGPT in preparatory testing activities. In: 2024 IEEE Frontiers in Education Conference (FIE), Washington, DC, USA, pp. 1–5. IEEE (2024). https://doi.org/10.1109/FIE61694.2024.10893214. https://ieeexplore.ieee.org/document/10893214/

28. Happe, A., Cito, J.: Getting pwn'd by AI: penetration testing with large language models. In: Proceedings of the 31st ACM Joint European Software Engineering Conference and Symposium on the Foundations of Software Engineering, San Francisco, CA, USA, pp. 2082–2086. ACM (2023). https://doi.org/10.1145/3611643.3613083. https://dl.acm.org/doi/10.1145/3611643.3613083

29. Helmy, M., Sobhy, O., ElHusseiny, F.: AI-driven testing: unleashing autonomous systems for superior software quality using generative AI. In: 2024 International Telecommunications Conference (ITC-Egypt), Cairo, Egypt, pp. 1–6. IEEE (2024). https://doi.org/10.1109/ITC-Egypt61547.2024.10620598. https://ieeexplore.ieee.org/document/10620598/

30. Hossain, S.B., Dwyer, M.: TOGLL: Correct and Strong Test Oracle Generation with LLMs (2024). https://doi.org/10.48550/arXiv.2405.03786. http://arxiv.org/abs/2405.03786. arXiv:2405.03786

31. ISO, IEC, IEEE: ISO/IEC/IEEE 24765 international standard, second edition: Systems and software engineering – vocabulary (2017). https://pascal.computer.org

32. ISTQB: Glossary of the international software testing qualifications board (2025). https://glossary.istqb.org

33. Kapoor, S.: AI-assisted test script generation for GUI applications. In: 2025 Fifth International Conference on Advances in Electrical, Computing, Communication and Sustainable Technologies (ICAECT), Bhilai, India, pp. 1–5. IEEE (2025). https://doi.org/10.1109/ICAECT63952.2025.10958949. https://ieeexplore.ieee.org/document/10958949/

34. Kaur, A.: An approach to extract optimal test cases using AI. In: 2020 10th International Conference on Cloud Computing, Data Science & Engineering (Confluence), Noida, India, pp. 649–654. IEEE (2020). https://doi.org/10.1109/Confluence47617.2020.9058244. https://ieeexplore.ieee.org/document/9058244/

35. Leu, B., Volken, J., Kropp, M., Dogru, N., Anslow, C., Biddle, R.: Reducing workload in using AI-based API REST test generation. In: Proceedings of the 5th ACM/IEEE International Conference on Automation of Software Test (AST 2024), Lisbon, Portugal, pp. 147–148. ACM (2024). https://doi.org/10.1145/3644032.3644449. https://dl.acm.org/doi/10.1145/3644032.3644449

36. Maia, C.J.D.L., Aguiar, Y.P.C.: AI-driven acceptance testing: first insights exploring the educational potential for test analysts. In: Proceedings of the XXIII Brazilian Symposium on Software Quality, Salvador, Bahia, Brazil. pp. 665–672. ACM (2024). https://doi.org/10.1145/3701625.3701691. https://dl.acm.org/doi/10.1145/3701625.3701691

37. Martin-Lopez, A.: AI-driven web API testing. In: Proceedings of the ACM/IEEE 42nd International Conference on Software Engineering: Companion Proceedings, Seoul, South Korea, pp. 202–205. ACM (2020). https://doi.org/10.1145/3377812.3381388. https://dl.acm.org/doi/10.1145/3377812.3381388

38. McGuinness, D.L., Van Harmelen, F., et al.: Owl web ontology language overview. W3C Recomm. **10**(10), 2004 (2004)

39. Mohacsi, S., Felderer, M.: AI-based enhancement of test models in an industrial model-based testing tool. In: 2021 IEEE International Conference on Software Analysis, Evolution and Reengineering (SANER), Honolulu, HI, USA, pp. 636–638. IEEE (2021). https://doi.org/10.1109/SANER50967.2021.00080. https://ieeexplore.ieee.org/document/9426031/

40. Naimi, L., Bouziane, E.M., Manaouch, M., Jakimi, A.: A new approach for automatic test case generation from use case diagram using LLMs and prompt engi-

neering. In: 2024 International Conference on Circuit, Systems and Communication (ICCSC), Fes, Morocco, pp. 1–5. IEEE (2024). https://doi.org/10.1109/ICCSC62074.2024.10616548. https://ieeexplore.ieee.org/document/10616548/

41. Olmez, M.M., Gehringer, E.: Automation of test skeletons within test-driven development projects. In: 2024 36th International Conference on Software Engineering Education and Training (CSEE&T), Würzburg, Germany, pp. 1–10. IEEE (2024). https://doi.org/10.1109/CSEET62301.2024.10663016. https://ieeexplore.ieee.org/document/10663016/

42. Peixoto, M., Baía, D., Nascimento, N., Alencar, P., Fonseca, B., Ribeiro, M.: On the effectiveness of LLMs for manual test verifications. In: 2025 IEEE/ACM International Workshop on Deep Learning for Testing and Testing for Deep Learning (DeepTest), Ottawa, ON, Canada, pp. 45–52. IEEE (2025). https://doi.org/10.1109/DeepTest66595.2025.00012. https://ieeexplore.ieee.org/document/11026915/

43. Prasetya, I.S.W.B., Shirzadehhajimahmood, S., Ansari, S.G., Fernandes, P., Prada, R.: An agent-based architecture for AI-enhanced automated testing for XR systems, a short paper. In: 2021 IEEE International Conference on Software Testing, Verification and Validation Workshops (ICSTW), Porto de Galinhas, Brazil, pp. 213–217. IEEE (2021). https://doi.org/10.1109/ICSTW52544.2021.00044. https://ieeexplore.ieee.org/document/9440175/

44. Primbs, S., Fein, B., Fraser, G.: AsserT5: Test Assertion Generation Using a Fine-Tuned Code Language Model (2025). https://doi.org/10.1109/AST66626.2025.00008. http://arxiv.org/abs/2502.02708. arXiv:2502.02708

45. Ragel, R.K.C., Balahadia, F.F.: Visual test framework: enhancing software test automation with visual artificial intelligence and behavioral driven development. In: 2023 IEEE 15th International Conference on Humanoid, Nanotechnology, Information Technology, Communication and Control, Environment, and Management (HNICEM), Coron, Palawan, Philippines, pp. 1–5. IEEE (2023). https://doi.org/10.1109/HNICEM60674.2023.10589222. https://ieeexplore.ieee.org/document/10589222/

46. Robinson, P., Ragusa, C.: Taxonomy and requirements rationalization for infrastructure in cloud-based software testing. In: 2011 IEEE Third International Conference on Cloud Computing Technology and Science, pp. 454–461. IEEE (2011)

47. Rous, B.: Major update to ACM's computing classification system. Commun. ACM **55**(11), 12 (2012)

48. Salatino, A.A., Thanapalasingam, T., Mannocci, A., Birukou, A., Osborne, F., Motta, E.: The computer science ontology: a comprehensive automatically-generated taxonomy of research areas. Data Intell. **2**(3), 379–416 (2020)

49. Schieferdecker, I.K.: Next-gen software engineering: AI-assisted big models. arXiv preprint arXiv:2409.18048 (2024)

50. Schieferdecker, I.K.: AI4SE - the AI for software engineering ontology (2025). https://github.com/schieferdecker/ai4se

51. Schieferdecker, I.K.: AI4ST - the AI for software testing ontology (2025). https://github.com/schieferdecker/ai4st

52. Schieferdecker, I.K.: Annex for 'a taxonomy for AI-augmented software testing' (2025). https://github.com/schieferdecker/ai4stpaper

53. Schieferdecker, I.K.: STC - the software testing concept ontology (2025). https://github.com/schieferdecker/stc

54. Shirzadehhajimahmood, S., Prasetya, I.S.W.B., Dignum, F., Dastani, M., Keller, G.: Using an agent-based approach for robust automated testing of com-

puter games. In: Proceedings of the 12th International Workshop on Automating TEST Case Design, Selection, and Evaluation, Athens Greece, pp. 1–8. ACM (2021). https://doi.org/10.1145/3472672.3473952. https://dl.acm.org/doi/10.1145/3472672.3473952

55. Sicilia, M., Cuadrado, J.J., García, E., Rodríguez, D., Hilera, J.R.: The evaluation of ontological representation of the SWEBOK as a revision tool. In: 29th Annual International Computer Software and Application Conference (COMPSAC), Edinburgh, UK, pp. 26–28 (2005)

56. Souza, É.F.d., Falbo, R.d.A., Vijaykumar, N.L.: ROoST: reference ontology on software testing. Appl. Ontol. **12**(1), 59–90 (2017)

57. Spillner, A., Bremenn, H.: The W-MODEL. Strengthening the bond between development and test. In: International Conference on Software Testing, Analysis and Review, pp. 15–17 (2002)

58. Spillner, A., Linz, T.: Software testing foundations: a study guide for the certified tester exam-foundation level-ISTQB® compliant. dpunkt. verlag (2021)

59. Stapic, Z., López, E.G., Cabot, A.G., de Marcos Ortega, L., Strahonja, V.: Performing systematic literature review in software engineering. In: Central European Conference on Information and Intelligent Systems, p. 441. Faculty of Organization and Informatics Varazdin (2012)

60. Strandberg, P.E., Frasheri, M., Enoiu, E.P.: Ethical AI-powered regression test selection. In: 2021 IEEE International Conference on Artificial Intelligence Testing (AITest), Oxford, United Kingdom, pp. 83–84. IEEE (2021). https://doi.org/10.1109/AITEST52744.2021.00025. https://ieeexplore.ieee.org/document/9564367/

61. Tebes, G., Olsina, L., Peppino, D., Becker, P.: TestTDO: a top-domain software testing ontology. In: CIbSE, pp. 364–377 (2020)

62. Tebes, G., Peppino, D., Becker, P., Matturro, G., Solari, M., Olsina, L.: Analyzing and documenting the systematic review results of software testing ontologies. Inf. Softw. Technol. **123**, 106298 (2020)

63. Usman, M., Britto, R., Börstler, J., Mendes, E.: Taxonomies in software engineering: a systematic mapping study and a revised taxonomy development method. Inf. Softw. Technol. **85**, 43–59 (2017) https://doi.org/10.1016/j.infsof.2017.01.006. https://www.sciencedirect.com/science/article/pii/S0950584917300472

64. Utting, M., Pretschner, A., Legeard, B.: A taxonomy of model-based testing approaches. Softw. Test. Verif. Reliab. **22**(5), 297–312 (2012)

65. Villalón, J.C.M., Agustin, G.C., Gilabert, T.S.F., de Jesús Jiménez Puello, J.: A taxonomy for software testing projects. In: 2015 10th Iberian Conference on Information Systems and Technologies (CISTI), pp. 1–6 (2015). https://doi.org/10.1109/CISTI.2015.7170545

66. Wang, H., Xu, T., Wang, B.: Deep multiple assertions generation. In: Proceedings of the 2024 IEEE/ACM First International Conference on AI Foundation Models and Software Engineering, Lisbon, Portugal, pp. 1–11. ACM (2024). https://doi.org/10.1145/3650105.3652293. https://dl.acm.org/doi/10.1145/3650105.3652293

67. Washizaki, H.E.: Guide to the Software Engineering Body of Knowledge (SWEBOK Guide), Version 4.0 (2024). http://www.swebok.org

68. Wille, C., Abran, A., Desharnais, J.M., Dumke, R.: The quality concepts and sub concepts in SWEBOK: an ontology challenge. In: International Workshop on Software Measurement (IWSM), Montreal, vol. 18 (2003)

69. Yao, Y., et al.: BugBlitz-AI: an intelligent QA assistant. In: 2024 IEEE 15th International Conference on Software Engineering and Service Science (ICSESS), Changsha, China, pp. 57–63. IEEE (2024). https://doi.org/10.1109/ICSESS62520.2024.10719045. https://ieeexplore.ieee.org/document/10719045/

70. Zhang, Y.: New approaches to automated software testing based on artificial intelligence. In: 2024 5th International Conference on Artificial Intelligence and Computer Engineering (ICAICE), Wuhu, China, pp. 806–810. IEEE (2024). https://doi.org/10.1109/ICAICE63571.2024.10863866. https://ieeexplore.ieee.org/document/10863866/

71. Zhu, H., Huo, Q.: Developing software testing ontology in UML for a software growth environment of web-based applications. In: Software Evolution with UML and XML, pp. 263–295. IGI Global (2005)

72. Zimmermann, D., Koziolek, A.: GUI-based software testing: an automated approach using GPT-4 and selenium WebDriver. In: 2023 38th IEEE/ACM International Conference on Automated Software Engineering Workshops (ASEW), Luxembourg, Luxembourg, pp. 171–174. IEEE (2023). https://doi.org/10.1109/ASEW60602.2023.00028. https://ieeexplore.ieee.org/document/10298721/

An Overview of Sound and Modest Approaches to Quantitative Model Checking from Sea to Space

Arnd Hartmanns$^{(\boxtimes)}$ (iD)

University of Twente, Enschede, The Netherlands
`a.hartmanns@utwente.nl`

Abstract. Quantitative system properties such as resilience, response times, and throughput are crucial measures in the design and opera-tion of complex cyber-physical systems. The formal methods community has developed a variety of approaches to evaluate and optimise such properties with clear correctness and optimality guarantees. In practice, however, every application poses new challenges that require adaptations and novel combinations of the "off-the-shelf" methods we usually present in scientific papers. In this extended abstract accompanying the author's FMICS 2025 invited presentation, we use recent case studies ranging from water management for storm surge protection to routing in satel-lite constellations to (i) contrast the different demands on model expres-siveness and tool capabilities of each application and (ii) highlight the capabilities of the MODEST TOOLSET to solve these challenges with the varied modelling, simulation, and verification approaches it implements. In addition to these examples, we outline how quantitative verification tools can deliver the correctness and optimality guarantees we would like to see.

1 Introduction

Cyber-physical systems (CPS) use discrete control strategies, often implemented in software, to operate physical components or processes. In contrast to the more traditional notions of embedded or hybrid systems, "CPS" tends to refer to larger-scale implementations that span a larger area and consist of many interact-ing (e.g. networked) components or agents. Many CPS such as railway signalling systems, chemical plants, or smart electricity grids are safety- and performance-critical: Failures can cause loss of lives, and insufficient performance can cause significant economic damage. Performance and safety may even be linked, e.g. when a sewage treatment plant cannot keep up with inflow during a rain event and consequently discharges a waste water overflow into the environment. Thus

This work was supported by the EU's Horizon 2020 programme under Marie Skło-dowska-Curie grant agreement no. 101008233 (MISSION), by the Interreg North Sea project STORM_SAFE, and by NWO VIDI grant VI.Vidi.223.110 (TruSTy).

A. Remke and B. Steffen (Eds.): FMICS 2025, LNCS 16040, pp. 21–36, 2025.
https://doi.org/10.1007/978-3-032-00942-5_2

properties such as reliability, resilience, throughput, and response times are key quality indicators to designers in the conception phase of the system, and (in terms of measurements and predictions) to operators once the system is up and running. These properties are inherently quantitative as they reason about real time aspects, probabilities, and expected values; and so are the system models required to study them, which need to incorporate those same aspects as well as represent physical laws and quantities (e.g. water levels, flows, the state of charge of batteries, etc.) together with the discrete state of the control software.

The formal methods and performance evaluation research communities have developed a plethora of approaches to address the challenge of analysing such properties (i.e. either determining their value, or finding a control strategy that optimises their value) on quantitative system models [6]. These approaches require a *formal model* to start with, which is typically given in a higher-level formalism such as stochastic variants of hybrid Petri nets [37] or the MOD-EST modelling language [12,41]. These formalisms are in turn equipped with a well-defined semantics that maps into a lower-level mathematical formalism ranging from simple Markov chains [7] to the highly expressive stochastic hybrid automata (SHA) [34]. Where the higher-level formalisms aim to be user-friendly interfaces for system modelling and design, the lower-level ones are reduced to the minimal necessary set of operations and concepts and thus more useful to specify analysis algorithms and create tool implementations for.

In this overview, we focus on the family of *quantitative automata-based formalisms* [44], the most expressive of which are the aforementioned SHA, and analysis methods based on probabilistic model checking (PMC) [4,5] and statistical model checking (SMC) [1]. Whereas PMC applies iterative numeric algorithms to an in-memory representation of the entire state space of the model, SMC performs a statistical evaluation of a large number of samples of the model's behaviour. SHA are expressive but also hard to analyse, so it is important to choose, for each case study, the "simplest" formalism appropriate for the level of abstraction required to solve the given set of properties of interest. We exemplify this choice using three case studies: of controlling water flow along a river in times of storm surges in the sea (Sect. 3.1), of optimising operations in an open-pit mine (Sect. 3.2), and of routing in satellite constellations (Sect. 3.3). Crucially, for none of them, previously developed analysis approaches worked "off-the-shelf", with each case study posing some particular complication that required additional modelling and analysis capabilities that we had to add to our algorithms and tools. These are collected in the MODEST TOOLSET [43], the capabilities of which we summarise in Sect. 2.

With analysis methods developed by the formal methods research community comes an expectation of *trustworthy results*: When an algorithm or tool returns a result, e.g. a probability $\tilde{p}$ for a reliability property, users expect that to equal the true, correct probability p for the model they made, or for it to come with a clearly stated correctness guarantee (such as an error ε so that $p \in \tilde{p} \pm \varepsilon = [\tilde{p} - \varepsilon, \tilde{p} + \varepsilon]$. Unfortunately, several commonly used algorithms, and moreso tool implementations, fail to achieve such a guarantee—an issue that has gained significant recent attention, leading to the development of explicitly *sound* PMC and SMC approaches, which we briefly survey in Sect. 4.

Prior Work. In earlier work [15] originating from an invited presentation at the MARS 2022 workshop, we similarly surveyed three case studies for their specific modelling and analysis requirements. One of them, on routing in satellite constellations, returns in this overview, while the other two case studies of this overview represent new developments and insights. The one on controlling water flow along a river is ongoing work that will require further investment in developing algorithms and scaling up tools to be truly solved.

2   The Modest Toolset

The MODEST TOOLSET [43] provides a collection of visualisation, model transformation, probabilistic model checking, and statistical model checking tools. It has been in development since 2008; it is written in C#, with small parts in C, and is available at modestchecker.net as precompiled binaries for common Linux distributions, macOS, and Windows on x86-64 and ARM-64 platforms.

Input and Output. As input languages, the MODEST TOOLSET supports MODEST as well as the JANI JSON-based model interchange format [19]. Its moconv tool can convert between the two and apply various transformations, such as applying the digital clocks transformation [55] to suitable probabilistic timed automata (PTA) [56] models. JANI is also supported by several other quantitative verification tools, notably the STORM probabilistic model checker [51], which can convert further higher-level formalisms (such as generalised stochastic Petri nets [8] and the PRISM language [54]) into JANI and thus allow the MODEST TOOLSET to analyse models written in these formalisms, too. The mosta tool visualises a model's symbolic semantics, helping in learning MODEST and in debugging models. The mopy tool converts a model into Python code implementing a first-state-next-state interface [13] that can be used to quickly prototype explicit-state verification algorithms.

PMC. The mcsta [44] tool implements PMC in an explicit-state fashion with a unique disk-based approach to mitigate the state space explosion problem. It includes efficient model reductions such as the essential states abstraction [30], and provides state-of-the-art algorithms [23] for model checking Markov automata (MA) [33,45]. Compared to other PMC tools like STORM or PRISM, mcsta puts a particular emphasis on providing sound results: It implements sound, floating point-correct, and verified PMC algorithms (see Section 4), and returns not only a single numeric result for each property, but also a clear statement on the correctness guarantees associated with that result.

SMC. The statistical model checker modes [18] complements mcsta's capabilities for cases where model checking cannot be applied, such as when facing state space explosion or models with non-Markovian probability distributions like stochastic timed automata (STA) [12]. SMC is, in essence, Monte Carlo simulation applied to formal models and properties. A constant-memory technique, it however incurs a runtime explosion when faced with rare events (as a prohibitively large number of samples would be needed to obtain an error that is smaller than the low probability of the rare event itself), and does not directly support nondeterministic models such as Markov decision processes (MDPs) [9,52]. The modes tool addresses these shortcomings by providing rare event simulation [65] via a highly automated implementation of importance splitting [16], and by offering lightweight strategy sampling [58] for MDP, PTA [28,49], and (with limitations) stochastic-time models like MA and STA [29]. Additionally, it defaults to sound statistical methods [21] (see Sect. 4), and can estimate quantities that are not expected values, such as quantiles or conditional value at risk [22].

3   Case Studies from Sea to Space

Over the past years, we tackled several case studies using the MODEST TOOLSET, finding that each came with its own requirements and specifics that often needed modelling facilities or analysis capabilities that were not yet available in the MODEST TOOLSET. The first case study we outline below, concerning river back-flooding, requires optimisation of SHA models; the second on open-pit mining needs a notion of partial observability not for inherent reasons but to make analysis feasible; and the final one on routing in space poses a distributed-information problem that we tried to tackle with PMC, SMC, and reinforcement learning.

3.1   Preventing River Backflooding in Storm Surges

The Interreg project STORM_SAFE (see interregnorthsea.eu/stormsafe, co-funded by the European Union) seeks to improve the digital resilience of crucial water infrastructures in the North Sea region through a collaboration between public authorities and universities, with a view towards applying state-of-the-art formal methods to a variety of systems in operation or being planned at the different partners.

One of these systems is the regulation of the river Mölndalsån, which flows through the city of Gothenburg, Sweden, into the North Sea. From a set of lakes in the hinterland, the river passes a sequence of sections and lakes with dams that have the ability to regulate its flow by opening or closing gates, until it reaches the much larger river Göta älv in central Gothenburg (see Fig. 1). The river flooded Gothenburg in 2006 [38], and its proper control has been a point of attention for the city since. Of particular interest is the scenario of an expected storm surge in the North Sea, which will lead to high sea water levels that propagate directly into Göta älv. In such a situation, the final gates that Mölndalsån passes through need to be closed to protect the city from the sea

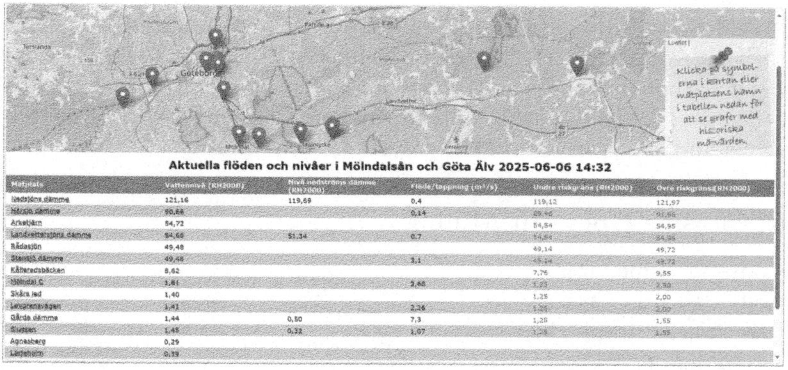

Fig. 1. Water levels of Mölndalsån along its sections and dams (from molndalsan.se)

water; yet at the same time, the river continues to receive inflow from upstream, which can in itself cause flooding as well. Thus a control strategy is needed that, based upon a short-term *forecast* of the sea levels, brings all the sections and lakes of the river into a state where they can buffer enough water inflow to survive the storm surge without flooding before sea levels return to normal.

Given the uncertainties in both weather and sea level forecasting, as well as in river water inflows, this is clearly a probabilistic system. A faithful representation of the flow dynamics of the river and in particular the gates results in a large system of rather nontrivial differential equations describing the physical behaviour of the river system and its gates. Thus we need to build and analyse an SHA model. Two types of analysis are needed: First, we need to find the control strategy that minimises the risk of flooding; second, we also would like to perform a sensitivity analysis w.r.t. the quality of the forecast, i.e. determine the maximal forecasting uncertainty that we can afford without raising the chance for flooding above a given probability threshold.

Unfortunately, the MODEST TOOLSET does not currently provide the means to check either property: For SHA, its prohver PMC tool [41] can compute upper bounds on maximum reachability probabilities via a combination of interval abstraction for continuous probability distributions and non-stochastic reachability analysis for the hybrid behaviour (currently provided by a modified version of PHAVER [35]). It cannot currently return the corresponding strategy, though—and this would also not be useful given the overapproximative nature of its solution. Using SMC, modes can simulate SHA that do not contain non-deterministic choices, using an engine based on numeric integration [60] (which in turn means it cannot provide almost any formal guarantees on the quality of the results due to the unknown integration error). Its strategy sampling features do not directly apply to systems with complex continuous dynamics [29]. Thus modes cannot help with the optimisation tasks of this case study either.

As a first step, we thus plan to employ a combination of (i) strategy optimisation via PMC on an abstract MDP model with (ii) validation of the strategy via

SMC on a detailed fully stochastic SHA model, similar in spirit to approaches taken earlier to synthesise strategies for lacquer production [14] and for battery-aware usage of nanosatellites [11]. Extending the capabilities of PMC tools to handle the two problems of the Mölndalsån case is a longer-term research challenge for us and the stochastic hybrid systems community.

3.2   Optimising Open-Pit Mining

In an open-pit mine, material needs to be transported by trucks from the extraction points to different places depending on if the material contains ore or is simply waste, as depicted in Fig. 2. This material transportation is one of the most important aspects that determine the mine's productivity. Consequently, given a mine setup of extraction and dumping point with associated production rates and travel times, we want to

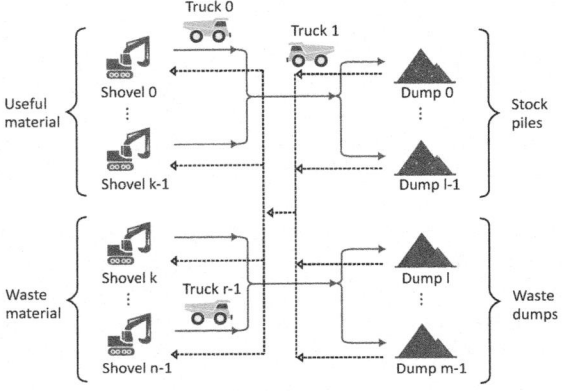

Fig. 2. Schematic view of the open pit mine [17]

find a strategy for distributing the trucks that minimises their waiting time (and any other possible non-productive time). This is also known as the *truck dispatching problem*. Using the MODEST TOOLSET, we proposed a flexible truck allocation approach to solve the problem based on an MA model of the mine and trucking operations [17]. The core property for which we need to find a (near-)optimal strategy is to maximise the amount of material moved within one shift of mine operations.

In principle, this could be solved directly by applying PMC to the MA model. Our property is a time-bounded expected reward property, however, for which the only available PMC algorithm today uses a discretisation approach [50]. This exacerbates the state space explosion problem of PMC by introducing many new states for the many discrete time steps needed for a reasonably precise result. We found that even checking the embedded MDP of small variants of this case study is infeasible; analysing the property of interest using a discretisation-based approach is thus out of the question [17].

Instead, we investigated using SMC in combination with the smart lightweight strategy sampling (LSS) [31,58] and (explicit table-based) Q-learning [66,67] techniques, both implemented in modes, which extend SMC from estimation to optimisation as required for this case study. The effectiveness of LSS depends on the probability of randomly sampling a (near-)optimal strategy out of the full strategy sampling space (which we restrict to the set of memoryless deterministic strategies in this case, since they can reasonably be implemented). That is, reducing the number of choices, or forcing multiple states to make the same choice based on some specific insights into the model, is advantageous. The latter is actually common in machine learning: Typically, only a projection of the model's states to selected *features* is presented to the learner. To tackle the open-pit mining problem, we thus extended modes with a notion of partial observability aimed at identifying features for LSS and Q-learning; we showed that this then in fact makes a difference for the two methods' outcomes. As part of that work, we additionally added a connection to the DTCONTROL tool [3] to modes which allows the resulting strategies to be turned into a more understandable and explainable representation in the form of decision trees.

3.3   Routing in Space

Satellite networks in low-Earth orbit are increasingly used to collect and distribute information across the globe. In sparse constellations (consisting of only a small number of satellites), real-time end-to-end connectivity from one point on Earth to another cannot be achieved; instead, such constellations leverage the store-carry-and-forward principle where nodes store

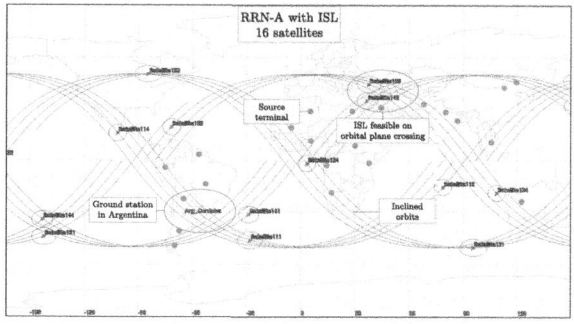

Fig. 3. Walker constellation DTN example [27]

received messages for later forwarding to other nodes in the network, once a communication window appears. The result is (necessarily) a *delay-tolerant network* (DTN).

In satellite constellations, the orbits are known with sufficient precision to calculate upcoming *contacts*, i.e. communication windows, over the next few days, giving rise to a *contact plan*. However, message transmissions may fail for various reasons such as unreliable (low-cost) components, contact mispredictions, or interference during the wireless communication. This gives rise to an *uncertain* contact plan where each contact is annotated with its probability of successful message transmission. Given a message's source and destination, and a limit n on the number of message copies present in the network to avoid exhausting the satellites' limited resources, we would like to compute the routing strategy that maximises the probability of message delivery within the time window covered by the contact plan. Due to the combination of randomness (in transmission failures) with nondeterministic decisions to be optimised (which contacts to use to send how many copies) in a discrete-time setting (a sequence of contacts), the simplest automata-based formalism we can use are MDPs. For them, scalable PMC approaches are implemented in a variety of tools [20].

However, PMC works with complete, global information. That is, when one satellite needs to decide how many message copies to send to a second satellite during a contact (or to send none at all), PMC assumes the satellite to have perfect information about the state of all other satellites, including the number of message copies they have. Our satellite could thus, for example, decide to send a copy only if some third satellite (that will have a contact with the final destination soon) did not manage to receive a message copy yet. This is clearly unrealistic; what we actually have is a *distributed-information* setting. We need to find a *distributed strategy* [36], or equivalently solve a *decentralised partially-observable MDP* (Dec-POMDP) [62]. These are undecidable problems. The L-RUCoP method [64] uses a PMC-based approximative approach to approach this problem, trying to find a good (but not necessarily optimal) strategy. It however runs out of memory quickly, e.g. for the larger instances of the realistic Walker constellation (depicted in Fig. 3) that we considered [27].

Instead, we turn to SMC with LSS and Q-learning again. As used for the open-pit mining case in Sect. 3.2, however, these are also global-information methods, just like plain PMC. We have thus extended LSS to consider distributed strategies only [26], and more recently added a *concurrent Q-learning* approach to modes that uses one separate learner per satellite, each seeing only the local state of their satellite [27]. For LSS, the distributed variant in fact improves the method's effectiveness, because it again reduces the space of strategies to sample from. For Q-learning, we found performance (in terms of the probability of message delivery that the returned strategy achieves) to be a little better than LSS, at the cost of higher memory usage [27].

4   Sound Quantitative Model Checking

In solving real case studies, the previous section showed that it is important to identify the right level of abstraction for modelling and analysis, and even then we may need to adapt existing PMC and SMC methods to actually work well for the case study at hand. Once we have a method that works, we then obviously expect it to deliver correct results. Unfortunately, the tools and algorithms used in quantitative verification have a mediocre track record when it comes to correctness guarantees: For PMC, the stopping criterion used for the widely implemented value iteration approach did not, in fact, guarantee the result to be ε-close to the true value [39]; and using a linear programming solver instead, which was often referred to as providing a "precise" result, can deliver arbitrarily wrong results, too [46]. In SMC, most tools used statistical methods that may return incorrect results more often than the user-specified confidence level would allow [21]. Additionally, when developing PMC and SMC tools in the typical academic context, we rarely use any formal methods approaches to check the tools themselves, leading to a high risk of implementation bugs.

Sound PMC. Traditionally, PMC tools by default use the value iteration algorithm, stopping iterations once the relative error is no larger than a user-specified ε. A common assumption was that the result $\tilde{v}$ would then be within

$\pm\varepsilon$ of the (unknown) true result v. Only 14 years after the arguably most widely used probabilistic model checker, PRISM, was first mentioned [2], the PMC community was made aware by Haddad and Monmege [39] that this method can lead to results that are arbitrarily far away from v. They also proposed an alternative algorithm, interval iteration (II) [40], which approximates the result from above and below (where value iteration would only approximate from below) and stops once the difference between the two approximations l and u is at most ε. Then $\frac{1}{2}(l+u)$ is guaranteed to be ε-close to v, and $[l, u]$ is guaranteed to contain v. We call such a result, and an algorithm that (only) produces such results, *sound*. Further sound PMC algorithms sparked by Haddad and Monmege's work are sound value iteration [63] and optimistic value iteration [47].

These algorithms are, however, always specified w.r.t. exact real or rational (on the usual assumption that all probabilities in a model are rational numbers) arithmetic. Yet their implementations typically use finite-precision IEEE 754 floating-point arithmetic for performance reasons, which involves rounding errors that can make the results unsound again [42,68]. We have recently shown, with an implementation in mcsta, that making use of the directed rounding modes that are part of IEEE 754 and implemented in all modern CPUs (though with very limited support from programming languages) allows implementing II at high performance without incurring incorrect results due to rounding errors [42].

Sound SMC. The results delivered by SMC come with *statistical guarantees*, e.g. that the true value v lies within $\pm\varepsilon$ of the returned estimate $\hat{v}$ in $(1 - \delta) \cdot 100\%$ of the times the SMC analysis is performed. Here, $1 - \delta$ is the *confidence level*; we often set $\delta = 0.05$. We call such results *sound*, too; the difference to the guarantee provided by sound PMC is that the result may be completely wrong with a-priori probability δ, which is unavoidable in a statistical Monte Carlo approach. Unfortunately, as we recently showed [21], most SMC tools use statistical methods such as confidence intervals based on the central limit theorem that, when parametrised with confidence level $1 - \delta$, may actually return an incorrect result with probability $\gg \delta$. For estimating probabilities, a good sound statistical method is the Clopper-Pearson interval [25]. For expected values, whether a good sound method is available depends on the specific type of property; we recommend in [21] different variants of using the Dvoretzky-Kiefer-Wolfowitz-Massart inequality (DKW) [32,59]. The modes tool now uses our recommended sound methods by default. It furthermore now supports estimating new quantities that are not means, in particular quantiles and the conditional value at risk, using the DKW [22].

Verified Algorithms and Tools. The soundness of the approaches detailed above has been proven in the classic "pen-and-paper" manner. Just as their manual implementation in tools, this leaves room for human errors that may invalidate the actual soundness. To exclude such errors, the algorithms may be formalised in the language of an interactive theorem proving (ITP) tool such as Isabelle/HOL [61] or Rocq (see rocq-prover.org); then an equally formalised theorem stating their soundness/correctness can be proven and the proof be machine-checked by the ITP tool. This reduces the amount of things that need to be trusted for the soundness to hold to the small core of the ITP tool.

To make the connection from the proven formalised algorithm to the correctness of an actual implementation, two alternative approaches can be used: Either an existing tool is extended with mechanisms to output a *certificate* in addition to the result, which is a compact extra output that can in turn be used by a verified certificate checker to assert the correctness of the result. Certification is widely used in e.g. SAT tools and the Software Verification Competition [10]. In SAT, for example, a certificate for a "satisfiable" result is simply a satisfying assignment for the formula's Boolean variables, which can very easily be checked. Certification is attractive because it is usually much less computational effort (given a good notion of certificate) than finding the result in the first place, so the performance of the certificate checker is not critical. Consequently, such checkers can be generated with little effort by refining their ITP formalisation into a program in a (slow) functional language that is semantically close to the language of the ITP tool (e.g. Standard ML for Isabelle/HOL). The alternative approach is to refine the proven formalised algorithm into an executable program, which however should be implemented in an efficient (imperative) programming language using efficient (imperative) low-level data structures. The correctness of all refinement steps then has to be proven using the ITP tool as well. The additional performance considerations typically make obtaining such a correct-by-construction implementation a higher effort.

The first certification approach for PMC algorithms such as II has recently become available [24], using Isabelle/HOL. It however needs additional information (a distance vector) aside from the vector of intervals produced by II, slightly complicating the PMC tool; then checking certificates turns out to be relatively slow compared to the often-fast PMC algorithms, so that it has an actual impact on the overall performance; and finally, the PMC algorithm implementations turn out to often generate invalid certificates (according to the criterion used by this approach) even for correct results.

We instead took the correct-by-construction implementation approach to improve the reliability of mcsta, using Isabelle/HOL in combination with the Isabelle Refinement Framework [57] to obtain high-performance implementations in LLVM bytecode. We first did so for the maximal end component decomposition that is a necessary preprocessing step to bring the MDP at hand into a form that is amenable to II [48]. We then formalised II, proving its soundness and convergence, and provably refined it into a sound floating-point implementation whose performance is on par with mcsta's previous unverified one [53].

5   Conclusion

We have surveyed the possibilities and challenges of applying PMC and SMC approaches as implemented in the MODEST TOOLSET to real-world problems. To handle the Mölndalsån case, we found that we lack tools and algorithms to approach the problem directly, and instead plan to make use of a two-step approach combining an abstract, imprecise optimisation step on an MDP discretisation with a subsequent validation on a detailed SHA simulation model. While the open-pit mining case can directly be modelled using MA, its challenge is state space explosion combined with a very simplistic PMC algorithm that exacerbates it; we instead make use of SMC with LSS and Q-learning, for which we added a way to select features to improve the effectiveness of the two methods. The space DTN routing case is seemingly even simpler, with MDP being a perfect fit for modelling—but it requires an analysis that considers distributed information for decentralised decision-making, turning it into an instance of an undecidable problem: so we again turn to SMC with LSS (adapted to consider distributed strategies) and Q-learning (using a concurrent Q-learning approach). All of these methods should return sound results, which has not always been the case in PMC and SMC algorithms and tools of the past; mcsta and modes however provide a choice of several sound approaches today.

Our overview raises the question whether, as a quantitative formal methods community, we will ever reach a point where our tools can *directly* be applied to most actual problems without requiring individual adaptation, extension, and new research. Will reality always be one step ahead; will the demands of case studies always increase with the capabilities of our tools? Or are we perhaps simply not talking and publishing about the multitude of examples (if they exist) where our methods *do* work straight away?

Acknowledgments. I thank my collaborators and co-authors on the work that I summarise in this overview: Mohammad Abdulaziz, Carlos E. Budde, Pedro R. D'Argenio, Juan A. Fraire, E. Moritz Hahn, Holger Hermanns, Benjamin L. Kaminski, Bram Kohlen, Peter Lammich, Tobias Meggendorfer, Annabell Petri, Fernando D. Raverta, Maximilian Schäffeler, Maximilian Weininger, Patrick Wienhöft, and many others.

References

1. Agha, G., Palmskog, K.: A survey of statistical model checking. ACM Trans. Model. Comput. Simul. **28**(1), 6:1–6:39 (2018). https://doi.org/10.1145/3158668
2. de Alfaro, L., Kwiatkowska, M., Norman, G., Parker, D., Segala, R.: Symbolic model checking of probabilistic processes using MTBDDs and the Kronecker representation. In: Graf, S., Schwartzbach, M. (eds.) TACAS 2000. LNCS, vol. 1785, pp. 395–410. Springer, Heidelberg (2000). https://doi.org/10.1007/3-540-46419-0_27
3. Ashok, P., Jackermeier, M., Křetínský, J., Weinhuber, C., Weininger, M., Yadav, M.: dtControl 2.0: explainable strategy representation via decision tree learning steered by experts. In: TACAS 2021. LNCS, vol. 12652, pp. 326–345. Springer, Cham (2021). https://doi.org/10.1007/978-3-030-72013-1_17
4. Baier, C.: Probabilistic model checking. In: Esparza, J., Grumberg, O., Sickert, S. (eds.) Dependable Software Systems Engineering, NATO Science for Peace and Security Series – D: Information and Communication Security, vol 45, pp. 1–23. IOS Press (2016). https://doi.org/10.3233/978-1-61499-627-9-1

5. Baier, C., de Alfaro, L., Forejt, V., Kwiatkowska, M.: Model Checking Probabilistic Systems. In: Clarke, E., Henzinger, T., Veith, H., Bloem, R. (eds.) Handbook of Model Checking, pp. 963–999. Springer, Cham (2018). https://doi.org/10.1007/978-3-319-10575-8_28

6. Baier, C., Haverkort, B.R., Hermanns, H., Katoen, J.P.: Performance evaluation and model checking join forces. Commun. ACM **53**(9), 76–85 (2010). https://doi.org/10.1145/1810891.1810912

7. Baier, C., Katoen, J.P.: Principles of Model Checking. MIT Press (2008)

8. Balbo, G.: Introduction to generalized stochastic Petri nets. In: Bernardo, M., Hillston, J. (eds.) SFM 2007. LNCS, vol. 4486, pp. 83–131. Springer, Heidelberg (2007). https://doi.org/10.1007/978-3-540-72522-0_3

9. Bellman, R.: A Markovian decision process. J. Math. Mech. **6**(5), 679–684 (1957)

10. Beyer, D., Strejcek, J.: Improvements in software verification and witness validation: SV-COMP 2025. In: Gurfinkel, A., Heule, M. (eds.) TACAS 2025. LNCS, vol. 15698, pp. 151–186. Springer, Cham (2025). https://doi.org/10.1007/978-3-031-90660-2_9

11. Bisgaard, M., Gerhardt, D., Hermanns, H., Krcál, J., Nies, G., Stenger, M.: Battery-aware scheduling in low orbit: the GomX-3 case. Formal Aspects Comput. **31**(2), 261–285 (2019). https://doi.org/10.1007/S00165-018-0458-2

12. Bohnenkamp, H.C., D'Argenio, P.R., Hermanns, H., Katoen, J.P.: MoDeST: a compositional modeling formalism for hard and softly timed systems. IEEE Trans. Software Eng. **32**(10), 812–830 (2006). https://doi.org/10.1109/TSE.2006.104

13. Bohnenkamp, H., Hermanns, H., Katoen, J.-P., Klaren, R.: The MODEST modeling tool and its implementation. In: Kemper, P., Sanders, W.H. (eds.) TOOLS 2003. LNCS, vol. 2794, pp. 116–133. Springer, Heidelberg (2003). https://doi.org/10.1007/978-3-540-45232-4_8

14. Bohnenkamp, H.C., Hermanns, H., Klaren, R., Mader, A., Usenko, Y.S.: Synthesis and stochastic assessment of schedules for lacquer production. In: 1st International Conference on Quantitative Evaluation of Systems (QEST 2004), pp. 28–37. IEEE Computer Society (2004). https://doi.org/10.1109/QEST.2004.1348013

15. Budde, C.E., D'Argenio, P.R., Fraire, J.A., Hartmanns, A., Zhang, Z.: Modest models and tools for real stochastic timed systems. In: Jansen, N., et al. (eds.) Principles of Verification: Cycling the Probabilistic Landscape – Essays Dedicated to Joost-Pieter Katoen on the Occasion of His 60th Birthday. Lecture Notes in Computer Science, vol. 15261, pp. 115–142. Springer (2024). https://doi.org/10.1007/978-3-031-75775-4_6

16. Budde, C.E., D'Argenio, P.R., Hartmanns, A.: Automated compositional importance splitting. Sci. Comput. Program. **174**, 90–108 (2019). https://doi.org/10.1016/J.SCICO.2019.01.006

17. Budde, C.E., D'Argenio, P.R., Hartmanns, A.: Digging for decision trees: a case study in strategy sampling and learning. In: Steffen, B. (ed.) 2nd International Conference on Bridging the Gap Between AI and Reality (AISoLA 2024). Lecture Notes in Computer Science, vol. 15217, pp. 354–378. Springer (2024). https://doi.org/10.1007/978-3-031-75434-0_24

18. Budde, C.E., D'Argenio, P.R., Hartmanns, A., Sedwards, S.: An efficient statistical model checker for nondeterminism and rare events. Int. J. Softw. Tools Technol. Transf. **22**(6), 759–780 (2020). https://doi.org/10.1007/S10009-020-00563-2

19. Budde, C.E., Dehnert, C., Hahn, E.M., Hartmanns, A., Junges, S., Turrini, A.: JANI: quantitative model and tool interaction. In: Legay, A., Margaria, T. (eds.) TACAS 2017. LNCS, vol. 10206, pp. 151–168. Springer, Heidelberg (2017). https://doi.org/10.1007/978-3-662-54580-5_9

20. Budde, C.E., et al.: On correctness, precision, and performance in quantitative verification. In: Margaria, T., Steffen, B. (eds.) ISoLA 2020. LNCS, vol. 12479, pp. 216–241. Springer, Cham (2021). https://doi.org/10.1007/978-3-030-83723-5_15

21. Budde, C.E., Hartmanns, A., Meggendorfer, T., Weininger, M., Wienhöft, P.: Sound statistical model checking for probabilities and expected rewards. In: Gurfinkel, A., Heule, M. (eds.) 31st International Conference on Tools and Algorithms for the Construction and Analysis of Systems (TACAS 2025). Lecture Notes in Computer Science, vol. 15696, pp. 167–190. Springer (2025). https://doi.org/10.1007/978-3-031-90643-5_9

22. Budde, C.E., Hartmanns, A., Meggendorfer, T., Weininger, M., Wienhöft, P.: Statistical model checking beyond means: Quantiles, CVaR, and the DKW inequality. In: 2nd International Joint Conference on Quantitative Evaluation of Systems and Formal Modeling and Analysis of Timed Systems (QEST-FORMATS 2025). Lecture Notes in Computer Science. Springer (2025, to appear)

23. Butkova, Y., Hartmanns, A., Hermanns, H.: A Modest approach to Markov automata. ACM Trans. Model. Comput. Simul. **31**(3), 14:1–14:34 (2021). https://doi.org/10.1145/3449355

24. Chatterjee, K., Quatmann, T., Schäffeler, M., Weininger, M., Winkler, T., Zilken, D.: Fixed point certificates for reachability and expected rewards in MDPs. In: Gurfinkel, A., Heule, M. (eds.) 31st International Conference on Tools and Algorithms for the Construction and Analysis of Systems (TACAS 2025). Lecture Notes in Computer Science, vol. 15697, pp. 130–151. Springer (2025). https://doi.org/10.1007/978-3-031-90653-4_7

25. Clopper, C., Pearson, E.: The use of confidence or fiducial limits illustrated in the case of the binomial. Biometrika **26**(4), 404–413 (1934). https://doi.org/10.1093/biomet/26.4.404

26. D'Argenio, P.R., Fraire, J.A., Hartmanns, A.: Sampling distributed schedulers for resilient space communication. In: Lee, R., Jha, S., Mavridou, A., Giannakopoulou, D. (eds.) NFM 2020. LNCS, vol. 12229, pp. 291–310. Springer, Cham (2020). https://doi.org/10.1007/978-3-030-55754-6_17

27. D'Argenio, P.R., Fraire, J.A., Hartmanns, A., Raverta, F.D.: Comparing statistical, analytical, and learning-based routing approaches for delay-tolerant networks. ACM Trans. Model. Comput. Simul. **35**(2), 10:1–10:26 (2025). https://doi.org/10.1145/3665927

28. D'Argenio, P.R., Hartmanns, A., Legay, A., Sedwards, S.: Statistical approximation of optimal schedulers for probabilistic timed automata. In: Ábrahám, E., Huisman, M. (eds.) IFM 2016. LNCS, vol. 9681, pp. 99–114. Springer, Cham (2016). https://doi.org/10.1007/978-3-319-33693-0_7

29. D'Argenio, P.R., Hartmanns, A., Sedwards, S.: Lightweight statistical model checking in nondeterministic continuous time. In: Margaria, T., Steffen, B. (eds.) ISoLA 2018. LNCS, vol. 11245, pp. 336–353. Springer, Cham (2018). https://doi.org/10.1007/978-3-030-03421-4_22

30. D'Argenio, P.R., Jeannet, B., Jensen, H.E., Larsen, K.G.: Reduction and refinement strategies for probabilistic analysis. In: Hermanns, H., Segala, R. (eds.) PAPM-PROBMIV 2002. LNCS, vol. 2399, pp. 57–76. Springer, Heidelberg (2002). https://doi.org/10.1007/3-540-45605-8_5

31. D'Argenio, P.R., Legay, A., Sedwards, S., Traonouez, L.M.: Smart sampling for lightweight verification of Markov decision processes. Int. J. Softw. Tools Technol. Transf. **17**(4), 469–484 (2015). https://doi.org/10.1007/S10009-015-0383-0

32. Dvoretzky, A., Kiefer, J., Wolfowitz, J.: Asymptotic minimax character of the sample distribution function and of the classical multinomial estimator. Ann. Math. Stat. **27**(3), 642–669 (1956). https://doi.org/10.1214/aoms/1177728174

33. Eisentraut, C., Hermanns, H., Zhang, L.: On probabilistic automata in continuous time. In: 25th Annual IEEE Symposium on Logic in Computer Science (LICS 2010), pp. 342–351. IEEE Computer Society (2010). https://doi.org/10.1109/LICS.2010.41

34. Fränzle, M., Hahn, E.M., Hermanns, H., Wolovick, N., Zhang, L.: Measurability and safety verification for stochastic hybrid systems. In: Caccamo, M., Frazzoli, E., Grosu, R. (eds.) 14th ACM International Conference on Hybrid Systems: Computation and Control (HSCC 2011), pp. 43–52. ACM (2011). https://doi.org/10.1145/1967701.1967710

35. Frehse, G.: PHAVer: algorithmic verification of hybrid systems past HyTech. Int. J. Softw. Tools Technol. Transf. **10**(3), 263–279 (2008). https://doi.org/10.1007/S10009-007-0062-X

36. Giro, S., D'Argenio, P.R.: Quantitative model checking revisited: neither decidable nor approximable. In: Raskin, J.-F., Thiagarajan, P.S. (eds.) FORMATS 2007. LNCS, vol. 4763, pp. 179–194. Springer, Heidelberg (2007). https://doi.org/10.1007/978-3-540-75454-1_14

37. Gribaudo, M., Remke, A.: Hybrid Petri nets with general one-shot transitions for dependability evaluation of fluid critical infrastructures. In: 12th IEEE High Assurance Systems Engineering Symposium (HASE 2010), pp. 84–93. IEEE Computer Society (2010). https://doi.org/10.1109/HASE.2010.27

38. Göteborgs stad, Härryda kommun, Mölndals stad: Mölndalsån – reglerad livsnerv genom tre kommuner. https://molndalsan.se/molndalsan.pdf. Accessed 06 June 2025

39. Haddad, S., Monmege, B.: Reachability in MDPs: refining convergence of value iteration. In: Ouaknine, J., Potapov, I., Worrell, J. (eds.) RP 2014. LNCS, vol. 8762, pp. 125–137. Springer, Cham (2014). https://doi.org/10.1007/978-3-319-11439-2_10

40. Haddad, S., Monmege, B.: Interval iteration algorithm for MDPs and IMDPs. Theor. Comput. Sci. **735**, 111–131 (2018). https://doi.org/10.1016/J.TCS.2016.12.003

41. Hahn, E.M., Hartmanns, A., Hermanns, H., Katoen, J.P.: A compositional modelling and analysis framework for stochastic hybrid systems. Formal Methods Syst. Des. **43**(2), 191–232 (2013). https://doi.org/10.1007/S10703-012-0167-Z

42. Hartmanns, A.: Correct probabilistic model checking with floating-point arithmetic. In: Fisman, D., Rosu, G. (eds.) TACAS 2022. LNCS, vol. 13244, pp. 41–59. Springer, Cham (2022). https://doi.org/10.1007/978-3-030-99527-0_3

43. Hartmanns, A., Hermanns, H.: The Modest Toolset: an integrated environment for quantitative modelling and verification. In: Ábrahám, E., Havelund, K. (eds.) TACAS 2014. LNCS, vol. 8413, pp. 593–598. Springer, Heidelberg (2014). https://doi.org/10.1007/978-3-642-54862-8_51

44. Hartmanns, A., Hermanns, H.: In the quantitative automata zoo. Sci. Comput. Program. **112**, 3–23 (2015). https://doi.org/10.1016/J.SCICO.2015.08.009

45. Hartmanns, A., Hermanns, H.: A Modest Markov automata tutorial. In: Krötzsch, M., Stepanova, D. (eds.) Reasoning Web. Explainable Artificial Intelligence. LNCS, vol. 11810, pp. 250–276. Springer, Cham (2019). https://doi.org/10.1007/978-3-030-31423-1_8

46. Hartmanns, A., Junges, S., Quatmann, T., Weininger, M.: A practitioner's guide to MDP model checking algorithms. In: Sankaranarayanan, S., Sharygina, N. (eds.) 29th International Conference on Tools and Algorithms for the Construction and Analysis of Systems (TACAS 2023). Lecture Notes in Computer Science, vol. 13993, pp. 469–488. Springer (2023). https://doi.org/10.1007/978-3-031-30823-9_24

47. Hartmanns, A., Kaminski, B.L.: Optimistic value iteration. In: Lahiri, S.K., Wang, C. (eds.) CAV 2020. LNCS, vol. 12225, pp. 488–511. Springer, Cham (2020). https://doi.org/10.1007/978-3-030-53291-8_26

48. Hartmanns, A., Kohlen, B., Lammich, P.: Efficient formally verified maximal end component decomposition for MDPs. In: Platzer, A., Rozier, K.Y., Pradella, M., Rossi, M. (eds.) 26th International Formal Methods Symposium (FM 2024). Lecture Notes in Computer Science, vol. 14933, pp. 206–225. Springer (2024). https://doi.org/10.1007/978-3-031-71162-6_11

49. Hartmanns, A., Sedwards, S., D'Argenio, P.R.: Efficient simulation-based verification of probabilistic timed automata. In: 2017 Winter Simulation Conference (WSC 2017), pp. 1419–1430. IEEE (2017). https://doi.org/10.1109/WSC.2017.8247885

50. Hatefi-Ardakani, H.: Finite horizon analysis of Markov automata. Ph.D. thesis, Saarland University, Germany (2017). http://scidok.sulb.uni-saarland.de/volltexte/2017/6743/

51. Hensel, C., Junges, S., Katoen, J.P., Quatmann, T., Volk, M.: The probabilistic model checker Storm. Int. J. Softw. Tools Technol. Transf. 24(4), 589–610 (2022). https://doi.org/10.1007/S10009-021-00633-Z

52. Howard, R.A.: Dynamic Programming and Markov Processes. MIT Press (1960)

53. Kohlen, B., Schäffeler, M., Abdulaziz, M., Hartmanns, A., Lammich, P.: A formally verified IEEE 754 floating-point implementation of interval iteration for MDPs. In: 37th International Conference on Computer Aided Verification (CAV 2025). Lecture Notes in Computer Science. Springer (2025). https://doi.org/10.1007/978-3-031-98679-6_6

54. Kwiatkowska, M., Norman, G., Parker, D.: PRISM 4.0: verification of probabilistic real-time systems. In: Gopalakrishnan, G., Qadeer, S. (eds.) CAV 2011. LNCS, vol. 6806, pp. 585–591. Springer, Heidelberg (2011). https://doi.org/10.1007/978-3-642-22110-1_47

55. Kwiatkowska, M.Z., Norman, G., Parker, D., Sproston, J.: Performance analysis of probabilistic timed automata using digital clocks. Formal Methods Syst. Des. 29(1), 33–78 (2006). https://doi.org/10.1007/S10703-006-0005-2

56. Kwiatkowska, M.Z., Norman, G., Segala, R., Sproston, J.: Automatic verification of real-time systems with discrete probability distributions. Theor. Comput. Sci. 282(1), 101–150 (2002). https://doi.org/10.1016/S0304-3975(01)00046-9

57. Lammich, P., Tuerk, T.: Applying data refinement for monadic programs to Hopcroft's algorithm. In: Beringer, L., Felty, A. (eds.) ITP 2012. LNCS, vol. 7406, pp. 166–182. Springer, Heidelberg (2012). https://doi.org/10.1007/978-3-642-32347-8_12

58. Legay, A., Sedwards, S., Traonouez, L.-M.: Scalable verification of Markov decision processes. In: Canal, C., Idani, A. (eds.) SEFM 2014. LNCS, vol. 8938, pp. 350–362. Springer, Cham (2015). https://doi.org/10.1007/978-3-319-15201-1_23

59. Massart, P.: The tight constant in the Dvoretzky-Kiefer-Wolfowitz inequality. Ann. Probab. 18(3), 1269–1283 (1990). https://doi.org/10.1214/aop/1176990746

60. Niehage, M., Hartmanns, A., Remke, A.: Learning optimal decisions for stochastic hybrid systems. In: Arun-Kumar, S., Méry, D., Saha, I., Zhang, L. (eds.) 19th ACM-IEEE International Conference on Formal Methods and Models for System

Design (MEMOCODE 2021), pp. 44–55. ACM (2021). https://doi.org/10.1145/3487212.3487339

61. Nipkow, T., Paulson, L.C., Wenzel, M.: Isabelle/HOL – a proof assistant for Higher-Order Logic. Springer (2002)

62. Oliehoek, F.A., Amato, C.: A Concise Introduction to Decentralized POMDPs. Springer Briefs in Intelligent Systems. Springer (2016). https://doi.org/10.1007/978-3-319-28929-8

63. Quatmann, T., Katoen, J.-P.: Sound value iteration. In: Chockler, H., Weissenbacher, G. (eds.) CAV 2018. LNCS, vol. 10981, pp. 643–661. Springer, Cham (2018). https://doi.org/10.1007/978-3-319-96145-3_37

64. Raverta, F.D., Fraire, J.A., Madoery, P.G., Demasi, R.A., Finochietto, J.M., D'Argenio, P.R.: Routing in delay-tolerant networks under uncertain contact plans. Ad Hoc Netw. **123**, 102663 (2021). https://doi.org/10.1016/j.adhoc.2021.102663

65. Rubino, G., Tuffin, B. (eds.): Rare Event Simulation using Monte Carlo Methods. Wiley (2009). https://doi.org/10.1002/9780470745403

66. Sutton, R.S., Barto, A.G.: Reinforcement Learning - An Introduction. Adaptive Computation and Machine Learning. MIT Press (1998)

67. Watkins, C.J.C.H., Dayan, P.: Q-learning. Mach. Learn. **8**, 279–292 (1992). https://doi.org/10.1007/BF00992698

68. Wimmer, R., Kortus, A., Herbstritt, M., Becker, B.: Probabilistic model checking and reliability of results. In: Straube, B., Drutarovský, M., Renovell, M., Gramata, P., Fischerová, M. (eds.) 11th IEEE Workshop on Design & Diagnostics of Electronic Circuits & Systems (DDECS 2008), pp. 207–212. IEEE Computer Society (2008). https://doi.org/10.1109/DDECS.2008.4538787

Verification

Verification

Proof Engineering in Logika: Synergistically Integrating Automated and Semi-automated Program Verification

Stefan Hallerstede[1]($\boxtimes$), Robby[2], John Hatcliff[2], Jason Belt[2], and David Hardin[3]

[1] Aarhus University, Aarhus, Denmark
sha@ece.au.dk
[2] Kansas State University, Manhattan, KS, USA
{robby,hatcliff,belt}@ksu.edu
[3] Collins Aerospace, Cedar Rapids, IA, USA
david.hardin@collins.com

Abstract. Recent work on industry-capable program verification technology has emphasized the need for greater predictability in the performance of SMT-based automated verification approaches. Moreover, foundational limitations of SMT necessitate some incorporation of manual proof steps, and researchers are considering the utility of handing off some verification obligations to more powerful semi-automated interactive proof assistants. In this paper, we describe how capabilities that are usually associated with expert-level semi-automated proof assistants can be integrated synergistically in a developer-friendly code-based proof language to address many of the limitations of traditional SMT-based automated verification. Our approach enables proofs of more powerful properties to be carried out directly in a familiar programming environment rather than in a separate proof assistant tool that often utilizes low-level encodings of program semantics in annotations that are unfamiliar to industry developers. Because the proof language is implemented at the same level of abstraction as the programming language, using familiar syntax, our approach can provide easier-to-understand visualizations of rewriting/simplification steps that better align with the developer's mental model of program execution (providing a better user experience). Our approach is implemented in the open-source Logika program verifier for Slang (a safety-critical subset of Scala). We evaluate the framework on a collection of examples, including libraries for high assurance embedded system data structures developed by engineers at Collins Aerospace.

1 Introduction

Program verification with SMT (Satisfiability Modulo Theories) solvers has made significant advances in recent years, enabling formal verification of increasingly complex software. However, there are several issues that frustrate developers and impede the adoption of formal verification techniques.

First, SMT-based program verifiers often suffer from "proof instability" (e.g. investigated by Zhou et al. [34]) – situations in which "semantically irrelevant changes to the query can have large effects on the SMT solver's response". E.g., simply renaming a variable might cause a previously verified procedure to take orders of magnitude longer to verify, or fail completely. Second, the effectiveness of SMT-based program verification depends heavily on solver heuristics and configuration choices to work around the general inherent incompleteness of SMT, creating significant usability challenges for developers [9]. Modern SMT solvers like Z3 and CVC5 employ hundreds of heuristic rules for, e.g.: (a) quantifier instantiation patterns, (b) theory combination strategies, (c) search-space prioritization, and (d) preprocessing transformations. These implementations differ substantially between solvers, leading to: (i) unpredictable performance profiles for similar verification tasks, (ii) non-portable verification results across solver versions (sometimes performance on certain tasks may regress [21]), and (iii) configuration sensitivity requiring expert-level tuning. To deal with the unpredictability as well as fundamental limitations of SMT, previous work has investigated handing off some verification obligations to more powerful interactive theorem provers, e.g., [23,27]. However, the community is struggling to find the most effective approaches for achieving these handoffs in ways that are easy to use, that achieve the best synergy between automated and semi-automated techniques, and that avoid disruptive steps in proof engineering workflows.

In this paper, we describe how capabilities (such as induction proofs for recursive data structures, term rewriting and simplification) that are usually associated with expert-level semi-automated proof assistants can be integrated in a developer-friendly code-level proof language. This stands in contrast to other "hand-off" approaches that require developers to complete the hand-off in a separate proof assistant tool that uses low-level encodings of program semantics in annotations that are unfamiliar to industry developers [19]. We show how these integrated capabilities can be synergistically combined with SMT to address the limitations of traditional SMT-based automated verification described above. Our approach is implemented in the open-source Logika program verifier for Slang. Previously, we gave an overview of Logika [32]. We described design goals for Logika, Logika's contract language, the incorporation of Logika into the widely-used IntelliJ IDE to form an *integrated verification environment* (IVE), and gave a one-page summary of capabilities of the initial version of Logika's proof language. In this paper, we report on our complete realization of the integrated proof language concept, and its application to industry-relevant examples. The specific contributions of this paper are as follows.

- We present our strategy for integrating associated semi-automated verification in an approach that seamlessly and synergistically integrates with Logika's symbolic execution SMT-based verification.
- We describe the language's support for inductive proofs for code that manipulates inductively defined data types.
- We illustrate explainability and visualization features that we have added in the IVE to help developer understanding of succeeding and failing proof steps.

– We describe Logika's rewriting and simplification proof methods that use approaches similar to partial evaluation and symbolic execution to simplify programming language terms appearing in proofs. Because the proof language is implemented at the same level of abstraction as the programming language, using familiar syntax, our approach can provide easier-to-understand visualizations of rewriting/simplification steps that better align with the developer's mental model of program execution.
– We illustrate the features above using a collection of examples that includes an embedded system data structure library developed at Collins Aerospace.

Slang and Logika are part of the Sireum framework for language processing, analysis, and verification developed at Kansas State University. The entire Sireum framework is publicly available [36] under an open source license, as are the code examples referenced in this paper [35].

2   Background

In this section, we summarize the rationale for Slang and Logika's design, drawing from the more detailed presentations in [13,31,32].

Slang: The Slang (safety-critical) dialect of Scala was designed "hand in glove" with Logika to achieve effective, efficient, and usable verification while also supporting development for programming language and model processing, targeting embedded systems. Slang retains some of the expressive higher-level features of Scala (classes, traits, higher-order functions) while restricting them to a form that enables more effective verification. A subset of Slang (called "Slang Embedded") is further restricted to constructs that can be translated to C and Rust appropriate for embedded systems without the need for dynamic memory allocation/automatic memory management. For a detailed overview of Slang features and design rationale, see [31].

Examples of Slang's restrictions of higher-level Scala features include: (a) a modified type system that strictly separates immutable from mutable types, and (b) restrictions on mutable object aliasing, allowing aliasing to only be introduced in a single programming construct (i.e., method invocation) under certain object separation constraints. These customizations reduce developer reasoning effort and significantly simplify formal analyses (i.e., reducing verification costs). Slang's *extension interfaces* (akin to those in the Bogor model checker [30]) allow Slang to interface with full Scala, Java or any other JVM-based language, and C/Rust libraries, as well as facilitating domain-specific customizations.

While Slang is a strict Scala subset, its programming language features are still rich enough to support large application development. The largest system implemented in Slang is Sireum itself (which includes Slang and Logika). This allows for self-application of Sireum tooling to its own Slang codebase. At this point, the Sireum codebase consists of 41 (Maven) modules with close to 391k lines of code as 84% Slang, 11.4% Scala, and 4.6% Java.[1]

---

[1]   https://github.com/sireum/kekinian/tree/04afeba.

In addition to using Slang with standard JVM-based Scala/Java tools and ecosystems, the Slang Embedded subset can be transpiled to C without requiring garbage collection at runtime (i.e., objects are globally/stack-allocated). For additional assurance, the translated C code can be compiled using the CompCert verified C compiler [26]. We are developing transpilation of Slang Embedded code and contracts to Rust (with Verus [24] contracts) as part of an ongoing DARPA PROVERS project led by Collins Aerospace.

Slang and Logika have primarily been used on industrial research projects on high-assurance model-based development at Collins Aerospace [6,7] and Galois [16,17]. Given an AADL [3] component-based system architecture model, the Sireum HAMR high assurance embedded system engineering framework generates AADL runtime services in Slang Embedded that can be deployed in various platforms, including the seL4 verified micro-kernel (via C) with formal evidence that architectural constraints are preserved, thus enabling guarantees of safe/secure inter-component spatial and temporal separations [6]. In collaboration with Collins Aerospace and seL4 developers, HAMR was used to build an experimental mission control subsystem running on seL4 for the Boeing CH-47 Chinook helicopter platform. Regarding the primary developer-facing tooling, the Sireum Integrated Verification Environment (IVE) – a customized version of IntelliJ IDEA – integrates various Sireum tools such as the Slang front-end (providing, e.g., type checking, refactoring, etc.), the Proyek incremental/parallel build tool, and Logika, all running as microservices in a background Sireum server. Moreover, we recently added VSCode integration for Sireum.

Logika: Slang's contract language is based on classical logic and supports assertions, pre/post-conditions, data type invariants, and global invariants for global states. Verification of code conformance to contracts is performed compositionally and employs multiple back-end solvers in parallel, including Alt-Ergo [8], CVC4 [5], CVC5 [4], and Z3 [29]. In principle, other theorem provers could also be employed. To provide a continuous user abstraction experience, however, a developer should be supported within Slang/Logika as much as possible. Current work on Logika focuses on proof constructions within Slang to allow this. Logika uses a forward verification approach based on symbolic execution instead of a backward approach based on weakest pre-condition computation. Based on two decades of experience of implementing symbolic execution tools for both Java and SPARK, we believe that the symbolic execution approach produces diagnostic information about verification steps that is much easier to understand and also allows a more intuitive summary of the underlying verification algorithm for engineers and students. The scalability of Logika is complemented by using incremental, focused, and parallel (distributable) verification algorithms. Verification results, developer feedback on verification status, and contract/proof editing are supported in the Sireum IVE. With the IVE, we are able to support testing concepts with conventional unit libraries for Scala (e.g., ScalaTest) as well as provide testing coverage concepts using IntelliJ's built in coverage facility.[2]

---

[2] See https://doc.sireum.org/venues/presentations/logika/tccoe22/ for a video of a 25-minute technical talk and demonstration of Logika's IVE user interface and server-based checking architecture.

```
// Definition by cases, equational                    Validity Check for Loop invariant at the beginning of while-loop at [28, 17]: Valid
// Specification of the factorial function            Validity Check for Loop invariant at the beginning of while-loop at [28, 25]: Valid
@abs def fac(n: Z): Z = n match {                     Validity Check for Loop invariant at the beginning of while-loop at [28, 33]: Valid
  case 0 ⇒ 1                                           Validity Check for Loop invariant at the end of while-loop at [28, 17]: Valid
  case m if m > 0 ⇒ m * fac(m - 1)                     Validity Check for Loop invariant at the end of while-loop at [28, 25]: Valid
  case _ ⇒ halt("Negative factorial")                 Validity Check for Loop invariant at the end of while-loop at [28, 33]: Valid
}
                                                      ; Result: Valid
                                                      ; Solver: /Users/hatcliff/Dev/Sireum/kekinian/bin/cvc5.com
// SMT proof of the iterative factorial function      ; Arguments: --lang=smt2.6 --rlimit=2000000 --tlimit=6000 --fu
@pure def fac_it(n: Z): Z = {                          ; Time: 0.017s
  Contract(
    Requires(n ≥ 0),                                   ; Sequent:
    Ensures(Res == fac(n))                             ;
  )                                                    ; n >= 0,
                                                      ; At(x, 0) == 1,
  var x: Z = 1; var m: Z = 0;                          ; At(m, 0) == 0,
  while (m < n) {                                       ; 0 <= At(m, 1),
    Invariant(Modifies(x, m),                          ; At(m, 1) <= n,
              0 ≤ m, m ≤ n, x = fac(m))                ; x == fac(At(m, 1)),
    m = m + 1                                          ; At(m, 1) < n,
    var y: Z = 0; var k: Z = 0                         ; m == At(m, 1) + 1,
    while (k < m) {                                     ; At(y, 0) == 0,
      Invariant(Modifies(y, k),                         ; At(k, 0) == 0,
                0 ≤ k, k ≤ m, y = k * x)               ; 0 <= At(k, 1),
      y = y + x; k = k + 1                             ; At(k, 1) <= m,
    }                                                  ; At(y, 1) == At(k, 1) * x,
    x = y                                              ; At(k, 1) < m,
  }                                                    ; y == At(k, 1) * x + x,
  return x                                             ; k == At(k, 1) + 1,
}                                                      ; 0 <= k,
                                                      ; k <= m
(n: Z)                                                 ; ⊢
                                                      ; y == k * x

                                                      Filter ...
```

Fig. 1. Fully automated verification of factorial using Logika SMT-based symbolic execution

3   Proof Language Principles

In this section, we summarize basic features of Logika's proof language using a very simple example – an iterative version of the factorial function implemented using addition as the only numerical operation. Figure 1 presents a version of the example in the Sireum IVE in which the proof language is not utilized, i.e., verification is performed automatically using SMT. At the top left of the function, a Slang (executable) specification function `fac` is defined. The Scala annotation `@abs` indicates that the function is "strictly pure" (it is a side-effect free construct that can be directly translated to the SMT-LIB expression language) and can be used in Logika specifications and proof contexts. However, in contrast to Slang's similar `@strictpure` functions (see [31] for a detailed discussion of Slang's function flavors), `@abs` functions will not be unfolded automatically unless explicitly requested in Logika's rewrite tactics (similar to Isabelle's `definition` and `fun` distinction as illustrated below). Then, the iterative version `fac_it` is defined with: (a) a contract precondition requiring the argument to be non-negative, and (b) a post-condition stating that the method return value (denoted as `Res`) is equal to the result of the specification function. As the developer types, Logika continuously runs in the background to check for possible run-time exceptions, assertion violations, and to verify that the code conforms to declared contracts.

Significant engineering efforts have been devoted to displaying verification results directly in terms of program features that the developer can recognize instead of lower level representations such as information flowing to/from the SMT solver. The engineering involves mapping Logika's three-address code intermediate representation and internal logic variables back to Slang-level program expressions and variables, and also maintaining mappings between program artifacts and SMT-LIB encodings. One of Logika's most distinguishing features is to make this verification information available to developers at each program point in the code via clickable annotations in the left margin of the editor. There are two types of information: the lightbulb icons ⚡ display *facts* roughly corresponding to statement level pre/post-conditions; and lightning bolt icons ⚡ display sequents representing verification conditions that are encoded as calls to the underlying configured SMT solvers.

As Logika works, it collects facts that it discovers by symbolically moving forward step-by-step through the code. Some of the accumulated facts are immediately apparent from the structure of each program statement (we will refer to these as *immediate facts*). Others are the result of deductions that it has made by calling the underlying SMT solvers (we will refer to those as *deduced facts*). Logika can display all the inferred facts that it has accumulated at any point in the program (via the lightbulb icons) to provide valuable hints about how to reason systematically about the program. These Slang-level inferred facts are computed based on Logika's internal symbolic execution path conditions that must hold at the particular program points, which are intuitive as they are directly in line with the regular (concrete) program execution.

The ⚡ annotations indicate the points at which Logika makes automated deductions that require interactions with its underlying SMT solvers. Logika terms these interactions as *summonings* because the power of SMT solving is being "summoned" to make a deduction that cannot be carried out using simple syntactic manipulation of the current facts. Clicking on ⚡ shows the details of the summoning. Generally, summonings occur for each line of a post-condition, for (implicit/explicit) assertions, invariants, for checking the precondition of a called method, and for code branches to determine the feasible path(s) along which verification should proceed. The right side of Fig. 1 shows selected aspects of clicking on ⚡ (annotated with a red circle) at the second loop invariant. The loop invariant contains three (implicitly conjoined) clauses, and for each of these, Logika establishes two verification conditions (VCs, one that requires the clause to hold at the beginning of the loop, and another for the end of the loop). From the six total VCs for the selected ⚡, the user has selected the final one (the end of the loop VC, the clause y == k * x). The display provides information about the underlying SMT solver invocation (e.g., cvc5 is invoked with the particular configured set of arguments). Below this, the sequent display is given with the relevant clause as the conclusion. The sequent antecedents hold the accumulated facts relevant to the verification. Annotations such as At(k,1) refer to the value of variable k as its second occurrence (zero-based counting) within the method.

```
63    @pure def fac_it(n: Z): Z = {
92        var k: Z = 0
93        while (k < m) {
94            Invariant(Modifies(y, k),
95                    0 ≤ k, k ≤ m, y = k * x)
96            Deduce(
97                1 (y = k * x) by Premise,
98                2 (y + x = k * x + x) by Simpl and 1
99            )
100           val yn = y + x
101           Deduce(
102               1 (yn = y + x) by Premise,
103               2 (y = yn - x) by Algebra and 1,
104               3 (y + x = k * x + x) by Premise,
105               4 ((yn - x) + x = k * x + x)
106                     by Rewrite(RS(), 3) and 2,
107               5 (yn = k * x + x) by Algebra and 4,
108               6 (yn = (k + 1) * x) by Algebra and 5
109           )
110           y = yn
111           k = k + 1
112       }
fac_it(n: Z)
```

```
Info: Matched:
Matched:
  (yn - x + x) ≡ (k * x + x)

After rewriting #3:
  (y + x) ≡ (k * x + x)

and/or after simplifying the step claim to:
  (y + x) ≡ (k * x + x)

Trace:

Begin rewriting (y + x) ≡ (k * x + x)  ...

Trace:

by [eval] substitution using #2 [y/yn - x]:
  yn - x
  ≡ y

∴ (yn - x + x) ≡ (k * x + x)
  ≡ (y + x) ≡ (k * x + x)

Filter trace ...
```

Fig. 2. Verification of factorial using proof language (excerpts)

Figure 2 presents verification excerpts of the same example with selected features of Logika's manual proof language. The excerpts include the body of the inner `while` loop (an additional assignment to an intermediate variable `yn` has been introduced to facilitate the illustration). Proof blocks are presented Logika's `Deduce(..)` construct, which includes a numbered list of proof steps. Each proof step has a claim and an associated justification (or tactic) to apply to prove the claim. In the first `Deduce`, the claim `y == k * x` is justified by `Premise` because it follows immediately, since the invariant is assumed to be true at the top of loop body following the usual Hoare logic approach. In general, any claim shown in a ☀ can be copy-pasted "as is" as `Premise` in the corresponding program point. In addition to serving as user feedback, ☀ claims as `Premises` facilitate integration of Logika automation and interactive verifications. The second proof step is proved using `Simpl`, which rewrites terms using known facts in the form of equations and capturing the semantics of Slang expressions (akin to partial evaluation). Using the operator `and`, the justification `Simpl` can be restricted to equality claims supplied as arguments (the claim of proof step 1 in this case). Note that the claim is proven without an external call to the SMT solvers (indicated by having the "check mark" ✓ icon instead of ⚡), thus illustrating one of the avenues for proof engineers to avoid the potential instability and increased overhead of SMT. `Simpl` can also be used without any `and` argument, in which case it can use any preceding proof step claim in scope for equality substitutions. We recently introduced `ESimpl` (not shown), which offers a backtracking variant of `Simpl` that can recover from detrimental substitutions that diverge from proving the stated proof step claim. Table 1 lists some of Logika's justifications.

Table 1. Logika manual proof step justifications

Justification	Informal desciption
Simpl	Simplify current clause in proof into known fact, or fail
ESimpl	Backtracking version of the above
Rewrite	Rewrite indicated clause in proof into current clause, or fail
Premise	Known fact
Subst	Substitute one term for another left-to-right ">" or right-to-left "<"
AllI, AllE	Complete set of natural deduction rules (not all shown here)
Auto	Summon unconstrained configured SMT solvers
Algebra	Summon SMT solvers specialized to unquantified arithmetics and logics

In the second `Deduce`, the second claim is proved using `Algebra`. This step is proven by an external call to SMT (as indicated by the bolt gutter annotation), but it uses SMT in a very limited way that is less costly and likely more stable: it only uses explicitly referenced claims (the claim from step 1 in this case) and does not include implicitly any facts from the context. Proof of the fourth claim illustrates Logika's `Rewrite` justification. In general, `Rewrite` takes an ordered rewrite set consisting of lemmas/theorems and references to `@abs` methods to unfold (not shown), and a proven claim to be rewritten. For the fourth claim, rewriting is applied to claim 3 and the rewrite set `RS()` is empty, but the rewriting is specified to utilize the equality claim 2 as a left-to-right rewrite rule. Rewrite sets `RS` are defined using Slang sequence types and can be specified inline or by given an annotated Slang value definition `@rw val`. Set union and difference work on `RS`, e.g., `myRewriteSet ++ otherSet -- RS(m _)`, which can also be stored in a `@rw val` or inlined. In practice, `RS` members are names of Slang definitions.

Thus, `Rewrite` gives yet another way to avoid invoking SMT for a proof. Logika's rewriting approach is similar to Isabelle's, but it is currently not as powerful. However, it does have several of the key capabilities (flexible definition of rewrite sets with controlled unfolding of definitions). Even in its current form, we have found that it is powerful enough to address most common scenarios. By avoiding having to export VCs using hard-to-understand encodings to an external theorem prover, the developer works directly in terms of the programming language syntax, definition constructs, and abstraction level in the same programming/verification environment. In addition, clicking on ✔ annotation for the claim provides a trace of the rewriting directly in terms of the program-level constructs. The right side of Fig. 2 shows the rewriting trace for claim 4. First, the trace illustrates that claim 3 is to be rewritten. Then, it is written using the indicated equality of claim 2 (left to right), by substituting y for yn - x. This yields a match with claim 4, thus proving the claim.

4   Case Study

To assess the utility of Logika's proof language, we used it to prove the correctness of several data structure libraries. One of those is a Slang implementation of a doubly-linked linked list (DLL) based on similar approaches used in embedded security devices at Collins Aerospace [14]. The initial Slang implementation

```
1     // DLL Node type
2     @datatype class Node[E](elem: E, used: B, left: DLLPool.PoolPtr, right: DLLPool.PoolPtr) {}
3
4     // DLL Pool
5     object DLLPool {
6        type PoolPtr = Z
7        type PoolMem[E] = MSZ[Node[E]]
8        val Null: PoolPtr = -1
9        //...(excerpts of helper properties for concrete representation)
10       @abs def isPointer[E](pool: PoolMem[E], p: PoolPtr): B = { p == Null || pool.isInBound(p) }
11       @abs def isValidPointer[E](pool: PoolMem[E], p: PoolPtr): B = { pool.isInBound(p) }
12       @abs def freeNodesProp[E](pool: PoolMem[E], free: Z): B = { free == count_free(pool) }
13       //...(excerpts of properties used in abstraction/refinement relation)
14       @abs def asList[E](pool: PoolMem[E], head: PoolPtr): List[E] =
15          if (isValidPointer(pool, head)) {
16             Cons(pool(head).elem, asList(pool, pool(head).right))
17          } else { Nil() }
18       //...
19    }
20
21    @record class DLLPool[@imm E](eDefault: E, poolSz: Z) {
22       val defaultNode: Node[E] = Node[E](eDefault, F, Null, Null)
23       val maxSz: Z = if (poolSz > 0) poolSz else 0
24       val pool: PoolMem[E] = MSZ.create(maxSz, defaultNode) // pool storage
25       var free: Z = maxSz // current # of free items in pool
26       var head: PoolPtr = Null // index of the current logical head Node
27       var tail: PoolPtr = Null // index of the current logical tail Node
28       // ...(excerpts of invariants for concrete representation)
29       @spec def freeNodes = Invariant( freeNodesProp(pool, free) )
30       // Type & function definitions (with contracts) for abstract list (see Figure 6 for example)
31       // ...
32       // Specification of abstraction relations (omitted)
33       // ...
34       // Operations (with contracts) for concrete representation (omitted)
35       // ...
36    }
```

Fig. 3. DLL excerpts - primary declarations and concept outline

was completed several years ago with only a few simple aspects verified because it was difficult to complete the verification with the earlier implementations of Logika. The recent Logika addition of proof language features and better support for abstraction and refinement has enabled us to significantly expand the scope of the proofs.

Abstractly, a list can be easily expressed algebraically using the constructors Nil and Cons for values of type List. However, for high assurance embedded devices, it is undesirable to use such list directly because its manipulation requires dynamic memory allocation, which introduces unpredictable behaviors. Instead, we use such list and its accompanying theorems indirectly as abstract specification and in proof only. The data representation chosen for the concrete DLL implementation is challenging for understanding and verification in that it is not obvious that a list is implemented. The logical ordering of elements in the DLL does not follow their physical ordering in pool memory. Allocating new element storage and subsequent reclaiming must be managed explicitly. There are also several fairly complex invariants that need to be maintained by each DLL operation.

4.1   Overview

Figure 3 presents some of the primary definitions in the DLL library. In the concrete DLL implementation, in order to avoid dynamic memory allocation and guarantee locality of all memory access, all data of the DLL is stored in a memory block of fixed size represented as a Slang mutable sequence (line 24). The pool holds items of type `Node`. Each node (line 2) includes a data element `elem` of type E, indices of `Nodes` to the logical `left` (towards the head of the list) and `right` (towards the tail of the list). `head` and `tail` are pool indices for the current logical head and tail of the list (see Fig. 4).

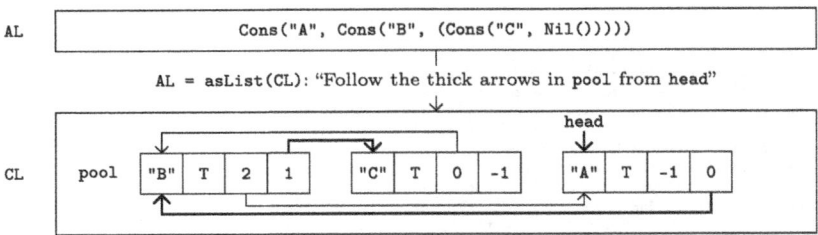

Fig. 4. DLL data structure and its list abstraction

Our verification strategy is as follows. Approximately 13 invariants are specified on the DLL structure. For example, Fig. 3 line 29 illustrates a simple invariant `freeNodes` that specifies that the pool variable `free` that holds a count of the number of free nodes in the pool matches the count computed by traversing the memory blocking and counting the nodes marked unused (note that the invariant uses the `freeNodesProp` helper property defined earlier in the figure). All DLL operations are proved to maintain the invariants. The `DLLPool` object contains approximately 20 helper methods with specification and proofs (starting at line 10, Fig. 3 shows some of the simpler ones like `isPointer`).

Next, we create an abstract operational specification of the DLL using an easily expressible and understandable inductively defined `List` type (for lack of space, these definitions are omitted since they correspond to the familiar cons-list data structure). Operations on `List` are written using the pure functional programming language features of Slang. This functional modeling style is common in theorem proving based on type theory.

Subsequently, a family of relations `asList` are defined as Slang specification methods that relate concrete DLL values to abstract `List` values (one of the methods is shown in Fig. 3 line 14. Figure 4 illustrates the relationship between the concrete and abstract values. At the top of the figure the abstract list is shown as an expression, at the bottom the concrete DLL implementation is shown where the `left` and `right` fields of a node point to other locations in the mutable sequence `pool`. The refinement relation between the two representations consists of reconstructing the abstract list by following the `right` pointers from the

head onwards. Subsequently, the concrete implementation of the DLL is verified against the abstract list model using refinement. In other words, we show that the concrete implementation is a simulation of the abstract list.

Figure 5 illustrates key concepts of the proof approach. Abstract list AL and concrete (implementation) list CL stored in the buffer are related by the relationship AL = asList(CL), describing the simulation of AL by CL. This simulation is used to relate abstract functions such as length that yields the length of a list to the CL function sizeOf that yields the length of a CL. In order for sizeOf to implement length correctly, the value returned by CL.sizeOf for a list must be equal to that AL.length if AL = asList(CL). (This is addressed in Fig. 8, discussed later). Similarly, the CL.cons simulates the abstract constructor Cons of the abstract list if the buffer is not full. (This is addressed in Fig. 9, discussed later).

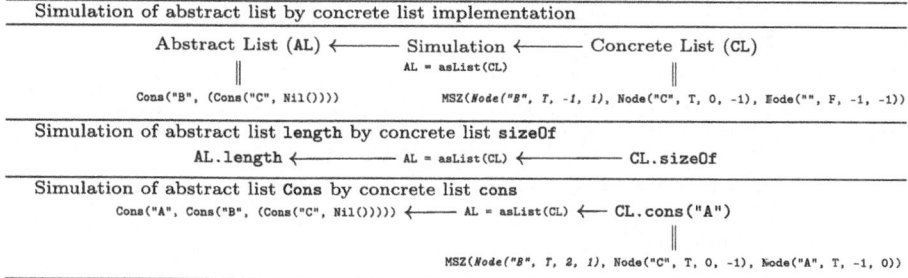

Fig. 5. Case Study Proof Approach

Generally speaking, proofs in the library dealing with more abstract concepts are more algebraic relying on rewriting, while pure implementation-level proofs require more complex properties that cannot be cast in the form of equations. The refinement relationship is an invariant of the concrete implementation and by mentioning both abstraction levels requires a mix of algebraic proofs and proofs that use properties with more complex shapes. In our experience, SMT solvers require some help from the user in order to achieve such proofs. In the approach that we follow, Slang's flexibility enables proofs to be carried out in supporting objects as much as possible and not in the code so as not to blur the implementation with more complex proofs.

4.2 Programming and Proof

The development and proof of the abstract list with its concrete implementation as doubly-linked list is separated into three parts:

(1) The abstract list modeled as an algebraic datatype List[E] with constructors Nil() and Cons(value, list), where value of generic type E and list

of type List[E]. Properties of abstract lists are proved a in corresponding List companion object (see theorem length_impl_with_acc_sum in Fig. 6).

(2) A doubly-linked list companion object DLLPool (see Fig. 3) with theorems relating to implementation concerns, the theorems about refinement, and related executable specification functions.

(3) The doubly-linked list class DLLPool[E] (see Fig. 3) with the implementation code and correctness proofs expressed in terms of theorems proved in (1) and (2).

```
1    @pure def length_impl_with_acc_sum[T](l: List[T]): Unit = {
2      Contract(Ensures(All{(acc: Z, bcc: Z) => bcc+l.len_acc(acc) == l.len_acc(bcc+acc)}))
3      (l: @induct) match {
4        case Cons(v, n) =>
5          Deduce(
6            1 (All{(acc: Z, bcc: Z) => bcc+n.len_acc(acc) == n.len_acc(bcc+acc)}) by Premise,
7            2 (Cons(v, n).length == 1 + n.length) by Simpl,
8            3 Let((acc: Z) => SubProof(
9              4 Let((bcc: Z) => SubProof(
10               5 (Cons(v, n).len_acc(bcc + acc) == n.len_acc(1 + (bcc + acc))) by Simpl,
11               6 (All{(bcc: Z) => bcc+n.len_acc(1+acc)==n.len_acc(bcc+1+acc)}) by AllE[Z](1),
12               7 (bcc + n.len_acc(1 + acc) == n.len_acc(bcc + (1 + acc))) by AllE[Z](6),
13               8 (bcc + Cons(v, n).len_acc(acc) == bcc + n.len_acc(1 + acc)) by Simpl,
14               9 (bcc+Cons(v, n).len_acc(acc) == Cons(v, n).len_acc(bcc+acc)) by Auto,
15               10 (bcc + l.len_acc(acc) == l.len_acc(bcc + acc)) by Auto
16             )),
17             11 (All{(bcc: Z) => bcc+l.len_acc(acc) == l.len_acc(bcc+acc)}) by AllI[Z](4)
18           )),
19           12 (All{(acc: Z, bcc: Z) => bcc+l.len_acc(acc) == l.len_acc(bcc+acc)}) by AllI[Z](3))
20         case Nil() => return
21    }}
```

Fig. 6. Example AL operation (high-level specification for DLL)

Abstract List Properties. Properties of abstractions are often needed to support refinement proofs. For instance, the refinement proof of CL sizeOf (see Fig. 8) needs to establish that the result Res equals AL list.length, the length of the corresponding abstract list. In the CL operation, Res is iteratively computed by a loop using a local variable res. To achieve res == list.length on termination, the progress in the computation of res must be recorded. This can stated as the universal claim All{(acc: Z) => acc + 1.length == 1.len_acc(acc)}. To help with proving the claim, we introduced the length_impl_with_acc_sum Logika method theorem shown in Fig. 6. The theorem is proven by using Logika's @induction (line 3). In the base case of Nil(), the theorem claim can be discharged automatically by SMT solving, thus there are no proof annotations (line 20). The inductive step of Cons(...) (line 4) illustrates the use of Logika's simplification and natural deduction tactics. The previous declaration of the @induct proof strategy (line 3) causes the induction hypothesis to be implicitly introduced in the fact set when in the Cons proof case (in the IVE, the fact would show up in ☀ annotation information). Because of this, the explicit statement of the induction hypothesis at line 6 can be discharged using the

Premise justification. Overall, some of the proof steps appear obvious, but none of the simplification steps using Simpl can be discharged by SMT solving due in part to the presence of uninterpreted functions, quantifier manipulation, etc. in the Slang-to-SMT encoding. To help direct SMT solving, we manually eliminate/instantiate and re-introduce the universal claim by using Logika universal quantifier elimination and introduction (AllE/AllI) rules (see lines 11 and 17). With quantifiers removed, and by judicious use of Simpl to prove facts to help SMT along, other parts of proof can be discharged via SMT solving using the Auto justification (lines 14 and 15).

This example illustrates nicely the common interplay between Logika SMT-based automated verification and interactive theorem proving found in many other parts of the DLL code, where automation is used as best as can be afforded using SMT solvers, coupled with some interactive proofs done using Logika's rewriting system. One very attractive aspect of our approach is that these activities are all integrated in a single tool (the IVE – built on a widely used IDE) and carried out using program-level features (instead of lower-level language encodings as they would appear in a separate theorem proving tool).

Implementation and Refinement Properties. Properties concerning the implementation of the doubly-linked list are stated and proved in the companion object DLLPool declared in Fig. 3 line 5. Figure 7 gives one example of such a property refines_p_not_Nil that states that if a provide concrete representation satisfies the refinement relation and there is a valid pointer p (i.e., the pointer does not reference an unused node), then the abstract list is not equal to Nil. Intuitively, the presence of rewriting and simplification tactics in the proof indicates that the claim to be proved is easily deduced by appealing to involved equalities, e.g., from function definition isValidPointer in line 5 in Fig. 7. The equality is a consequence of the definition of isValidPointer in line 11 in Fig. 3. Property refines_p_not_Nil is used in the refinement proof of function sizeOf below that needs to interpret low-level properties like isValidPointer(pool, p) in terms of high-level properties like 1 != Nil[E]().

```
1    @pure def refines_p_not_Nil[E](pool: PoolMem[E], p: PoolPtr, l: List[E]): Unit = {
2      Contract(Requires(isValidPointer(pool, p),refinesProp(pool, p, l)), Ensures(l != Nil[E]()))
3      Deduce(
4        1 (isValidPointer(pool, p)) by Premise,
5        2 (pool.isInBound(p)) by Rewrite(RS(isValidPointer _), 1),
6        3 (refinesProp(pool, p, l)) by Premise,
7        4 (asList(pool, p) == l) by Auto and 3,
8        5 (asList(pool, p) == Cons[E](pool(p).elem, asList(pool, pool(p).right)))
9            by RSimpl(RS(asList _)) and (1, 2),
10       6 (Cons[E](pool(p).elem, asList(pool, pool(p).right)) == l) by Subst_<(5, 4)) }
```

Fig. 7. Example low-level theorem from DLL companion object

Implementation of Side-Effect-Free CL Methods. We next illustrate in Fig. 8 the proof of a CL method sizeOf that traverses but does not modify the CL structure. Although the method uses imperative features, it has no visible external

```
1   @pure def sizeOf: Z = {
2     Contract(Requires(refinesProp(pool, head, list)),
3             Ensures(refinesProp(pool, head, list), Res == list.length))
4     var res: Z = 0
5     var p = head
6     @spec var l = list
7     Spec { length_impl_with_acc(list) } // apply lemma as method invocation
8     while (!isLeaf(p)) {
9       Invariant(Modifies(res, p, l),
10              refinesProp(pool, p, l), isPointer(pool, p), l.len_acc(res) == list.length)
11      Spec { length_impl_with_acc(l.tl); refines_p_not_Nil(pool, p, l)
12             refines_p_sublist(pool, p, l) }
13      res = res + 1
14      p = pool(p).right
15      Spec { l = l.tl }
16    }
17    return res
18  }
```

Fig. 8. Example low-level side-effect free CL method (with refinement proof)

side effects and so is annotated with the Slang @pure annotation. The postcondition indicates that, given that list is the abstract representation of the CL instance, sizeOf implements the abstract function list.length. The method contract also indicates that the refinement condition refinesProp(pool, head, list) is preserved. In the method body, the incrementally computed size of the DLL is stored in variable res. In order to relate the current value of res to the sublist it corresponds to, a @spec variable l is declared (line 6) that remembers the part of the corresponding abstract list that has not yet been visited (by leveraging Slang's copy-on-write semantics on mutable objects). The entire proof has been factored out into a set of lemmas. The lemma applications are stated as developer-friendly method invocations that are placed inside Spec blocks. Such lemma applications can be confirmed by inspecting the ☀ claims after the application program points (not shown). The final Spec block in line 15 only contains the update of the abstract list l = l.tl that corresponds to the low-level assignment p = pool(p).right in line 14, maintaining the relationship refinesProp(pool, p, l) stated in the invariant (see line 10). The use of the lemmas keeps the "noise" in the programs code produced by proof low. It also makes the interaction with the SMT solvers more stable due to the smaller amount of claims involving only the contracts of the involved method theorems but not the contained proofs, which reduces the load of the solvers.

Implementation of Side-Effecting CL *Methods.* Figure 9 shows the low-level CL function cons of DLL, which corresponds to the abstract list constructor Cons. Because the pool memory is limited in size, a call of cons only extends the CL if there is still space. This is expressed by the two cases of the contract of cons: the case free > 0 permits extending the list, the case free <= 0 leaves the CL unchanged. Note that free is proved to be the number of unused cells of the pool memory by means of the invariant freeNodes (see Fig. 3, line 29). The condition is reflected by the leading if-statement in line 7.

```
1    def cons(elem: E): Unit = {
2      Contract(Modifies(list),
3        Case(Requires(free > 0, refinesProp(pool, head, list)),
4            Ensures(refinesProp(pool, head, list), list == Cons(elem, In(list)))),
5        Case(Requires(free <= 0, refinesProp(pool, head, list)),
6            Ensures(refinesProp(pool, head, list))))
7      if (free > 0) {
8        if (isEmpty) {
9          head = 0; tail = 0
10         @spec val qool = pool
11         pool(0) = Node(elem, T, Null, Null)
12         Spec { count_free_on_alloc(qool, pool, 0); list = List.make(elem) }
13       } else {
14         val pnew: Z = findFreeNode()
15         @spec val qool = pool
16         pool(pnew) = Node(elem, T, Null, head)
17         Spec { unused_inv(qool, head, list, pool, pnew)
18               refines_new_head(pool, head, list, pnew, elem)
19               count_free_on_alloc(qool, pool, pnew) }
20         @spec val rool = pool
21         pool(head) = pool(head)(left = pnew)
22         Spec { list_coincidence(pool, rool, head); free_coincidence(pool, rool) }
23         head = pnew
24         Spec { list = Cons(elem, list) }
25       }
26       free = free - 1
27     }
28   }
```

Fig. 9. Example low-level side-effecting CL method (with refinement proof)

The library includes a number of other methods for finding items, and inserting and deleting items, and the same proof strategies are applied for those.

5 Illustrations

In addition to the full artifacts for the DLL example presented in this paper, we have prepared examples of varying complexity to further illustrate Logika's proof language features (see [35]).

- *Abstract list*: Inductive proof of $l = l.tl.tl$ for any list l. This development shows how a common inductive proof is carried out in Logika relying on rewriting and simplification to guide the proof.
- *Sequence sum*: In Logika, sequence induction is often done using while loops. This development shows how recursive properties are used in such proofs and how abstract properties are propagated to refinements.
- *Maximum of sorted sequence*: The maximum of a sequence of increasing values can be computed by returning the last value of the sequence. The proof of this is a program that computes the maximum value, confirming that the last value is the maximum. Except for the returned maximum, the entire program is enclosed in a Spec block. The program itself becomes a correctness annotation similar to typing information that confirms that values have the correct type.
- *Symbol table*: This example provides a symbol table that one might use, e.g., in a program/model implementation environment. The development demonstrates the use of function calls as theorem references and the replacement

of abstract predicates in pre-conditions by more efficient implementations without affecting the difficulty of the proofs. This approach is useful when compile-time and run-time-verification use are combined in practice.

Due to space constraints, in this paper we have focused on illustrating concepts. Full evaluations of efficiency gains and usability are part of our plans for future work. It is worth emphasizing, however, that we believe Logika provides a uniquely high degree of usability by the fact that it provides a continuous of abstraction on its streamlined automated and interactive theorem proving approach at the level that is familiar to regular system engineers in realistic development workflows and supported by industrial-scale programming/verification environments. Regarding efficiency, one of the motivations for our work was to provide pathways for reducing the time and instability of verification. Anecdotally, besides failing to discharge VCs in numerous situations, our early SMT-heavy versions of the case study code required minutes for full verification. By using simplification/rewriting instead of SMT calls and by using the proof language to minimize the size of constraint sets sent to SMT, we were able to not only succeed in verification, but also to reduce verification time of this example to a few seconds.

6   Related Work

The Why3 framework [10] is a good example of previous work that aims to provide support for both SMT and interactive theorem proving (ITP). It provides an intermediate language (WhyML - combining both imperative and functional features) for encoding behavior and specifications, and a VC generator that generates VCs dischargable using automated calls to a variety of SMT solvers (Z3, CVC4/CVC5, and Alt-Ego) or exportable to the Coq interactive theorem prover. Coq proof scripts for Coq-proven VCs can be re-incorporated back into the WhyML artifacts. SPARK 2014 [20] (a contract-based specification and verification framework for a safety-critical subset of Ada) is an example of a powerful industrial verification framework that uses Why3 as its verification engine. It translates SPARK programs into Why3 and relies on Why3 VC generation and verification framework to prove that SPARK programs conform to program contracts. This architecture provides combined automated SMT and theorem proving verification for SPARK programs. The difference with our work is that we aim to integrate SMT and *targeted* ITP directly within the programming language. Why3 is designed as an intermediate language and does not have the full support for developing, debugging, and execution that Slang does. When ITP is used, one must work with encodings of Why3 in Coq, whereas in Slang the developer works directly at the programming language level. When using SPARK 2014, diagnostic information is expressed in terms of Why3 encodings instead of directly in terms of the programming language. Moreover, when interactions with ITP are needed, users must understand a double-encoding – the encoding from SPARK 2014 to Why3, and then Why3 to Coq. An advantage of the SPARK 2014/Why3 approach is that one has access to the full power of a relatively mature theorem prover, whereas for our approach, we are currently providing a targeted set of tactics. As noted in [32], Logika's extension architecture can facilitate exporting VCs to any theorem prover in future work.

Dafny [25], Frama-C [22], AutoProof [11] and Verus [24] are examples of program verification frameworks used in industry that also aim to incorporate some notion of a proof language phrased in programming idioms. While these tools have many attractive features, including some that are not supported by Logika, their proof languages are not nearly as expansive as what we provide in Logika. AutoProof integrates verification support to Eiffel tapping into its contract language. Both Dafny and Verus provide specification lemmas (with no executable code) whose pre/post-conditions can be proved using SMT and then reused in other program contexts. Dafny supports calculation blocks that can include "hints" to lower-level SMT solvers. Verus authors are developing an approach to translate VCs to the Lean ITP, which the developer needs to discharge interactively in Lean [28]. This has the same tradeoffs (dealing with encodings and working in a separate less-user-friendly tool vs. full ITP power) as with the SPARK/Why3 architecture described above compared to our approach. Frama-C provides verification for C programs. Via a plug-in mechanism powerful verification techniques like abstract interpretation are available. Contract and verification annotations are kept in the comments. This make a tight integration of programming and proof concepts difficult. SED [18] uses annotations in comments and provides graphical visualizations of verification artifacts.

With a different objective than Logika, some of the approach to proof taken here has been used with Event-B [1] in the Rodin tool [2]. One of the design objectives of Rodin compared to its predecessor was to decompose large proof obligations and structure the remaining large proofs in such a way that the remaining sequents could be easily discharged by automated provers. Although Rodin is a tool for abstract modeling, the same approach to proof is at work in the presented work on Logika. It is not intended to eliminate the use of SMT (and other automated provers) from Logika but to make their use much more reliable and predictable.

7 Conclusion

Despite requiring "manual effort" and some level of expertise in formal methods, we believe there are significant benefits in integrating semi-automated proofs with automated program verifiers. A primary benefit is providing a pathway to continue verification progress when SMT-based automation becomes unstable or simply cannot prove true claims. Our goal in this paper has been to describe one particular approach that incorporates a proof language directly in the programming language and illustrate that it can work synergistically with SMT verification. We believe our approach is promising because the proof language emphasizes: (a) developer-friendly syntax and programming-like idioms, and (b) tool feedback like simplification/rewrite traces and SMT deductions are expressed directly in terms of program features (not lower-level encodings). We believe this approach is novel and applicable to other SMT-based automated program verifiers.

Regarding usability, an interesting anecdotal observation is that we teach Logika's full proof language as illustrated here in master's level courses in Aarhus University [13]. Logika's basic natural deduction steps and substitution are taught in an undergraduate programming logic course at Kansas State University, which has included 1000 students during the last six years (see [33] for online textbook). While we would not necessarily expect all industry engineers that apply Logika or other program verifiers to use the proof language features, one can imagine that having an integrated proof language makes it easier to hand-off to verification engineers that are capable of applying the features. Moreover, being able to have engineers working in a single environment (instead of having to hand off to an external theorem prover that has completely different abstractions/notations) makes user workflows smoother and artifact management easier.

There are likely other theorem proving techniques or finer-grain controls over deduction that could be added to our framework. We have focused on rewriting and simplification; combinations of tableau-based proof search and resolution-like techniques as in Isabelle's `blast` and `fastforce` tactics, which may be helpful for dealing with quantifier manipulation (which SMT-based solvers often struggle with), might be useful for adoption in Logika in the future. In general, Logika's extension architecture allows one to realize custom proof tactics as needed.

We are continuing applications on other industry-related examples. This includes verifying the correctness of the HAMR [15] run-time libraries providing real-time threading and communication being used in the Collins Aerospace DARPA PROVERS INSPECTA project, by using a similar refinement proof strategy presented in this paper. That is, we are proving that the Slang-based implementation of the libraries (deployed to, e.g., seL4 via C/Rust) are a refinement of a Slang purely functional executable reference semantics for the subset of AADL supported by HAMR that have also been formalized in Isabelle [12].

Acknowledgments. This work was primarily funded by a DARPA SBIR Phase 2 SIRFUR award, with some support from the DARPA CASE and PROVERS projects.

References

1. Abrial, J.R.: Modeling in Event-B - System and Software Engineering. Cambridge University Press, Cambridge (2010)
2. Abrial, J.R., Butler, M.J., Hallerstede, S., Hoang, T.S., Mehta, F., Voisin, L.: Rodin: an open toolset for modelling and reasoning in Event-B. Int. J. Softw. Tools Technol. Transf. **12**(6), 447–466 (2010)
3. of Automotive Engineers, S.: Architecture analysis & design language (AADL). Aerospace Standard AS5506 (2004)

4. Barbosa, H., et al.: cvc5: a versatile and industrial-strength SMT solver. In: TACAS 2022. LNCS, vol. 13243, pp. 415–442. Springer, Cham (2022). https://doi.org/10.1007/978-3-030-99524-9_24

5. Barrett, C., et al.: CVC4. In: Gopalakrishnan, G., Qadeer, S. (eds.) CAV 2011. LNCS, vol. 6806, pp. 171–177. Springer, Heidelberg (2011). https://doi.org/10.1007/978-3-642-22110-1_14

6. Belt, J., et al.: Model-driven development for the seL4 microkernel using the HAMR framework. J. Syst. Architecture (2022)

7. Cofer, D.D., et al.: Cyberassured systems engineering at scale. IEEE Secur. Priv. **20**(3), 52–64 (2022)

8. Conchon, S., Coquereau, A., Iguernlala, M., Mebsout, A.: Alt-ergo 2.2. In: SMT Workshop: International Workshop on Satisfiability Modulo Theories (2018)

9. de Moura, L., Passmore, G.O.: The strategy challenge in SMT solving. In: Bonacina, M.P., Stickel, M.E. (eds.) Automated Reasoning and Mathematics. LNCS (LNAI), vol. 7788, pp. 15–44. Springer, Heidelberg (2013). https://doi.org/10.1007/978-3-642-36675-8_2

10. Filliâtre, J.-C., Paskevich, A.: Why3 — where programs meet provers. In: Felleisen, M., Gardner, P. (eds.) ESOP 2013. LNCS, vol. 7792, pp. 125–128. Springer, Heidelberg (2013). https://doi.org/10.1007/978-3-642-37036-6_8

11. Furia, C.A., Nordio, M., Polikarpova, N., Tschannen, J.: Autoproof: auto-active functional verification of object-oriented programs. Int. J. Softw. Tools Technol. Transfer **19**(6), 697–716 (2017)

12. Hallerstede, S., Hatcliff, J.: A mechanized semantics for component-based systems in the HAMR AADL runtime. In: Cámara, J., Jongmans, S.S. (eds.) FACS 2023. LNCS, vol. 14485, pp. 45–64. Springer, Cham (2023). https://doi.org/10.1007/978-3-031-52183-6_3

13. Hallerstede, S., Hatcliff, J.: Robby: teaching with Logika: conceiving and constructing correct software. In: Sekerinski, E., Ribeiro, L. (eds.) FMTea 2024. LNCS, vol. 14939, pp. 106–123. Springer, Cham (2024). https://doi.org/10.1007/978-3-031-71379-8_7

14. Hardin, D., Slind, K.: Using ACL2 in the design of efficient, verifiable data structures for high-assurance systems. In: ACL2 Theorem Prover and its Applications (ACL2-2018). EPTCS, vol. 280, pp. 61–76 (2018)

15. Hatcliff, J., Belt, J., Robby, Carpenter, T.: HAMR: an AADL multi-platform code generation toolset. In: Margaria, T., Steffen, B. (eds.) ISoLA 2021. LNCS, vol. 13036, pp. 274–295. Springer, Cham (2021). https://doi.org/10.1007/978-3-030-89159-6_18

16. Hatcliff, J., Belt, J., Robby, Legg, J., Stewart, D., Carpenter, T.: Automated property-based testing from AADL component contracts. In: Cimatti, A., Titolo, L. (eds.) Formal Methods for Industrial Critical Systems (2023)

17. Hatcliff, J., Stewart, D., Belt, J., Robby, Schwerdfeger, A.: An AADL contract language supporting integrated model- and code-level verification. In: Proceedings of the 2022 ACM Workshop on High Integrity Language Technology. HILT 2022 (2022)

18. Hentschel, M., Bubel, R., Hähnle, R.: The symbolic execution debugger (SED): a platform for interactive symbolic execution, debugging, verification and more. Int. J. Softw. Tools Technol. Transfer **21**(5), 485–513 (2019)

19. Ho, S., Protzenko, J.: Aeneas: rust verification by functional translation. Proc. ACM Program. Lang. **6**(ICFP), 711–741 (2022)

20. Hoang, D., Moy, Y., Wallenburg, A., Chapman, R.: SPARK 2014 and GNATprove. Int. J. Softw. Tools Technol. Transf. **17**(6) (2015)

21. Jackson, D., Nelson, T., Schmitz, P.: Zelkova: SMT-based policy analysis at scale. In: Proceedings of the ACM SIGPLAN Conference on Programming Language Design and Implementation (PLDI), pp. 1–15. ACM (2020)
22. Kosmatov, N., Prevosto, V., Signoles, J.: Guide to Software Verification with Frama-C – Core Components, Usages, and Applications. Springer, Cham (2024)
23. Lattuada, A., et al.: Verus: a practical foundation for systems verification. In: Witchel, E., Rossbach, C.J., Arpaci-Dusseau, A.C., Keeton, K. (eds.) Proceedings of the ACM SIGOPS 30th Symposium on Operating Systems Principles, pp. 438–454. ACM (2024)
24. Lattuada, A., et al.: Verus: verifying Rust programs using linear ghost types. Proc. ACM Program. Lang. **7**(OOPSLA1), 286–315 (2023)
25. Leino, K.R.M.: Program Proofs. The MIT Press, Cambridge (2023)
26. Leroy, X., Blazy, S., Kästner, D., Schommer, B., Pister, M., Ferdinand, C.: CompCert–a formally verified optimizing compiler. In: ERTS 2016 (2016)
27. Martínez, G., et al.: Meta-F*: proof automation with SMT, tactics, and metaprograms. In: Caires, L. (ed.) ESOP 2019. LNCS, vol. 11423, pp. 30–59. Springer, Cham (2019). https://doi.org/10.1007/978-3-030-17184-1_2
28. Hatcliff, J., Belt, J., Moura, L., Ullrich, S.: The lean 4 theorem prover and programming language. In: Margaria, T., Steffen, B., Platzer, A., Sutcliffe, G. (eds.) CADE 2021. LNCS (LNAI), vol. 12699, pp. 625–635. Springer, Cham (2021). https://doi.org/10.1007/978-3-030-79876-5_37
29. de Moura, L., Bjørner, N.: Z3: an efficient SMT solver. In: Ramakrishnan, C.R., Rehof, J. (eds.) TACAS 2008. LNCS, vol. 4963, pp. 337–340. Springer, Heidelberg (2008). https://doi.org/10.1007/978-3-540-78800-3_24
30. Robby, Dwyer, M.B., Hatcliff, J.: Bogor: an extensible and highly-modular software model checking framework. In: 11th ACM SIGSOFT Symposium on Foundations of Software Engineering held jointly with 9th European Software Engineering Conference (ESEC/FSE), pp. 267–276. ACM (2003)
31. Robby, Hatcliff, J.: Slang: The Sireum Programming Language. In: Margaria, T., Steffen, B. (eds.) ISoLA 2021. LNCS, vol. 13036, pp. 253–273. Springer, Cham (2021). https://doi.org/10.1007/978-3-030-89159-6_17
32. Robby, Hatcliff, J., Belt, J.: Logika: The Sireum Verification Framework. In: Haxthausen, A.E., Serwe, W. (eds.) FMICS. LNCS, vol. 14952, pp. 97–116. Springer, Cham (2024). https://doi.org/10.1007/978-3-031-68150-9_6
33. Thorton, J.: Logical Foundations of Programming (online textbook for KSU CS 301). https://textbooks.cs.ksu.edu/cis301/index.html
34. Zhou, Y., Bosamiya, J., Takashima, Y., Li, J., Heule, M., Parno, B.: Mariposa: measuring SMT instability in automated program verification. In: Nadel, A., Rozier, K.Y. (eds.) FMCAD 2023, pp. 178–188. TU Wien Academic Press (2023)
35. Logika proof language case studies repository. https://github.com/santoslab/logika-proof-language-case-studies
36. Sireum website. https://sireum.org/

AutoSV-Annotator: Integrating Deductive and Automatic Software Verification

Lukas Armborst[1] [ID], Dirk Beyer[2] [ID],

Marieke Huisman[1] [ID], and Marian Lingsch-Rosenfeld[2] [ID]

[1] University of Twente, Enschede, The Netherlands
{l.armborst, m.huisman}@utwente.nl

[2] LMU Munich, Munich, Germany
{dirk.beyer, marian.lingsch-rosenfeld}@sosy.ifi.lmu.de

Abstract. Software model checking and deductive software verification have complementary strengths and weaknesses: software model checkers are more straight-forward to use, as they analyze the program without user input; but they do not yet support complicated data structures and expressive specifications. In contrast, deductive verifiers can verify expressive specifications and complex data structures modularly, but they require the user to specify the program behavior in detail, which is a time-consuming process. Due to their differing nature, the two approaches usually remain separate. However, for industrial usage, one requires both: ease of use as well as expressiveness. Therefore, we present AutoSV-Annotator, a toolchain that integrates the two approaches for C programs. The toolchain allows a user to iteratively refine the deductive annotations in a C program, calling a model checker to supplement the annotations at each iteration, guided by the already existing annotations. We show that our tool is able to annotate and prove many tasks from the SV-Benchmarks set. Our results show that the two strategies can indeed benefit from each other.

Keywords: Deductive software verification · Software model checking · Software validation · Verification witness · Cooperative verification

1 Introduction

Both deductive software verification and software model checking are popular among researchers and practitioners of software verification. Deductive software verifiers (e.g. VerCors [5], Frama-C [27], see also [33]) use user-provided specifications and annotations to modularly prove the program correct. In contrast, software model checkers (e.g. CPAchecker [8], Symbiotic [38], Ultimate [35]) use various algorithms (e.g. [12, 14, 22, 29, 39], mostly non-modular) to prove some properties of the program correct without requiring user input. Due to the different methodologies and the amount of user interaction required, cooperation between these approaches is challenging, but can help alleviate their respective shortcomings. The major bottleneck for deductive software verification is the need for explicit annotations, such as function pre- and postconditions or loop invariants. Writing the necessary annotations can be a time-consuming task, but it gives the developer control over the properties that are checked, and allows verifying complicated functional specifications

© The Author(s) 2025
A. Remke and B. Steffen (Eds.): FMICS 2025, LNCS 16040, pp. 59–77, 2025.
https://doi.org/10.1007/978-3-032-00942-5_4

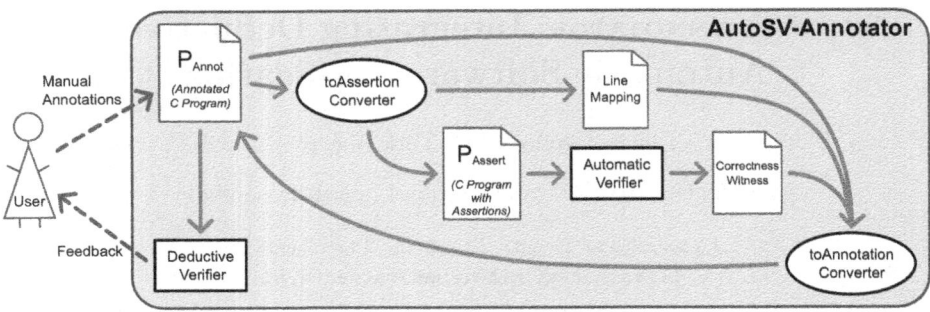

Fig. 1: Workflow integrating automatic and deductive verifiers, guided by the user (exchanged artifacts are red, user interactions blue and dashed)

over unbounded data. In contrast, the bottleneck of many model checkers is scaling to complex software systems, such as unbounded data structures or deeply nested loops. As the analyses are not modular, a failure to verify means there is not even a partial result. However, software model checkers require little input from the user, making them easier to use (thus, we also call them "automatic verifiers"). They often focus on standard properties such as the reachability of a specific program location.

Through cooperation, these tools can complement each other to reduce their respective disadvantages. This was shown by previous research [18], which generated annotations for FRAMA-C from a model checker and checked deductive annotations with model checkers. But in practice, it is unlikely that a single call to one verifier immediately overcomes the shortcomings of the other approach, e.g. by automatically generating all necessary deductive annotations. Instead, a user will usually have to go back and forth, adding or refining deductive annotations until one of the tools succeeds. Such an iterative approach is common in deductive verification, but integrating a model checker can help to speed it up, skipping many iterations compared to the purely deductive loop. To implement this, we developed AUTOSV-ANNOTATOR, which extends the ideas of [18] and integrates them into such a workflow loop, depicted in Fig. 1. This allows the user to seamlessly iterate between a C program with assertions for automatic software verifiers, and one with annotations for deductive verifiers. In particular, compared to [18], AUTOSV-ANNOTATOR implements a full loop and uses state-of-the-art witnesses, including those containing function contracts [7, 36]. This is an important improvement, as the modular deductive verifiers heavily rely on such contracts.

A user of AUTOSV-ANNOTATOR may have a C program with one postcondition indicating the intended behavior. Verifying with a deductive verifier (Fig. 1, left) will most likely fail, due to a lack of annotations. If it fails, AUTOSV-ANNOTATOR will convert the postcondition into an assertion for a model checker (center of Fig. 1, going left to right), and call a model checker. If the model checker provides a concrete counterexample, this shows the user more precisely than the deductive verifier where to change the annotations or the program, and why. Whenever the automatic verifier succeeds, it generates a software verification witness [7] that is converted into annotations, which are checked by the deductive verifier (Fig. 1, right to left on bottom). When the annotations are insufficient to prove the program correct, the user can refine the existing annotations with the feedback from the tool (Fig. 1, left). Even if the automatic verifier could not decide on a verdict, its output may give some useful information, like information about which loop it is currently unable to verify. In the next iteration, the user can then choose to let the *toAssertion Converter* abstract the program based on the existing deductive annotations, for example replacing an inner loop with its invariant. Not having to unroll the loop simplifies the automatic analysis, potentially now leading to a witness; AUTOSV-ANNOTATOR applies these findings automatically to the non-abstracted program with the help of a mapping between the lines of the two programs. Alternatively, the user may exploit the deductive verifier's modularity to prove entire modules deductively, while leaving other modules and the overall integration to automatic verifiers. This is useful for larger industrial systems, and when involving library calls. The user can focus the manual efforts on tasks with complex functional properties, such as recursive functions that the automatic verifier cannot handle, and let automatic verifiers handle the rest. Section 4.4 shows some example usages of the workflow.

Contributions. We present AUTOSV-ANNOTATOR, a toolchain that combines automatic and deductive verifiers into a cooperative workflow loop (Fig. 1). In particular:

- We transfer the results of previous work [18] from FRAMA-C with witnesses version 1.0 [13] to VERCORS for the new witness format version 2.0 [7].
- We evaluate the performance of VERCORS on witnesses version 2.0 extended by function contracts [36], which are important for modular deductive verifiers.
- We implement an automatic transformation of programs, based on their deductive annotations, to enhance the performance of automatic verifiers.
- We implemented AUTOSV-ANNOTATOR as a backend in METAVAL++[3], a tool providing multiple backends to interact with validation tasks (i.e. programs with witnesses), making the switch between tools as seamless as possible.
- We show that automatic verifiers' witnesses can help deductive tools prove many tasks in SV-Benchmarks correct, and we demonstrate the iterative workflow on case-studies.

Overview. Section 2 explains the underlying concepts, in particular automatic verification, verification witnesses and their validation, and deductive verification. In Sect. 3, we outline how AUTOSV-ANNOTATOR turns witnesses from automatic verifiers into annotations for deductive verifiers, and how the annotations of deductive verifiers can be used to help the automatic verifier. Afterwards, Sect. 4 shows the evaluation of our results for the two transformations, and the workflow loop as a whole. Section 5 discusses some of the limitations and avenues of future improvements.

1.1 Related Work

Our work falls in the broad category of cooperative verification [21], whose goal is to combine the strengths of different verification approaches. Previous work has focused particularly on combining different automatic verification approaches [15, 23, 34]. In contrast to the cooperation between automatic software verifiers, the cooperation

---

[3] https://gitlab.com/sosy-lab/software/metavalpp

between automatic and deductive verifiers has been studied less extensively. One example is Ivy [42], which combines deductive and interactive proving with model checking, but uses its own dedicated language, and hardware model checkers rather than software ones.

The most closely related work is a study using FRAMA-C [18], and we transfer their study to VERCORS in RQ 1. The previous work already describes the idea of transforming witnesses into deductive annotations, and annotations into assertions. Building on those ideas, we implement a toolchain for an iterative workflow, centered around the verification engineer. We also extend the existing approach in several important ways: We use the new witness format 2.0 extended with function contracts [7, 36], which is essential for the modular approach of deductive verifiers. We also use the deductive annotations to abstract the program, which can overcome some shortcomings of automatic verifiers, such as insufficient support of recursion. Overall, this improves the applicability and user experience.

In one step of the loop, we use the automatic verifier to obtain annotations for the deductive verifier. We do not aim to be an annotation generator, but use them as an exchange format between automatic and deductive verifiers and the user. Nevertheless, our work borders on the long research on generating specifications (see e.g. [40] for an overview of tools). Most relevant here are those that make use of existing tools. Some use the static analysis of Horn solvers [1, 31] similar to the automatic verifier here. Tools like Daikon [30] use templates for common specifications, and try sample executions of the program to see which template may apply. These test executions may be generated automatically and combined with deductive verifiers to check the generated specifications [32]. While all these focus on functional properties like us, there are also attempts to generate memory access specifications [6, 28]. Such specifications are also needed for VERCORS, but generating them is outside the scope of the model checkers investigated here. However, they complement our work, and it can be interesting to also cooperate with these tools, for instance by adding another loop to the workflow in Fig. 1.

A study on contract inference for FRAMA-C [3] similarly transforms (partial) deductive annotations into assertions, to then generate missing annotations automatically with Horn solvers. The project faced some challenges similar to us, for instance when translating annotations into executable C expressions, and sometimes use the same techniques to tackle them. Some of those techniques were already mentioned for Java [10]. However, the FRAMA-C study focuses on the case where the manual annotations are on the top level `main` function, which is explicitly transformed into a harness function that incorporates those annotations. In contrast, we support manual annotations more generally, for example allowing a recursive helper function to be annotated manually. Additionally, the study focuses on contract inference, while we also infer loop invariants.

2   Background

Deductive Verifiers. Deductive verifiers rely on specifications given as comments in the source code, which describe the desired properties and behavior of the program. Typically, the specifications use a contract style in the form of pre- and

```
1 //@ requires x>=0;
2 //@ ensures \result == 10*x;
3 int scale(int x) {
4   return x==0 ? 0 : 10+scale(x-1);
5 }
6
7 //@ ensures \result == 50;
8 int main() {
9   int i = 0, n = 100;
10  int a[n];
11  /*@ loop_invariant 0<=i && i<n
12        && (\forall int j=0 .. i;
13             a[j]==10*j); */
14  for(i=0; i<n; ++i) {
15    a[i] = scale(i);
16  }
17  assert(i==100);
18  return a[5];
19 }
```

```
- entry_type: "invariant_set"
  metadata:
    [...]
  content:
  - invariant:
      type: "loop_invariant"
      location:
        file_name: "fig2.c"
        line: 14
        column: 3
      function: "main"
      value: "0<=i && i<=n"
      format: "c_expression"
```

(a) Simple example program with (insufficient) VERCORS annotations

(b) Excerpt of a correctness witness

Fig. 2: An example program showing the style of VERCORS annotations (left), and an excerpt of a corresponding correctness witness using C expressions (right)

post-conditions and invariants, such as defined in the Java Modeling Language (JML) [41] or the ANSI/ISO C Specification Language (ACSL) [9]. Verifiers like FRAMA-C [27], OPENJML [26], and VERCORS [5] then use Hoare-style reasoning to prove the program correct with respect to those specifications. Even if no desired functional behavior is specified, the tool typically expects that no runtime errors occur, such as out-of-bounds array accesses, and it requires annotations like loop invariants to prove this. Due to this need for explicit annotations, deductive verification is less automated than model checking; but once sufficient annotations are provided by the user, the deductive verifier automatically proves that the program code adheres to those specification.

While details in the required annotations may vary between deductive verifiers, they typically use a modular approach to verify each function separately, based on its contract containing pre- and postconditions, and on other functions' contracts. When verifying a function like scale in Fig. 2a, its precondition x>=0 is assumed, and from this and scale's body, the postcondition \result==10*x is proven. Function calls in the body, like in this case the recursive call, are abstracted using the respective contract: scale checks that the recursive call satisfies its precondition before it is called, and then simply assumes its postcondition, without considering the actual recursive execution. If the function body contains a loop, like in main, this must be annotated with a loop invariant. To be invariant, it has to be *initialized*, i.e. it has to hold when the execution reaches the loop head for the first time, and it has to be *inductive*, i.e. the invariant together with the loop body need to imply the invariant again. This abstracts the loop, allowing to prove the program correct even for an unbounded number of loop iterations. Note that in the example in Fig. 2a, all these annotations result in a third of the lines being specifications, indicating the required effort of using deductive verification. And there is a difficult-to-spot error: The loop invariant should be i<=n rather than i<n, and is thus not actually inductive.

The approach of AUTOSV-ANNOTATOR works for various deductive C verifiers. While previous research [18] used FRAMA-C, our implementation focuses on VER-CORS [5]. It targets concurrent programs, which are especially error-prone, and has a wider range of input languages, including C extensions for GPU programs. In addition to the specifications mentioned above, VERCORS also requires annotations regarding the use of shared memory to ensure that concurrent threads do not interfere with each other, e.g. in a data race. It is built on permission-based separation logic [2], which extends Hoare logic with memory access permissions. Accesses to shared memory, such as global variables, is only allowed if the thread has sufficient permission for that location. Thereby, VERCORS can provide more precise guarantees for concurrent programs, but it also increases the efforts required from users when annotating a program. These annotations do not directly translate to properties checked by the automatic verifiers.

Software Model Checkers. Software model checkers [14, 25] like CPACHECKER [8] and UAUTOMIZER [35] take a program and a separate specification that indicates which properties to check (e.g. reachability of a program location), and automatically, i.e. without user interaction, try to check whether the program satisfies the properties. In the example in Fig. 2a, the wrapper function `assert` will raise an error if the given condition does not hold, and the property to check is the unreachability of that error. The verifiers use many different techniques, like k-Induction [29], CEGAR [24], and BMC [22]. These techniques focus on proving all paths of the program correct, in contrast to deductive verifiers which aim for a modular proof. For example, BMC will unroll the program to show its correctness, and can therefore not produce invariants. All automatic verifiers return a verdict, which is *True* if the specification holds for the program, *False* if it does not, and *Unknown* if the tool could not determine if it holds or not. Many automatic verifiers participate in the yearly software verification competition (SV-COMP) [19], which evaluates the verifiers on SV-Benchmarks, the largest set of benchmark C programs with associated expected verdicts. All verifiers participating in the competition use *software verification witnesses* [7, 13] to justify their verdict, either via a counterexample trace (called *violation witnesses*) or via a summary of why the program satisfies the specification (*correctness witnesses*). For this work, we focus on the latter.

Correctness Witnesses. Software verification witnesses allow tools verifying C programs to encode arguments supporting their verdict for a verification task in a machine-readable format. Correctness witnesses in version 2.0 [7] encode the proof found by an automatic verifier as a set of invariants. The invariants are encoded as C expressions and are matched to a location in the program. Figure 2b shows an example witness encoding parts of the loop invariant of the program on the left. The quantifier cannot be expressed as a C expression, and is therefore not included. Invariants are separated into *loop invariants* and *location invariants*: Loop invariants must hold after each evaluation of the loop condition. Thus, compared to the loop invariants in deductive verification, they are initialized, but not guaranteed to be inductive. Location invariants must hold for every path through a specified program location. Note the witness in Fig. 2b is only meant to illustrate the format, and was not actually produced by a verifier. Recently an extension of the correctness witness format was proposed [36], which allows to encode function contracts in the witness. This extension allows witnesses to make use of a restricted subset of ACSL annotations, \old, \result, and \at(x, Pre), which are used to refer to the state of the program before a function call, the return value of a function, and the state of the program at the beginning of the function.

Verification witnesses allow other tools, called *validators*, to independently check that the verdict provided by a verifier is correct. A validator may use the information contained in a witness to guide their proof search. Thereby, the validator's task is sometimes easier than the original verification. For example, the witness may contain an inductive invariant which accelerates the search for a fixpoint for that loop. Multiple validators exist, some based on automatic verifiers like CPACHECKER [16] and GOBLINT [43] and others on deductive verifiers like METAVAL++: this tool provides multiple backends for various interactions with a validation task, i.e. a program and a witness. One of these backends allows adding the invariants in the witness as annotations such that the annotated program can be verified using VERCORS [5] or FRAMA-C [27]. Starting in SV-COMP23 [11], there has been a dedicated track for the evaluation of validators.

3   AutoSV-Annotator

AutoSV-Annotator as shown in Fig. 1 is implemented as one of several backends of METAVAL++, which is a new tool currently under development. AutoSV-Annotator uses multiple components to exchange verification information between an automatic and a deductive verifier and verify the resulting annotated C program deductively. It is a sequential composition of the following components:

(1) The *toAssertion* converter transforms annotations into assertions, cf. Sect. 3.2. This component takes an annotated C program P_{Annot} and produces an abstracted C program P_{Assert} and a mapping between certain key lines that are in both P_{Assert} and P_{Annot}, such as function headers.
(2) An automatic verifier, which is run using FM-Weck [20] to allow for seamless integration of any SV-COMP verifier. FM-Weck is a tool which allows to download and run any tool participating in SV-COMP in in a container with all required dependencies. In addition, it provides a unified interface to pass inputs and get outputs from the tool. It takes P_{Assert} and a specification, for which we use the reachability of a dedicated function reach_error, and produces a correctness witness if the verifier could complete the verification successfully. If it cannot verify the program, AutoSV-Annotator aborts and tells the user that more information is required in form of annotations in P_{Annot}.
(3) The *toAnnotation* converter adds the contents of the witness as annotations back into P_{Annot}, cf. Sect. 3.1. This component takes P_{Annot} and a witness for P_{Assert}, modifies the line numbers in the witness using the mapping produced by the *toAssertion* converter, and produces an annotated C program P'_{Annot} similar to P_{Annot} but augmented with the information from the witness.
(4) A deductive verifier informs the user about the verification state of P'_{Annot}.

Therefore, the user only needs to interact with the annotated program to obtain further annotations from any SV-COMP tool as well as feedback whether a deductive verifier considers the program correct. The modular framework with well-defined interfaces such as the witnesses makes it possible to replace any of the components. In particular, it is already possible to exchange the automatic verifier thanks to FM-Weck [20]. This modularity avoids tool lock-in and makes it possible to always use the most up-to-date tools, compared to reimplementing automatic algorithms within deductive verifiers or vice versa.

3.1   To-Annotation Converter

In [18], the cooperation between deductive and automatic verifiers was analyzed by investigating each translation direction separately. In particular, the authors implemented a transformation from verification witnesses to annotations for the deductive verifier FRAMA-C. We reimplement and extend this transformation to generate annotations for both FRAMA-C and VERCORS. This implements the *toAnnotation* converter at the bottom right of Fig. 1. We implemented this as another backend of METAVAL++, different from the AUTOSV-ANNOTATOR backend. The modularity of METAVAL++ allows us to use this backend in isolation or as part of AUTOSV-ANNOTATOR. The transformation uses a witness in version 2.0 [7] with the proposed extension for function contracts [36] and encodes its contents as annotations in the format of the respective deductive verifier. Additionally, it adds some known annotations, for example the precondition of the dedicated `assert` function. In contrast to the previous work, we are able to use witnesses in version 2.0 [7] with the addition of function contracts [36] instead of 1.0 [13]. This makes the transformation much easier, since the new format contains a direct mapping to the program structure. We also added the support for function contracts, which is an important part of the deductive specification, due to the modular nature of those tools. In addition, we slightly transform the program, such as removing some GNU-C features, to make it more compatible with some deductive verifiers like VERCORS which cannot handle them.

3.2   To-Assertion Converter

We use specifications written for a deductive verifier to guide automatic verifiers to enhance their performance in two major ways: (1) Turning VERCORS annotations into **assertions** for model checkers, and (2) **abstracting the program** based on those annotations to improve the performance of the automatic verifier. In AUTOSV-ANNOTATOR, this represents the *toAssertion* converter at the center top of Fig. 1. Given that this is targeting VERCORS-specific annotations, we extended VERCORS to implement both components, reusing its existing infrastructure.

C Assertions. We turn VERCORS annotations, such as pre- and postconditions and loop invariants, into calls to a wrapper function, which calls the `reach_error` function if the assertion does not hold. Figure 3a shows this for the example from Fig. 2a. This encoding requires the asserted expression to be a valid expression in plain C. Therefore, we need to remove or replace all VERCORS-specific sub-expressions. Some are simple, such as turning the implication `A==>B` into the disjunction `!A||B`. Others are more complex, such as caching the value of `\old` expressions at the beginning of a function. Note that this caching deviates from the memory model of VERCORS in a few corner cases such as a loop invariant `a[i]==\old(a[i])+1`, where the local variable `i` with its current value is combined with the old state of the global variable `a`.

```
 1 int scale(int x) {                        27 int scale_abstract(int x) {
 2    assert(x>=0);                          28    assert(x>=0);
 3    int returnValue = x==0 ? 0             29    /* nothing to havoc in this case */
 4       : 10 + scale_abstract(x-1);         30    int returnValue;
 5    assert(returnValue == 10*x);           31    assume(returnValue == 10*x);
 6    return returnValue;                    32    return returnValue;
 7 }                                         33 }
 8                                           34
 9 int main() {                             35 int main() {
10    assert(1);                             36    /* ... */
11    int i = 0, n = 100;                    37
12    int a[n];                              38    int i = 0;
13    for(i=0; i<n; ++i) {                   39    assert(0<=i && i<=n &&
14       int j = nondet();                   40       (!(0<=j && j<i) || a[j]==10*j));
15       assert(0<=i && i<=n &&              41    i = nondet();
16          (!(0<=j && j<i) || a[j]==10*j)); 42    assume(0<=i && i<=n);
17       a[i] = scale(i);                    43    assume(i<n);
18    }                                      44    int idx = havoc();
19    int j = nondet();                      45    assume(0<=idx && idx<n);
20    assert(0<=i && i<=n &&                 46    a[idx] = havoc();
21       (!(0<=j && j<i) || a[j]==10*j));    47    i = havoc();
22    assert(i==100);                        48    assume(0<=i && i<=n);
23    int returnValue = a[5];                49    assume(!(i<n));
24    assert(returnValue==50);               50
25    return returnValue;                    51    /* ... */
26 }                                         52 }
```

(a) Example with assertions   (b) Abstracted example

Fig. 3: Example from Fig. 2, with the VERCORS annotations turned into C assertions (left) and with the loop abstracted based on the invariants (right). Note that the quantifier is dropped from Lines 42 and 48, as discussed below.

A major limitation are VERCORS' memory access permissions, whose encoding into C expressions would require maps that keep track of the permission amounts per variable. This would worsen the performance of an automatic verifier significantly due to the enlarged state space, since maps are not a native type in C. Therefore, we remove permission expressions completely. In most cases, this has no influence on functional properties, and will not affect the soundness of the automatic analysis. However, permissions may imply that two memory locations are distinct; this anti-aliasing information may need to be added back manually.

Another limitation are quantifiers such as ($\forall$ int i;...). For JBMC [10], two cases for quantified expressions are described, with different approaches to their encoding. The easier case is called *angelic*, where a universal quantifier is asserted or an existential quantifier is assumed. As `assert` statements are implicitly quantified to hold over all execution paths, such a universal quantifier can be encoded with a fresh local variable to replace the quantified variable (e.g. Lines 14 and 15 of Fig. 3a). The same holds for assumed existential quantifiers.

The other case is called *demonic*, where a universal quantifier is assumed, or an existential one asserted. This requires the encoding to use a loop to explicitly iterate over all possible values of the quantified variable. It is therefore only applicable in certain cases (where the variable's values are sufficiently restricted), and even then only in some simple cases can it be handled successfully by automatic verifiers. Instead, the verifier often struggles to apply the knowledge, which is encoded in the loop, to a later assertion. We therefore decided to only implement the angelic case, and remove the demonic quantifiers similar to permission expressions. This can have significant impact on the semantics of encoded annotations and lead to spurious verification failures. However, note that deductive verifiers themselves often struggle with existential quantifiers, so the angelic case of an asserted universal is much more frequent to occur in verified deductive annotations than the asserted existential. Thus, this limitation mostly impacts assumed universal quantifiers, such as when abstracting a program containing quantifiers with the techniques outlined below. Therefore, dropping demonic quantifiers will again mostly affect the completeness of the automatic analysis, not its soundness.

Figure 3a shows how the VERCORS annotations from Fig. 2a were transformed: The pre- and postcondition become assertions at the function start and **return**, respectively. The returned value is stored in a variable **returnValue** to facilitate VERCORS' \result keyword. The loop invariant is added as an assertion' after the loop condition is evaluated, with the quantifier encoded using a local variable.

Program Abstraction. Annotations also allow us to abstract parts of the program by replacing the body of a function with its contract, or a loop body with its loop invariants. This reflects how modular deductive verifiers usually handle the program. Abstracting the program generates an over-approximation of its actual behavior, since deductive annotations are typically over-approximations. When doing the abstraction, variables which are modified in the function or loop body need to be havocked, i.e. assigned a random value. During its verification, VERCORS uses its permission annotations to decide which variables to havoc. But since the program might not contain those, yet, we over-approximate by havocking all stack and heap locations that are targets of assignment statements.

For example, Fig. 3b shows the program from Fig. 2a after abstraction. The loop of **main** is replaced by a series of **assert**, **assume** and **havoc** statements. First, the invariant is asserted, to check that it is initialized. This is not strictly necessary for abstracting the loop, but rather part of the assertion encoding described above. Then, the loop counter is havocked and the invariant and the loop condition are assumed, to model the start of an arbitrary loop iteration. Afterwards, the assigned variables of the loop body are havocked, modeling the body's execution. Finally, the invariant is assumed again, as well as the negated loop condition, modeling the loop exit. Note that assuming the invariant turns the quantifier demonic, and it is therefore dropped. Function calls can be similarly abstracted. Figure 3b also shows an abstract version of **scale**, based on its contract. The user can indicate per call site whether the explicit version of the function shall be invoked (e.g. in **main** in Fig. 3a), or the abstract one (e.g. within **scale**).

These abstractions significantly impact the program, and thus also the verification performance. In general, it will speed up the verification. However, in some cases, the approximation may be too coarse and introduce spurious verification failures. In the example, dropping the quantifier means that the postcondition of **main** can no longer be proven.

4   Evaluation

First, we evaluate each part of the AUTOSV-ANNOTATOR workflow in isolation. We evaluate the conversion of a witness and a C program with assertions into an annotated C program (*toAnnotation* in Fig. 1) using RQ 1 and RQ 2. Then, RQ 3 evaluates the direction from annotated programs to programs with assertions (*toAssertion* in Fig. 1). Finally, RQ 4 brings both directions together to evaluate the full workflow loop. More precisely, we analyze the following:

RQ 1 Are loop invariants produced by automatic verifiers sufficient as annotations for VERCORS, i.e., do the results with FRAMA-C [18] transfer to VERCORS?

RQ 2 Does the extension to the witness format through function contracts improve the results from RQ 1?

RQ 3 Can the transformations from Sect. 3.2, based on an annotated and verified program, aid an automatic verifier in its verification?

RQ 4 Does the AUTOSV-ANNOTATOR toolchain improve the verification workflow compared to using each verifier separately?

Benchmark Environment. We use BENCHEXEC to ensure reliable benchmarking [17]. All benchmarks are performed on machines with an Intel Xeon E5-1230 CPU (4 physical cores with 2 processing units each), 33 GB of RAM, and running Ubuntu 22.04. We restrict all runs to a maximum of 15 min CPU time, 15 GB of RAM, and to 2 processing units. For the evaluation we use all tools which exported non-trivial correctness witnesses in version 2.0 at SV-COMP25 in their participating versions. These are CPACHECKER, UAUTOMIZER, and GOBLINT. For the deductive tools we used VERCORS in version 694fff57 and FRAMA-C in version 30.0. AUTOSV-ANNOTATOR is implemented as a backend of METAVAL+− which was used in version 90bb3cc7. All benchmarks used for RQ 1, RQ 2, and RQ 3 belong to SV-Benchmarks in its SV-COMP25 version, where we focus on the *ReachSafety Loops* and *ReachSafety Recursive* subsets, since they focus on programs requiring complex invariants or function contracts without the heap.

4.1   RQ 1: To-Annotation Converter

To evaluate if the results from [18] transfer to VERCORS, we export witnesses in version 2.0 for the *ReachSafety Loops* subset of SV-Benchmarks and validate them using VERCORS and FRAMA-C. In [18], the authors showed that when analyzing 434 tasks, each composed of a witness and a program, FRAMA-C using the EVA analysis could prove significantly more correct when using the information from the witness as annotations, compared to analyzing the program without that information. Similarly, we used several model checkers to automatically verify the benchmark programs and generate witnesses, and used the *toAnnotation* converter to create annotated versions of the program that can be checked with VERCORS and FRAMA-C. For nearly all programs, neither VERCORS nor FRAMA-C using the weakest precondition analysis could prove the task without the information of the witness. The comparison of the results when using witnesses can be seen in Table 1. It shows that, while FRAMA-C could validate more witnesses, the results are comparable between VERCORS and FRAMA-C (23% of all generated witnesses vs. 30%). There are two major reasons to explain the difference: (1) missing support for some C features from VERCORS, since it is originally a Java verification tool; (2) VERCORS requiring annotations for shared memory, via memory access permissions, which FRAMA-C does not always need.

Table 1: Validation of witnesses in version 2.0 using VERCORS and FRAMA-C

Tool	Witnesses	FRAMA-C	VERCORS
CPACHECKER	351	61	46
UAUTOMIZER	399	130	107
GOBLINT	123	76	46

However, we see that the success rate for both deductive tools is low, meaning the loop invariants produced by the automatic verifier are often not sufficient to prove the program correct with either deductive verifier. The reasons for this depend on the particular automatic tool being used, though some are common between them: (1) Most tools use abstract domains to encode their correctness arguments (e.g., as SMT formulas). Often, these abstract domains cannot be translated into C expressions, thus that particular piece of information is missing from the witness. Therefore, the invariant in the witness is not strong enough for the deductive tool. (2) Automatic tools are only interested in proving specific assertions over all paths in the program. Therefore, the invariants that they provide may not be inductive. One such case is when loops are completely unrolled. (3) Due to their modular nature, deductive verifiers need more annotations than loop invariants, for example function contracts.

> In summary, the generated invariants are sometimes sufficient to prove the program deductively, and the results from [18] mostly transfer to VERCORS.

4.2   RQ 2: Extensions to the To-Annotation Converter

The previous section shows that deductive verifiers often need stronger annotations than those produced by the automatic verifiers. In particular, they would benefit from function contracts, due to their modular analysis. Therefore, we use CPACHECKER to generate witnesses in the newly proposed format for function contracts [36] and validate them using VERCORS.

We compare the witnesses in version 2.0 with those with function contracts on the *ReachSafety Loops* and *ReachSafety Recursive* subsets of SV-Benchmarks. CPACHECKER exported 388 witnesses in total, of which VERCORS could validate 46 in version 2.0 and 69 with the addition of function contracts. This indicates that deductive verifiers benefit from additional information exported by the automatic verifier. However, this export should happen in a standardized form, and be supported by many automatic verifiers. Our results therefore emphasize the usefulness of extending the witness format, and we encourage tool developers to implement those extensions. A possible future addition is information about heap accesses, such as VERCORS' permissions or FRAMA-C's `modifies` clause.

> In summary, exporting function contracts from automatic verifiers proves useful for deductive verifiers. This encourages further extensions to the witness format, and a wider implementation of the existing format among automatic verifiers.

Table 2: Performance of different automatic verifiers on annotated and abstracted files; CPACHECKER + FC denotes the witnesses with function contracts exported by CPACHECKER; the number of tasks which could not be solved by the given verifier originally but could now be solved using the abstractions is given in grey.

		correctly solved by		
witness generator	files	CPACHECKER	UAUTOMIZER	GOBLINT
CPACHECKER	41	(0) 40	(0) 39	(0) 39
CPACHECKER + FC	64	(0) 62	(0) 61	(0) 61
UAUTOMIZER	100	(19) 91	(0) 90	(0) 89
GOBLINT	46	(5) 45	(0) 44	(0) 44

4.3 RQ 3: To-Assertion Converter

In the opposite direction, we annotate files with VERCORS specifications, and then use the *toAssertion* converter (cf. Sect. 3.2) to turn them into assertions for model checkers. We also use the abstractions described in Sect. 3.2 to replace loops and recursive function calls by their specification. To automate this, we use all automatically annotated programs from the previous sections that VERCORS successfully verified. For some of them, the simplification failed, so there are less tasks than could be validated by VERCORS as shown in Table 1. Manually annotated files are deferred to the following section, testing the entire loop.

The results are summarized in Table 2. Almost all simplified programs could be verified regardless of where the witness comes from or which verifier is chosen. This is not surprising since the abstracted programs no longer contain loops nor recursive functions, making them straight-line programs whose verification is usually easy. This is reflected in the average CPU time per task, which is more than 10 times slower for the original tasks when compared to the simplified tasks (101.5 s vs. 7.2 s). Note that in a few cases, a verifier could not prove a file that was abstracted based on its own witness. As explained in Sect. 3.2, such spurious verification failures can happen if the annotation is too coarse. However, Table 2 shows that such cases are rare. Additionally we see that thanks to the abstraction based on UAUTOMIZER and GOBLINT witnesses, CPACHECKER can now solve tasks that it previously could not solve.

> In summary, abstracting program structures using verified annotations can improve the automatic verifier's result and runtime. Verification failures due to the abstraction are rare.

4.4 RQ 4: The Full AUTOSV-ANNOTATOR Toolchain

Together, the directions evaluated above form the whole AUTOSV-ANNOTATOR workflow, which we have evaluated qualitatively on parts of SV-Benchmarks. Revisiting the example in Fig. 2a, assume that main's postcondition is initially the only deductive annotation. The automatic verifier is unable to handle the recursion, so as a first step the user annotates the recursive function, and uses the abstraction for the call in main. Running through METAVAL++, the automatic verifier can prove the file, but the generated witness and annotations enumerate all possible values for i and do not

```
1  int main() {
2    int x = 0;
3    while (nondet()) {
4      int n = nondet();
5      assume(n>=0);
6      x += scale(n);
7    }
8    assert(x % 2 == 0);
9    return 0;
10 }
```

```
- invariant:
    type: "loop_invariant"
    location:
      line: 3
      column: 3
      function: "main"
    value: "((( x >= 0) ? (x % 2) :
            ((x % 2) + 2)) == 0)"
    format: "c_expression"
```

(a) Partially annotated program

(b) Generated witness (excerpt, line number adjusted to match Fig. 4a)

Fig. 4: Example program (left) using the **scale** function of Fig. 2a that neither automatic nor deductive verifiers can verify on their own, but the partial annotations of Fig. 2a let VERCORS abstract the recursive function, which in turn allows ULTIMATE to generate a loop invariant (right) that helps VERCORS.

contain the knowledge of a[i]. So the user decides to manually add the invariant on Line 11-13. Due to the error (cf. Sect. 2), the deductive verifier marks the annotation as not inductive. The error is subtle enough that even an experienced verification engineer may lose time debugging it. Instead, the user runs AUTOSV-ANNOTATOR again, and the automatic verifier gives a concrete counterexample that indicates the error. The user fixes the issue, and the deductive verifier can prove the program correct. Meanwhile, the automatic verifier times out while proving the quantifier of the loop invariant. Even though it could prove the program originally by unrolling the loop, proving the more abstract property in the invariant is too difficult. This highlights the strengths of the automatic verifier by potentially providing a verdict early in the development and giving a concrete counterexample, and the strengths of the deductive verifier in handling the recursion and the quantifier.

Figure 4a shows another program that makes use of the same **scale** function. Neither CPACHECKER nor VERCORS can verify it on their own. AUTOSV-ANNOTATOR can prove the assertion without any additional annotations, deriving the loop invariant automatically. The corresponding witness (generated by ULTIMATE) is shown in Fig. 4b. The resulting annotated file is successfully verified by VERCORS. This shows the advantage of deductive function contracts, especially in the context of library functions like **scale**, and how the automatic verifier uses them to verify the program, fully annotating it in the process. It shows how the verification engineer can concentrate on more difficult parts (like abstracting the recursion in **scale**), while the automatic verifier handles more straight-forward tasks, like adding the condition of the **assert** in Fig. 4a as a loop invariant.

> In summary, the workflow combining both model checker and deductive verifier into an iterative loop can support the verification engineer, helping them to prove some examples that the tools individually struggled with.

4.5   Threats to Validity

Internal Validity. We used the benchmarking framework BENCHEXEC [17] to run the experiments, which uses the most modern Linux features for reliable benchmarking. In particular, BENCHEXEC makes sure to never run two different executions on the same physical core, in order to avoid interference of shared computing resources, which may result in differing time measurements. Many tools, for example CPACHECKER, use a portfolio of analyses, using the wall time to limit the time spent on certain algorithms. Therefore, there may be variance in the results if the time measurements are not precise enough.

In addition to the measurement imprecision, the implementation of our workflow loop may contain some bugs, but since the results of our transformations are always used as input for other verifiers, they are double-checked, raising our confidence in their correctness. The used verifiers may also contain bugs, but all are widely used and have been tested extensively.

External Validity. For this study, we concentrated on a subset of SV-Benchmarks, but it is unclear if the results generalize to other benchmarks. We assume that the results should generalize well; in particular if more information is exported from automatic tools. Section 4.2 shows that such an extension can improve the interaction. Additionally, Sect. 4.4 was a case study conducted by the developers of AUTOSV-ANNOTATOR; a complete user study to investigate the usefulness of the AUTOSV-ANNOTATOR workflow in practice remains as future work.

5 Discussion

The evaluation in the previous section shows that the AUTOSV-ANNOTATOR workflow works in practice, and can improve the work of the verification engineer. However, it also highlights some areas that merit further investigation:

- Some useful specifications cannot be expressed as C expressions, such as demonic quantifiers and memory access permissions. How can they be encoded, and how can automatic verifiers be extended to handle them? While there has been work to encode VERCORS' permission checks as runtime checks for Java [37], it remains future work to do so for C.
- The generated invariants are sometimes not strong enough for a deductive tool to prove the correctness of the program. Sometimes, this is due to the algorithm used not generating invariants, e.g. BMC. Other times, the tool cannot export all its knowledge, e.g. when there is no clear encoding into C expressions.
- VERCORS does not, or has restricted support for, some C language constructs. For example, bit operations are badly supported; and back-jumping gotos, which effectively create a loop, need to be annotated with loop invariants.
- When the automatic verifier times out, it is not always clear where in the program it got stuck. More detailed feedback can help the verification engineer decide where to put manual annotations to aid it.

While the latter two are related to tool implementation, the former two relate to the encoding of the exchange format, and may warrant further extensions of the witness format. Additionally, to fully evaluate the applicability of AUTOSV-ANNOTATOR to industrial cases, a more extensive user study on a larger example than discussed here would be needed. Such a study may involve users of different levels of expertise in formal verification, to further assess how users can best benefit from the toolchain.

6   Conclusion

In this paper, we develop and implement AUTOSV-ANNOTATOR, a workflow to cooperate between software model checkers and deductive software verifiers. Our work provides four major contributions. First, it applies the ideas explored previously [18] for FRAMA-C to the deductive verifier VERCORS. Second, we integrate the newly proposed extension of the witness format with function contracts [36]. Third, we provide program transformations that turn deductive annotations into assertions for software model checkers, and abstract loops and function calls to simplify the automatic analysis. Finally, we have implemented the workflow within METAVAL++, to integrate the steps into an automated pipeline.

Our evaluation shows that the toolchain can assist the verification engineer in proving properties of a program, both in cases where software model checkers could not verify without deductive guidance and where deductive verifiers were supported by software model checkers. But it also shows the limitations of the automation, for instance where more deductive annotations are required than the automatic verifier provides. This highlights the need of centering the workflow around the verification engineer, using an iterative approach like AUTOSV-ANNOTATOR.

Data-Availability Statement. A reproduction package that includes all software and data that we used for our experiments is available on Zenodo [4]. In addition, our tools are publicly available: METAVAL++ is on GitLab https://gitlab.com/sosy-lab/software/metavalpp and VERCORS is on GitHub https://github.com/utwente-fmt/vercors.

Funding Statement. This project was funded in part by the Deutsche Forschungsgemeinschaft (DFG) — 378803395 (ConVeY), and the Dutch Research Council (NWO) — VICI project 639.023.710 (Mercedes).

Disclosure of Interests. The authors have no competing interests to declare that are relevant to the content of this article.

References

1. Alshnakat, A., Gurov, D., Lidström, C., Rümmer, P.: Constraint-Based Contract Inference for Deductive Verification, pp. 149–176. LNCS 12345, Springer (2020). https://doi.org/10.1007/978-3-030-64354-6_6
2. Amighi, A., Haack, C., Huisman, M., Hurlin, C.: Permission-based separation logic for multithreaded java programs. LMCS **11**(1) (2015). https://doi.org/10.2168/LMCS-11(1:2)2015
3. Amilon, J., Esen, Z., Gurov, D., Lidström, C., Rümmer, P.: An Exercise in Mind Reading: Automatic Contract Inference for Frama-C. Springer (2024). https://doi.org/10.1007/978-3-031-55608-1_13
4. Armborst, L., Beyer, D., Huisman, M., Lingsch-Rosenfeld, M.: Reproduction package for FMICS 2025 Submission 'AutoSV-Annotator: Integrating Deductive and Automatic Software Verification'. Zenodo (2025). https://doi.org/10.5281/zenodo.15199589
5. Armborst, L., Bos, P., van den Haak, L., Huisman, M., Rubbens, R., Şakar, O., Tasche, P.: The VERCORS verifier: A progress report. In: Proc. CAV. pp. 3–18. Springer (2024). https://doi.org/10.1007/978-3-031-65630-9_1

6. Armborst, L., Huisman, M.: Using horn solvers to generate memory access permissions for deductive verification: A preliminary report (2024)

7. Ayaziová, P., Beyer, D., Lingsch-Rosenfeld, M., Spiessl, M., Strejček, J.: Software verification witnesses 2.0. In: Proc. SPIN. pp. 184–203. LNCS 14624, Springer (2024). https://doi.org/10.1007/978-3-031-66149-5_11

8. Baier, D., Beyer, D., Chien, P.C., Jakobs, M.C., Jankola, M., Kettl, M., Lee, N.Z., Lemberger, T., Lingsch-Rosenfeld, M., Wachowitz, H., Wendler, P.: Software verification with CPACHECKER 3.0: Tutorial and user guide. In: Proc. FM. pp. 543–570. LNCS 14934, Springer (2024). https://doi.org/10.1007/978-3-031-71177-0_30

9. Baudin, P., Cuoq, P., Filliâtre, J.C., Marché, C., Monate, B., Moy, Y., Prevosto, V.: ACSL: ANSI/ISO C specification language version 1.17 (2021), available at https://frama-c.com/download/acsl-1.17.pdf

10. Beckert, B., Kirsten, M., Klamroth, J., Ulbrich, M.: Modular verification of JML contracts using bounded model checking. In: Leveraging Applications of Formal Methods, Verification and Validation: Verification Principles. Springer (2020). https://doi.org/10.1007/978-3-030-61362-4_4

11. Beyer, D.: Competition on software verification and witness validation: SV-COMP 2023. In: Proc. TACAS (2). pp. 495–522. LNCS 13994, Springer (2023). https://doi.org/10.1007/978-3-031-30820-8_29

12. Beyer, D., Dangl, M.: Software verification with PDR: An implementation of the state of the art. In: Proc. TACAS (1). pp. 3–21. LNCS 12078, Springer (2020). https://doi.org/10.1007/978-3-030-45190-5_1

13. Beyer, D., Dangl, M., Dietsch, D., Heizmann, M., Lemberger, T., Tautschnig, M.: Verification witnesses. ACM Trans. Softw. Eng. Methodol. 31(4), 57:1–57:69 (2022). https://doi.org/10.1145/3477579

14. Beyer, D., Dangl, M., Wendler, P.: A unifying view on SMT-based software verification. J. Autom. Reasoning 60(3), 299–335 (2018). https://doi.org/10.1007/s10817-017-9432-6

15. Beyer, D., Haltermann, J., Lemberger, T., Wehrheim, H.: Decomposing software verification into off-the-shelf components: An application to CEGAR. In: Proc. ICSE. pp. 536–548. ACM (2022). https://doi.org/10.1145/3510003.3510064

16. Beyer, D., Lingsch-Rosenfeld, M.: CPACHECKER VALIDATOR 4.0 (competition contribution). In: Proc. TACAS (3). LNCS 15698, Springer (2025)

17. Beyer, D., Löwe, S., Wendler, P.: Reliable benchmarking: Requirements and solutions. Int. J. Softw. Tools Technol. Transfer 21(1), 1–29 (2019). https://doi.org/10.1007/s10009-017-0469-y

18. Beyer, D., Spiessl, M., Umbricht, S.: Cooperation between automatic and interactive software verifiers. In: Proc. SEFM. p. 111–128. LNCS 13550, Springer (2022). https://doi.org/10.1007/978-3-031-17108-6_7

19. Beyer, D., Strejček, J.: Improvements in software verification and witness validation: SV-COMP 2025. In: Proc. TACAS (3). LNCS 15698, Springer (2025)

20. Beyer, D., Wachowitz, H.: FM-WECK: Containerized execution of formal-methods tools. In: Proc. FM. pp. 39–47. LNCS 14934, Springer (2024). https://doi.org/10.1007/978-3-031-71177-0_3

21. Beyer, D., Wehrheim, H.: Verification artifacts in cooperative verification: Survey and unifying component framework. In: Proc. ISoLA (1). pp. 143–167. LNCS 12476, Springer (2020). https://doi.org/10.1007/978-3-030-61362-4_8

22. Biere, A., Cimatti, A., Clarke, E.M., Zhu, Y.: Symbolic model checking without BDDs. In: Proc. TACAS. pp. 193–207. LNCS 1579, Springer (1999). https://doi.org/10.1007/3-540-49059-0_14

23. Chalupa, M., Richter, C.: BUBAAK-SPLIT: Split what you cannot verify (competition contribution). In: Proc. TACAS (3). pp. 353–358. LNCS 14572, Springer (2024). https://doi.org/10.1007/978-3-031-57256-2_20

24. Clarke, E.M., Grumberg, O., Jha, S., Lu, Y., Veith, H.: Counterexample-guided abstraction refinement for symbolic model checking. J. ACM **50**(5), 752–794 (2003). https://doi.org/10.1145/876638.876643

25. Clarke, E.M., Grumberg, O., Peled, D.A.: Model Checking. MIT (1999)

26. Cok, D.: OpenJML: software verification for Java 7 using JML, OpenJDK, and Eclipse. In: 1st Workshop on Formal Integrated Development Environment, (F-IDE). pp. 79–92 (2014). https://doi.org/10.4204/EPTCS.149.8

27. Cuoq, P., Kirchner, F., Kosmatov, N., Prevosto, V., Signoles, J., Yakobowski, B.: FRAMA-C. In: Proc. SEFM. pp. 233–247. Springer (2012). https://doi.org/10.1007/978-3-642-33826-7_16

28. Dohrau, J.: Automatic Inference of Permission Specifications. Ph.D. thesis, ETH Zurich (2022)

29. Donaldson, A.F., Haller, L., Kröning, D., Rümmer, P.: Software verification using k-induction. In: Proc. SAS. pp. 351–368. LNCS 6887, Springer (2011). https://doi.org/10.1007/978-3-642-23702-7_26

30. Ernst, M.D., Perkins, J.H., Guo, P.J., McCamant, S., Pacheco, C., Tschantz, M.S., Xiao, C.: The DAIKON system for dynamic detection of likely invariants. Science of Computer Programming **69**(1–3), 35–45 (2007). https://doi.org/10.1016/j.scico.2007.01.015, Tool website: https://plse.cs.washington.edu/daikon/

31. Ezudheen, P., Neider, D., D'Souza, D., Garg, P., Madhusudan, P.: Horn-ICE learning for synthesizing invariants and contracts. Proc. ACM Program. Lang. **2**(OOPSLA) (2018). https://doi.org/10.1145/3276501

32. Galeotti, J., Furia, C., May, E., Fraser, G., Zeller, A.: Inferring loop invariants by mutation, dynamic analysis, and static checking. IEEE Trans. Softw. Eng. **41**, 1019–1037 (2015). https://doi.org/10.1109/TSE.2015.2431688

33. Hähnle, R., Huisman, M.: Deductive software verification: From pen-and-paper proofs to industrial tools. In: Computing and Software Science - State of the Art and Perspectives, pp. 345–373. LNCS 10000, Springer (2019)

34. Haltermann, J., Jakobs, M.C., Richter, C., Wehrheim, H.: Parallel program analysis via range splitting. In: Proc. FASE. pp. 195–219 (2023). https://doi.org/10.1007/978-3-031-30826-0_11

35. Heizmann, M., Bentele, M., Dietsch, D., Jiang, X., Klumpp, D., Schüssele, F., Podelski, A.: ULTIMATE AUTOMIZER and the abstraction of bitwise operations (competition contribution). In: Proc. TACAS (3). pp. 418–423. LNCS 14572, Springer (2024). https://doi.org/10.1007/978-3-031-57256-2_31

36. Heizmann, M., Klumpp, D., Lingsch-Rosenfeld, M., Schüssele, F.: Correctness Witnesses with Function Contracts. arXiv (1 2025). https://doi.org/10.48550/arXiv.2501.12313

37. Janssen, D.D.: Design and implementation of new features for runtime permission verification in concurrent Java programs using VerCors (May 2024)

38. Jonáš, M., Kumor, K., Novák, J., Sedláček, J., Trtík, M., Zaoral, L., Ayaziová, P., Strejček, J.: SYMBIOTIC 10: Lazy memory initialization and compact symbolic execution (competition contribution). In: Proc. TACAS (3). pp. 406–411. LNCS 14572, Springer (2024). https://doi.org/10.1007/978-3-031-57256-2_29

39. King, J.C.: Symbolic execution and program testing. Commun. ACM **19**(7), 385–394 (1976). https://doi.org/10.1145/360248.360252

40. Lathouwers, S., Huisman, M.: Survey of annotation generators for deductive verifiers. Journal of Systems and Software **211** (2024). https://doi.org/10.1016/j.jss.2024.111972
41. Leavens, G., Poll, E., Clifton, C., Cheon, Y., Ruby, C., Cok, D.R., Müller, P., Kiniry, J., Chalin, P.: JML Reference Manual (2007), dept. of Computer Science, Iowa State University. Available from http://www.jmlspecs.org
42. McMillan, K.L., Padon, O.: Ivy: A multi-modal verification tool for distributed algorithms. In: Lahiri, S.K., Wang, C. (eds.) Computer Aided Verification. Springer International Publishing (2020). https://doi.org/10.1007/978-3-030-53291-8_12
43. Saan, S., Erhard, J., Schwarz, M., Bozhilov, S., Holter, K., Tilscher, S., Vojdani, V., Seidl, H.: GOBLINT VALIDATOR: Correctness witness validation by abstract interpretation (competition contribution). In: Proc. TACAS (3). pp. 335–340. LNCS 14572, Springer (2024). https://doi.org/10.1007/978-3-031-57256-2_17

IC3 for Loop Invariant Generation in Deductive Analysis

Niklas van de Sand and Marcus Völker[✉] [iD]

RWTH Aachen University, Embedded Software (Informatik 11), Aachen, Germany
niklas.van.de.sand@rwth-aachen.de, voelker@embedded.rwth-aachen.de

Abstract. In this paper, we introduce a framework for programmable logic controller programs that combines a deductive verification approach on control flow automata with an inductive verification technique used to automatically derive loop invariants. The deductive verification is based on Hoare triples that are propagated through loop-free sections of the program using strongest postcondition and weakest precondition. Loop invariants are derived from loop pre- and postconditions with a modified version of the IC3 algorithm with predicate abstraction. While this approach is straightforward for programs with a single loop, programs with multiple loops require iterating potential loop invariants between the loops until an overall proof can be found. We demonstrate the efficacy of our approach by evaluating example programs, showing both improved performance compared to inductive verification of the complete program, and a push-button approach to deductive verification requiring – ideally – no user-supplied loop invariants.

Keywords: Deductive Verification · Program Analysis · Safety · Programmable Logic Controllers

1 Introduction

The more safety-critical the field a piece of software is used in, the more necessary it is to make sure that the software behaves correctly. This implies a direct need for the use of safety-assuring approaches in the context of industrial automation, where failures are potentially much more costly and harmful than in user-space applications on e.g. a desktop computer. To that end, many verification techniques have been developed for or lifted to the industrial domain, such as programmable logic controllers (PLCs) [2,4,11,17,25]. However, the nature of the industrial domain is that oftentimes, the technicians and engineers developing and overseeing these systems are not well-versed in the language of theoretical computer science. That is, special training or the addition of dedicated verification engineers is necessary to ensure techniques that place more of an onus on the developer of the system can be used in practice.

How important this is varies between different techniques; while comparatively simple analyses such as the various dataflow analyses [24] can usually be

A. Remke and B. Steffen (Eds.): FMICS 2025, LNCS 16040, pp. 78–104, 2025.
https://doi.org/10.1007/978-3-032-00942-5_5

performed without user interaction, model checking requires at least a formalisation of the requirement to be checked, which in turn requires understanding of the logic the model checker is using. Oftentimes, these are temporal logics such as linear temporal logic (LTL) [27], that need to be understood to be able to specify the requirements. Furthermore, if no dedicated model checker for the target domain is available, converting the system into the input description of the model checker – such as nuXmv [7] – requires additional work.

Maybe the hardest techniques to use for laypeople involve proofs over the program, such as deductive verification with Hoare logic [16]. Here, inference rules have to be applied – by hand – to prove that a program fulfils a given specification. While some of these inference rules can be and have been automated, e.g. with strongest postcondition/weakest precondition [13], a big intrinsic problem is the treatment of program loops, as they require additional information in the form of a loop invariant. That is, a formula that encodes some information about the variables that stays true over the whole loop execution has to be used to prove facts about the loop.

The big advantage of deductive verification over an approach such as model checking is the greatly reduced computational effort; while model checking requires instantiation of the program's reachable state-space (which in the worst case is exponential in the size of the program memory), deductive verification is for the most part based on purely syntax-driven rules and simple logical implications. One could say the effort is lifted from being purely computational to a requirement of the human having a deeper understanding of the program and being able to express this in a proof.

Unfortunately, as described, this runs directly counter to the necessities of verification in the context of industrial automation, where giving the human the ability to carry out a deductive proof is not easy or economical to fulfil. This is why considerable effort has been expended to attempt to automate deductive verification as much as possible, and where our contribution comes in as well:

We propose a framework for deductive verification specifically of PLC software and use a sophisticated algorithm for model checking to automatically derive loop invariants. As we only care about the loop invariants, and not model checking of the complete program, we can deploy the model checker on a much smaller scale. This keeps the computational complexity of model checking at a managable level, while the rest of the verification process uses the benefits of deductive reasoning.

This paper is structured as follows: In Sect. 2, we explain necessary preliminaries to later explain our approch: Hoare logic, predicate transformers, and the IC3 algorithm. In Sect. 3, we explain our contribution by intuitively building our algorithm up from these preliminaries from simple to general programs, and then giving a formal description in pseudocode. In Sect. 4, we present a quantitative evaluation of the runtime of our approach compared to using IC3 modelchecking on the whole program. Finally, in Sect. 5, we draw a short conclusion and discuss open questions for future work.

1.1   Related Work

We are neither the first to investigate the automated generation of invariants in deductive reasoning, nor the first to tailor verification techniques to the PLC domain, nor doing both. Verification of PLC code has been an active topic of research since Moon modelled ladder logic for verification [22]. Since then, many approaches tailored to PLC verification have been developed [2,11,25]. Our work here was implemented in the PLC code analysis tool Arcade [4,5,29], which has the same aim of bringing analysis techniques into the industrial domain.

In the verification community at large, much research has been done to automatically generate invariants for deductive reasoning, whether with abstract interpretation [10,30], learning [15,28], or generative AI [26].

Perhaps closest to our work in aim is the work by Lourenço et al. [19,20], who use deductive verification with automated invariant generation for analysis of programs written in ladder logic. They use the verification framework Why3 [14] which contains an invariant generator based on abstract interpretation. The main differences between our approaches are that we use a symbolic method with IC3 instead, and that we target Structured Text while they target ladder logic.

2   Preliminaries

In this section, we describe the necessary techniques for deductive and inductive verification that we use to build our verification framework: Hoare logic, predicate transformers and the IC3 algorithm.

2.1   Hoare Logic

In Hoare logic [16], the basic structure that proofs operate on is the *Hoare triple* $\{\varphi\}\, P\, \{\psi\}$. This has the meaning that if the propositional logic formula φ over the program variables in program (fragment) P holds, and P is executed, then afterwards the propositional logic formula ψ will hold. To prove that a Hoare triple is valid, inference rules can be used that operate on the syntax of P. While the reader is referred to literature for a full treatment of Hoare logic, there are two inference rules that we would like to mention here:

$$(\text{seq})\frac{\{\varphi\}\, S_1\, \{\vartheta\} \qquad \{\vartheta\}\, S_2\, \{\psi\}}{\{\varphi\}\, S_1; S_2\, \{\psi\}}$$

$$(\text{while})\frac{\{\vartheta \wedge c\}\, S\, \{\vartheta\}}{\{\vartheta\}\, \texttt{while } c \texttt{ do } S \texttt{ od}\, \{\vartheta \wedge \neg c\}}$$

These rules illustrate the different reasonings we need to be able to do in order to perform deductive verification. The sequence rule (seq) states that in order to prove $\{\varphi\}\, S_1; S_2\, \{\psi\}$, we need to find a predicate ϑ that holds in between the two components of the sequence. While this, in principle, needs human knowledge, as we will see below, this can easily be automated.

The rule for while is different. It also requires a predicate ϑ to be found, the *loop invariant*, but in this case, there is no general algorithm that can provide such a loop invariant, leaving a human to provide ϑ, typically through annotation in the source code when using a framework such as Viper [23].

2.2   Predicate Transformers

Hoare logic has a consequence rule allowing to strengthen preconditions and weaken postconditions.

$$\text{(conseq)}\ \frac{\varphi \to \varphi' \quad \{\varphi'\}\, S\, \{\psi'\} \quad \psi' \to \psi}{\{\varphi\}\, S\, \{\psi\}}$$

This implies that we have an interest to find the *weakest precondition* and the *strongest postcondition*, which we can then strengthen/weaken if necessary for the proof. These can be computed with *predicate transformers* [13], $SP_S(\varphi)$ and $WP_S(\psi)$. Given a predicate φ, SP_S computes the strongest postcondition ψ such that $\{\varphi\}\, S\, \{\psi\}$ is valid. Conversely, given a predicate ψ, WP_S computes the weakest precondition φ such that $\{\varphi\}\, S\, \{\psi\}$ is valid. These predicate transformers are defined recursively over the structure of S, e.g. $SP_{S_1;S_2}(\varphi) = SP_{S_2}(SP_{S_1}(\varphi))$ or $WP_{\mathtt{x:=e}}(\psi) = \psi\,[x/e]$. Note that we use what is otherwise called *weakest liberal precondition*, as we do not analyse loop termination. In our algorithm, we use these predicate transformers over paths through the control flow, but the concept is analogous and essentially boils down to combining the instructions in a path with the sequence combinator;.

2.3   IC3

IC3 [6], also known as *Property Directed Reachability* (PDR), is an algorithm originally conceived for Boolean model checking; that is, given a propositional transition formula $T(\bar{x}, \bar{x}')$, an initial configuration $I(\bar{x})$, and a characterisation of bad states $B(\bar{x})$, it calculates whether B is reachable from I given repeated application of T. The key idea is that the algorithm tries to find an invariant P under T (that is, $P(\bar{x}) \wedge T(\bar{x}, \bar{x}') \to P(\bar{x}')$) which is sufficiently strong to prove safety, i.e. $I(\bar{x}) \to P(\bar{x})$ and $P(\bar{x}) \to \neg B(\bar{x})$. In that sense, P is an overapproximation of the reachable state space, strong enough to prove safety, but (ideally) weak enough to be efficiently computable. Internally, this is accomplished by generating a telescoping sequence of frames $F_i(\bar{x})$, with the semantic that frame F_i overapproximates states reachable within the first i steps. Once two frames F_i and F_{i+1} are found that are identical, we have found an invariant that proves the whole program safe, while an irrefutable intersection of F_i and B proves that the program is unsafe. There are more subtle and inventive novelties to the IC3 approach specificially; the reader is referred to the related work for these, as in the context of our approach, this high-level view of IC3 suffices.

As mentioned above, IC3 itself is an algorithm for Boolean model checking. As we are interested in programs with more than just Boolean logic, and are, in the end, going to use IC3 to provide invariants for Hoare logic, we need to be able to express predicates over background theories that have more capabilities than just Boolean logic. Therefore, we also use the extension of IC3 with predicate abstraction [9], which replaces the Boolean variables in the formulas with predicates over the program variables, lifting the problem and the necessary solver from SAT to SMT.

This adds the possibility of spurious counterexamples into the algorithm, i.e., it is now possible for IC3 to report that there is a path from I to B via T, even though the path is only possible in the abstract world of predicate abstraction and not the actual program. Therefore, an additional step is added in which the counterexample is checked against the concrete state space. If the counterexample is realisable there, the specification is indeed violated, whereas an unrealisable counterexample shows that the abstraction is too coarse and must be refined. This is done with *Craig interpolation* [21]. Interpolation allows us to take two SMT formulas A and B that are unsatisfiable together and derive an *interpolant* J using only symbols common to A and B, with the properties $A \rightarrow J$ and $J \rightarrow \neg B$. Simply put, J is an explanation for the contradiction between A and B. We can then use this to derive additional predicates that need to be added into the abstraction by encoding the abstract and the concrete path with A and B, respectively. These additional predicates, due to the property of the interpolator, specifically remove the spurious counterexample from the abstraction.

3   Contribution

In this section, we present our deductive verification approach. The examples in this section, as is traditional for Hoare logic, use a simple While-language. Our implementation is for programs written in Structured Text [18], which are transformed into a *control flow automation* (CFA) representation by our parser. We distinguish CFAs from the common control flow graphs by requiring the program's instructions to be annotated to the edges, not the vertices. We annotate a Hoare triple to the program body, giving it a pre- and postcondition, which we aim to verify. As PLC code is executed cyclically, these conditions are to be taken to hold at the beginning and end of a cycle.

3.1   Iterative Computation of Loop Invariants

While we have developed a technique that can derive proofs for programs with arbitrary usage of loops, for didactical reasons it makes most sense to first consider the easiest case. That is, a program that consists of a single loop with code before and after it (which especially means no branching around the loop). A discussion of general programs with a more formalised approach follows in Sect. 3.3. In a general sense, we can represent this type of program as $S_1;$ `while` c `do` S_2 `od`$; S_3$. Given a pre- and postcondition, the Hoare triple we want to prove is

$$\{\varphi\}\, S_1; \texttt{while } c \texttt{ do } S_2 \texttt{ od}; S_3\, \{\psi\}$$

With the usage of predicate transformers the loop-free components S_1 and S_3 can be traversed automatically, giving

$$\{SP_{S_1}(\varphi)\}\, \texttt{while } c \texttt{ do } S_2 \texttt{ od}\, \{WP_{S_3}(\psi)\}$$

This is the best case, as we have the strongest possible precondition and the weakest possible postcondition for the loop itself. We will see later how this changes in more complex programs. The loop's precondition $SP_{S_1}(\varphi)$, together with a predicate $\texttt{pc} = entry(S_2)$ ensuring that we start at the beginning of the loop forms the initial configuration for IC3, i.e.

$$I(\bar{x}) = (SP_{S_1}(\varphi) \wedge \texttt{pc} = entry(S_2))$$

The loop's postcondition, on the other hand, can be encoded into B. For this, consider when the loop violates the Hoare triple: This happens when

1. The loop terminates, i.e.
   (a) The execution arrives at the top of the loop $\texttt{pc} = entry(S_2)$
   (b) The loop condition c is not fulfilled
2. and the annotated postcondition is violated

Putting these together, we get

$$B(\bar{x}) = (\texttt{pc} = entry(S_2) \wedge \neg c \wedge \neg WP_{S_3}(\psi))$$

The transition relation T is obtained from a simple encoding of S_2's CFA structure. Now, we have all the ingredients necessary to run IC3 on the loop. Once it terminates, we have one of two results: Case 1: IC3 reports that the bad states are unreachable, which allows us to extract the final frame F_k as loop invariant and use it as ϑ in the Hoare rule. Case 2: IC3 finds a non-spurious counterexample, which corresponds directly to an execution starting the loop in $SP_{S_1}(\varphi)$ and terminating outside of $WP_{S_3}(\psi)$, meaning the Hoare triple is incorrect. Take, for example, the simple program in Listing 1 and assume the precondition $\varphi = true$ and the postcondition $\psi = (res)$. As described above, we get a loop precondition

$$SP_{\texttt{db:=0;tmp:=0}}(true) = (db = 0 \wedge tmp = 0)$$

and a postcondition

$$WP_{\texttt{IF...FI}}(res) = ((2 \mid db \rightarrow true) \wedge (2 \nmid db \rightarrow false)) = (2 \mid db)$$

```
 1  db  := 0;
 2  tmp := 0;
 3  WHILE tmp < x DO
 4     db  := db + 2;
 5     tmp := tmp + 1
 6  OD;
 7  IF db MOD 2 = 0 THEN
 8     res := true
 9  ELSE
10     res := false
11  FI
```

Listing 1. Example Program with a single loop

These, together with the symbolic encoding of the loop body, form the input to IC3:

$$I(\bar{x}) = (db = 0 \land tmp = 0) \land (pc = 3)$$

$$T(\bar{x}, \bar{x}') = \begin{pmatrix} pc = 3 \rightarrow x' = x \land db' = db + 2 \land tmp' = tmp \land pc' = 4 \\ \land pc = 4 \rightarrow x' = x \land db' = db \land tmp' = tmp + 1 \land pc' = 3 \end{pmatrix}$$

$$B(\bar{x}) = (pc = 3 \land tmp \geq x \land (2 \nmid db))$$

IC3 can prove this correct, giving e.g. the invariant $\vartheta = F_k = (2 \mid db)$

3.2 Sequential Loops

We will again use a generic program with two loops to illustrate our approach:

$$\{\varphi\}\, S_1; \texttt{while } c_1 \texttt{ do } W_1 \texttt{ od}; S_2; \texttt{while } c_2 \texttt{ do } W_2 \texttt{ od}; S_3\, \{\psi\}$$

Here, the problem with the single loop approach becomes apparent: We cannot calculate either strongest postcondition or weakest precondition for a while loop, so we cannot annotate either of these loops with both a pre- and a postcondition, which we need in order to find $I(\bar{x})$ and $B(\bar{x})$ for IC3. Hence, the idea is to start with a precondition that is weaker than the actual strongest postcondition, and seeing if that is enough to prove the given Hoare triple. If not, we will have to add refinement steps in order to attempt the proof again. This is done by substituting *true* for the invariant ϑ_1 of the first loop, which has the effect (cf. the while rule) of attempting to prove the Hoare triple

$$\{\neg c_1\}\, S_2; \texttt{while } c_2 \texttt{ do } W_2 \texttt{ od}; S_3\, \{\psi\}$$

In this case, we obtain the single loop case and use predicate transformers and IC3 as described above. If the proof works, we are done, but if the proof does not work, this only means that this specific Hoare triple is incorrect, not that the original Hoare triple was incorrect. So now, we have to attempt to strengthen ϑ_1 until we can also derive an invariant ϑ_2, which in turn proves the original Hoare triple correct. We do this with a variation on counterexample-guided abstraction refinement; as the IC3 proof on the second loop fails, it gives us the violation of the loop's initial condition. In the context of Hoare logic, we found a conflict predicate κ for the Hoare triple $\{\varphi\}$ while c do S od $\{\psi\}$, such that $\kappa \to \varphi$, and $\{\kappa\}$ while c do S od $\{\neg\psi\}$, which proves the first Hoare triple incorrect. Our obligation now is to prove that κ can not actually occur in the precondition of the second loop, so we backpropagate $\neg\kappa$ with weakest precondition, which gives us a new Hoare triple

$$\{SP_{S_1}(\varphi)\}\, \texttt{while } c_1 \texttt{ do } W_1 \texttt{ od}\, \{WP_{S_2}(\neg\kappa)\}$$

If proving this Hoare triple with IC3 fails as well, we have found a counterexample and proven the Hoare triple on the complete program wrong. If it succeeds, we have a strengthened invariant ϑ_1 and can propagate it forward again. This back and forth between the two loops continues until we either find a violation as described, or we find invariants ϑ_1 and ϑ_2 that prove the Hoare triple correct.

3.3   Proving Complete Programs

Based on the intuitive description, we now explore the proper formalisation of the algorithm, which works on the general case of a program with arbitrarily combined loops. Note first that due to the way we handle loops, nested loops are not meaningfully different from an atomic loop; the body of the outermost loop is encoded as a transition predicate via its CFA, whether it contains further loops or not. Therefore, combining multiple loops into a program is only relevant in as far as the loops are put into a sequential or branching order. Our first step, therefore, is to calculate the dependencies of loops on one another, as well as which loops are directly (i.e., without passing another loop) reachable from the program entry, and which reach the program exit. This is accomplished with a simple depth-first search on the CFA once loops are identified, and yields a dependency graph. In our implementation, this is performed by a function LOOPDEPENDENCIES. An example is depicted in Fig. 1. Propagation of predicates between these loops, with the predicate transformers SP and WP, can then be performed along the edges of this dependency graph. The formal description of the algorithm is in Algorithm 1, which we will now explain. First, the CFA G of the program is searched for loops and the dependency graph is constructed. All loops are annotated with an initial invariant of *true*, and the global pre- and postcondition are propagated to give local pre- and postconditions for each loop, under the assumption of the invariant *true*. Here, we store separate preconditions for each predecessor of a loop, i.e. $\Phi(l)(l')$ is the precondition of l if we come from loop l'. This ensures we can update loop preconditions properly when only receiving updates from a single loop, otherwise we would have to start more complicated propagation steps inbetween. If there is a path between the entry and exit of G that does not contain a loop, it is possible to already find a contradiction in this step. Then, we initialise a stack of proof obligations with all the loops that are directly connected to the exit of the CFA, using the backpropagated postcondition. Now, until this stack is empty, we keep looking at the proof obligation on top of the stack, consisting of the loop and its postcondition. This obligation is analysed with IC3, using the annotated precondition, giving one of two possible results: An invariant ϑ or a conflict κ. If we get an invariant, we have proven the proof obligation (and return PROVEN), annotate the newly discovered invariant, propagate the postcondition resulting from the invariant forward, and pop the obligation from the stack. If we get a conflict, we have to check whether the loop is directly reachable from the entry. If it is, we have found a counterexample and return REFUTED. Otherwise, we backpropagate $\neg\kappa$ to the predecessor loops and add the resulting postcondition as new proof obligation. To illustrate the workings of the algorithm, let us consider an example, the code of which can be found in Listing 2. The program calculates the sum of x and y, provided both are non-negative. This gives us the Hoare triple $\{x \geq 0 \wedge y \geq 0\} \, P \, \{sum = x + y\}$ The program contains three loops, which we will now refer to (by their line numbers) as l_3, l_7 and l_{12} (we omit the CFA representation here for brevity). The entry reaches l_3, l_3 reaches the other loops, and those loops reach the exit. We initialise our Φ and Ψ annotations of these loops with strongest postcondition and weakest precondition, as described:

$$\Phi(l_3)(entry(G)) = (x \geq 0 \wedge y \geq 0 \wedge sum = 0 \wedge tmp = 0)$$
$$\Psi(l_3) = true$$
$$\Phi(l_7)(l_3) = (x \leq y \wedge (sum \geq x \vee sum \geq y))$$
$$\Psi(l_7) = (sum = x + y)$$
$$\Phi(l_{12})(l_3) = (x > y \wedge (sum \geq x \vee sum \geq y))$$
$$\Psi(l_{12}) = (sum = x + y)$$

There is no direct path from entry to exit, so we cannot try to trivially refute the Hoare triple. Therefore, the loops connected to the exit give us our first two proof obligations:

$$obligations = [(l_7, sum = x + y), (l_{12}, sum = x + y)]$$

We now run IC3 with

$$I(\bar{x}) = (x \leq y \wedge (sum \geq x \vee sum \geq y))$$
$$T(\bar{x}, \bar{x}') = (x' = x \wedge y' = y \wedge sum' = sum + 1 \wedge tmp' = tmp + 1)$$
$$B(\bar{x}) = (sum \geq y \wedge sum \neq x + y)$$

(we have projected away the program counter for brevity's sake) IC3 will find a counterexample here. Let us, for sake of brevity, assume the conflict is $\kappa = (x \leq y \wedge sum = x + 1)$, which is consistent with φ/I, and leads into $\neg\psi/B$. So, we leave this proof obligation on the stack for later and propagate $\neg\kappa$ backwards

```
 1  sum  :=  0;
 2  tmp  :=  0;
 3  WHILE  sum  <  x  AND  sum  <  y  DO
 4      sum  :=  sum  +  1
 5  OD;
 6  IF  x  ≤  y  THEN
 7      WHILE  tmp  <  y  DO
 8          sum  :=  sum  +  1;
 9          tmp  :=  tmp  +  1
10      OD
11  ELSE
12      WHILE  tmp  <  x  DO
13          sum  :=  sum  +  1;
14          tmp  :=  tmp  +  1
15      OD
16  FI
```

Listing 2. Example Program with three loops

to l_3 with weakest precondition. This leads to the new proof obligation $(l_3, x \le y \to sum \neq x + 1)$, which is then handled next, giving us the IC3 instance

$$I(\bar{x}) = (x \ge 0 \land y \ge 0 \land sum = 0 \land tmp = 0 \land pc = 3)$$
$$T(\bar{x}, \bar{x}') = (pc = 3 \to (sum' = sum + 1 \land pc' = 3))$$
$$B(\bar{x}) = (pc = 3 \land (sum \ge x \lor sum \ge y) \land x \le y \land sum = x + 1)$$

In this case, IC3 can prove the Hoare triple, so we extract the invariant, which we assume is $\Theta(l_3) = sum \le \min(x, y)$ (Note that this is an exceptionally good pick, in a real verification process this would likely need multiple refinement steps and be written more verbosely). This, combined with the negated loop condition, $(sum \ge x \lor sum \ge y)$, gives $sum \le \min(x, y) \land (sum = x \lor sum = y)$, which then is propagated forward to the two other loops,

$$2\Phi(l_7)(l_3) = (x \le y \land sum = x)$$
$$\Phi(l_{12})(l_3) = (x > y \land sum = y)$$

These preconditions are strong enough to prove the correctness of the Hoare triples of these two loops, giving invariants such as $\Theta(l_7) = (sum = x + tmp \land tmp \le y)$

3.4 Limitations

The biggest theoretical limitation comes from the fact that we use interpolation in the predicate abstraction for IC3. Interpolation is difficult in multiple ways; first, there are formulas that modern interpolators cannot handle. This is directly

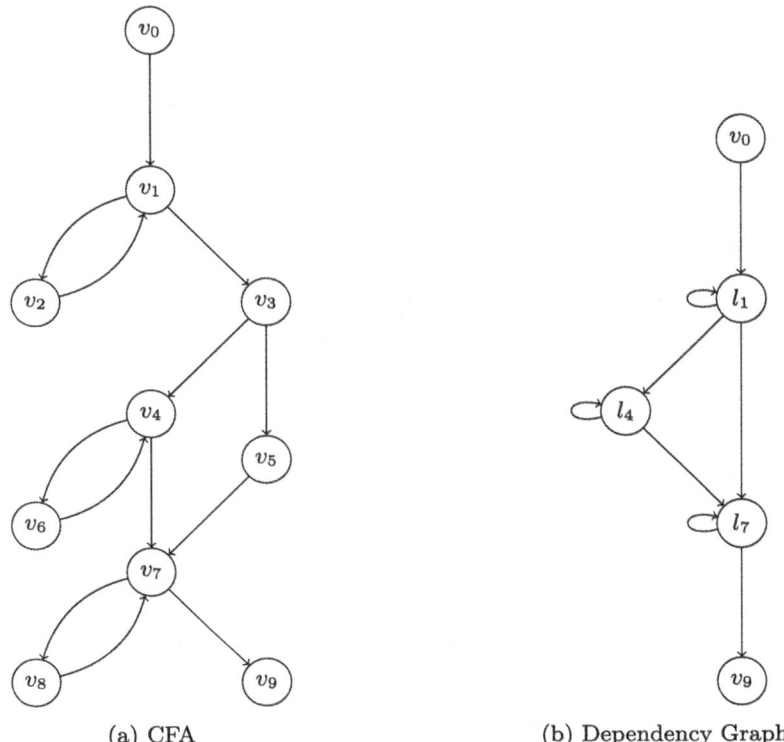

(a) CFA   (b) Dependency Graph

Fig. 1. Dependency Graph of loops for example CFA

connected to the operators used in the program itself, which end up in the T predicates for the loops, and then in the input to the interpolator. We have found that as soon as we stop using linear programs (for simplicity: with merely addition and subtraction), the interpolator has a good chance of not being able to generate interpolants, which directly limits the type of programs we can analyse (cf. A for the programs we did analyse in the end) Next, even if the interpolator can find an interpolant, there are stark differences in the quality of different generated interpolants. For example, say that the invariant of a loop that just increments x is $x > 0$, we have already derived the predicates $x = 0$ and $x = 1$, and the interpolator is trying to resolve a conflict between $x_p = 1 \land x = x_p + 1$ and $x = 0$. If we are lucky, the interpolator will find that indeed $x > 0$ explains this conflict. If we are unlucky, however, the interpolator will find $x = 2$ instead, which will negate the counterexample we have found, but we will run into the same problem again one loop iteration later, when $x_p = 2 \land x = x_p + 1$ and $x = 0$ are in conflict. Even if IC3 terminates eventually, it is possible that the generated invariant for the counterexample is too specific and while it blocks the currently requested proof obligation, it is not strong enough to prove correctness

---

Algorithm 1. Deductive Proof

1: **procedure** PROVEDEDUCTIVE(φ, CFA G, ψ)
2:      $loops \leftarrow$ LOOPS(G)
3:      $deps \leftarrow$ LOOPDEPENDENCIES($G, loops$)
4:      $\Theta \leftarrow [l \mapsto true \mid l \in loops]$
5:      $\Phi \leftarrow$ PROPAGATEPRE($G, loops, \varphi$)
6:      $\Psi \leftarrow$ PROPAGATEPOST($G, loops, \psi$)
7:      **if** SAT($\Phi(exit(G)) \wedge \neg\psi$) **then return** REFUTED
8:      $obligations \leftarrow$ stack($\emptyset$)
9:      **for** $l \in \{l$ reaches exit(G) $\mid l \in loops\}$ **do**
10:          $obligations$.push($(l, \Psi(l))$)
11:      **while** $\neg obligations$.empty() **do**
12:          $(l, \psi_l, k) \leftarrow obligations$.top()
13:          $result \leftarrow$ IC3($\bigvee_{l'} \Phi(l)(l'), T_l, \neg\psi_l$)
14:          **if** $result$ is ϑ **then**
15:              $\Theta(l) \leftarrow \Theta(l) \wedge \vartheta$
16:              **for** $(l', S) \in \{(l', S) \mid (l, S) \in deps(l')\}$ **do**
17:                  $\Phi(l')(l) \leftarrow \Phi(l')(l) \wedge SP_S(\Theta(l) \wedge \neg c_l)$
18:              $obligations$.pop()
19:          **else**
20:              $\kappa \leftarrow result$
21:              **if** $\exists_S(entry(G), S) \in deps(l) \wedge$ SAT($\varphi \wedge WP_S(\kappa)$) **then**
22:                  **return** REFUTED
23:              **for** $(l', S) \in deps(l)$ **do**
24:                  $obligations$.push($l', WP_S(\neg\kappa)$)
25:      **return** PROVEN

---

of the program, leading to another strengthening step. It is possible for this loop of consecutively generated invariants to never terminate.

4   Evaluation

To evaluate how well the approach performs, we evaluated it on a variety of test programs. We wrote nine programs ourselves and took five more from the software verification competition [3]. The body of programs is represented in Appendix A. These programs were then fed to a fuzzer to generate more test instances to artificially generate a bigger dataset. We then took all our generated programs (154 in total) and used monolithic IC3 as well as our deductive approach on them, measuring the run time with a timeout of 20 min. Looking under the hood of our implementation, we have implemented our analysis in the PLC software analysis tool ARCADE [4], which is currently written in C++. For SMT solving we use the SMT solver Z3 [12]. Unfortunately, Z3 removed the capability of performing Craig interpolation at some point, which is why we also use SMTInterpol [8]. The drawback is that SMTInterpol is written in Java, which forces us to communicate with it via operating system calls and the file system, which we expect slows down our implementaiton somewhat. This holds both for the monolithic IC3 and our approach. First, we should note that monolithic IC3 and our approach yield the same analysis results, giving credence to the validity of our implementation. Running both approaches on all programs gives the runtimes shown in Fig. 2. In all cases where the dot is above the red line, it means that the monolithic proof was slower than the deductive approach. Calculating more precise numbers, we can see that in roughly 93% of cases, the deductive proof is faster. Not depicted, however, are the two instances where the deductive approach failed to find a result in 20 min, while the monolithic approach could solve the problem. In cases where both approaches found a result, the average speedup was 68%, we should note though that most of this speedup happens on the fuzzed programs, with a speedup of only 39% for the original programs. We attribute this to the fuzzed programs being more likely to feature incorrect Hoare triples than can easily be refuted.

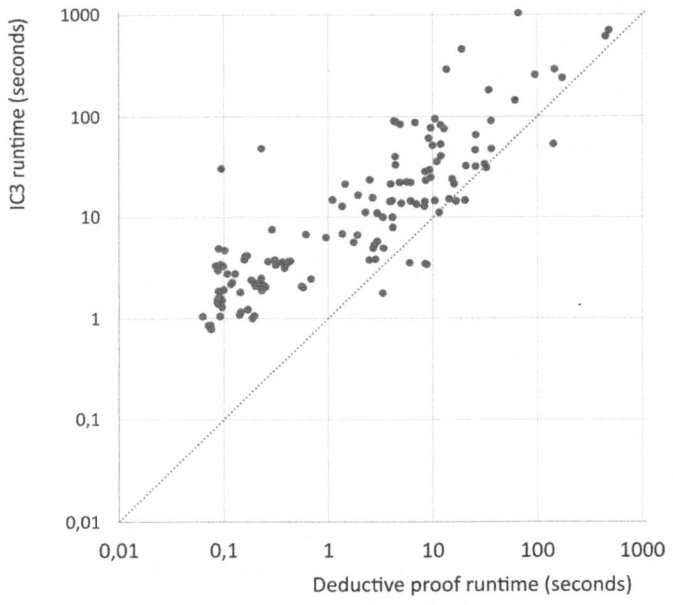

Fig. 2. Evaluation results

We also considered an optimisation where IC3 instances would be reused once a second proof obligation on the same loop is to be analysed, but were not able to extract consistent performance gains from this implementation. While more research might find a heuristic that identifies programs that benefit from an optimisation such as this, the average result was slowdown, so we will not consider it here.

5   Conclusion

We have presented an algorithm for deductive verification where loop invariants can be automatically derived with IC3. We have implemented it for verification of Structured Text programs running on a PLC in the context of industrial automation. The algorithm is capable of finding a deductive proof for a Hoare triple if it exists, though it is not guaranteed to terminate, based on the capricious behaviour of Craig interpolation. It did terminate in most cases where monolithic IC3 terminated, and on average manages a speedup compared to the pure model checking approach. We see this as a very promising step on the way of push-button deductive verification for the industrial use case.

5.1   Future Work

While the algorithm works, there are two major fronts for improvements that we are currently investigating. First, the algorithm currently cannot handle programs that the interpolator cannot handle. Different approaches to interpolation, such as Newton refinement [1] or specifically tailored interpolation algorithms might be able to increase the number of loops that IC3 with predicate abstraction can work on. Second, while our approach outperforms monolithic IC3, it appears to do so only by a constant factor, which is a far cry from the potential speed gains from using deductive verification in the first place. In the worst case, this is to be expected, as we are asking a question with inherently exponential complexity; however, IC3 is only one tool in the big toolbox of invariant generators. A possible approach might be to use faster and less complete techniques than model checking, both black-box and white-box, to first try to find workable invariants quickly, before turning to the sledgehammer that is inductive model checking. Another angle could be the treatment of nested loops. While small nested loops (such as two-dimensional array traversal) seem to make sense to handle monolithically, programs with a big outer loop and multiple smaller inner loops might benefit from a smarter approach, such as recursively using the algorithm on loop bodies to try and prove inner invariants before proving outer invariants. On the implementation side, we currently only work with programs without calls. In the PLC domain, recursion is forbidden, so calls are trivially inlineable, but one of the strengths of deductive verification is the composability from sub-proofs on functions, so adding this would allow for modular verification, though the onus on the developer would be to provide pre- and postconditions not just for the main program but also the other program organisation units. Finally, taking a step back to our aim of providing fast verification that is usable for technicians on the job, we have not fully eliminated specialised knowledge yet, as even without invariant annotation, pre- and postconditions still need to be annotated. We are currently investigating how other specification logics (such as LTL) that encode more than a single PLC cycle can be converted into a set of Hoare triples that prove it. Then, we hope to lift these results to specification formalisms more familiar to industry professionals, such as Petri Nets.

A   Test Programs

```
1   // post: (and (>= res 0) (or (= res i0) (= res (-
        i0))))
2
3   PROGRAM EXAMPLE
4   VAR
5       i0: INT;
6       tmp: INT;
7       res: INT;
8   END_VAR
9
10      tmp := 0;
11      res := 0;
12
13      IF i0 < 0 THEN
14          WHILE tmp > i0 DO
15              res := res + 1;
16              tmp := tmp - 1;
17          END_WHILE;
18      ELSE
19          WHILE tmp < i0 DO
20              res := res + 1;
21              tmp := tmp + 1;
22          END_WHILE;
23      END_IF;
24
25  END_PROGRAM
```

```
1   // pre: (and (< low i0) (< low i1) (> up i0) (> up
        i1))
2   // post: (and (<= low i0) (<= low i1) (>= up i0)
        (>= up i1) (or (= low i0) (= low i1)) (or (= up
        i0) (= up i1)))
3
4   PROGRAM EXAMPLE
5   VAR
6       i0: INT;
7       i1: INT;
8       control: BOOL;
9       low: INT;
10      up: INT;
11      tmp: INT;
12  END_VAR
13      tmp := 0;
14
```

```
15 │     IF i0 < i1 THEN
16 │         WHILE low < i0 DO
17 │             low := low + 1;
18 │         END_WHILE;
19 │     ELSE
20 │         WHILE low < i1 DO
21 │             low := low + 1;
22 │         END_WHILE;
23 │     END_IF;
24 │
25 │     WHILE up > i0 AND up > i1 DO
26 │         up := up - 1;
27 │     END_WHILE;
28 │
29 │     IF control THEN
30 │         tmp := i0;
31 │         i0 := i1;
32 │         i1 := tmp;
33 │     END_IF;
34 │
35 │ END_PROGRAM
```

```
 1 │ // pre: (> b 0)
 2 │ // post: (and (>= delta 0) (or (= delta (- a b))
   │    (= delta (- b a))))
 3 │
 4 │ PROGRAM EXAMPLE
 5 │ VAR
 6 │     a:  INT;
 7 │     b:  INT;
 8 │     a1: INT;
 9 │     b1: INT;
10 │     tmp: INT;
11 │     delta: INT;
12 │ END_VAR
13 │     a1 := a;
14 │
15 │     IF a1 < 0 THEN
16 │         a1 := - a1;
17 │     END_IF;
18 │
19 │     b1 := b;
20 │     delta := 0;
21 │
22 │     IF a < 0 THEN
```

```
23              tmp := a1;
24              WHILE tmp > 0 DO
25                  b1 := b1 + 1;
26                  tmp := tmp - 1;
27              END_WHILE;
28              delta := delta + b1;
29              b1 := - a;
30          END_IF;
31
32          WHILE a1 <> b1 DO
33              delta := delta + 1;
34              IF a1 < b1 THEN
35                  a1 := a1 + 1;
36              ELSE
37                  b1 := b1 + 1;
38              END_IF;
39          END_WHILE;
40
41  END_PROGRAM
```

```
1   // pre: (>= i0 0)
2   // post: (= r (* 2 i0))
3
4   PROGRAM EXAMPLE
5   VAR
6       i0: INT;
7       x: INT;
8     a: INT;
9       r: INT;
10  END_VAR
11
12    a := 0;
13      x := 0;
14
15      WHILE x < i0 DO
16          a := a + 2;
17          x := x + 1;
18      END_WHILE;
19
20      r := a;
21
22  END_PROGRAM
```

```
1   // pre: (and (>= i0 0) (>= i1 0))
2   // post: (= r (+ (* 2 i0) (* 3 i1)))
```

```
 3 |
 4 |
 5 | PROGRAM EXAMPLE
 6 | VAR
 7 |     i0: INT;
 8 |     i1: INT;
 9 |     x: INT;
10 |   a: INT;
11 |     b: INT;
12 |     r: INT;
13 | END_VAR
14 |
15 |   a := 0;
16 |     x := 0;
17 |
18 |     WHILE x < i0 DO
19 |         a := a + 2;
20 |         x := x + 1;
21 |     END_WHILE;
22 |
23 |     b := 0;
24 |
25 |     WHILE b < i1 DO
26 |         a := a + 3;
27 |         b := b + 1;
28 |     END_WHILE;
29 |
30 |     r := a;
31 |
32 | END_PROGRAM
```

```
 1 | // pre: (and (>= i0 0) (>= i1 0) (>= i2 0))
 2 | // post: (= r (+ (* 2 i0) (* 3 i1) (* 4 i2)))
 3 |
 4 | PROGRAM EXAMPLE
 5 | VAR
 6 |     i0: INT;
 7 |     i1: INT;
 8 |     i2: INT;
 9 |     x: INT;
10 |   a: INT;
11 |     b: INT;
12 |     c: INT;
13 |     r: INT;
14 | END_VAR
```

```
15
16   a  :=  0;
17     x  :=  0;
18
19     WHILE  x  <  i0  DO
20         a  :=  a  +  2;
21         x  :=  x  +  1;
22     END_WHILE;
23
24     b  :=  0;
25
26     WHILE  b  <  i1  DO
27         a  :=  a  +  3;
28         b  :=  b  +  1;
29     END_WHILE;
30
31     c  :=  0;
32
33     WHILE  c  <  i2  DO
34         a  :=  a  +  4;
35         c  :=  c  +  1;
36     END_WHILE;
37
38     r  :=  a;
39
40  END_PROGRAM
```

```
1  // post: (and (= 0 (+ a0 b0)) (= 0 (+ a1 b1)))
2
3  PROGRAM EXAMPLE
4  VAR
5      i0: INT;
6      i1: INT;
7      count: INT;
8      a0: INT;
9      a1: INT;
10     b0: INT;
11     b1: INT;
12     tmp: INT;
13  END_VAR
14     b0  :=  i0;
15     b1  :=  i1;
16     a0  :=  -  b0;
17     a1  :=  -  b1;
18     tmp  :=  0;
```

```
19
20        WHILE tmp < count DO
21            a0  := a0 - 1;
22            a1  := a1 + 1;
23            b0  := b0 + 1;
24            b1  := b1 - 1;
25            tmp := tmp + 1;
26        END_WHILE;
27
28 END_PROGRAM
```

```
1 // pre:  (>= a0 0)
2 // post: (and (>= b1 a0) (<= b1 (+ a0 12)))
3
4 PROGRAM EXAMPLE
5 VAR
6     a0: INT;
7     a1: INT;
8     b1: INT;
9 END_VAR
10    a1 := 0;
11    WHILE a1 < a0 DO
12        a1 := a1 + 5;
13    END_WHILE;
14
15    b1 := 0;
16    WHILE b1 < a1 DO
17        b1 := b1 + 7;
18    END_WHILE;
19
20 END_PROGRAM
```

```
1 // pre:  (and (>= x 0) (>= y 0))
2 // post: (= sum (+ x y))
3
4 PROGRAM EXAMPLE
5 VAR
6     x: INT;
7     y: INT;
8     sum: INT;
9     tmp: INT;
10 END_VAR
11
12     sum := 0;
13
```

```
14        WHILE x < y AND sum < x DO
15            sum := sum + 1;
16        END_WHILE;
17
18        IF x >= y THEN
19            tmp := x - y;
20            WHILE tmp < 2 * x DO
21                sum := sum + 1;
22                tmp := tmp + 1;
23            END_WHILE;
24        ELSE
25            sum := sum + y;
26        END_IF;
27
28 END_PROGRAM
```

```
1  // post: res
2  PROGRAM EXAMPLE
3  VAR
4    s: INT;
5    tmp: INT;
6    tmp2: INT;
7    res: BOOL;
8  END_VAR
9    s := 0;
10   res := TRUE;
11
12   WHILE tmp > 0 DO
13     tmp := tmp - 1;
14
15     IF s <> 0 THEN
16       s := s + 1;
17     END_IF;
18
19     IF tmp2 > 0 THEN
20       tmp2 := tmp2 - 1;
21       res := res AND (s = 0);
22     END_IF;
23   END_WHILE;
24 END_PROGRAM
25
26 // Adapted from the Competition on Software
        Verification sv-comp.sosy-lab.org/2024/
```

```
 1  // post: res
 2  PROGRAM EXAMPLE
 3  VAR
 4    i: INT;
 5    j: INT;
 6    pvlen: INT;
 7    tmp___1: INT;
 8    k: INT;
 9    n: INT;
10    tmp2: INT;
11    tmp3: INT;
12    tmp4: BOOL;
13    res: BOOL;
14  END_VAR
15    k := 0;
16    i := 0;
17
18    WHILE tmp2 > 0 AND i <= 1000000 DO
19      tmp2 := tmp2 - 1;
20
21      i := i + 1;
22    END_WHILE;
23
24    IF i > pvlen THEN
25      pvlen := i;
26    END_IF;
27
28    i := 0;
29
30    WHILE tmp3 > 0 AND i <= 1000000 DO
31      tmp___1 := i;
32      i := i + 1;
33      k := k + 1;
34    END_WHILE;
35
36    j := 0;
37    n := i;
38
39    tmp4 := TRUE;
40    res := TRUE;
41    WHILE tmp4 DO
42      res := res AND (k >= 0);
43      k := k - 1;
44      i := i - 1;
45      j := j - 1;
```

```
46
47       tmp4 := j < n;
48    END_WHILE;
49
50 END_PROGRAM
51
52 // Adapted from the Competition on Software
       Verification sv-comp.sosy-lab.org/2024/
```

```
1  // post: result
2  PROGRAM EXAMPLE
3  VAR
4    n0: INT;
5    n1: INT;
6    i0: INT;
7    i1: INT;
8    j1: INT;
9    k: INT;
10   result: BOOL;
11 END_VAR
12
13   i0 := 0;
14   k := 0;
15
16   WHILE i0 < n0 DO
17     i0 := i0 + 1;
18     k := k + 1;
19   END_WHILE;
20
21   i1 := 0;
22   WHILE i1 < n1 DO
23     i1 := i1 + 1;
24     k := k + 1;
25   END_WHILE;
26
27   j1 := 0;
28   result := TRUE;
29   WHILE j1 < n0 + n1 DO
30     result := result AND (k > 0);
31     j1 := j1 + 1;
32     k := k - 1;
33   END_WHILE;
34
35 END_PROGRAM
36
```

```
37  // Adapted from the Competition on Software
       Verification sv-comp.sosy-lab.org/2024/
```

```
 1  // pre: (> mid 0)
 2  // post: (= lo hi)
 3  PROGRAM EXAMPLE
 4  VAR
 5    lo: INT;
 6    mid: INT;
 7    hi: INT;
 8  END_VAR
 9
10    lo := 0;
11    hi := 2 * mid;
12
13    WHILE mid > 0 DO
14      lo := lo + 1;
15      hi := hi - 1;
16      mid := mid - 1;
17    END_WHILE;
18  END_PROGRAM
19
20  // Adapted from the Competition on Software
       Verification sv-comp.sosy-lab.org/2024/
```

```
 1  // pre: (and (>= i 0) (>= j 0))
 2  // post: res
 3  PROGRAM EXAMPLE
 4  VAR
 5    i: INT;
 6    j: INT;
 7    x: INT;
 8    y: INT;
 9    res: BOOL;
10  END_VAR
11    x := i;
12    y := j;
13
14    WHILE x <> 0 DO
15      x := x - 1;
16      y := y - 1;
17    END_WHILE;
18
19    res := TRUE;
20
```

```
21    IF  i = j THEN
22       res := y = 0;
23    END_IF;
24  END_PROGRAM
25
26  // Adapted from the Competition on Software
        Verification sv-comp.sosy-lab.org/2024/
```

References

1. Ball, T., Rajamani, S.: Generating abstract explanations of spurious counterexamples in c programs. Technical report MSR-TR-2002-09 (2002). https://www.microsoft.com/en-us/research/publication/generating-abstract-explanations-of-spurious-counterexamples-in-c-programs/

2. Beckert, B., Ulbrich, M., Vogel-Heuser, B., Weigl, A.: Regression verification for programmable logic controller software. In: Butler, M., Conchon, S., Zaïdi, F. (eds.) ICFEM 2015. LNCS, vol. 9407, pp. 234–251. Springer, Cham (2015). https://doi.org/10.1007/978-3-319-25423-4_15

3. Beyer, D.: State of the art in software verification and witness validation: SV-COMP 2024. In: Finkbeiner, B., Kovács, L. (eds.) TACAS 2024. LNCS, vol. 14572, pp. 299–329. Springer, Cham (2024). https://doi.org/10.1007/978-3-031-57256-2_15

4. Biallas, S., Brauer, J., Kowalewski, S.: Arcade.PLC: a verification platform for programmable logic controllers. In: Proceedings of the 27th IEEE/ACM International Conference on Automated Software Engineering, pp. 338–341. ASE 2012, ACM (2012), http://publications.embedded.rwth-aachen.de/file/3w

5. Bohlender, D., Hamm, D., Kowalewski, S.: Cycle-bounded model checking of PLC software via dynamic large-block encoding. In: Proceedings of the 33rd Annual ACM Symposium on Applied Computing, SAC 2018, Pau, France, April 09-13, 2018, pp. 1891–1898 (2018)

6. Bradley, A.R.: SAT-based model checking without unrolling. In: Jhala, R., Schmidt, D. (eds.) VMCAI 2011. LNCS, vol. 6538, pp. 70–87. Springer, Heidelberg (2011). https://doi.org/10.1007/978-3-642-18275-4_7

7. Cavada, R., et al.: The NUXMV symbolic model checker. In: Biere, A., Bloem, R. (eds.) CAV 2014. LNCS, vol. 8559, pp. 334–342. Springer, Cham (2014). https://doi.org/10.1007/978-3-319-08867-9_22

8. Christ, J., Hoenicke, J., Nutz, A.: SMTInterpol: an interpolating SMT solver. In: Donaldson, A., Parker, D. (eds.) SPIN 2012. LNCS, vol. 7385, pp. 248–254. Springer, Heidelberg (2012). https://doi.org/10.1007/978-3-642-31759-0_19

9. Cimatti, A., Griggio, A., Mover, S., Tonetta, S.: IC3 modulo theories via implicit predicate abstraction. In: Ábrahám, E., Havelund, K. (eds.) TACAS 2014. LNCS, vol. 8413, pp. 46–61. Springer, Heidelberg (2014). https://doi.org/10.1007/978-3-642-54862-8_4

10. Cousot, P., Halbwachs, N.: Automatic discovery of linear restraints among variables of a program. In: Proceedings of the 5th ACM SIGACT-SIGPLAN Symposium on Principles of Programming Languages, pp. 84–96. POPL 1978, Association for Computing Machinery, New York (1978). https://doi.org/10.1145/512760.512770

11. Darvas, D., Fernández Adiego, B., Blanco Viñuela, E.: Plcverif: a tool to verify plc programs based on model checking techniques (2015). https://doi.org/10.18429/JACoW-ICALEPCS2015-WEPGF092

12. de Moura, L., Bjørner, N.: Z3: an efficient SMT solver. In: Ramakrishnan, C.R., Rehof, J. (eds.) TACAS 2008. LNCS, vol. 4963, pp. 337–340. Springer, Heidelberg (2008). https://doi.org/10.1007/978-3-540-78800-3_24

13. Dijkstra, E.W.: Guarded commands, nondeterminacy and formal derivation of programs. Commun. ACM **18**(8), 453–457 (1975). https://doi.org/10.1145/360933.360975

14. Filliâtre, J.-C., Paskevich, A.: Why3 — where programs meet provers. In: Felleisen, M., Gardner, P. (eds.) ESOP 2013. LNCS, vol. 7792, pp. 125–128. Springer, Heidelberg (2013). https://doi.org/10.1007/978-3-642-37036-6_8

15. Garg, P., Löding, C., Madhusudan, P., Neider, D.: ICE: a robust framework for learning invariants. In: Biere, A., Bloem, R. (eds.) CAV 2014. LNCS, vol. 8559, pp. 69–87. Springer, Cham (2014). https://doi.org/10.1007/978-3-319-08867-9_5

16. Hoare, C.A.R.: An axiomatic basis for computer programming. Commun. ACM **12**(10), 576–580 (1969). https://doi.org/10.1145/363235.363259

17. Controllers, P.: Standard. International Electrotechnical Commission, Geneva, CH (2003)

18. Programmable Controllers - Programming Languages. Standard, International Electrotechnical Commission, Geneva, CH (2003)

19. Lourenço, C., Cousineau, D., Faissole, F., Marché, C., Mentré, D., Inoue, H.: Formal analysis of ladder programs using deductive verification. Research Report RR-9402, Inria (2021). https://inria.hal.science/hal-03199464

20. Lourenço, C.B., Cousineau, D., Faissole, F., Marché, C., Mentré, D., Inoue, H.: Automated verification of temporal properties of ladder programs. In: Lluch Lafuente, A., Mavridou, A. (eds.) FMICS 2021. LNCS, vol. 12863, pp. 21–38. Springer, Cham (2021). https://doi.org/10.1007/978-3-030-85248-1_2

21. Lyndon, R.C.: An interpolation theorem in the predicate calculus. Pac. J. Math. **9**(4), 129–142 (1959). http://dml.mathdoc.fr/item/1103039458

22. Moon, I.: Modeling programmable logic controllers for logic verification. IEEE Control Syst. Mag. **14**(2), 53–59 (1994)

23. Müller, P., Schwerhoff, M., Summers, A.J.: Viper: a verification infrastructure for permission-based reasoning. In: Jobstmann, B., Leino, K.R.M. (eds.) VMCAI 2016. LNCS, vol. 9583, pp. 41–62. Springer, Heidelberg (2016). https://doi.org/10.1007/978-3-662-49122-5_2

24. Nielson, F., Nielson, H.R., Hankin, C.: Algorithms. In: Principles of Program Analysis, pp. 365–392. Springer, Heidelberg (1999). https://doi.org/10.1007/978-3-662-03811-6_6

25. Ovatman, T., Aral, A., Polat, D., et al.: An overview of model checking practices on verification of PLC software. Softw. Syst. Model **15** (2016)

26. Pascoal Faria, J., Trigo, E., Abreu, R.: Automatic generation of loop invariants in Dafny with large language models. In: Hojjat, H., Caltais, G. (eds.) FSEN 2025. LNCS, pp. 138–154. Springer, Cham (2025). https://doi.org/10.1007/978-3-031-87054-5_10

27. Pnueli, A.: The temporal logic of programs. In: 18th Annual Symposium on Foundations of Computer Science (SFCS 1977), pp. 46–57 (1977). https://doi.org/10.1109/SFCS.1977.32

28. Ryan, G., Wong, J., Yao, J., Gu, R., Jana, S.: Cln2inv: learning loop invariants with continuous logic networks. In: International Conference on Learning Representations (2020). https://openreview.net/forum?id=HJlfuTEtvB

29. Simon, H., Kowalewski, S.: Mode-aware concolic testing for PLC software. In: Furia, C.A., Winter, K. (eds.) IFM 2018. LNCS, vol. 11023, pp. 367–376. Springer, Cham (2018). https://doi.org/10.1007/978-3-319-98938-9_21

30. Tasche, P., Herber, P., Huisman, M.: Automated invariant generation for efficient deductive reasoning about embedded systems. In: Madeira, A., Knapp, A. (eds.) SEFM 2024. LNCS, pp. 404–422. Springer, Cham (2025). https://doi.org/10.1007/978-3-031-77382-2_23

Backward Responsibility in Transition Systems Beyond Safety

Christel Baier[1,2], Rio Klatt[1,3], Sascha Klüppelholz[1],
and Johannes Lehmann[1,2(✉)]

[1] Technische Universität Dresden, Dresden, Germany
{christel.baier,sascha.klueppelholz,
johannes_alexander.lehmann}@tu-dresden.de, gtn809@alumni.ku.dk
[2] Centre for Tactile Internet with Human-in-the-Loop (CeTI), Dresden, Germany
[3] University of Copenhagen, Copenhagen, Denmark

Abstract. As the complexity of software systems rises, methods for explaining their behaviour are becoming ever-more important. When a system fails, it is critical to determine which of its components are responsible for this failure. Within the verification community, one approach uses graph games and the Shapley value to ascribe a responsibility value to every state of a transition system. As this is done with respect to a specific failure, it is called *backward responsibility*.

This paper provides tight complexity bounds for backward responsibility for reachability, Büchi and parity objectives. For Büchi objectives, a polynomial algorithm is given to determine the set of responsible states. To analyse systems that are too large for standard methods, the paper presents a novel refinement algorithm that iteratively computes responsibility and demonstrates its utility with a prototypical implementation.

1 Introduction

With modern computational systems becoming more complex and simultaneously less transparent to their users, there is growing demand for explaining which internal mechanisms lead to the exhibited behaviour of such systems. This is particularly true for cyber-physical systems and AI systems that are capable of solving complex tasks opaquely while interacting closely with their environment and users. Supporting perspicuity throughout the entire system lifecycle, from design-time over execution-time to inspection-time, therefore becomes an important feature that can improve all processes and workflows where humans

Authors are listed in alphabetical order. The authors are supported by the DFG through the Cluster of Excellence EXC 2050/1 (CeTI, project ID 390696704, as part of Germany's Excellence Strategy), the DFG grant 389792660 as part of TRR 248 (see https://perspicuous-computing.science) and by BMBF (Federal Ministry of Education and Research) in DAAD project 57616814 (SECAI, School of Embedded and Composite AI) as part of the program Konrad Zuse Schools of Excellence in Artificial Intelligence.

A. Remke and B. Steffen (Eds.): FMICS 2025, LNCS 16040, pp. 105–123, 2025.
https://doi.org/10.1007/978-3-032-00942-5_6

are in-the-loop, e.g. maintenance, debugging and system repair. Explainable AI is one example of a recent and rapidly growing research area that has emerged driven by the need for transparency, trust, and accountability in AI systems.

Orthogonal to explainable AI are recent trends towards explainable Formal Methods. Among others, these techniques aim to augment verification results in terms of mathematical concepts that explicate why a system model fulfils or violates its specification. Examples of such concepts are mathematical certificates like inductive invariants or deductive proofs [31] if the model satisfies its specification and counterexamples generated by a model checker or theorem prover in case of a specification violation (see e.g. [6, 14] for an overview). In the taxonomy of [34], the former are examples for forward-looking explications that take all possible behaviors of a model into account, while counterexamples and explications derived from them are backward-looking in the sense that they aim to explain a specific error scenario.

Counterexamples for regular linear-time properties are finite prefixes of computations, representing an ultimately periodic path that starts in an initial state and eventually enters a loop that is repeated ad infinity and that does not satisfy the property. Despite various techniques to generate short counterexamples [19, 20, 24], counterexamples can still be very long, which makes it difficult to identify the reason for the misbehavior. Motivated by this observation, multiple approaches have been proposed to explain counterexamples in terms of causality-based concepts or quantitative notions that measure the degree of responsibility of states or system components. Some of these approaches rely on Halpern and Pearl's notions of actual causality and interventions [22, 23]. The idea is to define causes as minimal sets of items that need to be modified (e.g. switching the truth value of atomic propositions in states) to avoid specification violations. The degree of responsibility of an individual item is then defined as $1/n$ where n is the size of a smallest cause containing that item. This approach has been used to define the degree of responsibility of states in the forward-looking [16] and the backward-looking [12] setting. Halpern and Pearl's notion of causality is also at the heart of [13, 26, 29, 30].

Other approaches to identify causes in counterexamples rely on Stalnaker's and Lewis' semantics of counterfactuals in terms of most similar computations that avoid the error scenario. This is formalised by distance functions on computations [21, 33]. Delta debugging [38] uses a divide-and-conquer technique to generate the most similar passing run. The difference between passing and failing runs can also be used statistically to assess which components of a program are most suspicious [27].

Another direction to explain counterexamples relies on Shapley values that have been introduced to measure the impact of individual players on the outcome of cooperative games [35][1]. Such Shapley-value based approaches have been first proposed for stochastic multi-player game structures [7] and for the forward-looking approach for temporal properties in transition systems [32]. In recent work, these approaches have been adapted to the backward-looking per-

---

[1] A recent discussions on the Shapley value can be found in [3, 36].

spective by explaining counterexamples for safety properties [5]. This has been extended by lifting responsibility from individual states to higher-level concepts such as components, modules and actors [5].

The current paper is in the line of these approaches, mostly of [5]. Given a transition system as operational model, a temporal objective representing the specification and a counterexample path, a state s has responsibility for the outcome if there is a set of states C such that C is not sufficient for satisfying the objective in the induced game, while $C \cup \{s\}$ is, i.e. s is responsible whenever it made a difference in whether the objective is satisfied. Responsibility is then quantified using the Shapley value.

Contribution. Our contribution is threefold. First, we provide complexity results for two decision problems (positivity and threshold) as well as the computation problem covering optimistic and pessimistic backward responsibility with reachability, Büchi and parity objectives (Sect. 4). This includes a polynomial-time algorithm that decides the optimistic positivity problem for Büchi objectives (Algorithm 1). Secondly, we present a refinement algorithm (cf. Algorithm 2 in Sect. 5) that allows for computing the set of states with positive responsibility. Thirdly, we provide a new version of our existing responsibility tool [5] extended with the refinement algorithm and the new objective classes. Section 6 experimentally evaluates the scalability and performance of the refinement algorithm and compares several heuristics. We show that for large models with few responsible states, the refinement algorithm can improve performance by several orders of magnitude.

A full version of this paper including detailed proofs is available at [9].

2 Preliminaries

We briefly present the notations for transition systems, games on graphs and Shapley values. For more details, see e.g. [8].

Transition Systems. A *transition system* is a tuple $\mathcal{T} = (S, \rightarrow, s_{init})$, where S is a finite set of *states*, $\rightarrow \subseteq S \times S$ is the *transition relation* (and we write $s \rightarrow t$ for $(s, t) \in \rightarrow$) and $s_{init} \in S$ is the *initial state*. A *run* on $\mathcal{T}$ is an infinite sequence of states $\rho = \rho_0 \rho_1 \ldots \in S^\omega$, where $\rho_0 = s_{init}$ and for all $i \in \mathbb{N}$, we have $\rho_i \rightarrow \rho_{i+1}$. A run ρ is *lasso-shaped* if there are finite state sequences $u, v \in S^*$ with $\rho = uv^\omega$ and a lasso-shaped run is *simple* if every state occurs at most once in v and no state from u also occurs in v. The set of all runs of $\mathcal{T}$ is denoted by $Runs(\mathcal{T})$. To simplify notations, we occasionally treat a run ρ as a set of states, where $s \in \rho$ if there is an $i \in \mathbb{N}$ with $s = \rho_i$. An *objective* is a set of runs $\Omega \subseteq Runs(\mathcal{T})$. A run ρ *fulfils objective* Ω if $\rho \in \Omega$, otherwise, it *violates* Ω. A transition system $\mathcal{T}$ *fulfils objective* Ω if $Runs(\mathcal{T}) \subseteq \Omega$.

For $F \in S$, a *safety objective* is given by $\Box \neg F = \{\rho \in Runs(\mathcal{T}) \mid \forall i \in \mathbb{N} : \rho_i \notin F\}$, a *reachability objective* is given by $\Diamond F = \{\rho \in Runs(\mathcal{T}) \mid \exists i \in \mathbb{N} : \rho_i \in F\}$ and a *Büchi objective* is given by $\Box \Diamond F = \{\rho \in Runs(\mathcal{T}) \mid \forall i \in \mathbb{N} \exists j > i : \rho_i \in F\}$.

For a *colouring function* $c\colon S \to \mathbb{N}$, a *parity objective* is given by $Parity\,(c) = \{\rho \in Runs(\mathcal{T}) \mid \max\{c(s) \mid s \in Inf(\rho)\}$ is even$\}$, where $Inf(\rho)$ denotes the states visited infinitely often in ρ.

Graph Games. A *game arena* between two Players Sat and Unsat is a tuple $\mathcal{A} = (S_{\mathrm{Sat}}, S_{\mathrm{Unsat}}, \to, s_{init})$, where S_{Sat} and S_{Unsat} are the *states controlled by Player* Sat *and Player* Unsat, respectively (and we write $S := S_{\mathrm{Sat}} \dot\cup S_{\mathrm{Unsat}}$), $\to\; \subseteq S \times S$ is the *transition relation* (and we write $s \to t$ for $(s,t) \in \to$) and $s_{init} \in S$ is the *initial state*. A *play* on $\mathcal{A}$ is an infinite sequence of states $\rho = \rho_0 \rho_1 \ldots \in S^\omega$, where $\rho_0 = s_{init}$ and for all $i \in \mathbb{N}$, we have $\rho_i \to \rho_{i+1}$. The set of all plays of $\mathcal{A}$ is denoted by $Plays(\mathcal{A})$.

Given a transition system $\mathcal{T} = (S, \to, s_{init})$ and $C \subseteq S$, the *corresponding two-player game arena* is defined by $\mathcal{T}[C] = (C, S \setminus C, \to, s_{init})$.

An *objective* is a set of plays $\Omega \subseteq Plays(\mathcal{A})$. A game is a tuple $\mathcal{G} = (\mathcal{A}, \Omega)$ of arena $\mathcal{A}$ and objective Ω. A play ρ is *winning* (with respect to Ω) if $\rho \in \Omega$. A *strategy* for Player Sat is a function $\sigma_{\mathrm{Sat}}\colon S_{\mathrm{Sat}} \to S$ such that $s \to \sigma_{\mathrm{Sat}}(s)$ for all $s \in S_{\mathrm{Sat}}$. Strategies for Player Unsat are defined analogously. A pair of strategies $\sigma = (\sigma_{\mathrm{Sat}}, \sigma_{\mathrm{Unsat}})$ induces a play $\rho = \rho_0 \rho_1 \ldots \in S^\omega$, where $\rho_0 = s_{init}$, $\sigma_{\mathrm{Sat}}(\rho_i) = \rho_{i+1}$ for $\rho_i \in S_{\mathrm{Sat}}$ and $\sigma_{\mathrm{Unsat}}(\rho_j) = \rho_{j+i}$ for $\rho_j \in S_{\mathrm{Unsat}}$. A game is *winning for Player* Sat if there is a strategy σ_{Sat} of Player Sat such that for all strategies σ_{Unsat} of Player Unsat, the induced play ρ satisfies the objective Ω (and we say that ρ is *winning for Player* Sat). Otherwise, the game is winning for Player Unsat. The *value* of the game is defined as $val(\mathcal{G}) = 1$ if $\mathcal{G}$ is winning for Player Sat and $val(\mathcal{G}) = 0$ otherwise. The *winning region* $Win(\mathcal{G})$ is the set of states from which Player Sat has a winning strategy.

Safety, reachability, Büchi and parity objectives for games are defined analogously to transition systems.

Shapley Values. Let $\mathcal{A} = \{A_1, \ldots, A_n\}$ be a set of *agents*. A *simple cooperative game* is a monotonic function $\gamma\colon 2^{\mathcal{A}} \to \{0,1\}$ and for $C \subseteq \mathcal{A}$, we call $\gamma(C)$ the *payoff of coalition* C. Shapley values [35] are a well-known concept from cooperative game theory. They distribute the payoff of a cooperative game based on how much each agent contributed to the outcome. For a simple cooperative game γ, the Shapley values are defined by the function $Shap_\gamma\colon \mathcal{A} \to [0,1]$ given by

$$Shap_\gamma(A) = \sum_{C \subseteq \mathcal{A} \setminus \{A\}} \frac{(|\mathcal{A}| - |C| - 1)! \cdot |C|!}{|\mathcal{A}|!}(\gamma(C \cup \{A\}) - \gamma(C)).$$

For $A \in \mathcal{A}$ and $C \subseteq \mathcal{A} \setminus \{A\}$, we call (C, A) a switching pair if $\gamma(C \cup \{A\}) - \gamma(C) = 1$, i.e. if $\gamma(C \cup \{A\}) = 1$ and $\gamma(C) = 0$. Switching pairs correspond to the non-zero summands in the above sum, which implies that $A \in \mathcal{A}$ has positive responsibility if and only there exists a switching pair (C, A) for some $C \subseteq \mathcal{A}$.

3   Responsibility Using the Shapley Value

This section briefly revisits the definition of backward responsibility from [5,10], which extends forward responsibility as defined by [32]. Backward responsibility differs from forward responsibility by assessing responsibility with respect to a specific run ρ. Throughout this section, let $\mathcal{T} = (S, \rightarrow, s_{init})$ be a transition system with objective Ω and simple lasso-shaped run $\rho = \rho_0 \rho_1 \ldots$ violating Ω.

The restriction to simple lasso-shaped runs ensures that ρ can be reproduced by a positional strategy, i.e. it is not necessary to remember whether a state has been visited previously. The objective classes analysed in this paper can be refuted with simple lasso-shaped runs.

To ensure the run ρ is followed, [5] introduces an *engraving* construction. For every state visited in ρ, all transitions are removed except for the one that follows ρ. The construction is only applied to the states of ρ that are not in a given set C.

Definition 3.1 (Engraving construction). Let $\mathcal{T}$ and ρ be as above and let $C \subseteq S$. The *engraved transition system* is given by $Engrave(\mathcal{T}, \rho, C) = (S, \rightarrow', s_{init})$ with $\rightarrow' = \{(s, t) \in \rightarrow \mid s \notin \rho \setminus C\} \cup \{(\rho_i, \rho_{i+1}) \mid i \in \mathbb{N} \text{ and } \rho_i \notin C\}$.

To determine the influence of some $C \subseteq S$ on fulfilling the objective, a graph game is constructed. For the behaviour of the remaining states $S \setminus C$, one can either "optimistically" assume they also try to fulfil the objectives or "pessimistically" assume that they try to prevent the objective from being fulfilled.

Definition 3.2 (Graph game). Let $\mathcal{T}$, Ω and ρ be as above and let $C \subseteq S$. Let $\mathcal{T}' = Engrave(\mathcal{T}, \rho, C)$ be the transition system obtained by engraving ρ in $\mathcal{T}$ except for the states in C. The *pessimistic graph game* is defined as $\mathcal{G}_{pes}[\mathcal{T}, \Omega, \rho, C] = (\mathcal{T}'[C], \Omega)$ and the *optimistic graph game* is defined as $\mathcal{G}_{opt}[\mathcal{T}, \Omega, \rho, C] = (\mathcal{T}'[C'], \Omega)$, where $C' = C \cup \{s \in S \mid s \notin \rho\}$. When $\mathcal{T}$, Ω and ρ are clear from context, we say that C *is winning in the pessimistic setting* if Player Sat wins $\mathcal{G}_{pes}[\mathcal{T}, \Omega, \rho, C]$ (and analogously for the optimistic case).

In the optimistic graph game, only states with engraved behaviour are controlled by Player Unsat. For simple lasso-shaped runs, Player Unsat thus has no decision power. Player Unsat may win nonetheless if the engraving prevents Player Sat from fulfilling the objective. The Shapley value now yields responsibility values.

Definition 3.3 (Responsibility values). Let $\mathcal{T}$, Ω and ρ be as above and let $C \subseteq S$. The *responsibility values* $Resp_{pes}[\mathcal{T}, \Omega, \rho]$ and $Resp_{opt}[\mathcal{T}, \Omega, \rho]$ are defined by the Shapley value of a function $2^S \rightarrow \{0, 1\}$ that maps $C \subseteq S$ to $val(\mathcal{G}_{pes}[\mathcal{T}, \Omega, \rho, C])$ in the pessimistic case and to $val(\mathcal{G}_{opt}[\mathcal{T}, \Omega, \rho, C])$ in the optimistic case.

Remark 3.4. Similar to the above, many other works also use the Shapley value for responsibility allocation [5,6,18,32,37] or rely on similar power indicies such as the *Banzhaf power index* [11]. An alternative technique allocates responsibility based on the smallest switching pair [2,15]. This is done by determining the smallest $C \subseteq S$ such that (C, s) is a switching pair and then defining the responsibility of s as $\frac{1}{|C|+1}$. However, the latter approach allocates more responsibility to a state with a single switching pair of size 3 than to a state with hundreds

Table 1. Overview of complexity results for the **positivity** and **comp**utation problem. The results are for completeness, except for those marked by ∈, which are for inclusion in the respective class.

	Forward [32]		Backward, opt			Backward, pess	
	Pos.	Comp.	Pos.	Comp.		Pos.	Comp.
Safety	NP#P		∈P [5]	∈P [5]		NP [5]	#P [5]
Reach.	NP#P		∈P(Proposition 4.2)	∈P(Proposition 4.6)		NP(Proposition 4.5)	#P(Proposition 4.8)
Büchi	NP#P		∈P(Proposition 4.3)	∈#P(Proposition 4.8)		NP(Proposition 4.5)	#P(Proposition 4.8)
Parity	NP#P		∈NP(Proposition 4.5)	∈#P(Proposition 4.8)		NP(Proposition 4.5)	#P(Proposition 4.8)

of switching pairs of size 4 – the global view of the Shapley value, on the other hand, ensures that the latter state has higher responsibility.

In the optimistic case, Player Sat controls every state $s \in S \setminus \rho$ and thus $\mathcal{G}_{opt}[\mathcal{T}, \Omega, \rho, C] = \mathcal{G}_{opt}[\mathcal{T}, \Omega, \rho, C \cup \{s\}]$. These states thus have no responsibility:

Lemma 3.5 (Responsible states for optimistic responsibility). *Let* $\mathcal{T}$, Ω *and* ρ *be as above. In the optimistic responsibility setting, only states on* ρ *can have a positive responsibility value.*

4   Complexity of Responsibility Computation Problems

This section studies the computational complexity of determining the set of responsible states and computing their responsibility value. Throughout this section, let $\mathcal{T} = (S, \rightarrow, s_{init})$ be a transition system with objective Ω and simple lasso-shaped run ρ violating Ω. Let $Resp \in \{Resp_{opt}, Resp_{pes}\}$.

Definition 4.1 (Responsibility problems). Given a state $s \in S$, the *positivity problem* asks whether $Resp[\mathcal{T}, \Omega, \rho](s) > 0$, the *threshold problem* asks whether $Resp[\mathcal{T}, \Omega, \rho](s) > t$ for a given threshold $t \in [0, 1]$ and the *computation problem* asks what the value of $Resp[\mathcal{T}, \Omega, \rho](s)$ is.

Table 1 gives an overview of the complexity of these problems for different objective classes, both for optimistic and pessimistic background responsibility. For completeness, the figure also includes the results for forward responsibility as given in [32]. For forward responsibility, the input of the problems does not include a run ρ violating Ω and the engraving step is omitted. The remaining steps are the same for the forward and backward view.

Recall that #P is a class of counting problems that ask how many accepting runs a non-deterministic Turing machine with polynomial runtime have (see e.g. Capter 9.1 in [4] for a formal introduction to #P). To obtain #P-completeness, we treat the computation problem as a counting problem producing a natural number (with the goal of counting the number of switching pairs).

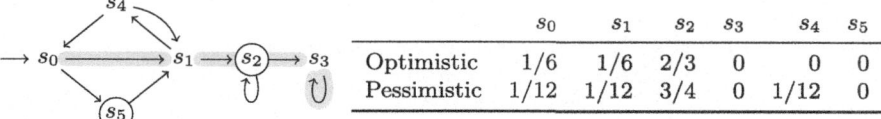

	s_0	s_1	s_2	s_3	s_4	s_5
Optimistic	1/6	1/6	2/3	0	0	0
Pessimistic	1/12	1/12	3/4	0	1/12	0

Fig. 1. A transition system with Büchi objective $\Box\Diamond\{s_2, s_5\}$ and the corresponding optimistic and pessimistic responsibility values. The grey highlighting indicates the violating run $\rho = s_0 s_1 s_2 s_3^{\omega}$.

4.1 Determining the Set of Responsible States

Deciding the optimistic positivity problem for safety objectives requires polynomial time [5]. We extend this result to reachability and Büchi objectives.

Proposition 4.2. *For reachability objectives, the optimistic positivity problem can be decided in polynomial time.*

Proof (sketch). If (C, s) is a switching pair for some $C \subseteq S$, then $(\varnothing, s)$ is also switching. Checking whether $(\varnothing, s)$ is a switching pair requires polynomial time.

Now let $\Omega = \Box\Diamond F$ be a Büchi objective. Unlike for reachability objectives, $(\varnothing, s)$ is no longer necessarily a switching pair for a responsible state s, as shown in Fig. 1: $(\{s_0\}, s_1)$ is a switching pair, but $(\varnothing, s_1)$ is not: Controlling s_0 and s_1 allows Player Sat to produce the accepting run $(s_0 s_5 s_1 s_4)^{\omega}$, while controlling only s_1 makes s_5 unreachable due to the engraving. The reachability positivity algorithm is therefore not applicable to transition systems with a Büchi objective. Nonetheless, there is an efficient algorithm for the optimistic positivity problem.

Proposition 4.3. *The optimistic positivity problem for Büchi objectives is decidable in polynomial time.*

For the proof, the following notation helps relate the states of ρ. For states $s, t \in \rho$ on the run, $s \preccurlyeq t$ if t is reachable from s in $Engrave(\mathcal{T}, \rho, S)$ and $s \prec t$ if $s \preccurlyeq t$ and not $t \preccurlyeq s$. A simple reachability analysis computes $\prec$ and $\preccurlyeq$ in polynomial time. We define the *lowest reachable state from* s as $\downarrow(s) = \rho_i$ such that Player Sat can reach ρ_i in $\mathcal{G}_{opt}[\mathcal{T}, F, \rho, \{s\}]$ and i is minimal. For $F \subseteq S$, the *lowest reachable state from* s *through* F is defined as $\downarrow_F s) = \rho_j$ such that there is an $f \in F$ for which Player Sat can reach f from s and t from f in $\mathcal{G}_{opt}[\mathcal{T}, F, \rho, \{s\}]$ and j is minimal. If no such state ρ_j exists, then $\downarrow_F s) = \bot$.

The algorithm for the optimistic positivity problem relies on the insight that if $C \cup \{s\}$ is winning and minimal, then either $C = \varnothing$ or the states are arranged as shown in Fig. 2. We have $C \cup \{s\} = \{s_{bottom}, s_{top}, s_1, \ldots, s_n\}$, where

- s_{bottom} can reach some Büchi state s_F and then continue to some state above $\downarrow_F s_{bottom})$, from which s_{top} is reached by following ρ,
- s_{top} can jump down to an earlier state of ρ to some state above $\downarrow'(s_{top})$, from which s_1 is reached by following ρ,

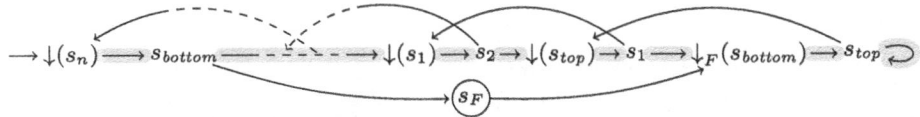

Fig. 2. For Büchi objectives, minimal non-singleton winning coalitions matches the depicted layout. Each arrow $s \rightarrow t$ indicates that there is a path from s to t, potentially visiting other states that are not depicted.

- s_1 can jump down to a state aboves $\downarrow(s_1)$, from which s_2 is reached, and so on, until $\downarrow(s_n)$ is reached, and
- from $\downarrow(s_n)$, state s_{bottom} is reachable again by following ρ.

It is easy to see that these states are able to enforce the winning loop. Every $t \in \{s_{top}, s_1, \ldots, s_n\}$ must "skip" some state that no other state in $C \cup \{s\}$ skips to ensure minimality of C. For example, in Fig. 2, $\downarrow(s_{top})$ is skipped only by the jump from s_1 to $\downarrow(s_1)$, so without controlling s_1, it would be impossible to go from s_{top} to s_{bottom}. State s_{bottom} is always necessary for winning to ensure that a Büchi state is reached. Minimality additionally required that no state in C is winning on its own. The following lemma formalises this structure.

Lemma 4.4 (Properties of a minimal coalition). *Let transition system $\mathcal{T}$, objective $\Box\Diamond F$ and run ρ be as above. If $C \subseteq S$ is a minimal winning coalition and $|C| > 1$, then*

(a) Player Sat has a winning play $\rho_{win} = uv^\omega$ in $\mathcal{G}_{opt}[\mathcal{T}, \omega, \rho, C]$ such that $u, v \in S^*$ and every state $s \in C$ occurs exactly once in the loop v in ρ_{win},

(b) there exists exactly one state $s_{bottom} \in C$ such that $\downarrow_F s_{bottom}) \preccurlyeq s_{top}$ for some state $s_{top} \in C$,

(c) we have $s_{bottom} \prec s \prec s_{top}$ for every state $s \in C \setminus \{s_{bottom}, s_{top}\}$ and

(d) for every state $s_i \in C \setminus \{s_{bottom}\}$, there exists a state $s_{skip} \in \rho$ with $s_{bottom} \prec s_{skip} \preccurlyeq \downarrow_F s_{bottom})$ such that $\downarrow(s) \prec s_{skip} \preccurlyeq s$ holds for s and no other $s' \in C \setminus \{s_{bottom}\}$.

Proof (sketch) First, (a) holds because ρ is simple lasso-shaped, so Player Unsat never has choices, enabling Player Sat to enforce a single winning run. For (b), consider the Büchi state in the loop of ρ_{win}. Choose as s_{bottom} the first state from C that occurs before this Büchi state and as s_{top} the first state from C that occurs after it. Then these states fulfil the required conditions. The uniqueness of s_{bottom} is shown by assuming there are two s_{bottom}, s'_{bottom} and showing that Player Sat can force a win by controlling only one of them, contradicting the minimality of C. For (c), if $s \preccurlyeq s_{bottom}$ were to hold for some $s \neq s_{bottom}$, Player Sat could win without controlling s and similarly, if $s_{top} \preccurlyeq s$ were to hold for some $s \neq s_{top}$, then Player Sat could win without controlling s_{top}. Finally, (d) holds with the following skip states: s_{top} skips $\downarrow_F s_{bottom})$, s_1 skips $\downarrow(s_{top})$

Algorithm 1. Deciding the optimistic positivity problem for Büchi objectives.

1: **function** IsResponsible(s)
2:    **if** $s \notin \rho$ **then**
3:        **return** false
4:    **if** IsWinning($\{s\}$) **then**
5:        **return** true
6:    **for** $s_{top} \succcurlyeq \downarrow_F s$) **do**
7:        **if** IsSbottom(s, s_{top}) **then**
8:            **return** true
9:    **for** $s_{bottom} \prec s$ with $\neg$IsWinning($\{s_{bottom}\}$) **do**
10:        **for** $s_{top} \succcurlyeq s$ with $s_{top} \succcurlyeq \downarrow_F s_{bottom}$) **do**
11:            **for** $s_{skip} \in \rho$ with $\downarrow(s) \prec s_{skip} \preccurlyeq s$ and $s_{bottom} \prec s_{skip} \preccurlyeq \downarrow_F s_{bottom}$) **do**
12:                **if** IsS$_i$($s, s_{bottom}, s_{top}, s_{skip}$) **then**
13:                    **return** true
14:    **return** false

15: **function** IsSbottom(s, s_{top})
16:    $C \leftarrow \{s, s_{top}\}$
17:    **for** $s' \in \rho$ with $s \prec s' \preccurlyeq s_{top}$ and $\neg$IsWinning($\{s\}$) **do**
18:        **if** $\neg(\downarrow_F s') \preccurlyeq s_{top}$ **then**
19:            $C \leftarrow C \cup \{s'\}$
20:    **return** IsWinning(C)

21: **function** IsS$_i$($s, s_{bottom}, s_{top}, s_{skip}$)
22:    C $\leftarrow \{s, s_{bottom}\}$
23:    **for** $s' \in \rho$ with $s_{bottom} \prec s' \preccurlyeq s_{top}$ and $\neg$IsWinning($\{s'\}$) **do**
24:        **if** $\neg(\downarrow_F s') \preccurlyeq s_{top}$ and $\neg(\downarrow(s') \prec s_{skip} \preccurlyeq s')$ **then**
25:            $C \leftarrow C \cup \{s'\}$
26:    **return** IsWinning(C)

---

and s_i for $1 < i \leq n$ skips $\downarrow(s_{i-1})$. In every case, if the respective state were not skipped, then C would not be minimal.

This lemma forms the base of Algorithm 1 to decide the optimistic positivity problem für Büchi objectives in polynomial time. The algorithm first covers the cases that $s \notin \rho$ or that s is winning on its own. The remainder of the algorithm checks whether s is part of a non-singleton minimal winning coalition, handling $s = s_{bottom}$ and $s \in \{s_{top}, s_1, \ldots, s_n\}$ separately. In the former case (lines 6–8 and IsSbottom), the algorithm iterates over every potential s_{top} and then checks whether there is a winning coalition C with the given s_{bottom} and s_{top}. For this, every state s' between s_{bottom} and s_{top} is added to C if it is neither winning on its own nor can reach s_{top} through F. If s_{top} were reachable through F, then s' could form a winning loop by going through F to s_{top} without ever visiting s_{bottom}. Finally, it is checked whether C is winning. If yes, then $(C \setminus \{s\}, s)$ is a switching pair as only s can reach s_{top} through F. If not, then no such coalition can exist, as C contains all states that are not winning already without s. The

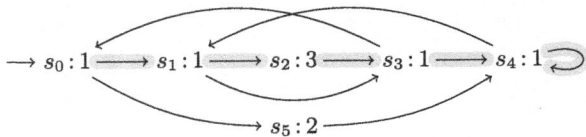

Fig. 3. The winning run in this transition system with parity objective requires jumping "forward" from s_1 to s_3, which is never required for Büchi objectives.

latter case (lines 9–13 and IsSi) first involves iterating over all potential s_{bottom}, s_{top} and skip states for s. The function IsSi then checks whether a coalition C of states between s_{bottom} and s_{top} exists such that no $s' \in C \setminus \{s\}$ is able to "jump" over s_{skip} (line 24). Once again, states that are winning on their own or that can reach s_{top} through F are excluded (line 23 and 24). If none of these checks succeed, then s has no responsibility. Correctness of the algorithm is formally shown in the full version ([9], Proposition B.1).

Optimistic Responsibility for Parity Objectives. The algorithm for the optimistic positivity problem for Büchi objectives relied on the insight that there is always a winning run with a certain shape (if there is a winning run at all). The loop of this run consists of a single "jump forward" (i.e. going from some state $s \in \rho$ to $s' \in \rho$ with $s \prec s'$ without following ρ). The remainder of the loop consists of jumps from $t \in \rho$ to $t' \in \rho$ with $t \succ t'$ and of segments of ρ, i.e. the loop contains only a single jump forward.

Figure 3 shows that this does not hold for parity objectives. States s_0, s_1, s_3 and s_4 are winning by following the loop $(s_0 s_5 s_4 s_1 s_3)^\omega$. This requires jumping forward from s_1 to s_3 (instead of following ρ via s_2) to avoid s_2 with colour 3. In the Büchi case, jumping "forward" is never necessary, as it is never useful to avoid a state. Due to this, the algorithm for Büchi objectives does not work for parity objectives and we thus only provide the following upper bound.

Proposition 4.5. *The optimistic positivity problem for parity objectives is in NP. The pessimistic positivity problem for reachability, Büchi and parity objectives is NP-complete.*

Proof (sketch). Inclusion in NP is shown by first guessing a coalition C and then verifying that (C, s) is a switching pair. For parity objectives, this is possible because solving parity games is known to be in NP $\cap$ CoNP. NP-hardness is shown by a reduction from the forward case, which is known to be NP-hard [32].

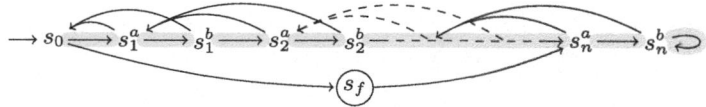

Fig. 4. Transition system with Büchi objective $\Box\Diamond\{s_f\}$ that has exponentially many minimal winning coalitions.

4.2   Computing the Responsibility Value

Proposition 4.6. *Solving the optimistic computation and threshold problem for reachability objectives requires polynomial time.*

Proof (sketch). Every state with positive responsibility has the same amount of responsibility. This induces an efficient algorithm by computing the set of responsible states R and assigning each state within the set responsibility $1/|R|$.

While Algorithm 1 efficiently checks whether a switching pair exists for a Büchi objective, computing responsibility values requires finding *all* switching pairs. This is computationally hard, as a system may have exponentially many minimal winning coalitions, as shown in Fig. 4: Every $C \in \{s_1^a, s_1^b\} \times \cdots \times \{s_n^a, s_n^b\}$ is a minimal winning coaltion.

Proposition 4.7. *For reachability objectives, the pessimistic threshold problem is NP-hard and in* PSPACE. *For Büchi and parity objectives, the optimistic and pessimistic threshold problems are in* PSPACE *and the pessimistic threshold problem is NP-hard.*

Proof (sketch). To compute the responsibility of state s in polynomial space, enumerate all coalitions C, determine whether they form a critical pair (C, s) (this takes polynomial time) and tally up the total responsibility. NP-hardness follows from the NP-hardness of the pessimistic positivity problem for reachability objectives (Proposition 4.5).

Proposition 4.8. *For Büchi and parity objectives, the optimistic computation problem is in* #P *and for reachability, Büchi and parity objectives, the pessimistic computation problem is* #P-complete.

Proof (sketch). Inclusion in #P is shown by constructing a non-deterministic Turing machine that guesses a coalition C and accepts if and only if (C, s) is switching. There is a one-to-one correspondence between switching pairs and accepting runs because solving reachability, Büchi and parity games is in UP ∩ CoUP, i.e. there exists a non-deterministic Turing machine that has exactly one accepting run if Player Sat wins the game (and analogously for Player Unsat). Hardness is shown by reduction from the forward case [32].

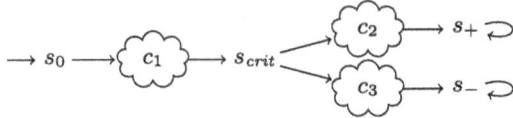

Fig. 5. Sketch of a large transition system with reachability property $\Diamond s_+$. If the clouds are acyclic, only s_{crit} has positive responsibility. The refinement algorithm from Sect. 5 can efficiently identify s_{crit} as responsible.

5 Computing Responsible States Using Refinement

Iterating all switching pairs to compute responsibility is infeasible in large models. However, many models only have a small set of responsible states, with most states bearing no responsibility. Existing implementations use some local criteria to identify states with no responsibility (e.g. states with only a single successor), but this local view does not capture the higher-level model structure. For example, the clouds in Fig. 5 represent a large number of states connected acyclically and have no responsibility for whether s_+ is eventually reached, even though the clouds might contain complex local structures. Existing approaches for dealing with large models include stochastic sampling [5] and grouping states into blocks [5,10]. The latter approach is efficient as long as the number of state blocks is limited, but requires manual specification of the state blocks.

This section presents an algorithm that automatically builds state blocks by iterative refinement. To output individual responsibility, we give a condition under which a block's responsibility corresponds to a state's individual responsibility. Let $\mathcal{T} = (S, \rightarrow, s_{init})$ be a transition system with objective Ω and run ρ that violates Ω, let $Resp \in \{Resp_{opt}[\mathcal{T}, \Omega, \rho], Resp_{pes}[\mathcal{T}, \Omega, \rho]\}$ be a responsibility metric and, for $C \subseteq S$, and let $\mathcal{G}[C] \in \{\mathcal{G}_{opt}[\mathcal{T}, \Omega, \rho, C], \mathcal{G}_{pes}[\mathcal{T}, \Omega, \rho, C]\}$ be the corresponding graph game.

Definition 5.1 (Block responsibility). Let $\mathfrak{S}$ be a partition of S. Every $B \in \mathfrak{S}$ is called a *state block*. For state $s \in S$, $[s]_{\mathfrak{S}}$ denotes the unique block in $\mathfrak{S}$ that contains s and for $S' \subseteq S$, $[S']_{\mathfrak{S}} = \bigcup_{s \in S'}[s]_{\mathfrak{S}}$. The *block responsibility* $Resp^{\mathfrak{S}}$ is defined by the Shapley value of the function $2^{\mathfrak{S}} \rightarrow \{0,1\}$ that maps $\mathcal{C} \subseteq \mathfrak{S}$ to $val(\mathcal{G}[flatten(\mathcal{C})])$, where $flatten(\mathcal{C}) = \bigcup_{B \in \mathcal{C}} B$. If $B \in \mathfrak{S}$ is a block and C is a union of blocks in $\mathfrak{S}$, then the pair (C, B) is called a *block-switching pair* if Player Sat wins $\mathcal{G}[C \cup B]$ and Player Unsat wins $\mathcal{G}[C]$. The set of blocks B for which some block-switching pair (C, B) exists is denoted by $HasBSP$.

A block $B \in \mathfrak{S}$ has positive block responsibility if and only if $B \in HasBSP$, but the responsibility value of a block is not equal to the sum of responsibility values of its members (see Fig. 6 in the full version [9] for a counterexample).

This equality only holds under the following restriction, which is used by the refinement algorithm as a termination condition.

Theorem 5.2. *If every block in HasBSP is a singleton, then for $s \in S$,*

$$Resp(s) > 0 \quad \textit{iff} \quad Resp^{\mathfrak{S}}([s]_{\mathfrak{S}}) > 0.$$

Algorithm 2. Refinement algorithm for computing the set of responsible states.

1: $\mathfrak{S} \leftarrow$ INITIALPARTITION()
2: $HasBSP \leftarrow$ COMPUTEHASSP($\mathfrak{S}$)
3: **while** $\exists B \in HasBSP$ *with* $|B| > 1$ **do**
4:      $R \leftarrow$ SELECTREFINEMENTS($\mathfrak{S}, HasBSP$)
5:      **for** $B \in R$ **do**
6:          $\mathfrak{S} \leftarrow (\mathfrak{S} \setminus B) \cup$ REFINE(B)
7:      $HasBSP \leftarrow$ COMPUTEHASSP($\mathfrak{S}$)
8: **return** $\{s \mid [s]_{\mathfrak{S}} \in HasBSP\}$

Proof. By contradiction, let $s \in S$ such that $Resp(s) > 0$, but $Resp^{\mathfrak{S}}([s]_{\mathfrak{S}}) = 0$. As $Resp(s) > 0$, there is some $C \subseteq S$ such that (C, s) is a switching pair. Conversely, $([C]_{\mathfrak{S}}, [s]_{\mathfrak{S}})$ is not a block-switching pair because $Resp^{\mathfrak{S}}(s) = 0$. As $C \cup \{s\} \subseteq [C]_{\mathfrak{S}} \cup [s]_{\mathfrak{S}}$, Player Sat wins $\mathcal{G}[[C]_{\mathfrak{S}} \cup [s]_{\mathfrak{S}}]$. Thus, Player Sat also wins $\mathcal{G}[[C]_{\mathfrak{S}}]$, as otherwise $([C]_{\mathfrak{S}}, [s]_{\mathfrak{S}})$ would be a block-switching pair. Let $C' = \{s \in C \mid [s]_{\mathfrak{S}} \in HasBSP\}$. As Player Sat wins $\mathcal{G}[[C]_{\mathfrak{S}}]$, Player Sat also wins $\mathcal{G}[[C']_{\mathfrak{S}}]$ – otherwise, one could construct a switching pair for some $[s']_{\mathfrak{S}}$ with $s \in C \setminus C'$, but the blocks of states in $C \setminus C'$ do not have switching pairs. As every block in $HasBSP$ is singleton, $[C']_{\mathfrak{S}} = C' \subseteq C$ and thus Player Sat wins $\mathcal{G}[C]$. This contradicts (C, s) being a switching pair. Now let $Resp^{\mathfrak{S}}([s]_{\mathfrak{S}}) > 0$. Then there exists a block-switching pair $([C]_{\mathfrak{S}}, [s]_{\mathfrak{S}})$. Then $[s]_{\mathfrak{S}} = \{s\}$ is singleton and thus $([C]_{\mathfrak{S}}, s)$ is also a switching pair, implying $Resp(s) > 0$.

This theorem forms the heart of the responsibility refinement algorithm (Algorithm 2). Heuristics INITIALPARTITION() produces a coarse initial partition. Each iteration first determines whether any blocks in $HasBSP$ are not singleton and selects some of these for refinement using heuristics SELECTREFINEMENTS($\cdot$). Each chosen block is then refined into two or more blocks by the heuristics REFINE($\cdot$). Different heuristics are evaluated in Sect. 6.

Theorem 5.3 (Correctness of refinement). *If* SELECTREFINEMENTS($\cdot$) *always selects at least one block and if* REFINE($\cdot$) *always produces at least two non-empty blocks, then Algorithm 2 terminates and a state s is contained in the algorithm's output if and only if $Resp(s) > 0$.*

Proof During every iteration of the loop (lines 3–7), the number of (non-empty) blocks in $\mathfrak{S}$ grows, because at least one block is refined and this refinement splits the block into at least two new blocks. Therefore, after finitely many iterations, the partition only contains singletons, unless the algorithm has already terminated. Once the partition only contains singletons, the loop condition (line 3) is no longer satisfied and the algorithm therefore terminates.

Line 8 is reached when all blocks in $HasBSP$ are singletons, so Theorem 5.2 is applicable. A block $[s]_{\mathfrak{S}}$ has positive group responsibility if and only if a block-switching pair for $[s]_{\mathfrak{S}}$ exists and by Theorem 5.2, s has positive (individual) responsibility exactly in this case. Therefore, Algorithm 2 outputs exactly the states with positive individual responsibility.

6   Experimental Evaluation

We have extended the implementation of [5] to support reachability and Büchi objectives and have added support for the refinement algorithm with several heuristics[2]. Compared to Algorithm 2, the implementation makes use of a few optimisations, such as ignoring singleton blocks from COMPUTEHASSP($\mathfrak{S}$) and caching the block-switching pairs from one iteration and using them as block-switching pair candidates in the next iteration.

For suitable models, the refinement algorithm reduces responsibility computation time by several orders of magnitude. All tests were run on an M2 MacBook Pro with 24 GB or RAM. Each result is the average of 10 runs.

Models. The evaluation uses the following models:

- dekker models Dekker's algorithm for mutual exclusion [17], with the objective of reaching the critical section infinitely often (to avoid deadlocks). 11 out of 23 states have positive responsibility.
- generals models the three generals problem [1], with the objective of either all three generals attacking or none of them attacking. 19 out of 27 states have positive responsibility.
- railway models a railway network with a misrouted train. The objective is to ensure the train does not get stuck in a loop. 4 out of 53 states have responsibility.
- station models Dresden main station with the objective of reaching the correct platform. 14 out of 75 tates have positive responsibility.
- philosophers models the dining philosophers problem with the objective of avoiding a deadlock. 22 out of 36 states have positive responsibility.
- clouds models the model from Fig. 5, where each cloud contains 100 000 states. Only a single state has positive responsibility.

Both station and clouds are intractable without refinement. We use a timeout of 30 min, but due to the exponential runtime, even a much longer timeout is unlikely to be sufficient. The refinement algorithm will deliver the biggest benefits in the models with many states, out of which only few are responsible, such as railway and, most significantly, clouds.

Initial Partition. To construct the initial partition, the tool first determines the set of *significant states*. This set includes every state that has non-deterministic behaviour (i.e. more than one outgoing transition) and that is both on paths that satisfy the objective and on those that do not. All other states cannot have positive responsibility and are therefore placed in a block that is never refined.

The significant states can optionally be split into n smaller blocks randomly. For $1 \leq n \leq 5$, the effect this has on runtime is depicted in Table 2 (for block selection heuristics *max* ($k = 1$) and splitting heuristics *frontier-random*). For every model, $n = 1$ is the fastest – sometimes more than an order of magnitude

---

[2] The code and model files of our implementation are available at [28].

Table 2. Comparison of runtimes for different initial partition sizes n. TO indicates that computation did not finish without 30 min.

	no refinement	$n = 1$	$n = 2$	$n = 3$	$n = 4$	$n = 5$
dekker	7.21 s	**6.4 ms**	12.7 ms	33.6 ms	83.9 ms	144.6 ms
generals	287.2 ms	**71.3 ms**	72.6 ms	75.7 ms	76.6 ms	77.1 ms
railway	129.06 s	**8.2 ms**	28.7 ms	86.4 ms	222.6 ms	446.4 ms
station	TO	**17.5 ms**	45.5 ms	126.2 ms	336.5 ms	861.1 ms
philosophers	816.3 ms	**813.6 ms**	817.0 ms	815.2 ms	826.3 ms	815.3 ms
clouds	TO	**4.40 s**	6.78 s	12.94 s	28.37 s	67.22 s

faster than $n = 5$. By keeping the number of blocks low, fewer potential block-switching pairs need to be checked. In philosophers and generals, many states have positive responsibility, so regardless of the initial partition, later iterations will deal with a partition that contains mostly singleton state blocks. Therefore, the performance difference is smaller for these models.

Choosing Refinement Blocks. In every iteration, the set of non-singleton blocks B with a block-switching pair (C, B) is determined. To choose which of these to refine, we provide three heuristics. Heuristics *random* chooses a block randomly, the heuristics *max* chooses the block where $|Win(C \cup B) \setminus Win(C)|$ is maximal and heuristics *min* chooses the block where it is minimal. Additionally, it is possible to refine k multiple blocks in a single iteration. Intuitively, a higher k might speed up refinement, as fewer iterations are needed.

Table 3 provides a runtime comparison (for initial partition $n = 1$ and refinement heuristics *frontier-all*). Each heuristics is evaluated for $k = 1$ and $k = 3$. It is evident that the difference in performance is small. This is likely because any block that has a block-switching pair needs to be refined eventually.

Table 3. Comparison of runtimes for different block selection heuristics. Heuristics *random* selects a block at random, while *max* and *min* select a block based on how much it increases the size of the winning region.

	random		max		min	
	$k = 1$	$k = 3$	$k = 1$	$k = 3$	$k = 1$	$k = 3$
dekker	8.4 ms	5.3 ms	6.0 ms	5.4 ms	5.9 ms	**5.1 ms**
generals	70.5 ms	69.8 ms	70.3 ms	69.3 ms	**69.0 ms**	69.9 ms
railway	10.3 ms	9.0 ms	9.5 ms	**8.5 ms**	10.9 ms	8.7 ms
station	18.5 ms	16.8 ms	16.9 ms	**16.6 ms**	22.0 ms	**16.6 ms**
philosophers	816.0 ms	814.1 ms	817.4 ms	**801.6 ms**	806.0 ms	821.8 ms
clouds	4.47 s	**4.42 s**	4.46 s	4.52 s	4.57 s	4.55 s

Table 4. Comparison of runtimes for splitting heuristics. TO indicates that computation did not finish without 30 min.

	no refinement	frontier		difference	
		-random	-all	-random	-all
`dekker`	7.21 s	5.5 ms	6.1 ms	**4.1 ms**	5.9 ms
`generals`	287.2 ms	**71.2 ms**	74.0 ms	71.6 ms	73.4 ms
`railway`	129.06 s	**8.4 ms**	9.4 ms	28.4 ms	48.2 ms
`station`	TO	17.4 ms	17.4 ms	**17.1 ms**	24.1 ms
`philosophers`	816.3 ms	**808.5 ms**	823.2 ms	811.2 ms	820.8 ms
`clouds`	TO	**4.43 s**	**4.43 s**	TO	TO

Refining Blocks. A non-singleton block B with a block-switching pair (C, B) is refined by selecting some states $B' \subseteq B \cap (Win(C \cup B) \setminus Win(C))$ and replacing block B by B' and $B \setminus B'$. The heuristics *difference-random* randomly selects a state from $B \cap Win(C \cup B) \setminus Win(C)$. The heuristics *difference-all* chooses all states from this set. To choose a better set B', we introduce the notion of the *frontier*: Given block-switching pair (C, B), the frontier includes every $s \in B \cap Win(C \cup B) \setminus Win(C)$ such that s has an outgoing transition to $Win(C)$. *frontier-random* randomly selects a single state from the frontier and *frontier-all* selects the entire frontier as B'. In the case of $B = B'$, we instead use the corresponding *difference* heuristics to ensure the algorithm progresses.

Example 6.1. Consider again the example `clouds` from Fig. 5. As initial partition, choose the singleton partition $\mathfrak{S}_0 = \{S\}$ with $S = \{s_0, s_{crit}, s_+, s_-\} \cup c_1 \cup c_2 \cup c_3$. Then $(\varnothing, S)$ forms a (non-singleton) block-switching pair. The winning region of $\varnothing$ is $c_2 \cup \{s_+\}$ and the winning region of S is $c_1 \cup c_2 \cup \{s_0, s_{crit}, s_+\}$. The frontier contains only s_{crit}, so block S is refined into $\{s_{crit}\}$ and $S \setminus \{s_{crit}\}$. In the next iteration, only $\{s_{crit}\}$ has a block-switching pair and as it is already a singleton, the algorithm terminates.

Table 4 shows that *frontier* significantly outperforms *difference* on `railway` and `clouds`. In the case of `clouds`, the algorithm would terminate in reasonable time only when randomly selecting the single responsible state out of 300 000 candidates, which is very unlikely to succeed. On the remaining models, the difference in performance is small. For these experiments, the initial partition $n = 1$ and block selection heuristics *max* ($k = 1$) was used.

Summary. Refinement is very effective on models with few responsible states. Even on unsuitable models such as `philosophers`, it does not increase runtime significantly. Using a singleton initial partition with *frontier* heuristics was the fastest, whereas block choice did not affect runtime meaningfully.

7 Conclusion

We have extended the definition of backward responsibility [5] to reachability, Büchi and parity objectives. The results for safety objectives transfer to reachability objectives, while the optimistic case is more difficult for Büchi objectives. Nonetheless, by exploiting the structure of minimal winning coalitions, the set of responsible states can be computed in polynomial time. Even though no polynomial algorithm for solving parity games is known, we have shown that the complexity bounds for responsibility in Büchi objectives also hold for parity objectives.

Secondly, we have presented a refinement algorithm that computes the set of states with positive responsibility. Our experimental evaluation shows that refinement can improve by orders of magnitude, especially in models that only have a small number of responsible states.

Future Work. The results from the prototypcial implementation of the refinement algorithm are promising. It is likely possible to improve performance further by developing better heuristics, more advanced control flow such as back-tracking if a split is not beneficial, parallelising the algorithm and caching results.

References

1. Akkoyunlu, E.A., Ekanadham, K., Huber, R.V.: Some constraints and tradeoffs in the design of network communications. In: Proceedings of the Fifth ACM Symposium on Operating Systems Principles, pp. 67–74 (1975)
2. Aleksandrowicz, G., Chockler, H., Halpern, J.Y., Ivrii, A.: The computational complexity of structure-based causality. J. Artif. Intell. Res. **58**, 431–451 (2017). https://doi.org/10.1613/JAIR.5229
3. Algaba, E., Fragnelli, V., Sánchez-Soriano, J.: Handbook of the Shapley Value. CRC Press (2019)
4. Arora, S., Barak, B.: Computational Complexity: A Modern Approach. Cambridge University Press (2009)
5. Baier, C., van den Bossche, R., Klüppelholz, S., Lehmann, J., Piribauer, J.: Backward responsibility in transition systems using general power indices. In: Thirty-Eighth AAAI Conference on Artificial Intelligence, AAAI 2024, Thirty-Sixth Conference on Innovative Applications of Artificial Intelligence, IAAI 2024, Fourteenth Symposium on Educational Advances in Artificial Intelligence, EAAI 2014, 20–27 February 2024, Vancouver, Canada, pp. 20320–20327. AAAI Press (2024). https://doi.org/10.1609/AAAI.V38I18.30013
6. Baier, C., et al.: From verification to causality-based explications (invited talk). In: 48th International Colloquium on Automata, Languages, and Programming, ICALP 2021, 12–16 July 2021, Glasgow, Scotland (Virtual Conference). LIPIcs, vol. 198, pp. 1:1–1:20. Schloss Dagstuhl - Leibniz-Zentrum für Informatik (2021). https://doi.org/10.4230/LIPICS.ICALP.2021.1
7. Baier, C., Funke, F., Majumdar, R.: A game-theoretic account of responsibility allocation. In: Proceedings of the Thirtieth International Joint Conference on Artificial Intelligence, IJCAI 2021, Virtual Event/Montreal, Canada, 19–27 August 2021, pp. 1773–1779. ijcai.org (2021). https://doi.org/10.24963/IJCAI.2021/244

8. Baier, C., Katoen, J.P.: Principles of Model Checking. MIT Press (2008)
9. Baier, C., Klatt, R., Klüppelholz, S., Lehmann, J.: Backward responsibility in transition systems beyond safety (2025). https://arxiv.org/abs/2506.05192
10. Baier, C., Klüppelholz, S., Lehmann, J.: Responsibility in actor-based systems. In: Rebeca for Actor Analysis in Action: Essays Dedicated to Marjan Sirjani on the Occasion of Her 60th Birthday, pp. 44–69. Springer, Cham (2025). https://doi.org/10.1007/978-3-031-85134-6_3
11. Banzhaf, J.F., III.: Weighted voting doesn't work: a mathematical analysis. Rutgers L. Rev. **19**, 317 (1964)
12. Beer, I., Ben-David, S., Chockler, H., Orni, A., Trefler, R.J.: Explaining counterexamples using causality. Formal Methods Syst. Des. **40**(1), 20–40 (2012). https://doi.org/10.1007/S10703-011-0132-2
13. Caltais, G., Guetlein, S.L., Leue, S.: Causality for general LTL-definable properties. In: Finkbeiner, B., Kleinberg, S. (eds.) Proceedings 3rd Workshop on formal reasoning about Causation, Responsibility, and Explanations in Science and Technology, CREST@ETAPS 2018, Thessaloniki, Greece, 21st April 2018. EPTCS, vol. 286, pp. 1–15 (2018). https://doi.org/10.4204/EPTCS.286.1
14. Chockler, H.: Causality and responsibility for formal verification and beyond. In: Gößler, G., Sokolsky, O. (eds.) Proceedings First Workshop on Causal Reasoning for Embedded and safety-critical Systems Technologies, CREST@ETAPS 2016, Eindhoven, The Netherlands, 8th April 2016. EPTCS, vol. 224, pp. 1–8 (2016). https://doi.org/10.4204/EPTCS.224.1
15. Chockler, H., Halpern, J.Y.: Responsibility and blame: a structural-model approach. J. Artif. Intell. Res. **22**, 93–115 (2004). https://doi.org/10.1613/JAIR.1391
16. Chockler, H., Halpern, J.Y., Kupferman, O.: What causes a system to satisfy a specification? ACM Trans. Comput. Log. **9**(3), 20:1–20:26 (2008). https://doi.org/10.1145/1352582.1352588
17. Dijkstra, E.W.: Over de sequentialiteit van procesbeschrijvingen (1962)
18. Friedenberg, M., Halpern, J.Y.: Blameworthiness in multi-agent settings. In: The Thirty-Third AAAI Conference on Artificial Intelligence, AAAI 2019, The Thirty-First Innovative Applications of Artificial Intelligence Conference, IAAI 2019, The Ninth AAAI Symposium on Educational Advances in Artificial Intelligence, EAAI 2019, Honolulu, Hawaii, USA, 27 January–1 February 2019, pp. 525–532. AAAI Press (2019). https://doi.org/10.1609/AAAI.V33I01.3301525
19. Gastin, P., Moro, P.: Minimal counterexample generation for SPIN. In: Bošnački, D., Edelkamp, S. (eds.) SPIN 2007. LNCS, vol. 4595, pp. 24–38. Springer, Heidelberg (2007). https://doi.org/10.1007/978-3-540-73370-6_4
20. Gastin, P., Moro, P., Zeitoun, M.: Minimization of counterexamples in SPIN. In: Graf, S., Mounier, L. (eds.) SPIN 2004. LNCS, vol. 2989, pp. 92–108. Springer, Heidelberg (2004). https://doi.org/10.1007/978-3-540-24732-6_7
21. Groce, A., Chaki, S., Kroening, D., Strichman, O.: Error explanation with distance metrics. Int. J. Softw. Tools Technol. Transf. **8**(3), 229–247 (2006). https://doi.org/10.1007/S10009-005-0202-0
22. Halpern, J.Y., Pearl, J.: Causes and explanations: a structural-model approach. Part i: Causes. Br. J. Philos. Sci. (2005). https://doi.org/10.1093/bjps/axi147
23. Halpern, J.Y., Pearl, J.: Causes and explanations: a structural-model approach. Part II: Explanations. Br. J. Philos. Sci. (2005). https://doi.org/10.1093/bjps/axi148
24. Hansen, H., Kervinen, A.: Counterexamples in O (n log n) Memory and O (n²) Time. In: Sixth International Conference on Application of Concurrency to Sys-

tem Design (ACSD 2006), 28–30 June 2006, Turku, Finland, pp. 133–142. IEEE Computer Society (2006). https://doi.org/10.1109/ACSD.2006.11

25. Jurdzinski, M.: Deciding the winner in parity games is in UP ∩ co-up. Inf. Process. Lett. **68**(3), 119–124 (1998). https://doi.org/10.1016/S0020-0190(98)00150-1

26. Kölbl, M., Leue, S., Schmid, R.: Dynamic causes for the violation of timed reachability properties. In: Bertrand, N., Jansen, N. (eds.) FORMATS 2020. LNCS, vol. 12288, pp. 127–143. Springer, Cham (2020). https://doi.org/10.1007/978-3-030-57628-8_8

27. Landsberg, D., Chockler, H., Kroening, D., Lewis, M.: Evaluation of measures for statistical fault localisation and an optimising scheme. In: Egyed, A., Schaefer, I. (eds.) FASE 2015. LNCS, vol. 9033, pp. 115–129. Springer, Heidelberg (2015). https://doi.org/10.1007/978-3-662-46675-9_8

28. Lehmann, J.: Tool to compute responsibility using refinement (2025). https://doi.org/10.5281/zenodo.15224560

29. Leitner-Fischer, F., Leue, S.: Causality checking for complex system models. In: Giacobbazzi, R., Berdine, J., Mastroeni, I. (eds.) VMCAI 2013. LNCS, vol. 7737, pp. 248–267. Springer, Heidelberg (2013). https://doi.org/10.1007/978-3-642-35873-9_16

30. Leitner-Fischer, F., Leue, S.: Spincause: a tool for causality checking In: Rungta, N., Tkachuk, O. (eds.) 2014 International Symposium on Model Checking of Software, SPIN 2014, Proceedings, San Jose, CA, USA, 21–23 July 2014, pp. 117–120. ACM (2014). https://doi.org/10.1145/2632362.2632371

31. Manna, Z., Pnueli, A.: Temporal verification of reactive systems: safety. Springer (1995). https://doi.org/10.1007/978-1-4612-4222-2

32. Mascle, C., Baier, C., Funke, F., Jantsch, S., Kiefer, S.: Responsibility and verification: importance value in temporal logics. In: 36th Annual ACM/IEEE Symposium on Logic in Computer Science, LICS 2021, Rome, Italy, 29 June–2 July 2021, pp. 1–14. IEEE (2021). https://doi.org/10.1109/LICS52264.2021.9470597

33. Parreaux, J., Piribauer, J., Baier, C.: Counterfactual causality for reachability and safety based on distance functions. In: Proceedings of the Fourteenth International Symposium on Games, Automata, Logics, and Formal Verification, GandALF 2023, Udine, Italy, 18–20 September 2023. EPTCS, vol. 390, pp. 132–149 (2023). https://doi.org/10.4204/EPTCS.390.9

34. Van de Poel, I.: The relation between forward-looking and backward-looking responsibility. In: Moral Responsibility: Beyond Free Will and Determinism, pp. 37–52. Springer (2011). https://doi.org/10.1007/978-94-007-1878-4_3

35. Shapley, L.S.: A value for n-person games. Contribution to the Theory of Games **2** (1953)

36. Winter, E.: The shapley value. In: Handbook of Game Theory with Economic Applications, vol. 3, pp. 2025–2054 (2002)

37. Yazdanpanah, V., Dastani, M., Jamroga, W., Alechina, N., Logan, B.: Strategic responsibility under imperfect information. In: Proceedings of the 18th International Conference on Autonomous Agents and MultiAgent Systems, AAMAS 2019, Montreal, QC, Canada, 13–17 May 2019, pp. 592–600. International Foundation for Autonomous Agents and Multiagent Systems (2019). http://dl.acm.org/citation.cfm?id=3331745

38. Zeller, A.: Isolating cause-effect chains from computer programs. In: Proceedings of the Tenth ACM SIGSOFT Symposium on Foundations of Software Engineering 2002, Charleston, South Carolina, USA, 18–22 November 2002, pp. 1–10. ACM (2002). https://doi.org/10.1145/587051.587053

Automotive and Railway

GRust: A Programming Language for Automotive Engineering

Émilie Thomé[1,2,3]($\boxtimes$), Xavier Denis[4], and Christine Tasson[3]

[1] LIP6, 75005 Paris, France
emilie.thome@lip6.fr
[2] Ampère, 31100 Toulouse, France
[3] ISAE-SUPAERO, 31400 Toulouse, France
[4] ETH Zurich, Zurich, Switzerland

Abstract. The increasing complexity of embedded automotive software necessitates a strong focus on safety. ISO 26262 mandates reliability in critical systems, ensuring secure and bounded memory usage, bounded execution time, and protection against division-by-zero and overflow errors. Automotive software is typically modeled in SIMULINK and STATE-FLOW, generating ISO 26262-compliant C code under a periodic execution paradigm. However, for data-driven applications such as automated driving, periodic execution leads to redundant computations and bus overloads, requiring manual optimization. To address these issues, we introduce GRust, a domain-specific language for automotive system modeling. GRust generates Rust implementations that enforce compile-time safety properties while optimizing execution through change propagation. Additionally, it integrates a verification wrapper of CREUSOT for formal property validation. This paper presents the design of GRust, its implementation, and verification capabilities, demonstrating its potential to improve both the reliability and efficiency of automotive software.

Keywords: Reactive system · Dataflow · Domain-specific language

1 Introduction

Context. Embedded software applications in vehicles are ubiquitous. To ensure the reliability and safety of these applications, automotive manufacturers can comply with the ISO 26262 standard. This standard defines safety requirements based on the criticality of software components criticality, ranging from ASIL A (low criticality, *e.g.* rear lights) to ASIL D (high criticality, *e.g.* airbags).

Automotive software components are inherently reactive systems, meaning that they must operate in *real time*, continuously responding to changes from the environment within strict timing and memory constraints. Given the complexity of automotive systems, which involve numerous concurrent processes, manually implementing these components in low-level languages is impractical and hazardous. Instead, high-level modeling languages are preferred, as they allow for

A. Remke and B. Steffen (Eds.): FMICS 2025, LNCS 16040, pp. 127–143, 2025.
https://doi.org/10.1007/978-3-032-00942-5_7

automatic generation of the low-level implementation of embedded controllers. A common approach in the industry is to use SIMULINK and STATEFLOW to model systems. These tools can generate C code that complies with ISO 26262. In most systems following the AUTOSAR architecture (standardized software framework in automotive industry), the generated code assumes periodic computation, which simplifies reasoning about time. However, as automated driving systems emerge, the amount of data being processed has significantly increased. Periodic execution in this context leads to inefficiencies, including redundant computations, increased communication leading to bus overload, and the need for manual code adjustments. Furthermore, highly algorithmic components—such as data fusion modules in Advanced Driver Assistance Systems (ADAS)—are often manually implemented in C rather than modeled in SIMULINK, creating additional challenges in its integration with other subsystems.

The ISO 26262 recommends static code analysis to enforce coding standards, prevent runtime errors, and ensure safe memory usage. While C remains the industry standard, it lacks built-in safety mechanisms to prevent such errors. In contrast, RUST offers stronger guarantees on memory safety, *e.g.* detecting invalid pointer access at compile-time, making it a strong candidate to become the new standard [26]. However, memory safety alone is not enough. Critical systems must ensure bounded execution time and memory usage, and the absence of division by zero and overflows in their most critical components.

Contribution. We introduce GRUST, a *domain-specific language* (DSL) designed for system modeling in the automotive context. GRUST introduces execution optimizations, such as reducing redundant computations and minimizing communication bus load by propagating state changes instead of relying on periodic execution. Inspired from synchronous languages, GRUST generates RUST code that guarantees at compile-time safe memory management, bounded memory usage and bounded execution time. To enhance the verification process, we also introduce GREUSOT, a wrapper of the formal verification tool CREUSOT [15], that enables the specification and verification of system properties beyond basic safety guarantees, including the absence of division-by-zero and overflow errors.

Outline. This paper is structured as follows. Section 2 introduces background on reactive systems programming. In particular the synchronous and the FRP paradigms on which GRUST relies. Section 3 introduces the syntax and execution of the GRUST language through an example borrowed from automotive. A complete description of GRUST's syntax is presented in Sect. 4, followed by details on the prototype compiler in Sect. 5. Section 6 demonstrates the use of GREUSOT to formally verify properties of the example system. Finally, we present related works in Sect. 7 and conclude in Sect. 8.

2   Background on Reactive Systems Programming

Reactive systems are continuously interacting with their environment. They can be found in various area ranging from critical systems to more common systems.

Domain-Specific Languages (DSL) have been designed to facilitate the conception of reliable reactive systems. Two widely used paradigms are *Synchronous Programming*, suited for critical reactive systems, and *Functional Reactive Programming* (FRP), primarily used for graphical user interfaces. Each approach offers unique advantages and trade-offs, reflecting its area of application.

Synchronous Programming. LUSTRE, the inspiring language of the SCADE development suite, is a state-of-the-art synchronous language [13,21] used in safety-critical domains such as civil aviation and nuclear energy. Many extensions of LUSTRE make it possible to prove or disprove safety properties of models, the most popular tools are Kind2 [8] and JKind [19], SMT-based model checkers.

In synchronous programming, time is discretized, information in the system behavior are modeled as infinite data flows called *streams*, and processes are modeled as sets of equations, called *nodes*, stating the dependencies between streams. Nodes are compiled into *finite-state machines*, ensuring deterministic execution, bounded memory usage, and predictable execution time. To efficiently and safely handle processes operating at different rates, called *clocks*, LUSTRE employs a *clock typing*. The system's fastest rate, called the *base clock*, dictates the time-step representing the computation deadline. Slower processes derive their clocks through *clock sampling*. However, correct clock usage requires a deep understanding of its semantics. Automata were added to LUSTRE [12] to address this engineering issue, enabling automatic and sound usage of clocks.

Functional Reactive Programming. FRP was originally introduced to ease animation development [16]. It models time-dependent values as *signals* (continuous values) and *events* (discrete occurrences). While early FRP languages offered great flexibility and were more expressive than synchronous languages, particularly in dynamically reconfiguring computations as system inputs change, they lacked constraints on causality (outputs only depend on current and previous inputs) and on memory usage, posing safety and efficiency challenges.

Two FRP subsets address these issues: Real-Time FRP [27] enforces bounded memory and execution time; Event-Driven FRP [28], where computations are triggered by discrete events and propagate changes accordingly. As an alternative, several authors have considered modal types to ensure productivity, causality and the absence of implicit space leaks [3,23].

GRUST *Domain-Specific Language.* GRUST is designed for engineers familiar with event-driven programming but not necessarily with synchronous or FRP paradigms. Programmers manage event and signal flows. Computation is triggered by input events or signal changes, using predefined flow operators inspired by the FRP paradigm or custom components based on the synchronous paradigm.

3   Example of an Adaptive Cruise Control System

Figure 1 presents a simplified Adaptive Cruise Control (ACC) service written in GRUST, illustrating key language constructs. The service imports vehicle data—

such as speed, radar distance, and driver activation—and computes a braking force to maintain safe following distance. This computation combines built-in reactive operators (`on_change`, `time`) with user-defined components and functions (*e.g.* `acc`, `safety_distance`). For brevity, some components (`convert`, `derive`) are not shown. Besides the intuitive introduction of the constructions appearing in this illustration, a detailed explanation of the syntax and of the execution behavior is provided in Sect. 4.

3.1 Syntax by Example

The GRUST language consists of three core elements: the service-modeling kernel GRFRP, the reactive library GREACT, and the component-modeling kernel GRSYNC. Let us describe them on the ACC example from Fig. 1.

Service-Modeling Kernel. In GRUST, a *service* is an entity that computes data flows. It is connected to the real system via an *interface*. Both are modeled using GRFRP, where data flows are categorized as *signals* for continuous values and *events* for discrete occurrences. Figure 1 defines the `adaptive_cruise_control` service (Lines 6–12) along with its interface to the system (Lines 1–4). Imports (Lines 1–3) define the input signals `speed_km_h` and `radar_m`, along with the event `acc_active`, which are received from sensors or other services. The braking force `brakes_m_s`, computed by the ACC service (Line 11), is exported (Line 4) to other services and actuators. The body of the service also defines local flows (`radar_e`, `cond`, `speed_m_s`, and `vel_delta`, Lines 7–10) in a declarative style.

Built-In Reactive Library. In services, exported and local flows are defined by flow operators. Built-in operators are provided by the GREACT library: `on_change` (Line 7) detects updates in the `radar_m` signal and creates the event `radar_e`; and `time` (Line 10) creates a signal representing the current execution time.

Component-Modeling Kernel. Beyond built-in operators, services can invoke user-defined flow operators called components. In Fig. 1, the service calls components `activate`, `convert`, `derive`, and `acc` (Lines 8–11) to produce the signals `cond`, `speed_m_s`, and `vel_delta`, as well as the exported signal `brakes_m_s`. The definitions of `activate` and `acc` are provided Lines 14–35.

Components, defined in the GRSYNC language, state the values of their output flows at each instant based on the values of input flows, treating values as time-step snapshots. They repeatedly compute output values from previous incoming input values. In the `activate` component (Line 28), the input events `acc_active` and `radar_e` are represented by the optional values `act` (`Activation?`) and `r` (`float?`); the question mark indicates uncertain presence.

A component determines output values through unordered equations that operate synchronously at each instant. The `activate` component, for instance, defines a boolean signal (`cond`, named `c` inside the component) using equations (Lines 29–34). There are different kind of equations in GRSYNC:

```
1   import signal car::state::speed_km_h        : float;
2   import signal car::sensors::radar_m         : float;
3   import event  car::hmi::acc_active          : Activation;
4   export signal car::actuators::brakes_m_s    : float;
5   // Adaptive Cruise Control service
6   service adaptive_cruise_control @[10, 3000] {
7     let event  radar_e: float = on_change(radar_m);
8     let signal cond: bool = activate(acc_active, radar_e);
9     let signal speed_m_s: float = convert(speed_km_h);
10    let signal vel_delta: float = derive(radar_m, time());
11    brakes_m_s = acc(cond, radar_m, vel_delta, speed_m_s);
12  }
13  // Filters the ACC on driver activation and when approaching FV
14  component acc(c:bool, d:float, v:float, s:float) -> (b:float) {
15    match c {
16      true => {
17        b = v^2 / (2. * (d - d_safe));
18        let d_safe: float = safety_distance(s, fv_v);
19        let fv_v: float = s + v;
20      }
21      false => {
22        b = 0.;
23        let (fv_v: float, d_safe: float) = (0., 0.);
24      }
25    }
26  }
27  // Activation condition of the ACC
28  component activate(act: Activation?, r: float?) -> (c: bool) {
29    when {
30      init => { d = 0.; active = false; approach = false; }
31      act? => { let active: bool = act == Activation::On; }
32      r? => { let d: float = r; let approach: bool = d < last d; }
33    }
34    c = active && approach;
35  }
36  // Safety distance computation
37  function safety_distance(sv_v: float, fv_v: float) -> float {
38    let (rho: float, b_max: float) = (1., 0.6*9.81);
39    let sv_d_stop: float = sv_v*rho + sv_v^2/(2.*b_max);
40    let fv_d_stop: float = fv_v^2/(2.*b_max);
41    return sv_d_stop - fv_d_stop;
42  }
43  // Activation type
44  enum Activation{ Off, On }
```

Fig. 1. Example of a GRUST program for an Adaptive Cruise Control system.

- standard equations define values through simple assignments (*e.g.* Line 34: `c = active && approach;`) or declaration (Line 32: `let d: float = r;`).
- when equations activate computations only upon discrete occurrences, event or rising edges, updating signals or emitting events. These equations include initialization of defined signals, as seen in Line 30, where `active` is initialized to `false` and updated in Line 31 upon `act?` event occurrence. This kind of equations is reminiscent of the transition system of a state machine.
- match equations select computations based on the values of matching signals. Unlike **when** equations, which execute on event arrivals, **match** ensures that a branch is always executed, meaning that the patterns are exhaustive. This kind of equations is reminiscent of the state definitions of a state machine.

Components can use memories of the last step with the **last** keyword (*e.g.* Line 32 in `activate`), allowing stateful computations. Execution within bounded time and bounded memory is verified at compile-time. For optimization purposes, GRUST distinguishes memory-less (combinatorial) computations called functions, such as `safety_distance` (Lines 37–42), which operate with ordered equations akin to traditional programming languages.

3.2 Execution by Example

The execution of the ACC service follows the scheme from Fig. 2: it propagates signals changes and events occurrences through its flow statements. All incoming flows (i.e. `acc_active`, `radar_m`, and `speed_km_h`) are timestamped. The GRE-ACT operator **time** gets its values from those timestamps (orange arrows in the scheme). A context keeps the current values of signals.

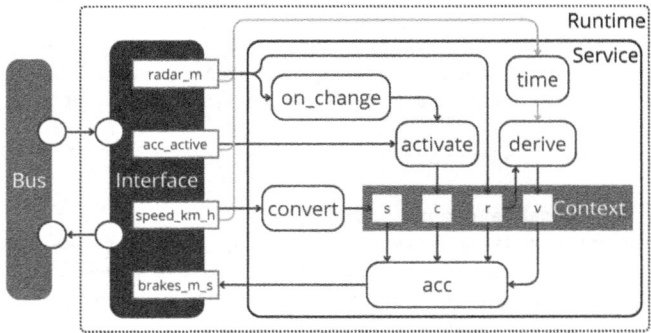

Fig. 2. Schematic execution for the Adaptive Cruise Control service Fig. 1.

When `speed_km_h` changes, it triggers the **convert** component, which updates s in the context. Concurrently, the timestamp updates the **time()** signal, which in turn triggers **derive**. The **derive** component retrieves the value of the signal r from the context and computes the updated value of v. Once s and v are updated, they propagate to the acc component, ensuring that all its inputs are up-to-date. The acc component then computes the current value of brakes_m_s. Finally, the value of brakes_m_s is sent through the bus, only if it has changed.

To prevent excessive updates and long absence of outputs, the ACC service adheres to timing constraints specified via @[10, 3000] (Line 6). This ensures that new values are produced at most every 10 ms and at least every 3000 ms. If inputs arrive before the 10 ms delay, they are stored in a buffer, waiting to be handled. Multiple arrivals of the same input within this delay represents a failure, detected at runtime and recovered by another (more robust) program.

Figure 3 shows the execution of the ACC service in a chronogram starting at an arbitrary time t. At this moment, the subject vehicle (controlled by the program) activates ACC while approaching the front car. At $t + 5$, computations are delayed because the service's minimal pause (defined by @[10, 3000] in Line 6) has not elapsed. The input speed_km_h is handled at $t + 10$, which updates speed_m_s. The braking rate is computed only when needed—specifically, when ACC is active, the front vehicle is approaching, and an update is required.

time	t	$t + 5$	$t + 10$	$t + 1010$	$t + 1210$
speed_km_h	129	131	131	131	128
radar_m	130	130	130	125	125
acc_active	On				
radar_e				125	
cond	false	false	false	true	true
speed_m_s	35.8	35.8	36.4	36.4	35.6
vel_delta	0	0	0	-5	-4.2
brakes_m_s	0	0	0	0.2	0.13

Fig. 3. Example of chronogram for an execution of the ACC service from Fig. 1. Imports changes and occurrences are red, updates of local flows and exports are blue. (Color figure online)

4   Syntax of GRUST

The GRUST language is composed of three elements: the service-modeling kernel GRFRP used to define computations on flows and their interaction with the system; the reactive library GREACT that offers built-in operators on flows; and the component-modeling kernel GRSYNC for user-defined operators on flows.

4.1   Syntax of GRFRP

This section presents the syntax of GRFRP, depicted in EBNF notation in Fig. 4. It combines the declaration of services, entities that compute data flows, and

InterDecl	::=	(**import** | **export**) FlowKind PATH: TY;
ServDecl	::=	**service** ID **@** [INT, INT] { FlowStmt* }
FlowStmt	::=	**let** (FlowKind ID: TY)* = FlowExpr; | ID* = FlowExpr;
FlowExpr	::=	ID | ID(FlowExpr*) | GReactExpr
FlowKind	::=	**event** | **signal**

Fig. 4. EBNF of GRFRP. Terminal symbols are in bold. Repetitions of X are denoted X*. PATH represents the abstract location of a flow in the system model. ID is an identifier composed of ASCII characters. INT is an integer. TY is a type.

their interaction with the real system via an interface. Inspired from the FRP paradigm, GRFRP defines flow computation in a declarative style.

In GRFRP, data flows are categorized as *signals* for continuous values and *events* for discrete occurrences. The value of a signal is always available but may change over time, while events values are only accessible when they occur.

The interface is declared by *imports* and *exports* of flows (InterDecl): the imported flows are produced by other entities in the system (sensors, or other services); the exported flows are produced by the program and made available for other entities in the system (actuators, or other services).

A service is an instantiation of flow computations. Its declaration (ServDecl) names the service, states timing constrains (**@** [INT, INT]) as minimal and maximal delays of execution in milliseconds, and provides the ordered list of flow statements ({ FlowStmt* }) that defines the behavior of the service. As explained in Sect. 3, services are not periodic, but follow time constraints, ensuring that new values are published between a minimum and maximum delay.

Flow statements are of two kinds: definitions (ID* = FlowExpr;) state the values of exported flows; declarations (**let** (FlowKind ID: TY)* = FlowExpr;) define the behavior of local flows. A single service and a single declaration can define an exported flow, but this is only verified locally and not system-wide.

Signals and events are defined by flow expressions composed of identifiers (ID), expressions from the GREACT library (GReactExpr), and calls of operators defined in the GRSYNC kernel (ID(FlowExpr*)). Both GREACT and GRSYNC are described in the following Sects. 4.2 and 4.3 respectively.

4.2 Syntax of GREACT

Inspired from ReactiveX [2], GREACT is a library that extends GRFRP expressions by offering built-in operators on flows. The syntax of GREACT operators is presented in Fig. 5, and Fig. 6 illustrates their behaviors.

The application of a GREACT operator (GReactExpr) creates new signals or events based on flow transformation, filtering, combinations, or timing. A signal can be transformed into an event containing its changes using the **on_change** operator; conversely, an event can be expanded into a signal using the **persist** operator. The timing of signals (*resp.* events) can be controlled by **scan** (*resp.* **sample**), which creates a signal (*resp.* an event) containing the values (*resp.*

GReactExpr   ::=   **on_change**(FlowExpr) | **persist**(FlowExpr)
            | **scan**(FlowExpr, INT) | **sample**(FlowExpr, INT)
            | **timeout**(FlowExpr, INT) | **merge**(FlowExpr, FlowExpr)
            | **throttle**(FlowExpr, (INT | FLOAT)) | **time**()

Fig. 5. EBNF for GReact expressions. Terminal symbols are in bold. INT and FLOAT are an integer and a float, respectively.

the optional last arrival) of the input over the ticks of the specified period in milliseconds. The **timeout** operator creates an event that emits unit values when the input (an event) has not arrived within the specified time, repeating the emission periodically until the input arrives, which resets the timeout.

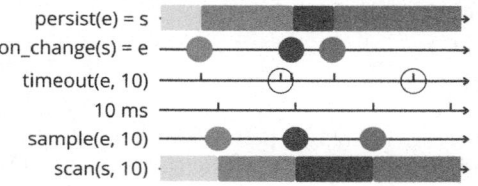

Fig. 6. Chronograms of some GReact operators (**10 ms** is used for **sample** and **scan**).

Two events can be combined into a single event using the **merge** operator, giving priority to the first listed event if they occur simultaneously. A signal containing only values whose difference is greater than a certain threshold can be created with **throttle**. Finally, the current time can be retrieved as a signal with the operator **time**.

4.3   Syntax of GRsync

This section presents the GRsync language, used for defining additional custom flow operators. Its syntax is fully illustrated in EBNF notation in Fig. 7. GRsync is highly inspired by Lustre-like languages [7,10,13], whose nodes bridge the gap between functional requirements and implementations of critical systems. Those languages use *clocks* to explicitly define when computations are performed. However, a correct usage of clocks requires a deep understanding of the formal semantics of the language. Constructs like **automaton** or **switch** ease the development of efficient systems. GRsync omits the explicit usage of clocks and offers other constructs to filter computations, presented in the following paragraphs, that are specific to the needs in the automotive industry.

User-defined flow operators are reusable building blocks of the system. They are modeled as *components* (CompDecl) if they use a finite number of buffers, or as *functions* (FunDecl) if they are memory-free.

The signature of a component (CompSign) declares its name, and the types and names of its input and output flows. The body of a component is a set of mutually recursive equations (EqSet), stating the values at every instant for the output flow based on the inputs. Ensuring that the output can be computed at every time step is checked at compile-time, as explained in Sect. 5.

The declaration of a function (FunDecl) is similar to traditional programming languages: the signature (FunSign) declares its name, the types and names of its

FunDecl	::=	FunSign FunBody
CompDecl	::=	CompSign EqSet
FunSign	::=	**function** ID ((ID: TY)*) → TY
CompSign	::=	**component** ID ((ID: TY)*) ↠ ((ID: TY)*)
FunBody	::=	{ Decl* **return** Expr; }
EqSet	::=	{ Eq* }
Eq	::=	Decl | ID* = Expr; | **init** ID = CST;
	|	**match** Expr { (Pat (**if** Expr)? ⇒ EqSet)* }
	|	**when** { InitBranch, (EPat (**if** Expr)? ⇒ EqSet)* }
Decl	::=	**let** (ID: TY)* = Expr;
InitBranch	::=	**init** ⇒ { (ID = CST;)* }
Expr	::=	CST | ID | **last** ID | **emit** Expr | OP(Expr*) | ID(Expr*)
	|	**match** Expr { (Pat (**if** Expr)? ⇒ Expr)* }
Pat	::=	CST | ID | _ | (Pat*)
EPat	::=	ID? | Expr | (EPat*)

Fig. 7. EBNF of GRSYNC. Terminal symbols are in bold. Repetitions of X are denoted X*. Option of X is denoted X?. ID is an identifier composed of ASCII characters. TY is a type. CST are constants. OP represents n-ary operators (*e.g.* addition).

input flows, and outputs' types; its body (FunBody) states the ordered intermediary computations (Decl*) necessary to return the output (**return** Expr;).

GRSYNC offers the five kinds of equations that follow.

Declaration (**let** (ID: TY)* = Expr;) declares the local identifiers ID*.
Instantiation (ID* = Expr;) gives a definition to the outputs ID*.
Initialization (**init** ID = CST;) initializes locally the signal ID.
Match (**match** Expr {(Pat (**if** Expr)? ⇒ EqSet)*}) selects at every instant the first branch whose pattern (Pat) matches the given expression (**match** Expr) and whose optional guard ((**if** Expr)?) holds. A pattern can be a constant (CST), a local identifier definition (ID), or a tuple ((Pat*)). Patterns must be exhaustive, ensuring that a branch is always selected.
When (**when** {InitBranch, (EPat (**if** Expr)? ⇒ EqSet)*}) selects the first branch whose eventful pattern (EPat) is satisfied and whose optional guard ((**if** Expr)?) holds. An eventful pattern can be an event detection (ID?), a rising edge (Expr), or a conjunction ((EPat*)). The activated branch performs updates of signals and emissions of events. Undefined signals in the branch keep their previous values, motivating their initialization in InitBranch.

Only declarations are used for intermediary computations in a function body.

Signals and events are defined by expressions composed of constants (CST), identifiers (ID), n-ary operations (OP(Expr*)), component or function calls (ID(Expr*)), match expressions that operate like the match equations, signal memories (**last** ID), and event emissions (**emit** Expr).

5   Implementation

The execution of GRust programs integrates two complementary paradigms: Functional Reactive Programming and Synchronous Programming. GRust combines GRfrp for managing asynchronous data flows and GRsync for time-step-based computations. This section details how these two sub-languages are compiled and executed, ensuring efficient and predictable system behavior.

5.1   Executing GRfrp Services

GRfrp services propagate signal updates and event occurrences using the push strategy of FRP [17]. A bus manages the communication between services, sending signal updates and event occurrences to the relevant interfaces. When an event occurs or a signal changes, all dependent flows are recomputed to maintain consistency, triggering a deterministic cascade of computations.

Instants of computation become unpredictable compared to periodic executions. However, real-time systems often rely on time (*e.g.* computing a derivative), so signals and events are timestamped. These timestamps define values of the signal **time()**, which provide a temporal reference for computations.

Flow operations in services require memory storage, called contexts. For example, the GReact operator **persist** retains the last occurrence of its input event. Components also require memory, which is detailed in the next section.

GRust restricts memory usage in components, also detailed in the next section, ensuring that only input changes can modify output values.

5.2   Compiling GRsync Components

A GRsync component computes output flow values based on both the current and past input values. It follows a state machine model, a common approach in Lustre-like languages [11], where its state stores all values needed for future computations. This includes referenced past values (via **last**) and the internal states of invoked components. The state size is finite and statically determined based on the number of identifiers using **last** and the number of called components. The step function of the state machine takes as input the current state and input values, and produces the next state and corresponding output values. Components equations are scheduled based on their dataflow at compile-time, ensuring that the outputs can be computed from the current state and inputs.

In contrast, functions, that are GRsync components without memory, are purely functional, computing outputs solely from the current input flow values.

In Lustre, nodes' step functions execute in synchronization with an externally defined clock, whereas in GRust, component clocks are driven by input changes within the service. Stateful computations are restricted to **when** equations, ensuring they activate only on input changes. As a result, components behave as purely combinatorial functions when inputs remain unchanged.

6   *G Reusot*

This section introduces GREUSOT, a GRUST wrapper of the CREUSOT deductive verifier. It begins with an overview of safety considerations in the automotive industry, followed by a presentation of the syntax of GREUSOT. Finally, a simplified version of the ACC example demonstrates its usage and limitations (see Fig. 9).

Safety Properties in Automotive. The compliance with the ISO 26262 standard guarantees the functional safety of electrical/electronic systems in automotive vehicles. It establishes Automotive Safety Integrity Levels (ASIL), which determine the safety measures required according to the probability of occurrence and severity of potential hazards. They are ranged from ASIL A for the less critical (*e.g.* heating and cooling) to ASIL D for the most critical (*e.g.* power steering). Hazards not affecting safety are identified as quality management (QM) and do not require safety measures.

Critical systems should not exhibit faults, including use of uninitialized memory, dereferencing of invalid pointers, overflows, division by zero, and memory leaks. Yet in-depth inspection of the code at runtime is often inefficient or impossible, which makes static bug detection extremely relevant for ASIL D systems.

GRUST compiles to RUST, a language that ensures memory safety while maintaining efficiency comparable to low-level languages. RUST enforces compile-time restrictions on shared memory mutation, preventing undefined behavior. However, some structures, like mutexes, require shared mutability and cannot be written in *safe* RUST. To address this, RUST allows encapsulated *unsafe* code within restricted APIs. The RUSTBELT project [22] provides a framework for proving the absence of undefined behavior for such APIs, including a formally verified mutex library. GRUST is composed of a synchronous kernel GRSYNC and an event-driven kernel GRFRP. The former targets safe RUST, while the latter abstracts the bus via the FUTURES library [1], not verified by RUSTBELT.

The deductive verifier CREUSOT [15] leverages RUST's memory safety to prove functional properties while reducing the amount of necessary specifications. It translates annotated RUST programs into WHY3 [18] which generates the proofs using automated solvers, such as Z3 [24], CVC4 [4], or Alt-Ergo [14]. By default, CREUSOT proves the absence of runtime errors, including the absence of division-by-zero and of arithmetic overflows across the entire program. Programmers can also specify and verify additional properties. GRUST includes GREUSOT, a wrapper of CREUSOT's specification language, for verifying GRSYNC components and functions.

Syntax of GREUSOT. Figure 8 presents the EBNF syntax of GREUSOT, which extends GRSYNC components and functions with formal specifications in their signatures.

A specification (Spec) consists of clauses (Clause*) that define pre-conditions (**requires**) and post-conditions (**ensures**). The **requires** clause states assumptions under which the **ensures** clause must always hold. Clause properties are

FunSign	::=	**function** ID ((ID: TY)*) $\rightarrow$ TY Spec
CompSign	::=	**component** ID ((ID: TY)*) $\rightarrow$ ((ID: TY)*) Spec
Spec	::=	Clause*
Clause	::=	(**requires** | **ensures**) { Term }
Term	::=	CST | ID | **last** ID | OP(Term*) | ID(Term*)
	|	Term $\Rightarrow$ Term | **forall** ID: TY, Term
	|	**when** EPat $\Rightarrow$ Term | **result**

Fig. 8. EBNF for GREUSOT specifications in components and functions declarations. Terminal symbols are in bold. Repetitions of X are denoted X*. ID is an identifier composed of ASCII characters. TY is a type. CST are constants. OP represents n-ary operators, such as conjunction or conditional.

expressed as terms, which can be constants (CST), identifiers (ID), memories of last executions (**last** ID), n-ary operations (OP(Term*)), function call (ID(Term*)), implications (Term $\Rightarrow$ Term), universal quantifiers (**forall** ID: TY, Term), event-based implications (**when** EPat $\Rightarrow$ Term), or the returned value of the specified function (**result**).

Compiling GREUSOT*Specifications.* Compilation of GRUST transforms **function** and **component** declarations into RUST functions, encoding their respective functions or state machines. Logical variants of functions are also generated for use in specifications. GREUSOT extends by lowering contracts to equivalent clauses on the output RUST code, using CREUSOT's **requires(..)** and **ensures(..)** macros. Components can refer to their state within specifications (**last** ID), in a **requires** clause this refers to the pre-state while in **ensures** it refers to the post-state.

GREUSOT specifications are verified by running **cargo creusot prove** on the output code. CREUSOT generates the proofs, leveraging several SMT solvers.

Example: Specifying the ACC System. The function **safety_distance** and the component **acc** from the ACC example in Sect. 3 are extended with GREUSOT specifications in Fig. 9. Because CREUSOT does not support floats, the program has been adapted with integers.

The function **safety_distance** is designed to be used with a subject vehicle speed between 0 and 50 meters per second (Line 17). The speed of the front vehicle must be lower than the subject vehicle's speed, with a maximum difference of 10 meters per second (Line 18). These constraints guarantee at Line 19 that the computed safety distance is always positive and does not exceed 150 m (maximum detection range of the radar), and ensures the absence of overflow.

The specification of the **acc** component assumes at Lines 2 and 3 that when the activation condition **c** is verified:

- vehicle speeds are within the valid range of **safety_distance** (vehicles are approaching, but not too fast),
- the distance between the vehicles is above a minimum threshold, ensuring that the subject vehicle can maintain a safe distance with maximum braking.

```
1  component acc(c: bool, d: int, v: int, s: int) -> (b: int)
2    requires { c => 0 < s && s <= 50 && 0 < s+v && v < 0 && -v <= 10 }
3    requires { c => d - safety_distance(s, s+v) > v^2/(2*6) }
4    requires { d < 150 }
5    ensures  { 0 <= b && b <= 6 }
6  {
7    match c {
8      true => {
9        b = compute_braking(d - d_safe, v);
10       let d_safe: int = safety_distance(s, fv_v);
11       let fv_v: int = s + v;
12     }
13     false => { let (fv_v: int, d_safe: int) = (0, 0); b = 0; }
14   }
15 }
16 function safety_distance(sv_v: int, fv_v: int) -> int
17   requires { 0 < sv_v && sv_v <= 50 }
18   requires { 0 < fv_v && fv_v < sv_v && sv_v - fv_v <= 10 }
19   ensures  { 0 < result && result < 150 }
20 { ... }
21 function compute_braking(d_grace: int, v: int) -> int
22 { ... }
```

Fig. 9. Usage of GREUSOT specifications in `safety_distance` function and `acc` component from the Adaptive Cruise Control example in Fig. 1.

Additionally, it assumes that d (distance detected by the radar) does not exceed 150 m (Line 4). The specification guarantees the absence of division-by-zero and overflow, and the braking rate stays within its bounds (Line 5). Proving the specifications of `acc` requires an intermediate function `compute_braking` to guide the solvers (Lines 22–23).

7   Related Works

GRUST combines principles from LUSTRE-like languages and FRP while introducing a different execution and composition model. Like LUSTRE, GRUST follows a synchronous dataflow approach, ensuring deterministic execution and compile-time verification of causality. However, while LUSTRE focuses on the computation of the stream of outputs given the stream of inputs, GRUST integrates the treatment of the interface with the environment. GRUST controls the flow of information, triggering updates only when necessary and thus avoiding the periodicity usually assumed.

Yet, the synchronous kernel of GRUST offers nothing more than what is already provided by existing LUSTRE-like languages. All its constructs can be translated into a well-defined LUSTRE version using clocks. The **when** equation remains an uncommon syntactic sugar, unlike the **match** equation that resembles a `switch`. The choice of these operators has been guided by the examples from the automotive domain.

From FRP, GRUST retains the handling of signal and event propagation [17], reducing unnecessary computations while maintaining a clear execution model. But it introduces stricter constraints on memory usage and recursion to ensure predictable execution.

GRUST shares similarities with Globally Asynchronous Locally Synchronous (GALS) architectures [6,9], which consist of synchronous components communicating asynchronously. They can be designed using the dataflow language Signal [20], that supports multi-clock computation. Prelude [25], a software architecture language, integrates synchronous processes running at different periods into a multi-periodic system. However, unlike these approaches, GRUST removes explicit clock definition, instead generating them at runtime based on input arrivals through the asynchronous bus. GRUST differs from the imperative synchronous language ESTEREL [5] whose syntax makes explicit use of control threads and whose notion of *signal* corresponds only to GRUST events.

8   Conclusion

We have presented a DSL tailored for the automotive industry with a syntax designed for engineers familiar with RUST, event-driven reasoning, and model-based design. It helps meet safety standards (such as ISO 26262) while reducing bus load at the interface between sensors, actuator and controllers. Mechanisms ensuring bounded memory and execution time, productivity, determinism and causality are hidden to the programmer, that can focus on modeling.

Indeed, GRUST introduces a novel composition and execution model that integrates principles from synchronous languages (like LUSTRE) with Function Reactive Programming (FRP). Structured around GRSYNC and GRFRP, it enables compositional design of control and dataflow, ensuring deterministic execution and event-driven updates to minimize unnecessary computations.

Moreover, ensuring the absence of failures like division-by-zero and overflows is essential for automotive software development, particularly for components requiring ISO 26262 ASIL D certification. GREUSOT is a proof of concept towards interfacing proof techniques with simplified industrial reactive software in RUST. The integration of formal verification techniques facilitates formal reasoning about program behavior, ensuring correctness properties such as the absence of runtime errors. However, proving that a program satisfies a specification will always be a hard task requiring expertise in proof techniques.

Future work. Will explore three directions. First, we will evaluate the DSL's ergonomics using realistic automotive models encoded by industry engineers. Second, we aim to extend GREUSOT's verification capabilities to support reasoning with differential equations (ODEs), enabling more expressive specifications (*e.g.* proving that planned dynamics maintain safety distances). Finally, optimizing execution, particularly for time-dependent signals, will further enhance GRUST's practical efficiency.

References

1. Futures: Zero-cost asynchronous programming in Rust. https://crates.io/crates/futures/
2. ReactiveX: An API for asynchronous programming with observable streams. https://reactivex.io/
3. Bahr, P., Graulund, C., Møgelberg, R.E.: Simply RATT: a fitch-style modal calculus for reactive programming without space leaks. Proc. ACM Program. Lang. 3(ICFP), 109:1–109:27 (2019). https://doi.org/10.1145/3341713
4. Barrett, C., et al.: CVC4. In: Gopalakrishnan, G., Qadeer, S. (eds.) CAV 2011. LNCS, vol. 6806, pp. 171–177. Springer, Heidelberg (2011). https://doi.org/10.1007/978-3-642-22110-1_14
5. Berry, G.: The foundations of esterel. In: Proof, Language, and Interaction, pp. 425–454. The MIT Press (2000)
6. Bormann, D., Cheung, P.: Asynchronous wrapper for heterogeneous systems. In: Proceedings International Conference on Computer Design VLSI in Computers and Processors, pp. 307–314 (1997). https://doi.org/10.1109/ICCD.1997.628884
7. Bourke, T., Pouzet, Ṁ.: Zélus: a synchronous language with odes. In: Belta, C., Ivancic, F. (eds.) Proceedings of the 16th International Conference on Hybrid Systems: Computation and Control, HSCC 2013, Philadelphia, PA, USA, 8–11 April 2013, pp. 113–118. ACM (2013). https://doi.org/10.1145/2461328.2461348
8. Champion, A., Mebsout, A., Sticksel, C., Tinelli, C.: The KIND 2 model checker. In: Chaudhuri, S., Farzan, A. (eds.) CAV 2016. LNCS, vol. 9780, pp. 510–517. Springer, Cham (2016). https://doi.org/10.1007/978-3-319-41540-6_29
9. Chapiro, D.M.: Globally-asynchronous locally-synchronous systems. Ph.D. thesis, Stanford University, USA (1985). https://searchworks.stanford.edu/view/1137794
10. Cohen, A., Gérard, L., Pouzet, M.: Programming parallelism with futures in lustre. In: Jerraya, A., Carloni, L.P., Maraninchi, F., Regehr, J. (eds.) Proceedings of the 12th International Conference on Embedded Software, EMSOFT 2012, Part of the Eighth Embedded Systems Week, ESWeek 2012, Tampere, Finland, 7–12 October 2012, pp. 197–206. ACM (2012). https://doi.org/10.1145/2380356.2380394
11. Colaço, J., Mendler, M., Pauget, B., Pouzet, M.: A constructive state-based semantics and interpreter for a synchronous data-flow language with state machines. ACM Trans. Embed. Comput. Syst. 22(5s), 152:1–152:26 (2023). https://doi.org/10.1145/3609131
12. Colaço, J., Pagano, B., Pouzet, M.: A conservative extension of synchronous data-flow with state machines. In: Wolf, W.H. (ed.) EMSOFT 2005, Jersey City, NJ, USA, 18–22 September 2005, 5th ACM International Conference on Embedded Software, Proceedings, pp. 173–182. ACM (2005). https://doi.org/10.1145/1086228.1086261
13. Colaço, J., Pagano, B., Pouzet, M.: SCADE 6: a formal language for embedded critical software development (invited paper). In: Mallet, F., Zhang, M., Madelaine, E. (eds.) 11th International Symposium on Theoretical Aspects of Software Engineering, TASE 2017, Sophia Antipolis, France, 13–15 September 2017, pp. 1–11. IEEE Computer Society (2017). https://doi.org/10.1109/TASE.2017.8285623
14. Conchon, S., Coquereau, A., Iguernlala, M., Mebsout, A.: Alt-ergo 2.2. In: SMT Workshop: International Workshop on Satisfiability Modulo Theories (2018)
15. Denis, X., Jourdan, J., Marché, C.: Creusot: a foundry for the deductive verification of rust programs. In: Riesco, A., Zhang, M. (eds.) Formal Methods and Software Engineering - 23rd International Conference on Formal Engineering Methods,

ICFEM 2022, Madrid, Spain, 24–27 October 2022, Proceedings. Lecture Notes in Computer Science, vol. 13478, pp. 90–105. Springer, Cham (2022). https://doi. org/10.1007/978-3-031-17244-1_6

16. Elliott, C., Hudak, P.: Functional reactive animation. In: Jones, S.L.P., Tofte, M., Berman, A.M. (eds.) Proceedings of the 1997 ACM SIGPLAN International Conference on Functional Programming (ICFP 1997), Amsterdam, The Netherlands, 9–11 June 1997, pp. 263–273. ACM (1997). https://doi.org/10.1145/258948.258973

17. Elliott, C.M.: Push-pull functional reactive programming. In: Weirich, S. (ed.) Proceedings of the 2nd ACM SIGPLAN Symposium on Haskell, Haskell 2009, Edinburgh, Scotland, UK, 3 September 2009, pp. 25–36. ACM (2009). https://doi. org/10.1145/1596638.1596643

18. Filliâtre, J.-C., Paskevich, A.: Why3—where programs meet provers. In: Felleisen, M., Gardner, P. (eds.) ESOP 2013. LNCS, vol. 7792, pp. 125–128. Springer, Heidelberg (2013). https://doi.org/10.1007/978-3-642-37036-6_8

19. Gacek, A., Backes, J., Whalen, M., Wagner, L., Ghassabani, E.: The JKIND model checker. In: Chockler, H., Weissenbacher, G. (eds.) CAV 2018. LNCS, vol. 10982, pp. 20–27. Springer, Cham (2018). https://doi.org/10.1007/978-3-319-96142-2_3

20. Gautier, T., Le Guernic, P., Besnard, L., Talpin, J.: The polychronous model of computation and Kahn process networks. Sci. Comput. Program. **228**, 102958 (2023). https://doi.org/10.1016/J.SCICO.2023.102958

21. Halbwachs, N., Caspi, P., Raymond, P., Pilaud, D.: The synchronous data flow programming language LUSTRE. Proc. IEEE **79**(9), 1305–1320 (1991). https:// doi.org/10.1109/5.97300

22. Jung, R., Jourdan, J., Krebbers, R., Dreyer, D.: Rustbelt: securing the foundations of the rust programming language. Proc. ACM Program. Lang. **2**(POPL), 66:1–66:34 (2018). https://doi.org/10.1145/3158154

23. Krishnaswami, N.R.: Higher-order functional reactive programming without space-time leaks. In: Morrisett, G., Uustalu, T. (eds.) ACM SIGPLAN International Conference on Functional Programming, ICFP 2013, Boston, MA, 25–27 September 2013, pp. 221–232. ACM (2013). https://doi.org/10.1145/2500365.2500588

24. de Moura, L., Bjørner, N.: Z3: an efficient SMT solver. In: Ramakrishnan, C.R., Rehof, J. (eds.) TACAS 2008. LNCS, vol. 4963, pp. 337–340. Springer, Heidelberg (2008). https://doi.org/10.1007/978-3-540-78800-3_24

25. Pagetti, C., Forget, J., Boniol, F., Cordovilla, M., Lesens, D.: Multi-task implementation of multi-periodic synchronous programs. Discret. Event Dyn. Syst. **21**(3), 307–338 (2011). https://doi.org/10.1007/s10626-011-0107-x

26. Ferrous Systems: Ferrocene: Rust compiler toolchain qualified at ISO 26262 (ASIL D) and IEC 61508 (SIL 4) (2025). https://ferrocene.dev/

27. Wan, Z., Taha, W., Hudak, P.: Real-time FRP. In: Pierce, B.C. (ed.) Proceedings of the Sixth ACM SIGPLAN International Conference on Functional Programming (ICFP 2001), Firenze (Florence), Italy, 3–5 September 2001, pp. 146–156. ACM (2001). https://doi.org/10.1145/507635.507654,

28. Wan, Z., Taha, W., Hudak, P.: Event-driven FRP. In: Krishnamurthi, S., Ramakrishnan, C.R. (eds.) PADL 2002. LNCS, vol. 2257, pp. 155–172. Springer, Heidelberg (2002). https://doi.org/10.1007/3-540-45587-6_11

Robust Spatio-Temporal Logic Semantics for Autonomous Driving Systems Falsification

Tiago Sequeira[1] and André Matos Pedro[2]([⊠]) [ID]

[1] VORTEX-CoLab, Vila Nova de Gaia, Portugal
`tiago.sequeira@vortex-colab.com`
[2] NOVA-LINCS & University of Beira Interior, Covilhã, Portugal
`matos.pedro@ubi.pt`

Abstract. Traditional industrial testing methods often fail to guarantee that a system behaves as expected due to the resource cost of exhaustively searching for defects. To minimize this cost, a promising alternative called *robustness-guided falsification* is emerging as a less exhaustive method that can handle the increasing complexity of autonomous driving systems. This approach attempts to identify counterexamples to a given system property by treating testing as an optimization problem with a robustness function to be minimized. This function quantifies how well the system satisfies a given property encoded as a logical formula, with values that indicate how close the system is to violating the property. In this paper, we apply robustness-guided falsification to a particular type of spatio-temporal logic, $LTL \times MS^{\leq}$, which integrates both temporal and spatial modalities to describe system behavior across time and space. We establish a correspondence between the Boolean semantics of the "subset or equal" relation and the degrees of robustness with signed Hausdorff distances, propose a robust semantics for $LTL \times MS^{\leq}$, and demonstrate how robustness-guided falsification can be applied to properties expressed in this logic. To evaluate our approach, we conducted an empirical case study in a traffic scenario. The results demonstrate the feasibility of this approach in falsifying spatio-temporal properties and support the adoption of counterexample generation for the verification of defects in realistic autonomous driving systems.

1 Introduction

Testing plays a critical role in building confidence in Autonomous Driving Systems (ADSs) that require high levels of assurance and regulatory compliance. However, traditional approaches such as exhaustive testing often fail to detect rare or corner-case bugs, mainly due to the large input space and high computational cost. To overcome these limitations, simulation- and optimization-based falsification techniques have emerged as promising alternatives to discover unintended behavior. Among these, robustness-guided falsification has been particularly effective in addressing the complexity of cyber-physical systems (CPSs) [20].

A. Remke and B. Steffen (Eds.): FMICS 2025, LNCS 16040, pp. 144–161, 2025.
https://doi.org/10.1007/978-3-032-00942-5_8

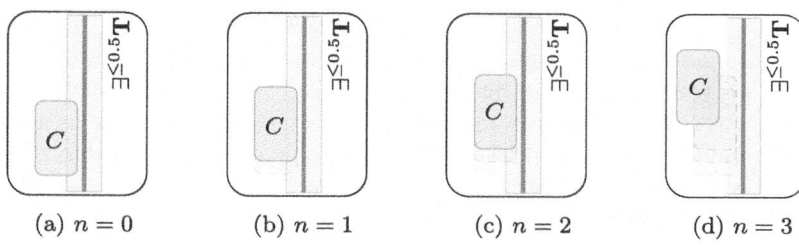

(a) $n = 0$ (b) $n = 1$ (c) $n = 2$ (d) $n = 3$

Fig. 1. Intuition of $LTL \times MS^{\leq}$ over a temporal sequence $n \in [0, 3]$, where each frame show the evolution between $\mathbf{T}$ (always static) and $\mathbf{C}$ (dynamic) objects.

Safety requirements of CPS can typically be expressed as system properties, where each property is formalized using temporal logic [11]. Although robustness measures the number of perturbations that a system tolerates until it no longer satisfies a given formula ϕ, the mapping between the behavior of the system and a robustness value, $r \in \mathbb{R}$, is given by a *robustness function*, which assigns a degree of satisfaction with respect to ϕ. Intuitively, a robustness value $r > 0$ indicates that the system satisfies ϕ with a safety margin, $r = 0$ indicates proximity to a violation, and $r < 0$ indicates a violation of ϕ. To search for a falsifying behavior, it uses stochastic sampling methods, where a robustness function (robust semantics) acts as an objective function that we want to minimize [1,8].

Robustness-guided falsification attempts to find a counterexample to a given property were first considered by Fainekos and Pappas for MITL [7]. They used a signed distance and quantified the degree of satisfaction (violation) of a signal with a given temporal property. Later, Donzé and Maler [6] extended the approach to STL by presenting robust semantics that capture the interaction between spatial robustness, the degree of satisfaction (violation) of a signal, and temporal robustness, *when* a signal satisfies the property, motivating the study of robust semantics for spatio-temporal logic.

In this work, we use a combination of Linear Temporal Logic with a fragment of Modal Metric Spaces ($LTL \times MS^{\leq}$) that can express a discrete time flow (with a strict precedence order $<$) of metric spaces with their respective topologies [9], where its formulas are constructed using a set of temporal and spatial operators to describe the behavior of a system over space and time.

Running Example. A scenario in which a vehicle must satisfy the requirement: "Vehicle $\mathbf{C}$ shall be within half a meter of reference trajectory $\mathbf{T}$". While C denotes a bounding box, T denotes the shape of a trajectory at time points $n \in \mathbb{N}$, as shown in Fig. 1. For $n = [0, 2]$, $\mathbf{C}$ overlaps with the space around $\mathbf{T}$, and the requirement is not valid for $n = 3$ as both $\mathbf{C}$ and $\mathbf{T}$ are disconnected. The shadows around $\mathbf{C}$ are their footprints at different time points, and for now just consider that $\exists^{\leq 0.5}\mathbf{T}$ means the expansion of $\mathbf{T}$ by 0.5 units.

Problem Statement. Consider testing the behavior of a ADS while driving on a road that must comply with road safety rules (e.g. the above requirement) defined by the International Vienna Convention [18]. The problem is to generate counterexamples using non-exhaustive testing techniques with low resource consumption for testing during development, training, or validation of the system. So we need to find a semantic function that assigns a robustness meaning to a logic fragment already used to describe a specific set of road traffic rules [4], $LTL \times MS^{\leq}$. In this way, we will be able to falsify properties of a given ADS using robustness-guided falsification.

Paper Contributions. First, we establish a correspondence between the Boolean evaluation of the "subset or equal" relation and a quantitative notion of robustness. Building on this, we provide robust semantics for $LTL \times MS^{\leq}$ that allows the evaluation of spatio-temporal properties with a degree of satisfaction. A new definition of the disconnected predicate of Region Connection Calculus (RCC) is proposed, along with robustness-based interpretations for other RCC predicates. Finally, we demonstrate the practical feasibility of robustness-guided falsification of $LTL \times MS^{\leq}$ properties through the running example.

Paper Structure. Section 2 introduces the syntax and semantics of $LTL \times MS^{\leq}$ terms and formulas, along with the Hausdorff distance. Section 3 then defines the robustness semantics for $LTL \times MS^{\leq}$. The semantic preservation of robust $LTL \times MS^{\leq}$ is demonstrated in Sect. 4, while Sect. 5 evaluates the feasibility of the proposed approach. Related work is discussed in Sect. 6, and Sect. 7 concludes the paper and outlines directions for future work.

2   Preliminaries

Definition 1 ($LTL \times MS^{\leq}$ - Syntax [9]). *The syntax of terms and formulas is defined by*

$$\varrho ::= p \mid \overline{\varrho} \mid \varrho_1 \sqcap \varrho_2 \mid \exists^{\leq a} \varrho \mid \varrho_1 \mathfrak{U} \varrho_2 \qquad \text{(terms)}$$
$$\varphi ::= \varrho_1 \sqsubseteq \varrho_2 \mid \neg\varphi \mid \varphi_1 \wedge \varphi_2 \mid \varphi_1 \, \mathcal{U} \, \varphi_2 \mid \varphi_1 \, \mathcal{S} \, \varphi_2, \qquad \text{(formulas)}$$

where $p \in \mathfrak{P}$ is a spatial variable, $a \in \mathbb{Q}$, and $\mathfrak{P}$ a nonempty set of variables. $\mathfrak{U}$ and $\mathcal{U}$ stand for the "Until" operator for terms and formulas, respectively, and $\mathcal{S}$ is the "Since" operator. $\exists^{\leq a} \varrho$ is an expansion of a term.

Definition 2 ($LTL \times MS^{\leq}$ - Terms Semantics). *A temporal metric model is a pair of the form $\mathfrak{M} = (\mathfrak{D}, \mathfrak{N})$ [2], where $\mathfrak{D} = (\Delta, d)$ is a metric space, Δ represents a non-empty set of points that reproduce the entire universe, d is a function of the form $\Delta \times \Delta \mapsto \mathbb{R}^{\geq 0}$ describing the distance between every two points in Δ, satisfying the identity of the indiscernible axioms, symmetry, and triangle inequality [14]. Valuation $\mathfrak{N}$ is a map that associates each spatial variable p and time point n with a set $\mathfrak{N}(p, n) \subseteq \Delta$. The valuation can be inductively extended to arbitrary $LTL \times MS^{\leq}$ terms such as*

$$\mathfrak{N}(\overline{\varrho}, n) \quad = \Delta - \mathfrak{N}(\varrho, n),$$
$$\mathfrak{N}(\varrho_1 \sqcap \varrho_2, n) = \mathfrak{N}(\varrho_1, n) \cap \mathfrak{N}(\varrho_2, n),$$
$$\mathfrak{N}(\exists^{\leq a} \varrho, n) \quad = \{x \in \Delta \mid \text{there exists a } y \in \mathfrak{N}(\varrho, n) \text{ such that } d(x, y) \leq a\},$$

$$\mathfrak{N}(\varrho_1 \mathfrak{U} \varrho_2, n) \quad = \bigcup_{m > n} \left(\mathfrak{N}(\varrho_2, m) \cap \bigcap_{k \in (n,m)} \mathfrak{N}(\varrho_1, k) \right)$$

Note that (n, m) means the open set for all $n, m \in \mathbb{N}$. The shorthands 'Eventually' $\diamondsuit$, 'Always' $\square$, and 'Next' $\odot$ are defined using $\mathfrak{U}$, as follows: $\diamondsuit \varrho \equiv \top \mathfrak{U} \varrho$, $\square \varrho \equiv \overline{\diamondsuit \overline{\varrho}}$, and $\odot \varrho \equiv \bot \mathfrak{U} \varrho$, where $\top$ and $\bot$ denote the universe and the empty set. Furthermore, the term union $\varrho_1 \sqcup \varrho_2$ can be expressed as $\overline{\overline{\varrho_1} \sqcap \overline{\varrho_1}}$. To easily understand the meaning of these shorthands, $\mathfrak{N}(\odot \varrho, n) = \mathfrak{N}(\varrho, n+1)$, $\mathfrak{N}(\diamondsuit \varrho, n) = \bigcup_{m > n} \mathfrak{N}(\varrho, m)$, and $\mathfrak{N}(\square \varrho, n) = \bigcap_{m > n} \mathfrak{N}(\varrho, m)$.

Definition 3 (Formulas Semantics [9]). *The truth values of formulas φ in a model $\mathfrak{M}$ are defined by the semantic function $A[\![\varphi]\!](\mathfrak{M}, n)$ as follows:*

$$A[\![\varrho_1 \sqsubseteq \varrho_2]\!] = \lambda(\mathfrak{D}, \mathfrak{N}), n. \; \mathfrak{N}(\varrho_1, n) \subseteq \mathfrak{N}(\varrho_2, n)$$
$$A[\![\neg \varphi]\!] = \lambda \mathfrak{M}, n. \; if A[\![\varphi]\!](\mathfrak{M}, n) = 1 \; then \; 0 \; else \; 1$$
$$A[\![\varphi_1 \wedge \varphi_2]\!] = \lambda \mathfrak{M}, n. \; A[\![\varphi_1]\!](\mathfrak{M}, n) = 1 \; and \; A[\![\varphi_2]\!](\mathfrak{M}, n) = 1$$
$$A[\![\varphi_1 \, \mathcal{U} \, \varphi_2]\!] = \lambda \mathfrak{M}, n. \; \exists m \in (n, \infty). \; A[\![\varphi_2]\!](\mathfrak{M}, m) = 1 \; and$$
$$\forall k \in (n, m). \; A[\![\varphi_1]\!](\mathfrak{M}, k) = 1$$
$$A[\![\varphi_1 \, \mathcal{S} \, \varphi_2]\!] = \lambda \mathfrak{M}, n. \; \exists m \in (0, n). \; A[\![\varphi_2]\!](\mathfrak{M}, m) = 1 \; and$$
$$\forall k \in (m, n). \; A[\![\varphi_1]\!](\mathfrak{M}, k) = 1$$

where n is a time point in the set of natural numbers $\mathbb{N}$, and λ denotes an anonymous function of the form $\lambda x_1, \ldots, x_n$. exp, e.g., $\lambda x, y$. $x + y$. For instance, the denotation of $+$ given by $[\![+]\!] = \lambda x, y$. $x + y$ reads as $[\![+]\!](3, 4) = (\lambda x, y \; . \; x + y)(3, 4) = 3 + 4 = 7$ with a function application. The satisfaction relation of a formula φ in a model $\mathfrak{M}$ is defined as $(\mathfrak{M}, n) \models \varphi$ iff $A[\![\varphi]\!](\mathfrak{M}, n) = 1$. We say $(\mathfrak{M}, n) \not\models \varphi$ iff $A[\![\varphi]\!](\mathfrak{M}, n) = 0$.

Note that $\varphi_1 \vee \varphi_2 \equiv \neg(\neg \varphi_1 \wedge \neg \varphi_2)$. Intuitively, $\exists^{\leq a} \varrho$ is the spatial expansion of ϱ by a units, $\mathfrak{U}$ and $\mathcal{U}$ stand for the binary operator "Until" for terms and formulas, respectively, and $\mathcal{S}$ is the "Since" operator. In addition, to write complex spatial patterns concisely, we use the definition of four RCC predicates: "Equal", "Disconnected", "Partially Overlapped" (O) and "Strictly Included", as exemplified in Fig. 2 . The definition of the RCC predicates is as follows:

$$\text{EQ}(\rho_1, \rho_2) := (\rho_1 \sqsubseteq \rho_2) \wedge (\rho_2 \sqsubseteq \rho_1), \tag{1a}$$
$$\text{DC}(\rho_1, \rho_2) := \text{EQ}(\rho_1 \sqcap \rho_2, \bot), \tag{1b}$$
$$\text{O}(\rho_1, \rho_2) \quad := \neg \text{DC}(\rho_1, \rho_2) \wedge \neg(\rho_1 \sqsubseteq \rho_2) \wedge \neg(\rho_2 \sqsubseteq \rho_1), \tag{1c}$$
$$\text{I}(\rho_1, \rho_2) \quad := (\rho_1 \sqsubseteq \rho_2) \wedge \neg(\rho_2 \sqsubseteq \rho_1). \tag{1d}$$

Example 1 (Overlap and Temporal Overlap). To formalize the requirement of the running example "a vehicle must follow a line", we consider $\mathbf{C}$ as a spatial term with a bounding box shape, $\mathbf{T}$ as another spatial term representing a line, as a reference trajectory, and $\exists^{\leq 0.5}\mathbf{T}$ as the space around $\mathbf{T}$, which is a thin bounding box with rounded corners due to expansion with a constant size of 0.5 units. The formula (2) does not satisfy every snapshot in Fig. 1.

$$\mathsf{O}\left(\mathbf{C}, \exists^{\leq 0.5}\mathbf{T}\right) \tag{2}$$

To complete the formalization, we combine (2) with the modality $\mathcal{U}$, which captures changes over time, as follows:

$$\Box\left[\mathsf{O}\left(\mathbf{C}, \exists^{\leq 0.5}\mathbf{T}\right)\right]. \tag{3}$$

Note that $\Box$ means 'Always' and is a shorthand for $\Box\varphi \equiv \neg\Diamond\neg\varphi$, where $\Diamond$ stands for 'Eventually' and is defined as $\Diamond\varphi \equiv \top\mathcal{U}\varphi$.

2.1 Hausdorff Distances

Let A and B be two sets, $A \subset \Delta$, and $B \subset \Delta$. The Hausdorff distance [12] between A and B is a measure of how different the sets are. It can be given by

$$d_H(A, B) = \max\left\{\vec{d}_H(A, B), \vec{d}_H(B, A)\right\} \tag{4}$$

where $\vec{d}_H(A, B) = \sup_{a\in A} \inf_{b\in B} d(a, b)$ and $\vec{d}_H(B, A) = \sup_{b\in B} \inf_{a\in A} d(a, b)$ are the *directed* Hausdorff distances between A and B and B and A, respectively, where sup stands for the supremum operator and inf for the infimum operator as usual. Informally, these directed distances mean the greatest distance from a point in A to its nearest correspondent point in B. Equivalently the Hausdorff distance can also be defined as:

$$d_H(A, B) = \inf\{\epsilon \geq 0 \mid A \subseteq B_\epsilon \text{ and } B \subseteq A_\epsilon\},$$

where $A_\epsilon = \bigcup_{a\in A}\{x \in \Delta \mid d(x, a) \leq \epsilon\}$ and $B_\epsilon = \bigcup_{b\in B}\{x \in \Delta \mid d(x, b) \leq \epsilon\}$ mean two generalized balls of radius ϵ, close to the definition of our $\exists^{\leq}$ term.

There are several important properties to mention about the Hausdorff distance. d_H is guaranteed to be finite *if and only if* A and B are bounded sets; $d_H(A, B) = 0$ does not necessarily mean $A = B$, it means that A and B have the same closure (e.g., $A = \{x \in \mathbb{R} \mid x < 2\}$ and $B = \{x \in \mathbb{R} \mid x \leq 2\}$); in general $\vec{d}_H(A, B) \neq \vec{d}_H(B, A)$, i.e., $\vec{d}_H$ is not a metric because it does not satisfy the symmetry axiom; and if $\vec{d}_H(A, B) = 0$ then $A \subseteq B$. So we have to find a way to get meaningful information about the interior of B, since $\vec{d}_H(A, B) = 0$ means that $A \subseteq B$. To capture these cases, we introduce the notion of signed distances.

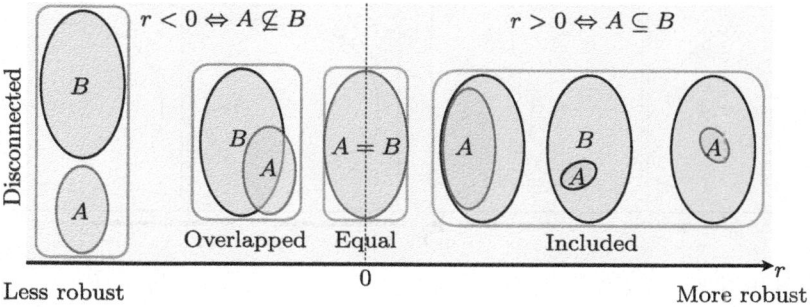

Fig. 2. The four RCC predicates between two spatial regions A and B and their respective robustness w.r.t. $A \subseteq B$. The two leftmost relations, "Disconnected" and "Partially Overlapped", have $r < 0$. The right side shows the cases where $A \subseteq B$ holds. The rightmost example is the most robust case, A is small relative to B and close to its center. On the left (satisfaction side) r is close to 0, A and B are about the same size with their boundaries close to each other.

Definition 4. *Signed (oriented) distances [13]. We define a signed distance function between a point $x \in \Delta$ relative to the set $\Omega \subseteq \Delta$, as*

$$sd_\Omega(x) := \begin{cases} d_\Omega(x), & \text{if } x \notin \Omega \\ -d_{\Delta \setminus \Omega}(x), & \text{if } x \in \Omega \end{cases}, \tag{5}$$

where $d_\Omega(x) := \inf_{y \in \Omega} d(x, y)$ and $d_{\Delta \setminus \Omega}(x) := \inf_{y \in \Delta \setminus \Omega} d(x, y)$.

Note that unlike $sd_\Omega(x)$, $d_\Omega(x)$ does not allow to capture information about the interior of Ω, since $d_\Omega(x) = 0$ for all $x \in \Omega$.

3   Robust $LTL \times MS^{\leq}$

The main difference between $LTL \times MS^{\leq}$ with boolean semantics and its robust variant is the definition of $\sqsubseteq$. The boolean semantics assigns a boolean value (true or false), while the robust semantics assigns a degree (a positive or negative value) to the truth value. To be able to distinguish between true and false, we need to introduce a sign. Given that the negative value means that the formula evaluates to false, we come up with the construction of the signed Hausdorff distance function `Dist` between two non-empty sets as follows:

$$\mathtt{Dist}(A, B) := \begin{cases} \vec{d}_H\left(A, \overline{B}\right), & \text{if } A \subseteq B \\ -\vec{d}_H\left(A, B\right), & \text{if } A \not\subseteq B \end{cases}, \tag{6}$$

where $\vec{d}_H$ is the *directed* Hausdorff distance. By combining $\vec{d}_H$ and the signed distance function, we can measure how "deep" or "far" one spatial term is relative to another. In practice, Fig. 2 shows our intuition about the robustness of "$\subseteq$". Moreover, Fig. 3 illustrates the motivation for defining the *subset or equal*

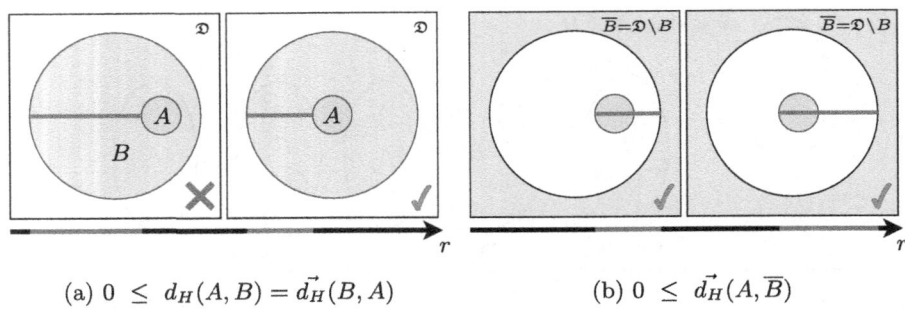

(a) $0 \leq d_H(A, B) = \vec{d_H}(B, A)$ (b) $0 \leq \vec{d_H}(A, \overline{B})$

Fig. 3. Difference of the directed Hausdorff distances between (a) two sets $A \subseteq B$ and (b) two sets $A \subseteq \overline{B}$. The directed Hausdorff distance between subsets closer to the boundary of their superset and the superset itself would give a higher distance than those closer to the center of the superset.

relation as $\vec{d_H}(A, \overline{B})$, if $A \subseteq B$, instead of just $\vec{d_H}(A, B)$. This gives us a distance r, which is our level of robustness. So we got the $LTL \times MS^{\leq}$ robust meaning for the formula $\rho_1 \sqsubseteq \rho_2$, which we will compute at a given time n by $\texttt{Dist}(\mathfrak{R}(\rho_1, n), \mathfrak{R}(\rho_2, n))$ as in (6).

Robustness of $LTL \times MS^{\leq}$ Formulas with $\sqsubseteq$. Let us use the Example 1. Let $\mathbf{C}$ be a compact set and let $\mathbf{T}$ be an unbounded curve, expanded by 0.5 units $\exists^{\leq 0.5}\mathbf{T} = \mathbf{T}'$. We will only consider the non-temporal part of (1c) between two spatial terms. Before we continue, a small change is required when using the "Disconnected" predicate due to the unsuitable definition of (6). Note that (1c) applies to (1b), which explicitly refers to the empty set $\perp$. From (1b) and (1a), DC is defined as $\texttt{DC}(\rho_1, \rho_2) = \texttt{EQ}(\rho_1 \sqcap \rho_2, \perp) = (\rho_1 \sqcap \rho_2 \sqsubseteq \perp) \wedge (\perp \sqsubseteq \rho_1 \sqcap \rho_2)$. If we try to measure the robustness of this predicate by directly applying our signed distance function (6) to it, we will end up computing the directed Hausdorff distances between the empty set and another set (which may or may not be empty). The Hausdorff distance has no meaning for empty sets, so it is undefined. Apart from the explicit mention of the empty set, another issue with (1b) is that we are trying to measure the distance between the two terms (their intersection) with respect to $\perp$, not the actual distance between ρ_1 and ρ_2. Intuitively, if ρ_1 and ρ_2 are separated, the robustness value should be the Hausdorff distance between them. And if they are not disconnected, we should still be able to assign a negative robustness in this case. We assume that two terms are disconnected if and only if they are contained in each other's complements. A concise way to redefine it, preserving the truth values of the Boolean semantics, that is also compatible with $\vec{d_H}$ is

$$\texttt{DC}(\rho_1, \rho_2) = \rho_1 \sqsubseteq \overline{\rho_2} \wedge \rho_2 \sqsubseteq \overline{\rho_1}. \tag{7}$$

This change will be enough as we will see later and also preserve the Boolean semantics $LTL \times MS^{\leq}$. Since the overlap is defined according to the definition above and our disconnected predicate is rewritten, we can proceed with the formulation of our robust semantics.

So, let us try to give meaning to the predicates (1a) and (1d). These predicates can be defined as follows:

$$\texttt{rEQ}(A, B) := \inf\{\texttt{Dist}(A, B), \texttt{Dist}(B, A)\}, \tag{8a}$$

$$\texttt{rI}(A, B) := \inf\{\texttt{Dist}(A, B), -\texttt{Dist}(B, A)\}. \tag{8b}$$

Informally, we can start seeing that we can replace every $\wedge$ operator by inf, and ($\neg$) by ($-$). We can continue to give meaning to (1b) and (1c). The other predicates can be defined by

$$\texttt{rDC}(A, B) := \inf\{\texttt{Dist}(A, \overline{B}), \texttt{Dist}(B, \overline{A})\}, \tag{9}$$

$$\texttt{rO}(A, B) := -\sup\{\texttt{rDC}(A, B), \texttt{Dist}(A, B), \texttt{Dist}(B, A)\}. \tag{10}$$

Now, from (9) and (10), we can write the robust expression of (2) as

$$\texttt{rO}(\mathbf{C}, \mathbf{T}') = -\sup\{\texttt{rDC}(\mathbf{C}, \mathbf{T}'), \texttt{Dist}(\mathbf{C}, \mathbf{T}'), \texttt{Dist}(\mathbf{T}', \mathbf{C})\}.$$

So, we have two cases. Between $\mathbf{C}$ and $\mathbf{T}'$ there is an overlap, which corresponds to $r > 0$; and $\mathbf{C}$ and $\mathbf{T}'$ are disconnected, which means $r < 0$. Figure 1c shows that $\mathbf{C}$ overlaps the trajectory $\mathbf{T}'$ and satisfies (2) $(r > 0)$, while Fig. 1d shows that $\mathbf{C}$ does not overlap the trajectory $\mathbf{T}'$ and does not satisfies (2) $(r < 0)$.

Let us turn our attention to how to compute the robustness value for the first case. To compute the aforementioned signed distances, we recall that $\mathbf{C} \not\sqsubseteq \mathbf{T}'$ and $\mathbf{T}' \not\sqsubseteq \mathbf{C}$, then $\texttt{Dist}(\mathbf{C}, \mathbf{T}') = -r_1$, and $\texttt{Dist}(\mathbf{T}', \mathbf{C}) = -\infty$. And also $\mathbf{C} \not\sqsubseteq \overline{\mathbf{T}'}$ and $\mathbf{T}' \not\sqsubseteq \overline{\mathbf{C}}$, so $\texttt{Dist}(\mathbf{C}, \overline{\mathbf{T}'}) = 0$, and $\texttt{Dist}(\mathbf{T}', \overline{\mathbf{C}}) = -\infty$. So the robustness value is $r_1 > 0$ as follows:

$$\texttt{rO}(\mathbf{C}, \mathbf{T}') = -\sup\{\inf\{-\infty, 0\}, -r_1, -\infty\}$$

$$= -\sup\{-\infty, -r_1, -\infty\} = r_1 > 0.$$

Now, let us turn our attention to the second case. In this case, we still have $\mathbf{C} \not\sqsubseteq \mathbf{T}'$ and $\mathbf{T}' \not\sqsubseteq \mathbf{C}$, thus $\texttt{Dist}(\mathbf{T}', \mathbf{C}) = -\infty$ and $\texttt{Dist}(\mathbf{C}, \mathbf{T}') = -r_1$. However, if $\texttt{O}(\mathbf{C}, \mathbf{T}')$ does not hold, then the subset relation $\mathbf{C} \sqsubseteq \overline{\mathbf{T}'}$ and $\mathbf{T}' \sqsubseteq \overline{\mathbf{C}}$ is satisfied. Thus, the corresponding directed Hausdorff distances are $\texttt{Dist}(\mathbf{C}, \overline{\mathbf{T}'}) = r_1 < \infty$ and $\texttt{Dist}(\mathbf{T}', \overline{\mathbf{C}}) = \infty$. Applying (3) to these four signed distances, the robustness value for this scenario is given by

$$\texttt{rO}(\mathbf{C}, \mathbf{T}') = -\sup\{\inf\{\infty, r_1\}, -r_1, -\infty\} = -r_1 < 0.$$

After these computations, it seems to be giving the robustness value properly.

Robustness of $LTL \times MS^{\leq}$ Formulas with $\sqsubseteq$ and $\mathcal{U}$. Until now, we have only considered a single frame in $\mathfrak{M}$ and its robustness at a single time point. However, to compute a robustness value for each time point, we need to incorporate the time modality $\mathcal{U}$. The property (3) uses $\square$. From $\square$ and $\diamondsuit$, we find that

$\Box\varphi$ is equal to $\neg(\top\,\mathcal{U}\,\neg\varphi)$. Intuitively, $(\mathfrak{M}, n) \models \neg(\top\,\mathcal{U}\,\neg\phi)$ means that $(\mathfrak{M}, n)$ satisfies a formula ϕ if for any $n > 0$, $\mathcal{A}[\![\phi]\!](\mathfrak{M}, n)$ is true. So, we can construct a disjunction that will infinitely often enumerate formulas with $\bigcirc$, such as

$$\bigwedge_{m>n}\left[(\underbrace{\bigcirc\ldots\bigcirc}_{m\times}\phi)\right].$$

Now, consider that ϕ is equal to (2) and that we map ($\wedge$) to (inf) as before. With some abuse of notation, we can express the robustness of $\Box$ for (3) as

$$\inf_{m>n}\left\{\mathbf{r0}\left(\mathbf{C}_{(m)}, \exists^{\le 0.5}\mathbf{T}\right)\right\} \text{ with } \mathbf{C}_{(i)} := \underbrace{\bigodot\ldots\bigodot}_{i\times}C, \tag{11}$$

where $\mathbf{C}_{(i)} = \mathfrak{N}(\mathbf{C}, i)$. Now, from the semantics of $\mathcal{U}$ [4], we translate $\phi_1\,\mathcal{U}\,\phi_2$ into

$$\bigvee_{m>n}\left[\underbrace{\bigcirc\ldots\bigcirc}_{m\times}\phi_2 \wedge \bigwedge_{k\in(n,m)} \underbrace{\bigcirc\ldots\bigcirc}_{k\times}\phi_1\right],$$

and we can give a robust meaning to $\mathcal{U}$ following the same reasoning for $\Box$. Now, consider that we map ($\vee$) to (sup), a similar way to the map we did for ($\wedge$) to (inf) and ($\neg$) to ($-$). Thus, the robust meaning for $\neg(\top\,\mathcal{U}\,\neg\phi)$ is given by

$$-\sup_{m>n}\left\{\inf\left\{-\mathbf{r0}\left(\mathbf{C}_{(m)}, \exists^{\le 0.5}\mathbf{T}\right), \inf_{k\in(n,m)}\top\right\}\right\},$$

which is indeed the same as (11) but is more general as $\mathcal{U}$. This concludes the robustness meaning of $\mathcal{U}$.

Robust $LTL \times MS^{\le}$ (r$LTL \times MS^{\le}$). To achieve our goal of providing robust semantics, we define $\rho_1 \sqsubseteq \rho_2$ according to (6). However, the Hausdorff distance is not defined when a set is evaluated as $\bot$ or $\top$. Thus, we need to redefine the function $\texttt{Dist}_{\bot,\top}$ to treat these corner cases. $\texttt{Dist}_{\bot,\top}$ is defined as

$$\texttt{Dist}_{\bot,\top}(A, B) := \begin{cases} \texttt{Dist}(A, B) & \text{if } A \subset \Delta, B \subset \Delta, A \ne \emptyset, \text{ and } B \ne \emptyset \\ f_\infty(A, B) & \text{otherwise} \end{cases}, \tag{12}$$

where $f_\infty(A, B) = +\infty$ if $A \subseteq B$, and $-\infty$ otherwise. Therefore, we are now able to define the r$LTL \times MS^{\le}$ semantics using $\texttt{Dist}_{\bot,\top}$.

Definition 5 (Formulas Semantics of rLTL × MS$^{\le}$). *The robust values of the formulas φ in a model $\mathfrak{M}$ are inductively defined by the semantic function $\mathcal{R}[\![\varphi]\!](\mathfrak{M}, n)$ as follows:*

$$\mathcal{R}[\![\varrho_1 \sqsubseteq \varrho_2]\!] \quad = \lambda \mathfrak{M}, n. \ \mathtt{Dist}_{\perp,\top}(\mathfrak{R}(\varrho_1, n), \mathfrak{R}(\varrho_2, n)),$$

$$\mathcal{R}[\![\neg \varphi]\!] \quad = \lambda \mathfrak{M}, n. \ -\mathcal{R}[\![\varphi]\!](\mathfrak{M}, n),$$

$$\mathcal{R}[\![\varphi_1 \wedge \varphi_2]\!] \quad = \lambda \mathfrak{M}, n. \ \inf\{\mathcal{R}[\![\varphi_1]\!](\mathfrak{M}, n), \mathcal{R}[\![\varphi_2]\!](\mathfrak{M}, n)\}, \tag{13}$$

$$\mathcal{R}[\![\varphi_1 \mathcal{U} \varphi_2]\!] \quad = \lambda \mathfrak{M}, n. \ \sup_{m > n}\left\{\inf\left\{\mathcal{R}[\![\varphi_2]\!](\mathfrak{M}, n), \inf_{k \in (n,m)} \mathcal{R}[\![\varphi_1]\!](\mathfrak{M}, k)\right\}\right\},$$

$$\mathcal{R}[\![\varphi_1 \mathcal{S} \varphi_2]\!] \quad = \lambda \mathfrak{M}, n. \ \sup_{m < n}\left\{\inf\left\{\mathcal{R}[\![\varphi_2]\!](\mathfrak{M}, n), \inf_{k \in (m,n)} \mathcal{R}[\![\varphi_1]\!](\mathfrak{M}, k)\right\}\right\}.$$

where n is a time point in the set of natural numbers $\mathbb{N}$.

From the shorthand $\varphi_1 \vee \varphi_2 \equiv \neg(\neg\varphi_1 \wedge \neg\varphi_2)$, we can derive that

$$\mathcal{R}[\![\varphi_1 \vee \varphi_2]\!] = \lambda \mathfrak{M}, n. \ -\inf\{-\mathcal{R}[\![\varphi_1]\!](\mathfrak{M}, n), -\mathcal{R}[\![\varphi_2]\!](\mathfrak{M}, n)\} \tag{14}$$
$$= \lambda \mathfrak{M}, n. \ \sup\{\mathcal{R}[\![\varphi_1]\!](\mathfrak{M}, n), \mathcal{R}[\![\varphi_2]\!](\mathfrak{M}, n)\}.$$

However, it is essential to show that the robust interpretation provided by (13) preserves the original semantics of the $LTL \times MS^{\leq}$ formula.

4   Semantic Preservation of R$LTL \times MS^{\leq}$

In this section, we formalize the correspondence between the robust semantics of r$LTL \times MS^{\leq}$ and the classical semantics of $LTL \times MS^{\leq}$, establishing semantic preservation via an abstraction relation. First, we demonstrate the soundness of the predicates.

Lemma 1 (The robust 'Overlapped' predicate is sound). $\mathtt{r0}(A, B) > 0$ *if* $\mathtt{0}(A, B)$ *and* $\mathtt{r0}(A, B) < 0$ *if* $\neg\mathtt{0}(A, B)$ *for all* A, B

Proof (sketch). Assume that $\vec{d}_H(A, \overline{B}) = r_1'$, $\vec{d}_H(B, \overline{A}) = r_2'$, $\vec{d}_H(A, B) = r_1 < \infty$, and $\vec{d}_H(B, A) = r_2 < \infty$. Assume also that $A \subset \Delta$, $B \subset \Delta$, $A \neq \emptyset$, and $B \neq \emptyset$. We have to show that

$$\inf\{-\mathtt{rDC}(A, B), -\mathtt{Dist}(A, B), -\mathtt{Dist}(B, A)\} > 0 \text{ if } \mathtt{0}(A, B) \text{ for all } A, B, \text{ and}$$

$$\inf\{-\mathtt{rDC}(A, B), -\mathtt{Dist}(A, B), -\mathtt{Dist}(B, A)\} < 0 \text{ if } \neg\mathtt{0}(A, B) \text{ for all } A, B.$$

1. Case when $\mathtt{0}(A, B)$. Consider that $\mathtt{0}(A, B)$ holds, then $\mathtt{r0}(A, B) > 0$:

$$\mathtt{r0}(A, B) = \inf\{-\inf\{-r_1', -r_2'\}, r_1, r_2\} > 0$$
$$= -\sup\{\inf\{-r_1', -r_2'\}, -r_1, -r_2\} > 0 \tag{15}$$

2. Case when $\neg\mathtt{0}(A, B)$ and $A \cap B = \perp$. If A is disconnected from B, $A \subseteq \overline{B}$ and $B \subseteq \overline{A}$ hold, then $\mathtt{Dist}(A, \overline{B}) = \vec{d}_H(A, B) = r_1$ and $\mathtt{Dist}(B, \overline{A}) = \vec{d}_H(B, A) = r_2$. Also $A \not\subseteq B$ and $B \not\subseteq A$, then $\mathtt{Dist}(A, B) = -\vec{d}_H(A, B) = -r_1$ and $\mathtt{Dist}(B, A) = -\vec{d}_H(B, A) = -r_2$. Thus, the robustness value is

$$\mathtt{r0}(A, B) = -\sup\{\inf\{r_1, r_2\}, -r_1, -r_2\} = -\inf\{r_1, r_2\} < 0. \tag{16}$$

3. Case when $\neg 0\,(A, B)$ and $A = B$. We have $\vec{d}_H(A, B) = r_1 = 0$, $\vec{d}_H(B, A) = r_2 = 0$, $\vec{d}_H(A, \overline{B}) = r_1' < \infty$, and $\vec{d}_H(B, \overline{A}) = r_2' < \infty$. Since $A = B \Rightarrow A \subseteq B$, the first branches of $\text{Dist}(A, B)$ and $\text{Dist}(B, A)$ are chosen. Moreover $A \not\subseteq \overline{B}$ and $A \not\subseteq \overline{A}$, thus the second branches of $\text{Dist}(B, \overline{A}) = -\vec{d}_H(B, \overline{A})$ and $\text{Dist}(A, \overline{B}) = -\vec{d}_H(A, \overline{B})$ are chosen. So the robustness value is

$$\text{r0}\,(A, B) = -\sup\left\{\inf\left\{-r_1', -r_2'\right\}, 0^+, 0^+\right\} < 0. \tag{17}$$

The result is $-0^+ = 0^-$. This means that even the smallest change in the location of the spatial terms will produce a positive robustness value. It also means that a negative robustness value will result when one of the terms shrinks and moves 'into' the other term.

4. Case when $\neg 0\,(A, B)$ and $A \subset B$. Since $A \subset B \Rightarrow A \subseteq B$, $\text{Dist}(A, \overline{B}) = -\vec{d}_H(A, \overline{B}) = -r_1' > -\infty$, as $A \not\subseteq \overline{B}$ and $A \subseteq B$, $\text{Dist}(B, \overline{A}) = -\vec{d}_H(B, \overline{A}) = -r_2' > -\infty$, as $B \not\subseteq \overline{A}$ and $A \subseteq B$, $\text{Dist}(A, B) = \vec{d}_H(A, \overline{B}) = r_1' < \infty$ as $A \subseteq B$, and $\text{Dist}(B, A) = -\vec{d}_H(B, A) = -r_2 < \infty$, as $B \not\subseteq A$. Then, applying (3), the robustness value is $\text{r0}\,(A, B) = -r_1' < 0$. Note that if we flip the subset relation i.e. $B \subseteq A$, we would have $-r_2' < 0$ instead.

Now, assume that A or B can be $\top$ or $\bot$. These are the corner cases $+\infty$ if $A \subseteq B$ and $-\infty$ otherwise. They are covered by the definition of $\text{Dist}_{\bot,\top}$.   □

The soundness lemmas for the remaining predicates are omitted as they follow analogous reasoning and do not offer additional information.

We proceed with the correspondence of both semantics. Let $v \in \{0, 1\}$ and $v' \in \mathbb{R} \setminus \{0\} \cup \{-\infty, +\infty\}$ two values. $\approx$ is a preservation function defined by $v' \approx v$ if $v = 1$ and $v' > 0$, or $v = 0$ and $v' < 0$. $v' \not\approx v$ otherwise. Therefore, this abstraction relation maps robust satisfaction values to their corresponding classical Boolean values. This mapping enables us to relate the classical semantics of an $LTL \times MS^{\le}$ formula, denoted by $\mathcal{A}$, to the robust semantics of its $rLTL \times MS^{\le}$ counterpart, denoted by $\mathcal{R}$. Specifically, when composed with this relation, the robust semantics yield the classical interpretation.

Lemma 2 (Semantic Preservation). *If $LTL \times MS^{\le}$ is equipped with semantics $\mathcal{A}$, and $rLTL \times MS^{\le}$ with the semantics $\mathcal{R}$ then we have $\approx \circ \mathcal{R} = \mathcal{A}$.*

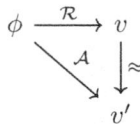

Proof (sketch). The proof proceeds by structural induction on ϕ.

1. The base case is $\phi = \varrho_1 \sqsubseteq \varrho_2$. So, we have to show

$$\text{Dist}(\mathfrak{R}\,(\varrho_1, n), \mathfrak{R}\,(\varrho_2, n)) > 0 \approx \mathcal{A}[\![\varrho_1 \sqsubseteq \varrho_2]\!](m, n) \text{ for all } m, n.$$

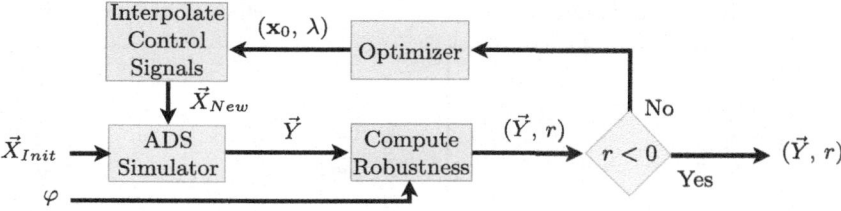

Fig. 4. Falsification loop workflow between simulator, robustness function $\mathcal{R}[\![\varphi]\!]$, optimization algorithm, and interpolation of control signals (new state $\mathbf{x}_0$ and control points λ). The inputs are the initial guess $\vec{X}_{Init}$ and formula φ while the outputs are $\vec{Y}$ and r.

We show if $\texttt{Dist}(\mathfrak{R}(\varrho_1, n), \mathfrak{R}(\varrho_2, n)) > 0$ then $\mathcal{A}[\![\varrho_1 \sqsubseteq \varrho_2]\!](m, n)$, and $\mathcal{A}[\![\varrho_1 \not\sqsubseteq \varrho_2]\!](m, n)$ otherwise. Assume that $\texttt{Dist}(\mathfrak{R}(\varrho_1, n), \mathfrak{R}(\varrho_2, n)) < 0$. This is direct, ρ_1, ρ_2 overlap. Lemma 1 shows the other way around. Assume that $\texttt{Dist}(\mathfrak{R}(\varrho_1, n), \mathfrak{R}(\varrho_2, n)) < 0$. This is direct, ρ_1, ρ_2 are disconnected. The proof for the other way around is skipped as it is similar to Lemma 1. Assume that $\texttt{Dist}(\mathfrak{R}(\varrho_1, n), \mathfrak{R}(\varrho_2, n)) = 0^+$ or $\texttt{Dist}(\mathfrak{R}(\varrho_1, n), \mathfrak{R}(\varrho_2, n)) > 0^+$. Therefore, ρ_1, ρ_2 are equal or included, $\varrho_1 \sqsubseteq \varrho_2$.

2. Inductive case when $\phi = \neg\varphi$. We have to show $-\mathcal{R}[\![\varphi]\!](m, n) \approx \mathcal{A}[\![\neg\varphi]\!](m, n)$ for all m, n. Assume $\mathcal{A}[\![\neg\varphi]\!](m, n) = 1$ then $\mathcal{R}[\![\varphi]\!](m, n) < 0$, while $\mathcal{R}[\![\neg\varphi]\!](m, n) = -\mathcal{R}[\![\varphi]\!](m, n) > 0$. Assume $\mathcal{A}[\![\neg\varphi]\!](m, n) = 0$ then $\mathcal{R}[\![\varphi]\!](m, n) > 0$, while $\mathcal{R}[\![\neg\varphi]\!](m, n) = -\mathcal{R}[\![\varphi]\!](m, n) < 0$.

3. Inductive case when $\phi = \varphi_1 \wedge \varphi_2$. We have to show $inf\{\mathcal{R}[\![\varphi_1]\!](m, n), \mathcal{R}[\![\varphi_2]\!](m, n)\} > 0 \approx \mathcal{A}[\![\varphi_1 \wedge \varphi_2]\!](m, n)$ for all m, n. We skip this case and the inductive cases when $\phi = \varphi_1 \, \mathcal{U} \, \varphi_2$ and $\phi = \varphi_1 \, \mathcal{S} \, \varphi_2$. $\qquad\Box$

5   Empirical Evaluation

To evaluate our approach, we employ robustness-guided falsification, extending the method proposed in [1] to incorporate the $rLTL \times MS^{\leq}$ semantics defined in (13). This enables us to reformulate the task of finding counterexamples to a given system and property as the following optimization problem:

$$\arg\min \mathcal{R}[\![\varphi]\!](\mathbf{x}_0) \text{ such that } \mathcal{R}[\![\varphi]\!](\mathbf{x}_0) = r < 0, \tag{18}$$

where $\mathbf{x}_0$ represents the initial conditions and the acceleration input signal of the system under test. Figure 4 illustrates the complete falsification loop.

To demonstrate the practicality of our falsification workflow, we examine two properties that an ADS is expected to satisfy. The first property, denoted by ϕ_1 and defined in (3), is associated with the robust semantics presented in (11). The second property, denoted by ϕ_2, is given by

$$\Diamond \left[\neg \mathsf{0} \left(\mathbf{C}, \exists^{\leq 0.5} \mathbf{T} \right) \right]. \tag{19}$$

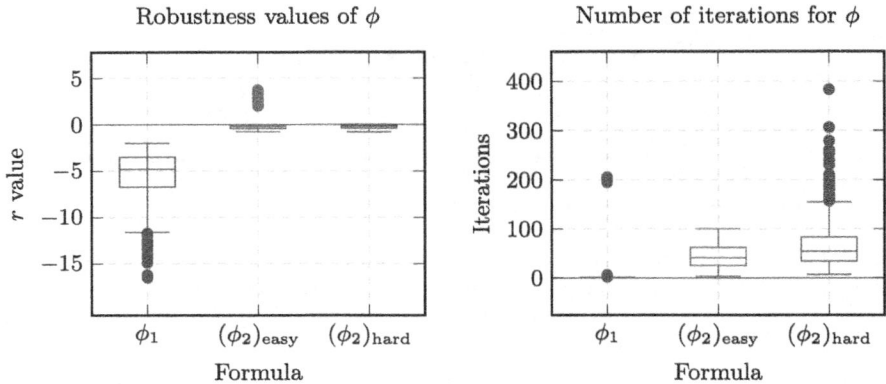

Fig. 5. Robustness values vs Iterations for SA with 1000 runs.

Note that $\neg\phi_1$ is equal to ϕ_2. Consequently, the robust semantics of ϕ_2 is expressed as:

$$- \inf_{m>n} \left\{ \mathtt{r0}\left(\mathbf{C}_{(m)}, \exists^{\le 0.5}\mathbf{T}\right) \right\} = \sup_{m>n} \left\{ -\mathtt{r0}\left(\mathbf{C}_{(m)}, \exists^{\le 0.5}\mathbf{T}\right) \right\}. \qquad (20)$$

Although the falsification of ϕ_1 is relatively straightforward – requiring that the term $\mathbf{C}$ does not overlap with $\exists^{\le 0.5}\mathbf{T}$ at *at least* one time point – the falsification of ϕ_2 is less intuitive. Since ϕ_2 contains the negation of $\mathtt{0}\left(\mathbf{C}, \exists^{\le 0.5}\mathbf{T}\right)$, falsifying ϕ_2 effectively means ensuring that $\mathbf{C}$ and $\exists^{\le 0.5}\mathbf{T}$ overlap. In practical terms, falsification of ϕ_2 corresponds to ensuring that $\mathbf{C}$ follows the reference trajectory $\mathbf{T}$ within a tolerance of 0.5 units. Achieving this requires the predicate $\mathtt{r0}\left(\mathbf{C}_{(m)}, \exists^{\le 0.5}\mathbf{T}\right)$ to hold at every time point m, making the falsification of ϕ_2 computationally more demanding than that of ϕ_1. As illustrated in Fig. 5, the average number of iterations required to falsify ϕ_1 is significantly lower than for ϕ_2. Generally speaking, falsifying formulas involving $\diamondsuit$ is more challenging than those involving $\square$ when using the robustness-based formulation in (18).

For ϕ_1, the initial guess is a trajectory that perfectly follows the reference trajectory, giving an initial robustness of $r = 0.5$. For ϕ_2, we consider two variants: $(\phi_2)_{\text{easy}}$, where the initial trajectory $\mathbf{C}$ runs parallel to $\exists^{\le 0.5}\mathbf{T}$ with an initial robustness of $r = 3.5$; and $(\phi_2)_{\text{hard}}$, where $\mathbf{C}$ increasingly deviates from $\exists^{\le 0.5}\mathbf{T}$, resulting in an initial robustness of approximately $r \sim 35$.

We selected Uniform Sampling (US) as the baseline for comparison with the Simulated Annealing (SA) method [5] and the Cross Entropy (CE) method. For SA, the initial temperature parameter is $T_0 = 5$ with a step amplitude of $\alpha = 0.05$. For CE, we sampled 10 traces from a Gaussian distribution. From these, we selected two trajectories with the lowest robustness values. These trajectories were then used to update the mean of the Gaussian distribution, while the standard deviation was kept fixed at $\alpha = 0.05$. For each property, we per-

Metric	US			SA			CE		
	ϕ_1	$(\phi_2)_{easy}$	$(\phi_2)_{hard}$	ϕ_1	$(\phi_2)_{easy}$	$(\phi_2)_{hard}$	ϕ_1	$(\phi_2)_{easy}$	$(\phi_2)_{hard}$
Success rate	1	0	0	1	0.94	1	1	1	1
Min. robust.	-127.98	–	–	-16.48	-0.78	-0.81	-20.35	-0.85	-0.84
Mean robust.	-43.39	–	–	-5.44	-0.10	-0.23	-9.65	-0.29	-0.23
Max. robust.	-2.18	–	–	-2.05	3.93	-0.004	-4.29	-0.004	-0.002
Min. iter.	1	500	500	1	3	7	1	1	4
Mean iter.	1	500	500	1.32	45.95	64.1	1	6.57	12.08
Max. iter.	1	500	500	6	500	383	1	23	62

Fig. 6. Performance metrics for formulas ϕ_1 and ϕ_2 (easy and hard variants) over US, SA, and CE methods. The metrics are the success rate of falsification with 1000 runs, the min, mean, and max of the robustness values, and the min, mean, and max number of iterations to falsification.

form 1000 falsification attempts per optimizer, with each attempt limited to a maximum of 500 iterations.

System Under Test and Simulation. The system models a simplified vehicle whose motion is governed by the acceleration vector $\mathbf{a}$. At any given time, the position of the vehicle $\mathbf{x}$ is represented by the spatial term $\mathbf{C}_{(i)}$. The state of the system is defined as $\mathbf{q} = (\mathbf{x}, \mathbf{v}, \mathbf{a})$, where $\mathbf{v}$ denotes the velocity vector. Given that the input signal $\mathbf{a}$ is known throughout the simulation window, the full state trajectory $\mathbf{q}$ can be reconstructed at each time point i by integrating $\mathbf{a}$. Moreover, the system will run for $t \in [0, 10]$, at an acquisition rate of 10Hz, in two dimensions $\Delta = [-20, 20]^2$. Regarding the search space, it is determined by the initial state of the system $\mathbf{q}_0 = (\mathbf{x}_0, \mathbf{v}_0, \mathbf{a}_0)$, and the acceleration control points λ, spaced by $1\,s$. Thus, the dimension of the search space is: $2 \times (|\mathbf{q}_0| + |\lambda|) = 2 \times 3 + 2 \times 10 = 26$. The admissible bounds for the initial position are $\mathbf{x}_0 = [-5, 5] \times [-15.25, -14.75]$, for $\mathbf{v}_0$ is $[-1, 1]^2$, and $\lambda_i \in [-3, 2]^{20}$. Furthermore, we impose a smoothness constraint on the input signal, which requires that the change in acceleration between consecutive time steps satisfies $|\mathbf{a}_{i+1} - \mathbf{a}_i| \leq 2$.

By choosing a spline to interpolate the acceleration input signal between control points, we can merge the simulation and interpolation steps. Consider a piecewise cubic trajectory between two consecutive control points $\mathbf{x}(t) = \mathbf{A}t^3 + \mathbf{B}t^2 + \mathbf{C}t + \mathbf{D}$, by enforcing Hermite constraints, we can ensure a C^1 continuous trajectory with its second derivative (acceleration) continuous, although not differentiable. So, assuming a piecewise linear acceleration signal, we can reconstruct $\mathbf{q}$ in dense time,

$$\mathbf{x}_i(t) = \mathbf{x}_{i-1} + \mathbf{v}_{i-1}t_i + \frac{\mathbf{a}_{i-1}}{2}t_i^2 + \frac{\mathbf{a}_i - \mathbf{a}_{i-1}}{6}t_i^3, \quad \text{for all } t_i.$$

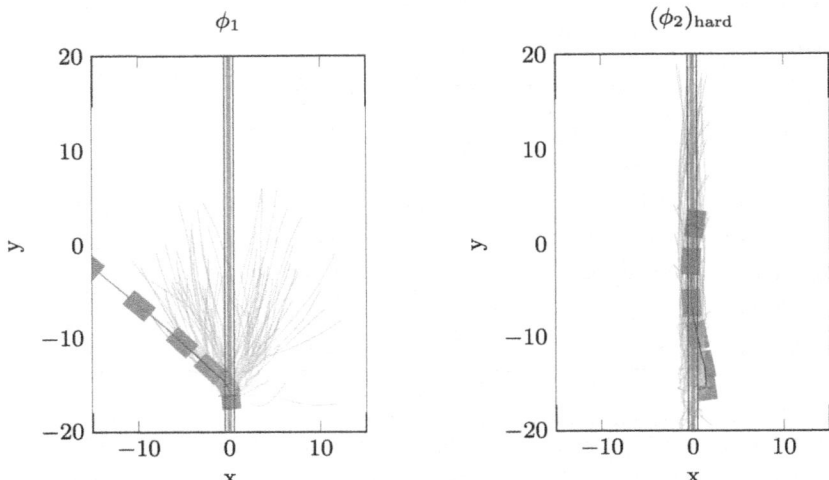

Fig. 7. Multiple trajectories generated using the SA method for the property (3) and its negation, corresponding to ϕ_1 and $(\phi_2)_{\text{hard}}$, respectively. Red squares indicate the points on the trajectory with maximum robustness across 1000 runs.

Evaluation Results. Figure 6 shows the results of our experiments. US is the best optimizer for finding trajectories with low robustness value with respect to ϕ_1 and the worst with respect to both variants ϕ_2. Since US generates, according to a uniform distribution, new $\mathbf{x}_0$ within admissible intervals, this is the easiest way to generate a trajectory that rapidly deviates from $\exists^{\leq 0.5}\mathbf{T}$. While SA and CE sample according to a Gaussian distribution, the steps between iterations are much more conservative than US, which may seem like a drawback, analyzing the mean robustness values are -5.44 and -9.65, respectively. However, considering the average number of iterations until falsification, SA (1.32) and CE (1) show the same performance compared to US.

The falsification results of the variants ϕ_2 show a clear advantage for the CE method. For $(\phi_2)_{\text{easy}}$, the average number of iterations is ~ 46 for SA and ~ 7 for CE. This large difference is due to the CE work with 10 trajectories per iteration, which leads to a longer computation time compared to SA, but the steps are much more fine-grained than the ones sampled by SA, leading to fewer iterations needed to falsify the properties.

Although SA did not falsify $(\phi_2)_{\text{easy}}$ in some runs (success rate 0.94 and maximum $r = 3.93$), Fig. 5 shows that these runs were outliers, and the robustness values obtained were heavily concentrated around the average robustness value $r = 0.1$. In fact, the same is true for $(\phi_2)_{\text{hard}}$, and in this case the success rate is 1, better than the *easy* variant.

For $(\phi_2)_{\text{hard}}$, which has an initial robustness value of $r \sim 35$, a 10x increase, CE in particular has a good performance of only ~ 12 iterations until falsification. In this variant, the differences between iterations until falsification between

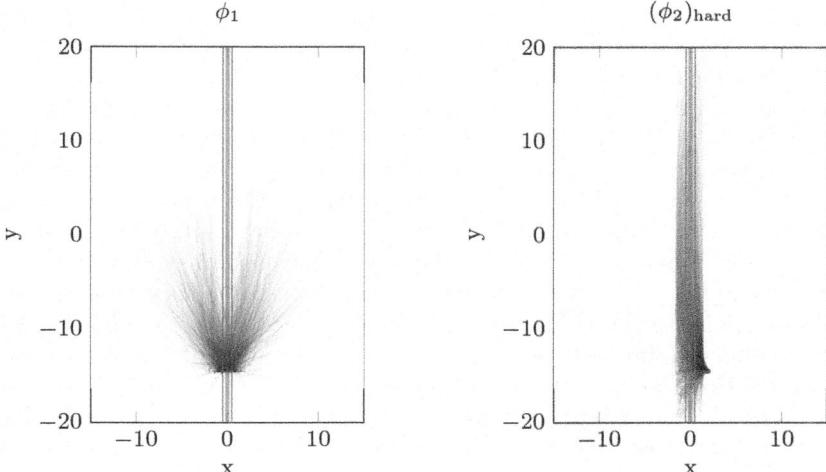

Fig. 8. Density maps of multiple trajectories generated using the SA method for the property (3) and its negation, corresponding to ϕ_1 and $(\phi_2)_{\text{hard}}$, respectively.

CE and SA are even clearer. On average, CE only takes ~ 12 iterations to falsify $(\phi_2)_{\text{hard}}$, while SA takes ~ 64. However, the robustness values in both methods are virtually the same, which makes sense, there is a small variation of trajectories of $\mathbf{C}$ that overlap $\mathbf{T}$ with 0.5 units of tolerance. Both methods found solutions that are close to the global minimum.

Figure 7 presents example trajectories generated by SA during attempts to falsify (ϕ_1) and $(\phi_2)_{hard}$. The squares indicate the position and orientation of the vehicle, showing a leftward motion for (ϕ_1) and a forward motion for $(\phi_2)_{\text{hard}}$. Figure 8 illustrates the distribution of falsified trajectories on 1000 SA runs, with the highest density corresponding to the initial position of the vehicle. It is evident that the trajectories diverge from the reference trajectory in the case of (ϕ_1), while they tend to converge to the reference trajectory in $(\phi_2)_{\text{hard}}$.

6   Related Work

Signal Spatio-Temporal Logic (SSTL) [19], Spatial-Temporal Logic (SpaTeL) [10], and Spatio-Temporal Reach and Escape Logic (STREL) [3], are three different spatial extensions of STL, which are equipped with Boolean and quantitative semantics. In all these cases, the interpretation and computation of the degree of satisfaction of the respective spatio-temporal formulas is based on the robustness concept presented by Donzé and Maler [6].

There are classes of spatio-temporal logic closely related to $LTL \times MS^{\leq}$ that have been equipped with alternative notions of satisfaction degrees. For example, Li et al. [15] introduced the Spatio-Temporal Specification Language (STSL), a fragment of $STL \times S4_u$, which defines both Boolean and quantitative semantics. STSL employs two atomic predicates: the *subset or equal* relation between two spatial terms and a threshold predicate on a signal (characteristic of STL). Similarly to $LTL \times MS^\leq$, STSL includes the *subset or equal* relation between spatial entities; however, its Boolean semantics are evaluated differently. Specifically, the *value* of a term is computed using an alternative definition of $\mathfrak{N}$. In their case, the satisfaction of the formula $(w, t) \models \rho_1 \sqsubseteq \rho_2$ is given by the condition $\mathfrak{N}(\rho_1, w, t) \leq \mathfrak{N}(\rho_2, w, t)$, where $\mathfrak{N}$ denotes the valuation of a term in a metric space. Li et al. [16] applied robustness-guided falsification and parameter synthesis techniques to test an adaptive cruise control system and to plan quadrotor trajectories according to STSL specifications. In their setting, spatial terms correspond to closed intervals $[a, b]$, with the valuation $\mathfrak{N}$ defined as $b - a$.

Our notion of robustness is based on the interpretation of a quantified *subset or equal* relation. We considered the generalization of the signed distance used in [7], a signed distance between two sets [13], instead of a point and a set. In our work, we assumed two-dimensional terms in simple shapes, circles, and bounding boxes, which makes non-trivial the quantification of *subset or equal*.

Madsen et al. [17] also studied this quantification of the relation $\sqsubseteq$ to establish a formal comparison between two STL formulas. They have considered signed Hausdorff distances, symmetric difference measures, and a convex combination between the two. Additionally, the spatial sets under consideration were restricted to boxes.

7   Conclusions and Future Work

We have presented a *robust semantics* for $LTL \times MS^\leq$, as well as a new definition of DC and empirically validated its feasibility through robust-guided falsification. For future work, we intend to extend our approach by applying robust-guided falsification and parameter synthesis within a more realistic ADS simulation environment, such as through integration with the CARLA simulator. We also plan to apply a more sophisticated ADS model and explore its applicability to other domains, such as warehouse robotics. Additionally, the current collision detection mechanism, which operates at each time point, offers opportunities for optimization, including the use of spatial data structures, such as quad-trees, to improve efficiency.

Acknowledgments. This work is supported by the European Union/Next Generation EU, through the Recovery and Resilience Plan (PRR)[Project Route 25 with Nr. C645463824-00000063].

References

1. Abbas, H., Fainekos, G., Sankaranarayanan, S., Ivancic, F., Gupta, A.: Probabilistic temporal logic falsification of cyber-physical systems. ACM Trans. Embed. Comput. Syst. **12**(2s):95:1–95:30 (2013)

2. Aiello, M., Pratt-Hartmann, I., van Benthem, J.: Handbook of Spatial Logics. Springer, Cham (2007)
3. Bartocci, E., Bortolussi, L., Loreti, M., Nenzi, L.: Monitoring mobile and spatially distributed cyber-physical systems. In: MEMOCODE, pp. 146–155. ACM (2017)
4. de Matos Pedro, A., Silva, T., Sequeira, T.F., Lourenço, J., Seco, J.C., Ferreira, C.: Monitoring of spatio-temporal properties with nonlinear SAT solvers. Int. J. Softw. Tools Technol. Transf. **26**(2), 169–188 (2024)
5. Delahaye, D., Chaimatanan, S., Mongeau, M.: Simulated annealing: from basics to applications. In: Handbook of Metaheuristics, pp. 1–35 (2019)
6. Donzé, A., Maler, O.: Robust satisfaction of temporal logic over real-valued signals. In: Chatterjee, K., Henzinger, T.A. (eds.) FORMATS 2010. LNCS, vol. 6246, pp. 92–106. Springer, Heidelberg (2010). https://doi.org/10.1007/978-3-642-15297-9_9
7. Fainekos, G.E., Pappas, G.J.: Robustness of temporal logic specifications for continuous-time signals. Theor. Comput. Sci. **410**(42), 4262–4291 (2009)
8. Fainekos, G.E., Sankaranarayanan, S., Ueda, K., Yazarel, H.: Verification of automotive control applications using s-taliro. In: American Control Conference, ACC 2012, Montreal, QC, Canada, 27–29 June 2012, pp. 3567–3572. IEEE (2012)
9. Gabelaia, D., Kontchakov, R., Kurucz, Á., Wolter, F., Zakharyaschev, M.: Combining spatial and temporal logics: expressiveness vs. complexity. J. Artif. Intell. Res. **23**, 167–243 (2005)
10. Haghighi, I., Jones, A., Kong, Z., Bartocci, E., Grosu, R., Belta, C.: Spatel: a novel spatial-temporal logic and its applications to networked systems. In: HSCC, pp. 189–198. ACM (2015)
11. Hasuo, I., Ishikawa, F.: Safety Assurance Under Uncertainties: From Software to Cyber-Physical/Machine Learning Systems. CRC Press (2025)
12. Jungeblut, P., Kleist, L., Miltzow, T.: The complexity of the Hausdorff distance. Discret. Comput. Geom. **71**(1), 177–213 (2024)
13. Kraft, D.: Computing the Hausdorff distance of two sets from their distance functions. Int. J. Comput. Geom. Appl. **30**(01), 19–49 (2020)
14. Kurucz, A., Wolter, F., Zakharyaschev, M.: Modal logics for metric spaces: open problems. In: We Will Show Them! Essays in Honour of Dov Gabbay, vol. 2, pp. 193–108. College Publications (2005)
15. Li, T., et al.: STSL: a novel spatio-temporal specification language for cyber-physical systems. In: QRS 2020), pp. 309–319. IEEE (2020)
16. Li, T., et al.: Runtime verification of spatio-temporal specification language. Mob. Netw. Appl. **26**(6), 2392–2406 (2021)
17. Madsen, C., et al.: Metrics for signal temporal logic formulae. In: CDC, pp. 1542–1547. IEEE (2018)
18. United Nations. Vienna convention on road traffic (1968). https://unece.org/DAM/trans/conventn/Conv_road_traffic_EN.pdf. Accessed 11 Apr 2025
19. Nenzi, L., Bortolussi, L., Ciancia, V., Loreti, M., Massink, M.: Qualitative and quantitative monitoring of spatio-temporal properties with SSTL. Log. Methods Comput. Sci. **14**(4) (2018)
20. Zhang, Z., Lyu, D., Arcaini, P., Ma, L., Hasuo, I., Zhao, J.: Falsifai: falsification of AI-enabled hybrid control systems guided by time-aware coverage criteria. IEEE Trans. Softw. Eng. **49**(4), 1842–1859 (2023)

Data-Driven Synthesis of Stochastic Fault Trees for Proactive Maintenance of Railway Vehicles

Laura Carnevali[1], Alessandro Fantechi[1], Gloria Gori[1]([✉]),
Denis Vreshtazi[1], Alessandro Borselli[2], Maria Rosaria Cefaloni[2],
and Lucio Rota[2]

[1] DINFO, University of Florence, Florence, Italy
{laura.carnevali,alessandro.fantechi,gloria.gori}@unifi.it,
denis.vreshtazi@edu.unifi.it
[2] Trenord s.r.l., Milan, Italy
{alessandro.borselli,mariarosaria.cefaloni,lucio.rota}@trenord.it

Abstract. The spreading of sensor technologies has enabled railway operators to collect increasing amounts of granular data on relevant events of components and systems of railway vehicles and infrastructure, presenting unprecedented opportunities to develop predictive failure models. Our research introduces a novel methodology for synthesizing stochastic fault tree models by strategically integrating extensive diagnostic data logs, maintenance records, and domain-specific knowledge to predict component and system-level reliability dynamics. To demonstrate the potential of the approach, we apply it to the traction control unit of a fleet of regional passenger trains, showing a scalable framework for predictive failure assessment across diverse railway vehicle configurations. By leveraging existing diagnostic infrastructure without requiring additional sensor investments, our approach represents a pathway from reactive diagnostic practices to proactive maintenance strategies.

1 Introduction

Synthesizing maintenance strategies in complex cyber-physical systems, particularly in transportation systems, represents a critical challenge at the intersection of reliability engineering and operational economics. The railway industry exemplifies this challenge, as it faces a striking contrast in maintenance capabilities across its fleet generations. Modern high-speed trains are equipped with sophisticated sensor networks that enable comprehensive condition monitoring and predictive maintenance (PdM) features. However, a significant fraction of the operating fleet consists of older vehicles that rely primarily on traditional time-based maintenance plans. While these legacy vehicles may already incorporate multiple basic diagnostic functions for fault detection and reporting, they lack advanced predictive capabilities, despite being more prone to failures and requiring more frequent corrective maintenance interventions [4,14]. This technological

© The Author(s), under exclusive license to Springer Nature Switzerland AG 2025
A. Remke and B. Steffen (Eds.): FMICS 2025, LNCS 16040, pp. 162–181, 2025.
https://doi.org/10.1007/978-3-032-00942-5_9

gap in railway fleets creates a compelling opportunity for innovation. The older vehicles are typically equipped with diagnostic sensors (monitoring vibration, temperature, electrical current, mechanical stress, etc.), primarily used to help maintenance engineers or drivers to detect anomalies and trigger maintenance alerts. However, data collected by these sensors also contain valuable patterns and trends that, if properly analyzed, could predict impending failures [14]. The challenge lies in developing methodologies that can effectively leverage this existing diagnostic infrastructure for predictive purposes without requiring further costs for sensor network upgrades. Furthermore, when fault-to-failure propagations (i.e., errors propagating in components up to cause their failure) and failure-to-fault propagations (i.e., component failures acting as external faults for other components) have probabilistic characterization in time, quantitative evaluation of stochastic models of the system failure logic enables derivation of metrics of dependability [18,29,31], supporting early validation of design choices and development of predictive analytics for proactive fault management [30].

Fault Tree Analysis (FTA) has long been established as a reliable method for analyzing system failures in various domains. Its structured approach to mapping failure pathways and understanding component interdependencies makes it particularly suitable for complex systems like the ones onboard railway vehicles. While FTA has traditionally been used in system design and reliability analysis, its application in real-time PdM represents a possible opportunity. The incorporation of dynamic probability assessment into Fault Trees (FTs), especially using real-time sensor data, offers a promising perspective for enhancing their utility in operational contexts.

This paper presents a novel application of FTA to bridge the said gap between the available diagnostic infrastructure and the lack of advanced predictive capabilities, by exploiting existing sensor networks in railway vehicles. Our approach leverages FaultFlow [7,8,26], an open-source library developed by our research group at the University of Florence, to analyze component and system failures, transforming traditional FTs into dynamic predictive models, continuously updated with probability assessments derived from operational sensor data. Given the hierarchical nature of railway systems, where train-level reliability depends on coach-level system reliability, our methodology employs a dual-model approach: FTA for detailed coach-level analysis of system failures and Reliability Block Diagrams (RBDs) for train-level reliability assessment considering system redundancy and operational constraints. The proposed methodology offers several advantages:

1. Cost-effectiveness by using of existing basic diagnostic infrastructure.
2. Integration with established diagnostic systems and maintenance protocols.
3. Transparent decision-making processes based on well-understood FT models.
4. Applicability to legacy railway vehicles with no extensive sensor upgrades.

We applied the approach to a railway case study provided by Trenord s.r.l., predicting the reliability of Traction Control Units (TCUs) on legacy vehicles. In particular, the key scientific contributions of this work include:

- Converting raw diagnostic data into stochastic models, providing an artifact[1] to replicate the experimental results, available under the AGPLv3 licence.
- Validating the feasibility of using FTA for real-time failure prediction.
- Showing how to apply the approach in a case study using real world data.

The remainder of this paper is organized as follows: Sect. 2 provides some related works, Sect. 3 discusses the background, Sect. 4 describes the methodology for fault detection by adapting diagnostic sensor data to FT-based predictive model. The problem definition and case study are presented in Sect. 6. Section 7 presents and discusses the results and their implications. Finally, Sect. 8 concludes the paper pointing out directions for future research.

2   Related Work

Fault detection and diagnosis, as well as PdM, have been extensively explored for railway systems, spanning various approaches from data-driven methods to model-based techniques. Several data-driven methods have demonstrated effectiveness for real-time fault detection and diagnosis in traction systems. Liu et al. [20] applied deep Principal Component Analysis (PCA) for detecting incipient faults in electrical drives, showing significant improvements over traditional methods in terms of early detection capabilities. Similarly, Chen et al. [12] developed adaptive observers to estimate system states and detect sensor faults in traction systems of high-speed trains, achieving robust performance even under variable operating conditions.

Beyond traction systems, PdM techniques have been successfully applied to other critical train components, with specific focus on door systems which frequently experience operational issues affecting service availability. When multiple doors are deactivated due to system issues, service interruptions become inevitable, highlighting the importance of early anomaly detection. Ribeiro et al. [28] employed statistical anomaly detection techniques to predict failures in automatic door systems, while Wang et al. [35] exploited sequential pattern mining to identify abnormal operational signatures in door functioning data. Other critical components have also benefited from data-driven approaches. Davari et al. [14] implemented a Sparse Autoencoder (SAE) network for early failure detection in Air Production Units (APUs), analyzing both analog and digital sensor data to identify anomalies indicative of potential air leakage problems or other failure modes before they manifest as critical issues.

For system-level reliability analysis, various FT analysis tools have been developed with varying capabilities and modeling approaches. Several tools focus on Dynamic Fault Trees (DFTs) [29], which offer enhanced expressivity by modeling dependencies among component behaviors, including dependent events, spare components, and different operational modes, e.g., DFTCalc [1], SAFEST [34], DFTRES [6], and SHyFTOO [13]. Other notable contributions include

---

[1] https://doi.org/10.5281/zenodo.15613737.

DFTSim [5], RAATS [22], MatCarloRE [21], and RADYBAN [23]. To manage the increased complexity in analyzing the underlying stochastic processes, these tools either constrain duration distributions within the Markovian setting or employ simulation-based solution methods. More general-purpose tools for quantitative evaluation of stochastic models (not specific for dependability evaluation) include SHARPE [32] (for generalized stochastic Petri nets), CPN IDE [33] (for colored Petri nets), TimeNET [36] (for deterministic and stochastic Petri nets), Möbius [15] (for various formalisms including stochastic activity networks), and ORIS [25] (for stochastic time Petri nets). Other tools such as LIFT [24] have addressed learning of static FTs from observed data, with focus on the FT structure rather than on the distribution of the time to FT events.

To perform FTA, we selected the FaultFlow library [7,8,26], which performs complete state space analysis and derives importance measures of faults. Specifically, the Birnbaum measure estimates the impact of the occurrence of a fault on the system time-to-failure Cumulative Distribution Function (CDF), while the Fussell-Vesely measure estimates such impact by taking into account the occurrence probability of any minimal cut set (i.e., minimal combination of faults that induces the system failure) containing the fault. Overall, these measures provide invaluable insights into the contribution of each subsystem to system-level failures, enabling more targeted maintenance strategies.

The considered case study presents train-level reliability where coach redundancy and operational constraints must be considered, which can be easily represented with standard combinatorial reliability models. We exploited RBDs to analyze the train reliability through librbd [9], an efficient open-source library that supports the numerical computation of the reliability curve for all RBD basic blocks.

Particularly relevant to our work is the research by Ferdous et al. [16], who developed data-driven machine learning approaches to predict faults in traction control units of legacy trains. However, their approach significantly differs from ours in two key aspects, i.e., it operates at the train level rather than the more granular coach level, and it relies predominantly on non-explainable black-box machine learning systems In contrast, our methodology leverages domain knowledge to create an explainable framework that operates at the coach level, enabling more precise fault detection and diagnosis. Our approach aligns with recent trends in quantitative dependability evaluation of train control systems in presence of uncertainty, as surveyed by Carnevali et al. [11], while providing the flexibility needed for modern heterogeneous train compositions.

3   Background

3.1   FaultFlow: Model-Driven Dependability Evaluation

FaultFlow [7,8,26] is a Java library for quantitative evaluation of dependability of component-based systems, leveraging a Model-Driven Engineering (MDE) approach to analyze complex failure behaviors. FaultFlow models the hierarchical structure of the system and the behavior of fault propagations within it, considering both intra-component propagations from a component fault to its failure, and inter-component propagations where a component failure comprises a fault of a higher-level component. In particular, the system structure is specified using a SysML Block Definition Diagram (BDD), while the system failure logic is modeled by a Stochastic Static Fault Tree (SSFT) made of: leaf nodes modeling internal faults; logical gates modeling conditions that activate propagation of a combination of faults into a component failure, i.e., AND (the output event occurs if all input events occur), OR (the output event occurs if any input event occurs), and VOT(k/N) (the output event occurs if at least k of the N input events occur); and, propagation nodes modeling durations of propagations.

The timing of fault occurrences and fault propagations is characterized by non-Markovian Probability Density Functions (PDFs) in the class of Expolynomial functions, potentially with bounded support, allowing for flexible fitting of analytical distributions from statistical data. FaultFlow calculates the Cumulative Distribution Function (CDF) of the time to failure for any failure defined in the SSFT, including the top-level system failure. If the SSFT does not include repeated events, FaultFlow also derives importance measures of faults, characterizing how each fault contributes to a system failure over time.

The typical workflow in FaultFlow consists of the following steps and model-to-model transformations: i) the metamodel instance of the system can be automatically created by parsing a JSON file encoding the BDD and the SSFT or, alternatively, it can be programmatically created using the FaultFlow API; ii) the metamodel instance is stored in a database; iii) for a specific failure mode, the metamodel instance can be transformed into a Stochastic Time Petri Net (STPN), which an be analyzed by the Sirio library of the ORIS tool [25], or into extended UML statecharts termed Hierarchical Semi-Markov Processes with parallel regions (HSMPs) [3,17], which can be analyzed by the Pyramis library [10,27]; iv) both stochastic analyses yield the time-to-failure CDF.

In the MDE perspective, FaultFlow provides the following advantages:

- High-level modeling: BDDs and SSFTs facilitate comprehension of complex models with respect to STPNs and UML statecharts, also by domain experts.
- Support for non-Markovian duration distributions: FaultFlow provides flexibility and accuracy in representing real-world systems compared to tools limited to exponential distributions, fitting only the mean value of observed statistics. Specifically, FaultFlow accepts any analytic form in the class of exponomial functions [32] (defined as the sum of products of exponential and polynomial terms), with the same representation over the entire domain or piecewise-defined over multiple sub-domains. If the SSFT does not include repeated events, FaultFlow also accepts any distribution in numerical form.
- Automated analysis: FaultFlow automates the transformation of BDDs and SSFTs into STPNs and HSMPs, and their subsequent stochastic analysis.
- Open-source availability: FaultFlow usage and extension are encouraged.

3.2   Librbd: Highly Effective Hierarchical Reliability Analysis

The librbd C library [9,19] supports the evaluation of redundancy behavior of complex systems by performing the analysis of Reliability Block Diagrams (RBDs). Specifically, librbd performs numerical evaluation of reliability for compositions of RBD basic blocks, providing computational efficiency, multiplatform support, and open-source availability under the AGPLv3 licence. The library can be effectively used in combination with FaultFlow in redundancy analysis scenarios, exploiting the time-to-failure CDF of system components derived by FaultFlow.

4   Process Description

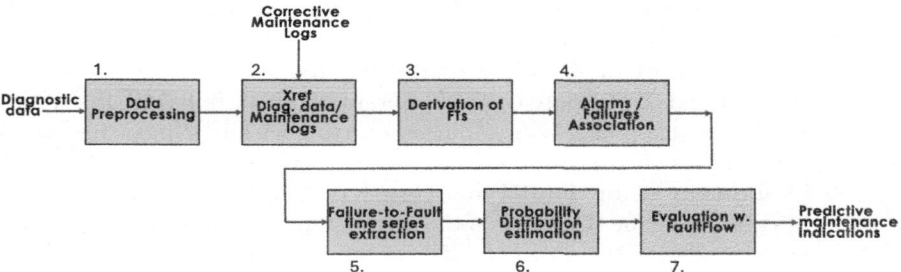

Fig. 1. Predictive maintenance workflow.

The proposed process of elaborating diagnostic data to establish a PdM system involves several methodological steps, each critical to ensure the reliability and accuracy of the predictive framework. In the following sections we describe step by step the workflow shown in Fig. 1. The process has been shaped over the railway case study at hand: it is however presented in rather general terms, in an effort to define a generic data-driven model-based PdM technique. Details on the implementation of each step in our case study are provided in Sect. 6.

Step 1: Data preprocessing. Raw diagnostic data are initially collected on a central server and preprocessed to improve their usability and relevance. Temporal alignment is performed to synchronize data points from various sensors or sources to a common timeline. Duplicate entries, which may arise from overlapping logs or redundant systems, are identified and filtered to prevent overrepresentation. A subset of diagnostic alarms is then selected based on their relevance to known failure modes, reducing noise and focusing on indicators with diagnostic significance.

Step 2: Cross-referencing diagnostic data with corrective maintenance logs. Historical corrective maintenance records are integrated with diagnostic data logs. This step enables the identification of correlations between specific alarms and actual failure events, providing a foundation for understanding failure patterns and causal relationships.

Step 3: Derivation of the fault tree structure. FTs model the hierarchical relationships between system components and potential failure modes. They can be derived from system schematics or safety analysis documents, ensuring alignment with system architecture and failure pathways.

Step 4: Association of alarms with failure events. Alarms from the diagnostic system are systematically linked to specific failure events. This step establishes a mapping that allows predictive algorithms to infer potential failures based on real-time alarm data.

Step 5: Extraction of time series. Time-series data capturing the temporal evolution of faults leading to failures are extracted from the combined logs. This dataset serves as a basis for analyzing the progression of faults over time and identifying early warning indicators.

Step 6: Estimation of probability distributions. The fault-to-failure time series are analyzed to compute time-to-fault and fault-to-failure PDFs, which quantify the likelihood of specific failures occurring within defined time intervals, providing insights into the system behavior under varying conditions.

Step 7: Evaluation using FaultFlow. The FT structure and the computed PDFs are used to define the SSFT of the system failure logic. Then, FaultFlow can be used to derive the duration CDF of failure processes (not necessarily top-level failures) and importance measures of faults.

4.1   Exploitability of Results

The time-to-failure CDFs (i.e., unreliability functions) derived by our analysis support maintenance planning and optimization in multiple ways. Through these applications, diagnostic data analyzed by our framework are effectively used to build a comprehensive PdM system capable of anticipating failures, optimizing maintenance schedules, and significantly enhancing overall system reliability while reducing operational costs and service disruptions.

Maintenance Planning. The reliability curves of TCUs can be mathematically combined to evaluate various redundancy policies, such as the train composition configurations discussed in Sect. 7.2. Specifically, by aggregating the coach-level unreliability functions according to specific redundancy rules (e.g., the constraint that non-functioning TCUs cannot be adjacent), maintenance engineers can quantitatively assess the reliability implications of different train configurations. This enables informed decisions about optimal fleet composition based on reliability requirements and operational constraints.

Threshold-Based Maintenance Triggering. A particularly valuable application of reliability functions is the establishment of threshold-based maintenance policies. By defining critical reliability thresholds (e.g., 0.9, 0.8, or 0.7), maintenance interventions can be automatically triggered when the computed system reliability falls below these levels. This approach transforms traditional time-based maintenance into a more efficient reliability-centered strategy.

Maintenance Resource Optimization. The reliability functions also facilitate optimal allocation of maintenance resources. By quantitatively predicting when specific components or subsystems will reach critical reliability thresholds, maintenance teams can prioritize interventions based on both criticality and timing, preventing the allocation of resources to components that still maintain acceptable reliability levels while ensuring timely attention to degrading subsystems.

4.2   Remarks

We notice that some of the steps 1–7 described above are tricky and require a deep expertise. At the same time, the quality of the initial data is also crucial. For example, while combining diagnostic and corrective maintenance data is a robust way to identify causal relationships between alarms and failures, this step assumes that corrective maintenance logs are detailed, accurate, and sufficiently granular to match with diagnostic data, which is not always the case. In fact, in our case study, corrective maintenance requests and logs are usually filled manually by train drivers and maintainers. Therefore, the effectiveness here depends heavily on the quality and completeness of the maintenance records.

The definition of the SSFT structure is also a crucial step. Using system schematics or safety analyses ensures that the SSFT structure is grounded in the system actual architecture. This step requires domain expertise and can be resource-intensive. The same problem occurs in associating alarms with failure events, which comprises a critical task for predictive models. This step assumes that historical data sufficiently captures the range of possible failure scenarios and that alarms are consistently reliable indicators to properly understand temporal dynamics and enabling time-based predictions. However, extracting these series requires well-labeled and time-stamped data, which can be difficult if the logs are incomplete or inconsistently recorded. It also assumes that the progression of faults can be meaningfully captured from the available data.

Finally, computing probability distributions of the duration of fault and failure processes is a standard means for quantifying uncertainty and making probabilistic predictions. However, the accuracy of these distributions depends on having a large and representative dataset modeling fault and failure behaviors. In this perspective, potential challenges include:

– **Data quality:** The entire process hinges on the availability of high-quality and well-structured data. On the other hand, inconsistent, sparse, or biased data can undermine the results.

- **Scalability:** Deriving the SSFT structure and manually associating alarms with failure events might not scale well for very large or complex systems.
- **Adaptability:** The process assumes that past patterns are indicative of future behavior. While generally valid, evolving system configurations or environmental conditions could reduce the accuracy of the predictions.
- **Expert involvement:** Several steps (e.g., SSFT structure derivation, alarm association) require domain expertise, which may introduce subjectivity or bottlenecks in the process.

5   Case Study Context

5.1   Railway Asset

Our case study is performed in collaboration with Trenord, a railway operator in Northern Italy, and involves a regional railway system comprising over 400 trains that serve approximately 700,000 passengers daily through approximately 2,200 service routes. The maintenance of this extensive rolling stock is conducted across six dedicated maintenance facilities.

Currently, maintenance needs are identified through a manual, expert-driven approach. The importance of PdM for this railway operator extends beyond organizational advantages in maintenance management and operational cost reduction; it represents a critical improvement in service reliability for passengers. The ability to predict failures would enable the operator to recall trains to maintenance facilities in advance, removing them from service before failures occur. In contrast, with the current reactive approach, both operators and passengers experience disruptions when failures happen during active service, necessitating corrective maintenance interventions that impact service continuity and passenger experience.

The trains we consider in this study, which make up most of the fleet, are equipped each with 18 diagnostic devices per vehicle, integrated with an onboard diagnostic platform responsible for capturing and transferring diagnostic data to a wayside system for analysis. While this system captures diagnostic information, it currently lacks an automated PdM mechanism capable of anticipating potential failures proactively.

This research focuses on developing a PdM solution specifically targeting the Traction Control Unit (TCU), a critical and complex on-board system.

5.2   Preliminary Data Analysis

Dataset Characteristics. The dataset provided by the railway operator encompasses two primary data types collected over a three-year period:

1. **Diagnostic data** (5,278,950 records):
   - Comprises fault, problem, and malfunction records for the TCU
   - Captures diagnostic events and alerts rather than precise sensor measurements

  – Each data point is a tuple which includes:
    • Coach where the event occurred
    • Event timestamp
    • Alert type and code
    • Geospatial information (latitude, longitude)
    • Train velocity
    • Coach identification
2. **Maintenance data** (473 records):
  – Includes both corrective and scheduled maintenance activities
  – Corrective maintenance: Interventions resulting from service-related faults
  – Scheduled maintenance: Planned activities according to the rolling stock maintenance schedule

Initial Data Analysis. Our preliminary investigation focuses exclusively on onboard diagnostic data to assess the feasibility of developing a predictive model. The research currently prioritizes predicting the number of critical alerts, which domain experts consider an indicator of potential system failures.

6   Application of the Process to the Case Study

In this section, we illustrate the application of our methodology to the case study and we provide some lessons learned.

Step 1: Data preprocessing. Raw diagnostic data on trains are collected on a central server using multiple data acquisition boards on each train. These boards somehow overlap and can possibly detect the same event with slight time-disalignments, therefore the task of synchronizing data w.r.t. a common timeline can be tricky. An information that may be useful is the train position and the known train length, but for the purposes of our analysis we decided to apply a simpler algorithm. In particular, for each coach we extracted the data coming from different acquisition boards separately and we proceeded to data fusion only after cleaning and selection phases. A subset of diagnostic alarms is then selected based on their relevance to known failure modes, reducing noise and focusing on indicators with diagnostic significance. Here we focus on the alarms concerning the failure of main TCU subsystems. These alarms are shown to the driver on the Driver Machine Interface (DMI) and are the ones that may trigger a manual maintenance request. First, we filtered data by train, by coach, by causing system, and by data acquisition board.

Step 2: Cross-referencing diagnostic data with corrective maintenance logs. We considered logs containing the following information: data and author of the request; train and coach identifiers; system identifier and issue; and, closure date. These logs are filled out manually, sometimes with coarse information. Anyway, we used the maintenance logs to split raw data in temporal sequences going from the end of a corrective maintenance intervention

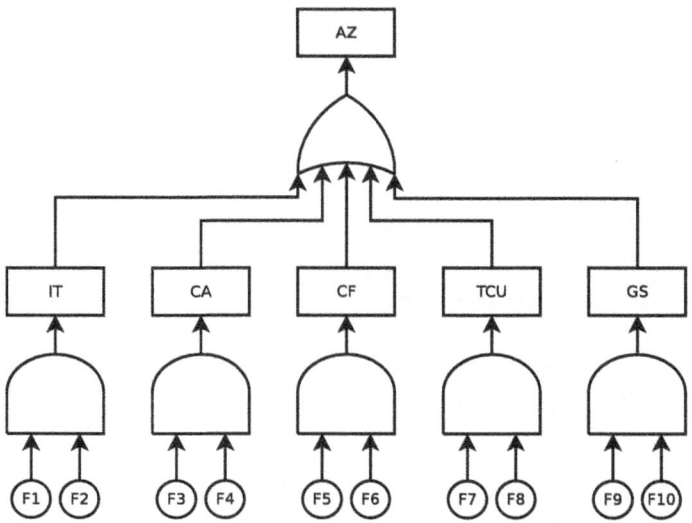

Fig. 2. High level system fault tree with main components.

to the raise of the first following request. This step helped us to identify correlations between specific alarms and to detect alarm sequences that lead to a system failure.

Step 3: Derivation of the fault tree structure. We constructed the SSFT structure on the basis of the list of alarms and electrical system schematics. Figure 2 shows the higher-level layer.

The top-level event is represented by the "AZ" box, which represents the system level failure or malfunction. The connections leading down from AZ represent the different potential causes or contributing factors. These are due to subsystem failures, in particular:

1. IT: Traction Inverter;
2. CA: Step down Chopper
3. CF: Braking Chopper
4. TCU: Train Control Unit board
5. GS: Inverter Static Group

Each of these lower-level subsystems (i.e., IT, CA, CF, TCU, GS) has further basic failure events represented by the numbered nodes F1, F2, ..., F10. The tree-like structure with AND gates models the fact that multiple lower-level failures would need to occur to ultimately lead to the top-level AZ failure.

In the traction system, no redundant components are inherently present. This might initially appear counterintuitive for a system with high availability requirements: indeed, redundancy is effectively implemented at the train composition level. More details are given in Sect. 7.2.

Step 4: Association of alarms with failure events. The railway operator provided a list with the identifier, description, and severity of each alarm. In this study, we considered the high-severity alarms and linked them to specific subsystem failures. The alarms were partitioned into two groups, i.e., visible to the driver and visible only to the maintainers. The alarm description helped us to link the referred subsystem or component, but there were cases (especially among the lower-severity alarms) in which this connection was not clear. In this step, the help of the railway operator was crucial.

Step 5: Extraction of time series. In this step, the diagnostic data were partitioned into separate files, one for each coach. For every corrective maintenance record, we identified the first occurrence of each selected alarm (among the various data acquisition boards) and computed the time difference between the alarm and the preceding maintenance event. Specifically, let M_i and M_{i+1} be two consecutive maintenance events, with associated timestamps $M_i(t_i)$ and $M_{i+1}(t_{i+1})$. For each alarm type A_x, we selected the timestamp of its *first occurrence* within the interval $(M_i(t_i), M_{i+1}(t_{i+1}))$, denoted as $A_x(t_1)$, and computed the delay from the preceding maintenance:

$$\Delta t_x = A_x(t_1) - M_i(t_i)$$

For this case study, data from 23 coaches across 5 trains was extracted.

Step 6: Estimation of probability distributions. The inter-event times Δt_x were modeled using an exponential distribution. For each alarm type A_x, the goal is to estimate the parameter λ_x of the exponential distribution:

$$f(t; \lambda_x) = \lambda_x e^{-\lambda_x t}, \quad t \geq 0$$

The maximum likelihood estimate (MLE) of λ_x under complete (non-censored) data is:

$$\hat{\lambda}_x = \frac{n}{\sum_{i=1}^{n} t_i}$$

where t_i is the observed time to the first alarm after the i-th maintenance and n is the number of observation windows (M_i, M_{i+1}) where the alarm appeared.

However, not every alarm A_x occurs between every pair of maintenance events. In such cases, the alarm is said to be *right-censored*: we only know that the event did not occur within the observation window (M_i, M_{i+1}), but not whether or when it might occur after.

To correctly account for this censoring, we define:

- t_i: the time between M_i and the first alarm occurrence, or the duration of the observation window (if censored).
- $\delta_i \in \{0, 1\}$: an indicator variable, where $\delta_i = 1$ if the alarm occurred (i.e., uncensored), and $\delta_i = 0$ otherwise.

The likelihood function accounting for censoring becomes:

$$L(\lambda_x) = \prod_{i=1}^{n} \left[\lambda_x e^{-\lambda_x t_i} \right]^{\delta_i} \cdot \left[e^{-\lambda_x t_i} \right]^{1-\delta_i} = \lambda_x^{\sum \delta_i} e^{-\lambda_x \sum t_i}$$

Maximizing this likelihood yields the censored MLE estimate:

$$\hat{\lambda}_x = \frac{\sum_{i=1}^n \delta_i}{\sum_{i=1}^n t_i}$$

This approach correctly incorporates both observed and censored times, resulting in a statistically safe estimation of the distribution of the considered time parameter (i.e., time-to-fault or fault-to-failure time).

Step 7: Evaluation using FaultFlow. We implemented the model in the FaultFlow library to compute the time-to-failure CDF for the full AZ system and for the subsystems IT, CA, CF, TCU board, GS, as well as the Birnbaum and the Fussell-Vesely importance measures of faults. We also used the `librbd` library to perform reliability analysis.

7   Results and Discussion

We present the experimental results obtained by using the FaultFlow library and the `librbd` library to analyze our case study. All experiments were performed on an Apple M3 CPU 8 Core @ 4.06 GHz with 16 GB RAM, running MacOS. The experiments performed using the FaultFlow library took nearly 2.7 s, while those performed using the `librbd` library took nearly 15 ms.

7.1   TCU Unreliability Analysis

In the following, we present the results of the FaultFlow analysis for the considered TCU, including the system-level time-to-failure CDF (also referred to as the unreliability function) and the importance measures of component faults.

Figure 3 shows the time-to-failure CDF of the coach traction system, representing the probability that at least one alarm occurs within time t. The steep rise in the curve indicates a rapid decrease in reliability. Notably, after approximately 300 h, the probability of experiencing at least one critical alarm reaches 0.7. This signifies a significant degradation in reliability within the initial operational period. Furthermore, the curve approaches 1.0 around 750 h, suggesting that it is almost certain that at least one critical alarm occurs within this time interval. This early and substantial unreliability points out the need for proactive rather than reactive maintenance. Analyzing more details in the diagnostic logs in conjunction with this CDF enables the identification of specific alarm patterns and their frequency within the first 500 h of operation.

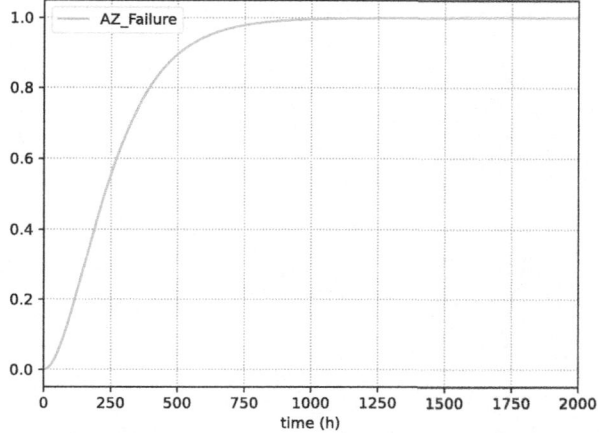

Fig. 3. CDF of the time to the AZ failure.

Figure 4 displays the Birnbaum importance measure for each fault, illustrating the relative influence of individual components on the system failure probability. It is evident that not all alarms contribute equally to the overall unreliability. Faults F3 and F4, associated with the step-down chopper, and F1 and F2, associated with the traction inverter, emerge as the most impactful. Specifically, F3 exhibits the highest Birnbaum importance measure, peaking around 10^6 h, followed closely by F4. This highlights their critical role in determining the system's overall reliability. Prioritizing the monitoring and maintenance of these components is crucial, as their failure has a more significant impact on the system's unreliability compared to other faults.

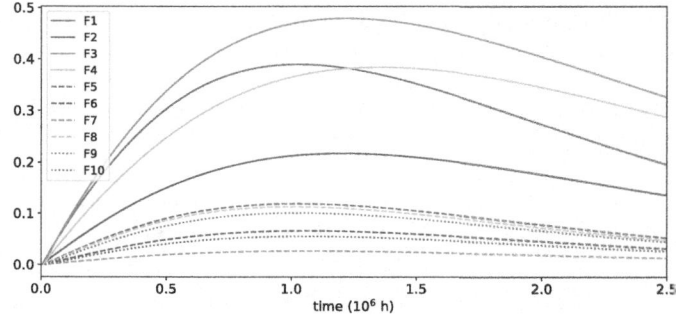

Fig. 4. Birnbaum importance measures of faults.

Figure 5 presents the Fussell-Vesely importance measure of each fault. Consistently with the Birnbaum measure, faults F3 and F4 dominate the ranking,

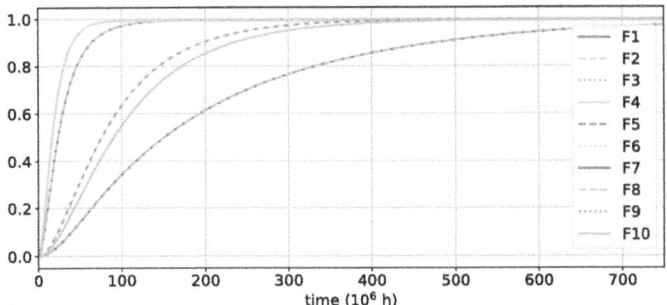

Fig. 5. Fussell Vesely importance measures of faults.

particularly within the early operational period. F3 and F4 show a rapid increase in their Fussell-Vesely importance measure, being close to 1.0 within 200–300 $\cdot 10^6$ h. This highlights their critical role in the failure behavior of the traction system and suggests that their failure is highly likely to lead to a system failure. This consistency across both importance measures strongly reinforces the need to prioritize these components in diagnostics and maintenance planning. This could involve more frequent inspections or sensor-based monitoring of critical components. The consistently high importance measures for F1, F2, F3, and F4 (Figs. 4 and 5) indicate that predictive maintenance efforts should be heavily concentrated on the traction inverter and step-down chopper).

7.2   Train Reliability Analysis

The considered trains are composed by powered coaches, each with a TCU, as shown in Fig. 6. Operational continuity can be maintained even with up to two TCUs excluded from service (except for the train configuration with three coaches, for which only one failed TCU is tolerated) provided that these non-functioning units are not positioned consecutively within the train configuration.

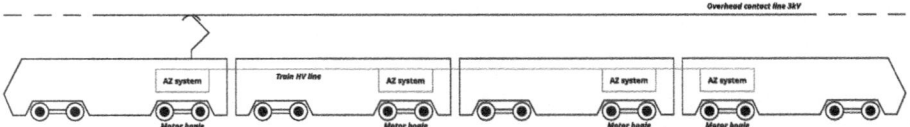

Fig. 6. A train configuration with 4 coaches.

We considered trains composed of 3, 4, 5 or 6 coaches. We used FaultFlow to derive the unreliability of the TCU of each coach, as described in Sect. 7.1, and then we used librbd to evaluate the overall train reliability. Specifically, the reliability of the 3-coach configuration is evaluated as the reliability of an RBD

consisting of a 2oo3 block (modeling the fact that 2 out of 3 TCUs are functioning); the reliability of the 4-coach configuration is evaluated as the reliability of
the RBD shown in Fig. 7, consisting of the parallel composition of: a 3oo4 block
(modeling the fact that 3 out of 4 TCUs are functioning), and three sequences
of four blocks, modeling the conditions under which the system is functioning
although 2 TCUs are non-functioning (i.e., the TCUs of coaches 1 and 3, or the
TCUs of coaches 2 and 3 are functioning, or the TCUs of coaches 2 and 4 are
functioning); and so on. Note that, in doing so, we are safely underestimating
the system reliability, given that the same events (i.e., the fact that the TCU
of a specific coach is not functioning) affect different compositions of blocks of
the RBD, and that these events are dependent and positively correlated but are
considered independent of each other in the quantitative evaluation [2].

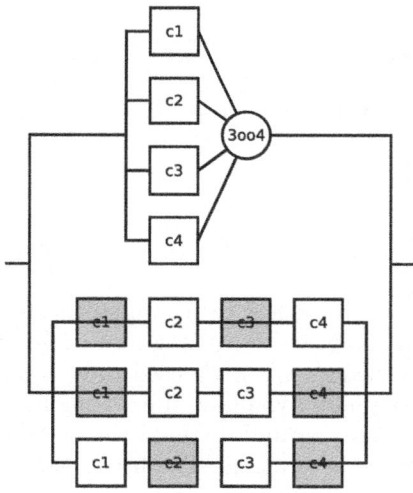

Fig. 7. RBD for a train with 4 coaches (grey blocks identify the failed coaches).

Figure 8 shows the reliability of the train configurations made of n coaches
with $n \in \{3, 4, 5, 6\}$. A train with 3 coaches is the most reliable, due to the
fact that with this configuration we have fewer combinations of possible failures
and only the failure of a single coach is tolerated. For the configurations with
4, 5, and 6 coaches, the adjacency constraint becomes increasingly restrictive
and significantly reduces the number of functioning system states. The adjacency requirement eliminates many potential operational configurations where
non-adjacent coaches could theoretically maintain system functionality, thereby
creating a more conservative reliability assessment. This fact also explains why
the reliability curves for a larger number of coaches show steeper degradation
patterns, as the system becomes more vulnerable to failures that violate the
spatial continuity requirement rather than just the minimum operational capac-
ity. Also note that the adjacency constraint serves as a simplification that may

be overly restrictive compared to usual operational flexibility, also making the obtained results an understimation of the actual reliability curves.

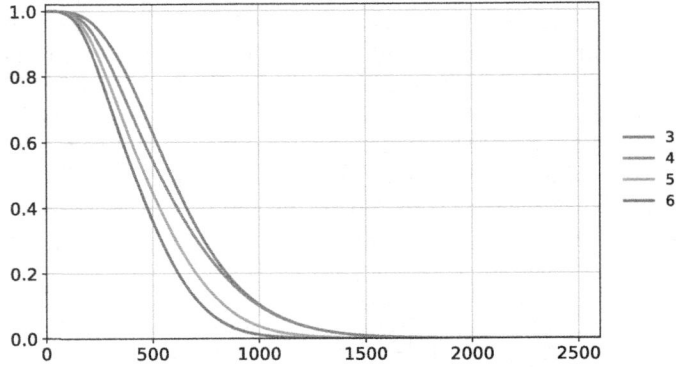

Fig. 8. Reliability of trains composed of 3, 4, 5 and 6 coaches.

8   Conclusions

We have presented a novel approach to derive stochastic fault tree models by strategically integrating extensive diagnostic data logs, maintenance records, and domain-specific knowledge. Then, we used these models to predict component and system-level reliability dynamics, supporting the definition of proactive maintenance strategies by exploiting existing diagnostic infrastructure, without requiring additional sensor investments. The feasibility and effectiveness of the approach are preliminarily demonstrated on a railway case study concerning the traction control unit of a fleet of regional passenger trains,

We have remarked how the success of the approach depends on the quality of data, discussing potential threats to validity. Specifically, addressing potential data limitations as well as validating the system extensively in real-world scenarios will be crucial for thoroughly assessing its reliability and effectiveness.

The study presented in this paper has been prompted by the need of railway industry for availability of efficient and robust techniques and tools for predictive maintenance. Our research presents a systematic approach to bridge the gap between diagnostic and predictive maintenance in railway vehicles. By developing a methodology that leverages existing sensor diagnostic data, we have demonstrated the potential of transforming legacy systems into proactive maintenance frameworks. In particular, key scientific contributions of our work include:

- establishing a replicable process for converting diagnostic data into predictive maintenance models;

- validating the feasibility of fault tree analysis for real-time failure prediction;
- showing the approach application in a case study using real-world data.

While our initial results are promising, several challenges and limitations warrant further investigation. In particular, this study leverages only a subset of available diagnostics alarms related to the TCU, hence this approach can be extended to other onboard systems to improve the accuracy of the overall reliability estimation. Future research directions include:

- exploiting machine learning algorithms that can dynamically adjust predictive models based on evolving system characteristics;
- investigating methods to improve data quality and reduce uncertainty in maintenance logs;
- exploring cross-domain applications of our predictive maintenance approach.

Acknowledgements. This study was carried out within the MUR PRIN 2022 PNRR P2022A492B project ADVENTURE (ADVancEd iNtegraTed evalUation of Railway systEms) and the MOST – Sustainable Mobility National Research Center and received funding from the European Union NextGenerationEU (PIANO NAZIONALE DI RIPRESA E RESILIENZA (PNRR) – MISSIONE 4.

References

1. Arnold, F., Belinfante, A., Van der Berg, F., Guck, D., Stoelinga, M.: DFTCALC: a tool for efficient fault tree analysis. In: Bitsch, F., Guiochet, J., Kaâniche, M. (eds.) SAFECOMP 2013. LNCS, vol. 8153, pp. 293–301. Springer, Heidelberg (2013). https://doi.org/10.1007/978-3-642-40793-2_27
2. Baccelli, F., Makowski, A.M.: Multidimensional stochastic ordering and associated random variables. Oper. Res. **37**(3), 478–487 (1989)
3. Biagi, M., Vicario, E., German, R.: Extending the steady state analysis of hierarchical semi-Markov processes with parallel regions. In: European Workshop on Performance Engineering, pp. 62–77 (2018)
4. Binder, M., Mezhuyev, V., Tschandl, M.: Predictive maintenance for railway domain: a systematic literature review. IEEE Eng. Manage. Rev. **51**(2), 120–140 (2023)
5. Boudali, H., Nijmeijer, A., Nijmeijer, A., Stoelinga, M.I.A.: DFTSim: a simulation tool for extended dynamic fault trees. In: 42nd Annual Simulation Symposium (ANSS 2009), p. 31. Association for Computing Machinery (2009)
6. Budde, C.E., Ruijters, E., Stoelinga, M.: The dynamic fault tree rare event simulator. In: Gribaudo, M., Jansen, D.N., Remke, A. (eds.) QEST 2020. LNCS, vol. 12289, pp. 233–238. Springer, Cham (2020). https://doi.org/10.1007/978-3-030-59854-9_17
7. Carnevali, L., Cerboni, S., Montecchi, L., Vicario, E.: Faultflow: an MDE library for dependability evaluation of component-based systems. IEEE Trans. Dependable Secure Comput. 1–18 (2025). https://doi.org/10.1109/TDSC.2025.3532340
8. Carnevali, L., Cerboni, S., Picano, B., Scommegna, L., Vicario, E.: An observation metamodel for dependability tools. In: 2024 19th European Dependable Computing Conference (EDCC), pp. 169–172. IEEE (2024)

9. Carnevali, L., Ciani, L., Fantechi, A., Gori, G., Papini, M.: An efficient library for reliability block diagram evaluation. Appl. Sci. **11**(9) (2021). https://doi.org/10.3390/app11094026

10. Carnevali, L., German, R., Santoni, F., Vicario, E.: Compositional analysis of hierarchical UML statecharts. IEEE Trans. Soft. Eng. **48**(12), 4762–4788 (2021)

11. Carnevali, L., Giandomenico, F.D., Fantechi, A., Gnesi, S., Gori, G.: Quantitative dependability evaluation of train control systems in presence of uncertainty: a systematic literature review. IEEE Trans. Intell. Transp. Syst. **26**(4), 4298–4314 (2025). https://doi.org/10.1109/TITS.2025.3530112

12. Chen, H., Jiang, B.: A review of fault detection and diagnosis for the traction system in high-speed trains. IEEE Trans. Intell. Transp. Syst. **21**(2), 450–465 (2020). https://doi.org/10.1109/TITS.2019.2897583

13. Chiacchio, F., Aizpurua, J.I., Compagno, L., D'Urso, D.: Shyftoo, an object-oriented Monte Carlo simulation library for the modeling of stochastic hybrid fault tree automaton. Expert Syst. Appl. **146**, 113139 (2020)

14. Davari, N., Veloso, B., Ribeiro, R.P., Pereira, P.M., Gama, J.: Predictive maintenance based on anomaly detection using deep learning for air production unit in the railway industry. In: 2021 IEEE 8th International Conference on Data Science and Advanced Analytics (DSAA), pp. 1–10 (2021). https://doi.org/10.1109/DSAA53316.2021.9564181

15. Deavours, D.D., et al.: The Mobius framework and its implementation. IEEE Tran. Soft. Eng. **28**(10), 956–969 (2002)

16. Ferdous, R., Spagnolo, G., Borselli, A., Rota, L., Ferrari, A.: Identifying maintenance needs with machine learning: a case study in railways. In: 2024 IEEE 32nd International Requirements Engineering Conference Workshops (REW), pp. 22–25 (2024). https://doi.org/10.1109/REW61692.2024.00008

17. Homm, D., German, R.: Analysis of hierarchical semi-Markov processes with parallel regions. In: Remke, A., Haverkort, B.R. (eds.) MMB&DFT 2016. LNCS, vol. 9629, pp. 92–106. Springer, Cham (2016). https://doi.org/10.1007/978-3-319-31559-1_9

18. Kabir, S.: An overview of fault tree analysis and its application in model based dependability analysis. Expert Syst. Appl. **77**, 114–135 (2017)

19. Librbd Library (2025). https://github.com/marcopapini/librbd

20. Liu, J., Zhang, Y., Han, J., He, J., Sun, J., Zhou, T.: Intelligent hazard-risk prediction model for train control systems. IEEE Trans. Intell. Transp. Syst. **21**(11), 4693–4704 (2020). https://doi.org/10.1109/TITS.2019.2945333

21. Manno, G., Chiacchio, F., Compagno, L., D'Urso, D., Trapani, N.: MatCarloRe: an integrated FT and Monte Carlo Simulink tool for the reliability assessment of dynamic fault tree. Expert Syst. Appl. **39**(12), 10334–10342 (2012)

22. Manno, G., Chiacchio, F., Compagno, L., D'Urso, D., Trapani, N.: Conception of repairable dynamic fault trees and resolution by the use of RAATSS, a Matlab® toolbox based on the ATS formalism. Reliab. Eng. Syst. Saf. **121**, 250–262 (2014)

23. Montani, S., Portinale, L., Bobbio, A., Codetta-Raiteri, D.: RADYBAN: A tool for reliability analysis of dynamic fault trees through conversion into dynamic Bayesian networks. Reliab. Eng. Syst. Saf. **93**(7), 922–932 (2008)

24. Nauta, M., Bucur, D., Stoelinga, M.: LIFT: learning fault trees from observational data. In: McIver, A., Horvath, A. (eds.) QEST 2018. LNCS, vol. 11024, pp. 306–322. Springer, Cham (2018). https://doi.org/10.1007/978-3-319-99154-2_19

25. Paolieri, M., Biagi, M., Carnevali, L., Vicario, E.: The ORIS tool: quantitative evaluation of non-Markovian systems. IEEE Trans. Softw. Eng. **47**(6), 1211–1225 (2021)

26. Parri, J., Sampietro, S., Vicario, E.: FaultFlow: a tool supporting an MDE approach for timed failure logic analysis. In: European Dependable Computing Conference, pp. 25–32. IEEE (2021)
27. Pyramis Library (2025). https://github.com/oris-tool/pyramis
28. Ribeiro, R.P., Pereira, P., Gama, J.: Sequential anomalies: a study in the railway industry. Mach. Learn. **105**, 127–153 (2016)
29. Ruijters, E., Stoelinga, M.: Fault tree analysis: a survey of the state-of-the-art in modeling, analysis and tools. Comput. Sci. Rev. **15**, 29–62 (2015)
30. Salfner, F., Lenk, M., Malek, M.: A survey of online failure prediction methods. ACM Comput. Surv. **42**(3), 1–42 (2010)
31. Stamatis, D.H.: Failure Mode and Effect Analysis: FMEA from Theory to Execution. Quality Press (2003)
32. Trivedi, K.S., Sahner, R.: Sharpe at the age of twenty two. ACM SIGMETRICS Perform. Eval. Rev. **36**(4), 52–57 (2009)
33. Verbeek, E., Fahland, D.: CPN IDE: an extensible replacement for CPN Tools that uses Access/CPN. In: International Conference on Process Mining Doctoral Consortium and Demo Track, pp. 29–30 (2021)
34. Volk, M., Sher, F., Katoen, J.P., Stoelinga, M.: SAFEST: fault tree analysis via probabilistic model checking. In: Annual Reliability and Maintainability Symposium (RAMS), pp. 1–7. IEEE (2024)
35. Wang, Y., Du, X., Lu, Z., Duan, Q., Wu, J.: Improved LSTM-based time-series anomaly detection in rail transit operation environments. IEEE Trans. Industr. Inf. **18**(12), 9027–9036 (2022)
36. Zimmermann, A.: Modelling and performance evaluation with TimeNET 4.4. In: Bertrand, N., Bortolussi, L. (eds.) QEST 2017. LNCS, vol. 10503, pp. 300–303. Springer, Cham (2017). https://doi.org/10.1007/978-3-319-66335-7_19

Cyber-Physical Systems

Promise-Driven Modeling: A Structured Approach for Modeling Cyber-Physical Systems

Felix Schaber[1(✉)], Atif Mashkoor[2,3], and Michael Leuschel[2,3]

[1] Hitachi Rail, Vienna, Austria
felix.schaber@urbanandmainlines.com
[2] Johannes Kepler University, Linz, Austria
[3] Heinrich Heine University, Düsseldorf, Germany

Abstract. This work proposes structuring formal models using promise theory and System Theoretic Process Analysis (STPA). Promise theory enables reasoning about a system's dependency structure and information locality, a common source of complexity in cyber-physical systems. STPA, on the other hand, provides the safety constraints that a formal model must satisfy. The core idea behind the proposed approach is to prioritize modeling those parts of the system requirements that are least likely to change in later stages, hence supporting early validation through animation. We illustrate our approach by applying it to a moving block system - a prototype of a novel train protection system in the railway domain, which is currently being investigated as part of Europe's Rail Joint Undertaking.

1 Introduction

It is well known that errors discovered in the early stages of system development are significantly less costly to fix than those found later [1]. Modeling is often promoted as a way to catch errors early, thereby reducing overall costs. However, as system complexity grows, so does the complexity of the model.

Consequently, errors introduced in early modeling stages can also become increasingly expensive. This makes choosing the right abstraction and refinement structure at the onset of modeling essential. Getting this right on the first attempt is a known challenge, particularly for cyber-physical systems, where it is often unclear which part of the system should be modeled first and at what level of detail.

When the system is safety-critical, the model must also support reasoning about safety properties. To address this, we use System Theoretic Process Analysis (STPA) [2] to decompose the system into individual controllers and identify the safety constraints associated with each controller.

The work of Felix Schaber has been partly funded by the European Union ▓ Grant Agreement # 101102001.

We introduce promise-driven modeling as a solution to the challenges mentioned above. Promise-driven modeling is based on the principle that behaviors least likely to change during model evolution are modeled first. Prioritizing design decisions by their likelihood of change is a generally considered best practice [3]. This reduces the risk of discovering the need for high-level changes late in the modeling process. High-level changes often ripple through the refinement chain, making them resource-intensive.

We iteratively build the model from small natural language descriptions of behavior, understandable by domain experts. These descriptions are then formalized using promise theory and integrated into the formal model. Promises enable us to express these behaviors. They allow the modeling of dependencies between agents within the system and locality of information - two key sources of complexity in cyber-physical systems.

We demonstrate promise-driven modeling by applying it to the moving block system case study - a prototype of a novel train protection system in the railway domain. Our approach creates a verified and validated formal model and a list of promises describing model behavior. Lessons learned during this case study are described in Sect. 5.

This paper makes the following contributions:

- A modeling and refinement strategy that supports iterative development and early model validation.
- A refinement criterion based on the stability of promised behavior.
- Validation of the promise-driven modeling approach through a real-world case study from the railway domain.

The remainder of this paper is structured as follows: Sect. 2 provides the relevant background. Promise-driven modeling is introduced in Sect. 3 and applied to the moving block system case study in Sect. 4. Sections 5 and 6 discuss lessons learned and related work, respectively. Section 7 presents our conclusions and outlines future work.

2   Background

2.1   System Theoretic Process Analysis

System Theoretic Process Analysis (STPA) [2] performs a top-down safety analysis based on system theory. Safety is described as emergent system behavior, and the system is decomposed into hierarchical control loops. A controller is very general and includes humans, automated controllers, or organizations. Controllers provide control actions and receive feedback from their environment. Each controller has a process model, describing its view of the state of other controllers. In a particular context (i.e., process model state) and worst-case environmental conditions, unsafe control actions will lead to an unsafe system state [2]. Concrete scenarios describing how an unsafe controller action may occur are called loss scenarios. Controller constraints are derived from unsafe control actions and shall prevent them from happening.

2.2   Promise Theory

Promise theory describes which interactions are necessary for cooperative behavior between agents [4]. Its goal is to construct an understanding of the overall system by reasoning about the behavior of the individual agents. Behavior is anything that an observer can see. An agent can be anything that produces behavior (i.e., this includes STPA controllers). Promises encode these behaviors. Promises can be kept (promised behavior realized) or broken (promised behavior not realized). A promise $\pi_n : S \xrightarrow{\pm b|c} R$ with name n is made between two agents, S (sender) and R (receiver), and constrains the behavior of S. The promised behavior is encoded in the body b and is conditional on keeping another promise c. If the condition c is not maintained, the behavior of S is not constrained by π_n.

A central concept of the promise theory is autonomy. This implies agents are independent of each other by default. Conditional promises can be used to modify this default and encode the system's dependency structure. Autonomy also means that agents only promise their behavior, ensuring locality. Both promises and agents can be fine-grained (refined) as needed.

2.3   Event-B

Event-B is a state-based formal modeling language built on predicate logic and set theory [5]. It consists of machines and contexts, which specify the dynamic and static parts of the model, respectively. Events contain actions that allow the transition between states and include free variables called event parameters. Guards constrain the activation of an event. Invariants are predicates that shall hold for every state. Event-B has a special INITIALISATION event, which is always fired first. Another key ingredient of Event-B is refinement, which enables the gradual addition of details and helps structure the proofs. Once discharged, proof obligations (POs) ensure that an Event-B model always satisfies its invariants and that refinement is correct. In addition to verification, Event-B models can be validated using ProB using validation obligations [6]. Rodin [7] is the modeling environment and toolset for the Event-B language.

3   Promise-Driven Modeling

Promise-driven modeling aims to systematically build, verify, and validate a formal model from the results of an STPA [2] analysis. It structures the model-building process by allowing validation early and often. By providing systematic guidance on which parts of the system should be modeled when, it ensures that the right model is built and aims to reduce costly, large-scale reworks of the model.

Promise-driven modeling starts with the controller constraints found by applying STPA (see Sect. 2 for an overview of STPA). Figure 1 shows the high-level process of promise-driven modeling. The individual steps of promise-driven modeling are described in more detail below.

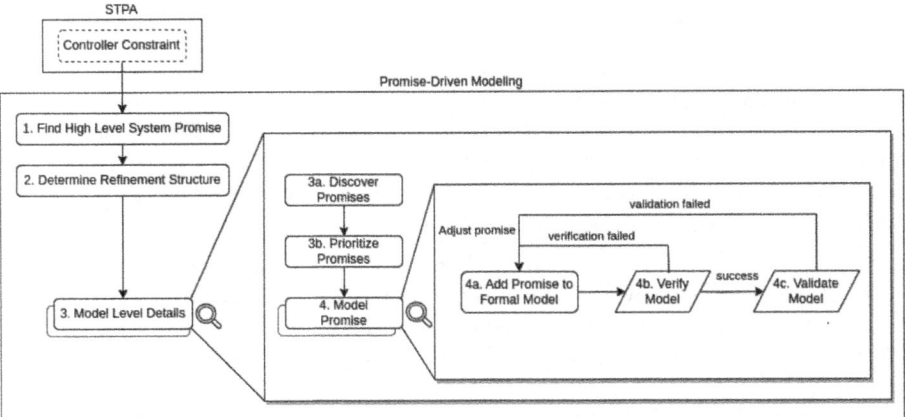

Fig. 1. Overview of promise-driven modeling. Details are provided in Sect. 4.

1. Find High-Level System Promise. From the STPA controller constraints, a high-level system promise is derived. It defines the formal model's abstract modeling goal and completion criterion and limits its scope. This scope defines the system's high-level agents and the variables the model must include to assess the system promise. It consists of all behaviors necessary to determine whether the system promise is kept. Cyber-physical systems typically include physical behavior, as hazards relate to the system's physical states.

2. Determine Refinement Structure. To further structure model complexity, the model is refined into levels. The refinement is based on the concept of observation levels presented by Mashkoor and Jacquot [8]. Observation levels group behaviors based on abstraction criteria. Here, the abstraction criterion is the likelihood of a change in behavior during modeling. Well-established and stable behaviors at the time of modeling have a lower likelihood of change (see Sect. 4.2 of the case study for concrete examples). Behaviors with a similar likelihood of change are part of the same level. Behaviors less likely to change shall be contained in lower levels (modeled first), while behaviors more likely to change are contained in higher levels (modeled later). Each level delimits a formal model sub-scope, describing to what level of detail the behavior shall be modeled.

3a. Promise Discovery. Model-level details are divided into substeps. The levels are modeled one by one. The promises and dependencies of all agents observable at this level's sub-scope are described for each level. This exploratory step is best performed in dialogue with domain experts. The goal is to find the promised behavior (promise body) for all promises and their potential dependencies on other promises (promise conditions). The sub-scope also serves as a termination criterion, limiting the promise discovery process to a sensible level of detail.

3b. Promise Prioritization. Promises are prioritized by their likelihood of change. This likelihood is based on two questions:

1. What would need to change for the promised behavior to change, given that the promise dependencies are fulfilled?
2. On what other promise does it depend, and how stable are these other promises?

The answers to these questions are used to prioritize the promises into priority groups. The primary criterion is the answer to question 1, while the answer to question 2 is used as a tiebreaker. If both criteria are equal for two promises, they belong to the same priority group. For promises of the same priority group, the modeler can choose which to model first.

4a. Add Promise to Formal Model. Each promise is added to the formal model in order of priority. This ensures that the most stable behavior is verified and validated first, reducing the likelihood of resource-intensive, retroactive changes to already verified and validated parts of the model. The details of this step will depend on the formal modeling language chosen.

4b. Verify Model. This step ensures that the model is built correctly. Details will again depend on the formal modeling language and verification technique (e.g., proof, model checking) chosen.

4c. Validate Model. Multiple techniques can be used here. First, animation and visualization help experts check the detailed behavior of the model without requiring expertise in the formal modeling toolset used. Second, the natural language form of promises (from which the formalization is later derived) allows domain experts to validate the promise behavior and dependencies without needing to delve into the details of the formal model. As the formal model is derived and traced to these promises, it is immediately clear where changes are required if a promise is incorrect or incomplete.

Testing against the loss scenarios found as part of the STPA analysis can also indicate that the model captures the level of detail required from the safety analysis, as already proposed in [9].

If the validation succeeds, the modeling proceeds with the following promise. Otherwise, it returns to step 4a, adjusting the promise until verification and validation succeed.

4   Moving Block System Case Study

Promise-driven modeling is demonstrated using an industrial case study. This case study analyses a novel type of train protection system called the moving block system.

The moving block system (MBS) controls the movement authorities (MAs) sent to trains [10]. An MA limits how fast and how far a train may run safely.

On the train, these MAs are enforced by an onboard unit (OBU). The OBU calculates the braking curve and enforces the onset of braking if the train driver brakes too late to keep the train within the limits of the MA.

The MAs are proposed to MBS from an external system. MBS can decide to grant or reject the proposal for an MA. Only granted MAs are sent to the train. MAs contain mode profiles describing the responsibility split between MBS, OBU, and the train driver for avoiding collisions. In this paper, we concentrate on full-supervision modes, where the MBS is solely responsible for ensuring that the track is clear until the MA is clear of trains and obstacles (known at the time of the request). The OBU can request a new MA from the MBS (MA request).

The OBU sends train data (TrainData) to MBS, estimates the physical train position, and periodically sends train position reports (TPRs). Trackside train detection systems (TTDs), installed at fixed sections along the tracks, also detect physical train presence, and information about train presence is sent to MBS.

An STPA for this system was already performed as part of the previous work [9]. This case study builds upon the controller constraints found in the existing STPA. We focus on the following particularly interesting controller constraint from the pre-existing STPA in this case study:

Controller Constraint. MBS shall not provide full supervision to the OBU when the MA may intersect with other trains or obstacles known at the time of the MA request.

The intersection of full supervision MAs is prevented by other controller constraints that are not part of this paper's case study. For further details and a high-level scope of the STPA analysis, the interested reader is referred to [9]. The following sections describe the process outlined in Fig. 1 in more detail.

4.1 High-Level System Promise (Step 1)

The complexity of this controller constraint comes from the statement concerning the position of all other trains or obstacles. This includes the position of trains or other obstacles that have moved since they were last known to MBS. A worst-case estimation is usually necessary because MBS does not know the exact positions. This worst-case estimation must be held until the MA region is released for the next train.

Therefore, the scope of the formal model must model these boundaries of the train positions and other obstacles. This depends on the train's physical behavior and the OBU's supervision functions. The promise of $TrainBehavior$ represents this behavior.

The model describes the physical train presence as variables $Rear(t)$ and $Front(t)$ where $Rear(t) < Front(t)$ and $t \in Trains$. The potential train presence is described by the promise body $regionOccupied$, which must always contain the true physical train presence. Stated more formally, the $regionOccupied$ must fulfill

$$\forall t \in trains : Rear(t) \ldots Front(t) \subseteq regionOccupied(t)$$

This determination is limited by the information available to MBS at the time of the MA request. It is, therefore, conditional on the information received from the train (TPR and $TrainData$) and the TTD reports ($TrackOccupation$). The content of these reports is described in Sect. 4.2.

Based on these considerations, the informal controller constraint can be encoded formally by the system promise π_{TP} given below:

$$\pi_{TP} : FM \xrightarrow{+regionOccupied|TrainData,TPR,TrackOccupation,TrainBehavior} MBS$$

Therefore, the purpose of the train protection formal model FM is to reason about the promise π_{TP} to MBS.

4.2 Determine Refinement Structure (Step 2)

Model Scope. The controller constraint's scope includes all physical train behavior affecting the position of the train's front and rear ends. For simplification, the scope excludes the time derivatives of position (i.e., train speed or acceleration is not modeled). This also implies that the detailed train braking curve is not modeled. The train is modeled to run along a single track.

The promise with the highest complexity is $TrainBehavior$. It describes the physical process by which the train's front and rear positions can change. This includes controlled train behavior, like driving forward, and uncontrolled behavior, like train rollback or train stretching and compression during braking and acceleration. The behavior of train splitting and joining is also included.

The agents responsible for providing inputs to MBS at runtime are the train's OBU and the TTD installed at fixed locations along the track. In contrast, $TrainBehavior$ is a dependency resolved during modeling time and derived from physical knowledge about the train's behavior.

Model Levels. The dependencies of the system promise are decomposed, taking a closer look at their likelihood of change. The OBU made promises about $TrainData$ and TPR. This behavior is shaped by specifications agreed through the industry like $UNISIG$ subset 026 [11]. Similarly, $TrackOccupation$ reports for new systems are guided by the $EULYNX$ set of standards (e.g., [12]). While these standards are relatively stable, they can and most likely will be modified by change requests in the future.

1. Level. The physical part of $TrainBehavior$ does not depend on an agreed-upon specification. Instead, it is shaped by the actual physical behavior of trains. This behavior is stable as it does not depend on potential future agreements or policy boundary changes. It is, therefore, the most stable of the π_{TP} dependencies. This level also includes the physical behavior of TTD, as detecting physical train presence is considered very stable.

2. Level. The scope is expanded to include the *OBU* as a new agent. *TrainBehavior* is further limited by supervision functions of the *OBU*. These supervision functions are specified in *UNISIG* subset 26 [11] and depend on the MA mode. Although on-board behavior is relatively stable, it depends on sensors (e.g., odometry) and actuators (e.g., brakes), which have limited precision/reliability and whose implementation details are more likely to change. Therefore, the supervision part of *TrainBehavior* is considered less stable than the physical part and modeled in the second level.

3. Level. Describes the promises about *TrainData* and *TPR* made by the OBU and *TrackOccupation* made by TTD. Changing these promises can, in principle, be done by adding/removing a data field at the interface. Therefore, they are considered less stable and are modeled last. It also includes behavior and data reported by the train integrity monitoring system (*TIMS*). The sub-scope of this level distinguishes between physical reality and the information measured and reported to MBS.

For example, there is a distinction between *physicalTrainFront*, representing physical reality not observable directly by the *OBU*, the estimated front end, and overreading, calculated by the odometry of the *OBU*, and *reportedEstimatedFront* transmitted to the MBS using TPRs from the OBU.

4.3   Model Level Details (Step 3)

The formal model is now built, verified, and validated for each level defined in the previous step. The individual steps are described below.

Promise Discovery (Step 3a). The goal of promise discovery is to find all promises required to describe the behavior within the scope of the current observation level. It is an iterative step, enumerating all promises and connecting them with their dependencies. First, all agents observable at the current scope are listed. Second, the promises between these agents are explored, and links between the promises are modeled as conditions.

This step requires in-depth domain knowledge and is best performed closely with domain experts. For this dialog, starting with a natural language description of promise bodies is helpful. Section 4.4 describes their refinement into formal statements.

Table 1 gives a statistic for all promises discovered per level.

Table 1. Total number of promises per observation level and Event-B machine

Level	1		2		3		
Machine	m0	m1	m2	m3	m4	m5	m6
# Promises	7	6	14	5	4	3	1

The agents of Level 1 are the physical train and its coupling, the track, and the TTDs installed along fixed track sections. Due to space constraints, a selection of informal promise bodies of Level 1 is summarized in Table 2.

For these promises, their dependencies are shown in Table 3.

Promise Prioritization (Step 3b). The likelihood of change prioritizes the promises in the previous step.

For example, the stability of the promise body in $\pi_{trainRollback}$ is assessed as very strong, as all trains essentially exhibit this behavior. In contrast, the stability of $\pi_{trainRearFollowsFront}$ is weak because the physical train length can change when the train accelerates or brakes. $\pi_{trainRollback}$ will, therefore, be in an earlier priority group (higher priority) than $\pi_{trainRearFollowsFront}$.

The ability of TTD to detect trains as described by $\pi_{ttdDetectsTrain}$ is also assessed as very strong. However, a change in TTD occupancy only occurs if no other train is already inside the TTD. In the moving block system, this dependency is not always fulfilled. Therefore, the dependency stability is classified as weak and is modeled in a later dependency group (lower priority) than $\pi_{trainRollback}$. All dependency classifications for the selected promises are found in Table 4.

4.4   Model Promises (Step 4)

This step starts by formalizing and adding the previously found promises to the formal model. After adding each promise, the resulting formal model is verified and validated.

Table 2. Selected promises from model Level 1

Promise ID	Promiser	Promisee	Promise Body
trainRollback	Train	Track	The train rear moves backward during rollback
trainRearFollowsFront	Train	Track	The train rear moves forward together with the train front
trainStretching	Train	Track	Physical stretching of train buffers during acceleration.
trainRelaxation	Train	Track	Physical relaxation of train buffers after acceleration. If the train is braked, the buffers are relaxed once the brakes are released.
trainCompression	Train	Track	Physical compression of the train buffers during braking.
ttdDetectsTrain	Train	TTD	The TTD changes to occupied if at least one train is located inside the section
ttdDetectsClearance	Train	TTD	The TTD changes to free if no train is located inside the section
trainJoin	Coupling	Train	Two trains are physically joined by the coupling and move as a single physical train afterwards.
trainSplit	Coupling	Train	Train car separates from the train. Train is (manually) decoupled or the coupling itself breaks apart

Add Promises to Formal Model (Step 4a). Here, the informal promise body is translated into a formal statement. How this step is performed depends on the formal modeling language chosen. We use the Event-B language [7] for the moving block system case study. The promises can add Event-B events or variables, and the conditions are typically translated into guards of the events. An example of the promises with the highest priority is given below.

According to the priority groups, $\pi_{trainRollback}$ is modeled first. To describe the changes in train position, variables for *physicalTrainFront* and *physicalTrainRear* are added to the model. The possible locations are modeled as natural numbers; a typing invariant ensures they stay within a bounded set of locations.

$\pi_{trainRollback}$ is then modeled as event *trainRollBackward*, where the actions subtracts *physicalTrainFront* and *physicalTrainRear* by 1. The conditions of $\pi_{trainRollback}$ listed in Table 3 are not part of the current levels' scope and are, therefore, modeled at a later level.

At the current stage, this model would fail verifications. Multiple applications of *trainRollBackward* can lead to a train position smaller than 0, violating the typing invariant. Therefore, a missing constraint was identified, describing the behavior at the network border. We make the modeling choice that behaviors crossing network borders shall be excluded from the formal model. This is expressed in a new promise $\pi_{networkClosed}$, which is added to the list of modeled promises. Its behavior constrains all events only to allow train movements

Table 3. Dependencies of the promises listed in Table 2

Promise ID	Dependencies
trainRollback	Cond1: the train is not braking Cond2: the train is not at standstill
trainRearFollowsFront	Cond1: the train has not lost its integrity Cond2: the train is driving with relaxed buffers
trainStretching	Cond1: the train is initially at standstill Cond2: the train is not braked
trainRelaxation	Cond1: train buffer is compressed Cond2: train is not braked
trainCompression	Cond1: the train is driving before the brakes are applied
ttdDetectsTrain	Cond1: the occupancy only changes when no other train is inside the TTD
ttdDetectsClearance	Cond1: the occupancy only changes when no other train remains inside the TTD
trainJoin	Cond1: train 1 is physically standing directly behind train 2 Cond2: train 1 can only join if the front train (train 2) is at standstill
trainSplit	Cond1: a train can split at any position between the cars Cond2: a train can only split if it has multiple cars

Table 4. Stability assessment of promises listed in Table 3

Promise ID	Stability body	Stability dependencies	Priority group
trainRollback	very strong	strong	1
trainRearFollowsFront	weak	weak	5
trainStretching	weak	strong	4
trainRelaxation	weak	strong	4
trainCompression	weak	strong	4
ttdDetectsTrain	very strong	weak	2
ttdDetectsClearance	very strong	weak	2
trainJoin	very strong	weak	2
trainSplit	strong	medium	3

that keep the train inside the network border. By documenting this promise and making it part of the modeling process, future model users know precisely how it affects the model and where changes are necessary if this promise is not kept.

The next priority group contains the promises relating to TTDs and train joining. As the occupancy state is directly affected by *trainRollBackward*, we model it first. This entails creating the context *trainTTDCtx*, which describes the *TTD_locations* along the tracks. The TTDs are then partitioned into two sets *clearTTD* and *occupiedTTD*. Axioms ensure that the initial members of these sets are consistent with the initial train positions. To ensure that all events update the membership correctly, the invariant *newclearTTD-correct* is introduced. The resulting invariants are shown in Fig. 2.

```
machine m0 sees trainTTDCtx
variables physicalTrainFront trains physicalTrainRear clearTTD occupiedTTD trainLength
invariants
  @type1 trains ⊆ Trains
  @type2 physicalTrainFront ∈ trains → locations
  @type3 physicalTrainRear ∈ trains → locations
  @type4 occupiedTTD ⊆ TTDs
  @type5 clearTTD ⊆ TTDs
  @type6 partition(TTDs,occupiedTTD,clearTTD)
  @newclearTTD-correct clearTTD = { s | s∈TTDs ∧
      (∀t·t∈trains ⇒ TTD_locations(s) ∩ physicalTrainRear(t)..physicalTrainFront(t) = ∅)}
```

Fig. 2. Invariants before adding *trainJoin* event.

The promises relating to TTD are not modeled as a separate event. Instead, the *clearTTD* and *occupiedTTD* are updated each time the train position changes. Many promises within the current level scope may modify the train's position.

To avoid unnecessary generation of additional proof obligations for each of these events, the new abstract event *abstractTrainMove* is created. This event is responsible for updating the TTD occupancy correctly when the train position changes, as shown[1] in Fig. 3.

```
event abstractTrainMove
  any t newFront newRear newClearTTD newOccupiedTTD
  where
    @typ1 t ∈ trains
    @prom1-1 pNetworkClosed = TRUE ⇒ newFront ∈ locations // -networkClosed
    @prom1-2 pNetworkClosed = TRUE ⇒ newRear ∈ locations // -networkClosed
    @hlp-newclear newClearTTD = { s | s∈TTDs ∧
                    (∀tt·tt∈trains ⇒ TTD_locations(s) ∩
                    (physicalTrainRear⩤{t↦newRear} )(tt) (physicalTrainFront⩤{t↦newFront})(tt) = ∅)}
    @hlp-newoccupied newOccupiedTTD = TTDs \ newClearTTD
  then
    @prom2-1 physicalTrainFront(t) = newFront
    @prom6   physicalTrainRear(t) = newRear
    @prom21  clearTTD = newClearTTD           // -ttdDetectsClearance
    @prom22  occupiedTTD = newOccupiedTTD      // -ttdDetectsTrain
  end
```

Fig. 3. Event *abstractTrainMove*.

The new train position is given by the parameters *newFront* and *newRear*. In addition, $\pi_{networkClosed}$ is encoded in the guards using an implication, allowing one to reason about the model behavior when this promise is broken. The TTD occupations are updated by the set comprehension of *newClearTTD*. Here, *newOccupiedTTD* is simply the complement of *newClearTTD*.

This allows moving the *trainRollBackward* event into a new machine that refines *abstractTrainMove*, reducing the number of proof obligations generated. *trainRollBackward* only assigns values to the parameters of *abstractTrainMove*, as shown in Fig. 4.

```
event trainRollBackward
extends abstractTrainMove
  where
    @newFront newFront = physicalTrainFront(t) - 1
    @newRear  newRear  = physicalTrainRear(t) - 1
end
```

```
event reportTTDOccupied
  any ttd newReportedState
  where
    @typ1 ttd ∈ occupiedTTD
    @hlp1 newReportedState = reportedTTDState ⩤ {ttd ↦ Occupied}
    theorem @hlp1-2 newReportedState∈TTDs → SectionStates
  then
    @prom1 reportedTTDState = newReportedState
end
```

Fig. 4. Event *trainRollBackward*.

Fig. 5. Event *reportTTDOccupied* using theorem guard *hlp1-2*.

The last promise from the current priority group is $\pi_{trainJoin}$. It is modeled by event *trainJoin*. The created train length is the sum of the individual trains' lengths. A new variable *trainLength* is added to remember this information. Condition 1 from Table 3 is encoded as a guard. Condition 2 is encoded at a later modeling level, as the motion states are not in the scope of Level 1. The event is shown in Fig. 6.

---

[1] The figures are corrected for a rendering error in the Camille Text Editor. Without correction, the overriding relation (⩤) would be erroneously rendered as ∃ .

```
event trainJoin
  any t1 t2
  where
    @typ1 t1 ∈ trains ∧ t2 ∈ trains
    @typ2 t1 ≠ t2
    @prom1cond1 physicalTrainFront(t1) = physicalTrainRear(t2) - 1 // +trainJoin
  then
    @prom1-1 trains = trains \ {t1}                                                    // +trainJoin
    @prom1-2 physicalTrainRear = {t1} ◁ (physicalTrainRear ⩤ {t2 ↦ physicalTrainRear(t1)})      // +trainJoin
    @prom1-3 physicalTrainFront = {t1} ◁ (physicalTrainFront)                          // +trainJoin
    @prom1-4 trainLength = {t1} ◁ (physicalTrainRear ⩤ {t2 ↦ trainLength(t1) + trainLength(t2)})// +trainJoin
end
```

Fig. 6. Event *trainJoin*.

The following sections describe insights and pitfalls when verifying the model based on the complete list of promises.

Verification (Step 4b). After adding each new promise, the model is verified by discharging the proof obligations generated by Rodin [7]. In addition to the provers bundled with Rodin, the SMT Solvers and the Atelier B provers plugin [13] are required to discharge many proofs. All POs are discharged, the vast majority of them automatically (see Fig. 7). If the POs cannot be discharged, the ProB2 (Dis)prover plugin for Rodin [14] is used to search for counterexamples on machine refinements instantiated with concrete values. Examples of POs requiring further manual investigation are given below.

For model Level 1, the more complex POs to discharge are related to the TTD occupation. Adding theorems encoding the properties of *clearTTD* and *occupiedTTD* is required to discharge these POs (see Fig. 8).

Many manually discharged proof obligations are related to theorems in variants or guards, e.g., adding a theorem guard giving typing hints helped discharging some POs (e.g., see *hlp1-2* in Fig. 5). The ML solver of the Atelier B provers plugin can then discharge the theorem PO.

Element Name	Total	Auto	Man.	Rev.	Und.
Total	254	249	5	0	0
trainCtx	4	4	0	0	0
trainTTDCtx	5	5	0	0	0
trainProtection_m0	34	34	0	0	0
trainProtection_m1	24	23	1	0	0
trainProtection_m2	86	86	0	0	0
trainProtection_m3	45	45	0	0	0
trainProtection_m4	29	27	2	0	0
trainProtection_m5	15	14	1	0	0
trainProtection_m6	12	11	1	0	0

Fig. 7. Proof statistics for the full Event-B Model.

```
theorem @occupiedTTD-correct ∀ttd·(ttd ∈ occupiedTTD ⇒
        (∃t·t∈trains ∧ trains≠∅ ∧ (TTD_locations(ttd) ∩ physicalTrainRear(t)‥physicalTrainFront(t) ≠ ∅)))
theorem @clearTTD-correct ∀ttd·(ttd ∈ clearTTD ⇒
        (∀t·t∈trains ⇒ TTD_locations(ttd) ∩ physicalTrainRear(t)‥physicalTrainFront(t) = ∅))
```

Fig. 8. Theorems required to discharge TTD POs.

Validation (Step 4c). Validation of the model is done at multiple steps throughout the modeling process. First, all promises found during promise discovery are discussed with a domain expert as described in Sect. 4.3. The formal model created from these promises can become very large, requiring a different communication tool.

Here, visually animating an instantiated refinement of the model using VisB [14] is very useful for discussions (see Fig. 9). It demonstrates to the domain expert how the actual model behaves.

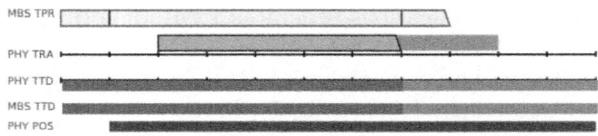

Fig. 9. VisB visualization used for discussion with domain experts.

Specific model flaws, e.g., out-of-bound train locations, are immediately apparent in the visualization. It is also helpful for modeling experts to understand why some POs regarding the overall system state cannot be discharged. For example, the VisB animation highlighted a flaw where the train could leave its potential area of movement (*PHY POS* in Fig. 9) by excessive rollbacks. The model contained a promise to limit rollback distance. However, this promise was added to the formal model so that a specific sequence of events could lead to an excessive rollback regardless. Visualization of the instantiated model aids in understanding why this is the case and changes the formal model accordingly.

5   Lessons Learned

When to Validate Promises with Domain Experts? Ideally, the model should be validated in dialogue with domain experts after adding each new promise to the formal model. However, domain experts may not always be available, so it is often impractical to have a joint validation session after every added promise. A practical compromise can be a joint validation session after completing each model level. If potentially missing promises are discovered during model verification, this can warrant an ad-hoc validation session, where existing promises are modified or new promises are added.

Rodin Auto-tactic Configuration Significantly Affects the Number of Manual Proofs. Many POs (ca. 1/3) required manual discharge using the default Rodin auto-tactic. While most of them could quickly be discharged by the SMT solver, the default configuration needed a separate manual activation for every PO. This can lead to many mouse clicks when the model is large. Changing the auto-tactic used by Rodin to include SMT solvers and Atelier-B provers significantly reduced the number of manual POs. The order of the provers in the auto-tactic matters. Proof replay was much slower if the PO was discharged using the ML or PP provers. This dramatically increases the Rodin model build time for a model with over 250 POs. Only using the slower provers (ML and PP) when the SMT solver was unsuccessful significantly decreased the time required for proof replay. For larger, industrial models, this difference in verification time can affect user acceptance and, therefore, the willingness to use the Rodin toolset.

How Theorem Guards Can Help Verification. For variables modified in the event actions, the automated provers sometimes could not show that all typing invariants hold. A helpful strategy here was to add a guard to the event, connecting the variable types before and after the event (see, e.g., *hlp1-2* in Fig. 5). This effectively generates a new hypothesis for the solver. If the PO is successfully discharged with the additional guard, the guard is converted into a theorem guard, and the resulting PO is discharged. Conversion into a theorem guard is necessary to ensure that model behavior is not changed inadvertently.

6   Related Work

STPA and Formal Methods. Thomas described how STPA can be used for formalizing safety requirements [15]. He proposed achieving completeness by exhaustively searching the state space. Colley and Butler proposed formalizing system requirements in Event-B iteratively, leveraging a workflow built on refinements [16]. They describe the construction of a formal model derived from STPA safety constraints. In contrast to this work, they do not use observation levels or explain how a refinement hierarchy shall be extracted from the requirements. Howard et al. [17] give a method for combined safety and security analysis of critical infrastructure formalized in Event-B [18].

Formalization. The European Train Control System (ETCS) has been studied extensively in the formal methods community. E.g., [19] discusses the formal verification of ETCS as a case study, and [20,21] discuss the use of formal methods in the railway domain, while [22] describes the use of the B-Method in particular. There are several industrial Event-B models for the safety analysis of railway systems, e.g., [23–25].

Validation of Formal Models. Validation is an essential topic for the industrial application of formal models. Specifically for railway applications, [26] discusses demonstrating and validating an ETCS system using B. A workflow with particular emphasis on validation, called validation-driven development, is described in [27]. It builds upon validation obligations [6] as the validation analog to proof obligations. Validation-driven development could be combined with the promise-driven modeling proposed in this paper.

7   Conclusion and Outlook

This work presents promise-driven modeling to structure formal models' creation, verification, and validation. Promises are used to model and refine informal behavior descriptions into formal statements systematically. The efficacy of the promise-driven modeling approach is shown using Europe's Rail moving block system case study, which is modeled, verified, and validated using the formal method Event-B. We provide lessons learned during verifying and validating this industrial case study.

In the future, we would like to explore ways to instantiate the model at runtime with real-world data and integrate it with an existing demonstrator of the moving block system. In addition, some parts of the model have a more natural representation in B than in Event-B. It would, therefore, be interesting to explore ways to integrate B and Event-B models and the existing moving block demonstrator into a combined system that is interoperable at runtime.

References

1. Leveson, N.: Engineering a Safer World: Systems Thinking Applied to Safety (2012). ISBN 978-0262533690
2. Leveson, N., Thomas, J.: STPA Handbook, p. 188 (2018). https://psas.scripts.mit.edu/home/get_file.php?name=STPA_handbook.pdf
3. Leveson, N.G.: Design and assurance of control software. IEEE Trans. Softw. Eng. **51**(3), 666–672 (2025). https://doi.org/10.1109/TSE.2025.3539975. ISSN 0098-5589, 1939-3520, 2326-3881. Accessed 30 Mar 2025
4. Bergstra, J.A., Burgess, M.: Promise Theory: Principles and Applications. tAxis, Oslo (2014). ISBN 978-1-4954-3777-9
5. Abrial, J.-R.: Modeling in Event-B - System and Software Engineering. Cambridge University Press (2010). ISBN 978-0-521-89556-9
6. Mashkoor, A., Leuschel, M., Egyed, A.: Validation obligations: a novel approach to check compliance between requirements and their formal specification. In: 2021 IEEE/ACM 43rd International Conference on Software Engineering: New Ideas and Emerging Results (ICSE-NIER), pp. 1–5 (2021). https://doi.org/10.1109/ICSE-NIER52604.2021.00009
7. Abrial, J.-R., et al.: Rodin: an open toolset for modelling and reasoning in event-B. Int. J. Softw. Tools Technol. Transfer **12**, 447–466 (2010)
8. Mashkoor, A., Jacquot, J.-P.: Observation-level-driven formal modeling. In: 2015 IEEE 16th International Symposium on High Assurance Systems Engineering (HASE), Daytona Beach, Shores, FL, USA, pp. 158–165. IEEE (2015). ISBN 978-1-4799-8111-3. Accessed 24 Mar 2025
9. Schaber, F., Mashkoor, A., Leuschel, M.: Towards a novel approach to railway safety using STPA and promise theory. In: Liu, S. (ed.) Software Fault Prevention, Verification, and Validation, vol. 15393, pp. 263–279. Springer, Singapore (2025). https://doi.org/10.1007/978-981-96-1621-3_17. Accessed 23 Mar 2025

10. Versluis, N.D., et al.: Real-time railway traffic management under moving-block signalling: a literature review and research agenda. Transp. Res. Part C: Emerg. Technol. **158**, 104438 (2024). https://doi.org/10.1016/j.trc.2023.104438. ISSN 0968090X. Accessed 05 Apr 2025

11. UNISIG. SUBSET-026 System Requirements Specification (2023). https://www.era.europa.eu/system/files/2023-09/index004_-_SUBSET-026_v400.zip

12. EULYNX. Interface Specification SCI-TDS. https://rail-research.europa.eu/wp-content/uploads/2023/06/20230628-Interface-specification-SCI-TDS-Eu.Doc.44-v4.0-2.A.pdf

13. Déharbe, D., Fontaine, P., Guyot, Y., Voisin, L.: SMT solvers for Rodin. In: Derrick, J., et al. (eds.) ABZ 2012. LNCS, vol. 7316, pp. 194–207. Springer, Heidelberg (2012). https://doi.org/10.1007/978-3-642-30885-7_14

14. Werth, M., Leuschel, M.: VisB: a lightweight tool to visualize formal models with SVG graphics. In: Raschke, A., Méry, D., Houdek, F. (eds.) ABZ 2020. LNCS, vol. 12071, pp. 260–265. Springer, Cham (2020). https://doi.org/10.1007/978-3-030-48077-6_21

15. Thomas, J.: Extending and Automating a Systems-Theoretic Hazard Analysis for Requirements Generation and Analysis. SAND2012-4080, 1044959 (2012). https://doi.org/10.2172/1044959

16. Colley, J., Butler, M.: A Formal, Systematic Approach to STPA Using Event-B Refinement and Proof (2013). https://eprints.soton.ac.uk/352155/1/STPAandEventB.pdf

17. Howard, G., et al.: Formal analysis of safety and security requirements of critical systems supported by an extended STPA methodology. In: 2017 IEEE European Symposium on Security and Privacy Workshops (EuroS&PW), Paris, pp. 174–180. IEEE (2017). https://doi.org/10.1109/EuroSPW.2017.68

18. Howard, G., et al.: A methodology for assuring the safety and security of critical infrastructure based on STPA and event-B. Int. J. Critical Comput.-Based Syst. **9**, 56–74 (2019)

19. Platzer, A., Quesel, J.-D.: European train control system: a case study in formal verification. In: Breitman, K., Cavalcanti, A. (eds.) ICFEM 2009. LNCS, vol. 5885, pp. 246–265. Springer, Heidelberg (2009). https://doi.org/10.1007/978-3-642-10373-5_13

20. ter Beek, M.H., et al.: Adopting formal methods in an industrial setting: the railways case. In: ter Beek, M.H., McIver, A., Oliveira, J.N. (eds.) FM 2019. LNCS, vol. 11800, pp. 762–772. Springer, Cham (2019). https://doi.org/10.1007/978-3-030-30942-8_46

21. Ferrari, A., et al.: Survey on formal methods and tools in railways: the ASTRail approach. In: Collart-Dutilleul, S., Lecomte, T., Romanovsky, A. (eds.) RSSRail 2019. LNCS, vol. 11495, pp. 226–241. Springer, Cham (2019). https://doi.org/10.1007/978-3-030-18744-6_15

22. Butler, M., et al.: The first twenty-five years of industrial use of the B-method. In: ter Beek, M.H., Ničković, D. (eds.) FMICS 2020. LNCS, vol. 12327, pp. 189–209. Springer, Cham (2020). https://doi.org/10.1007/978-3-030-58298-2_8

23. Butler, M., et al.: Formal modelling techniques for efficient development of railway control products. In: Fantechi, A., Lecomte, T., Romanovsky, A. (eds.) RSSRail 2017. LNCS, vol. 10598, pp. 71–86. Springer, Cham (2017). https://doi.org/10.1007/978-3-319-68499-4_5

24. Comptier, M., Deharbe, D., Perez, J.M., Mussat, L., Pierre, T., Sabatier, D.: Safety analysis of a CBTC system: a rigorous approach with event-B. In: Fantechi, A.,

Lecomte, T., Romanovsky, A. (eds.) RSSRail 2017. LNCS, vol. 10598, pp. 148–159. Springer, Cham (2017). https://doi.org/10.1007/978-3-319-68499-4_10

25. Sabatier, D.: Using formal proof and B method at system level for industrial projects. In: Lecomte, T., Pinger, R., Romanovsky, A. (eds.) RSSRail 2016. LNCS, vol. 9707, pp. 20–31. Springer, Cham (2016). https://doi.org/10.1007/978-3-319-33951-1_2

26. Hansen, D., et al.: Validation and real-life demonstration of ETCS hybrid level 3 principles using a formal B model. Int. J. Softw. Tools Technol. Transfer **22**(3), 315–332 (2020). https://doi.org/10.1007/s10009-020-00551-6

27. Stock, S., Mashkoor, A., Egyed, A.: Validation-driven development. In: Li, Y., Tahar, S. (eds.) ICFEM 2023. LNCS, vol. 14308, pp. 191–207. Springer, Singapore (2023). https://doi.org/10.1007/978-981-99-7584-6_12

Ensuring Integration Conditions During the Update of Cyber-Physical Systems at Runtime

Janis Kröger[1]([✉]), Ingo Stierand[2], and Martin Fränzle[1]

[1] Carl von Ossietzky Universität Oldenburg, Oldenburg, Germany
{janis.kroeger,martin.fraenzle}@uni-oldenburg.de
[2] German Aerospace Center - Institute of Systems Engineering for Future Mobility,
Oldenburg, Germany
ingo.stierand@dlr.de

Abstract. This paper addresses the challenge of maintaining system integrity and safety during the update processes of cyber-physical systems. We propose an approach that enables updates during operation of small subsets of components, and minimizes system downtime by utilizing the inactive states of system components. The underlying contract-based design (CBD) methodology ensures that integration conditions are maintained. The approach builds upon a CBD framework that supports the specification of operating modes and formal reasoning about integration conditions, thereby providing a mechanism for managing dependencies and maintaining consistency across updates. We demonstrate the practicality of our approach with an example, highlighting how the proposed method can lead to more efficient, safe, and user-accepted updates.

Keywords: Update Process · Updates at Runtime · Contract-based Design · Operating Modes

1 Introduction

Cyber-physical systems are becoming increasingly complex both in terms of hardware and software. For example, highly-automated vehicles are employing centralized high-performance platforms to execute resource-intense software functions such as sensor processing and perception. This trend towards software enables flexible system development along the whole product lifecycle, where regular software updates provide for maintenance of system integrity, introduce new features and enhancements, improve performance, and ensure regulatory compliance as operational conditions change.

Each update may introduce new risks to the system's safety. It is crucial that modifications do not compromise the system's functionality, a goal that necessitates a proper (incremental) safety process. This is the subject of ongoing

This work has been funded by the *Federal Ministry of Education and Research* (BMBF) as part of *AutoDevSafeOps* (01IS22087{Q,C}).

A. Remke and B. Steffen (Eds.): FMICS 2025, LNCS 16040, pp. 203–221, 2025.
https://doi.org/10.1007/978-3-032-00942-5_11

research [24, 32]. However, not only the modification but also the update process itself can pose a safety risk, for example, if system functions must be disabled in order to be updated. This issue can be avoided by updating the system only in a state of standstill. In the automotive domain, updates of vehicle software traditionally are performed in car repair shops, i.e., when disabled functions do not affect the system. This is about to change with over-the-air (OTA) updates, where the vehicle can be updated, e.g., in the garage of the end customer. Results from [15] indicate that the frequency of updates will continue to increase in the future. Updating during standstill has its drawbacks. Long system downtimes may not be acceptable to users. For some systems, such as critical infrastructure, prolonged outages may simply not be viable. To overcome these challenges, updates during system operation have been proposed. Existing strategies, like hot-swapping, enable execution of the current and the updated version in parallel, but require additional resources. This approach does not scale well for larger updates as the amount of required hardware resources may become unreasonable.

This paper proposes an alternative approach to enable updates during operation without bringing the entire system to a standstill. It leverages the states of individual system components, thus reducing the scope of outages from the system level to the component level. An update for a particular component can be carried out whenever two conditions are met: (1) the component is inactive in particular operational conditions, and (2) this inactivity period is sufficiently long for the update to be completed.

Components may change significantly their interface behavior and even interfaces due to an update. If such changes would violate any integration condition, the perimeter of the update needs to be extended, hence involving more components. The paper employs a contract-based design (CBD) methodology, which provides for the necessary formal reasoning about the involved integration conditions. The approach involves the use of operation modes for components. The employed contract language provides the possibility for specification of modes as presented in [22], and for reasoning about integration conditions of updates. The paper builds on these results and introduces modes that allow switching between different behaviors at appropriate time points. More precisely, it enables changing from "previous" behavior into one that enables the update of a component, and to switch to the "new" behavior after the update is completed. The presented method ensures the integrity of the system during updates, while also aiming at minimizing downtime. To this end, a decision procedure based on CBD is presented to determine minimal sets of components that need parallel updates, as well as orderings for sequences of updates that maintain integration conditions.

The paper does not consider technical update procedures, i.e., how data is transmitted and played into the system hardware. Also security issues are out of scope of the paper. The focus is on formally sound consideration of how updates can be performed while maintaining relevant integration conditions of the systems as part of the safety process.

The paper is structured as follows. Section 2 discusses related work. Section 3 provides an overview on the common concepts, which lay the foundation for a discussion of the approach in Sect. 4. Section 5 provides an application scenario to demonstrate the approach. Section 6 concludes the paper.

2   Related Work

Update Process: In order to extend the lifetime of a cyber-physical system by applying updates, it is necessary to integrate the development and deployment of updates into the development process, or more precisely, into the life cycle of the system. Traditionally, this is applied in the context of DevOps cycles [18,23]. There are various projects such as Step-UP!CPS [30] that have addressed the integration of contract-based design [14,16] and over-the-air updates [31] into the DevOps cycle. The execution of an update inevitably takes time. Rakow and Kröger [29] have divided the execution of an update into different phases and described responsibilities across these phases, which are specified by contracts to make the update process predictable and verifiable. Updating components is an intensely studied problem. Existing work considers, among others, dynamic adaption problems [19], dependencies [25], conditions and classifications of updates [27] [28] and changes in the specification [12]. However, there are still gaps in the application of rigorous system design with contract-based design to an agile DevOps cycle. Especially system updates in operation, and the associated verification obligations in the transition phase between two system versions during the update have not yet been addressed.

Update Types: Geisberger and Broy [11] provided a basic classification of system changes that do not require to shut down the system. The classification goes along the type of adjustments that a change entails. Guissouma et al. [14] and Bebawy et al. [3] developed this further in a context in which the system is considered as a component model with interfaces and specifications. Both specifically examine the influence of the individual update types on the interfaces, implementation, and specification of system components. The categories - adaptive, perfective, and corrective updates - each describe different goals and effects of software updates. Adaptive updates aim to adapt the software to changing environments, perfective updates improve performance or functionality, and corrective updates fix bugs. These different update types have a particular impact on updating components with dependencies, as we will see in Sect. 4.2.

Mode Management: There are different methods for specifying and managing operating modes within the context of the development of CPS. These include e.g. state charts proposed by David Harel [17] as well as tools such as AUTOSAR [1], which provides the possibility to install, remove and update software on an AUTOSAR Adaptive Platform [2]. Additionally, there are approaches for use of modes in CBD, as demonstrated by Kröger et al. [21,22]. Our paper builds upon the mode specifications presented in these articles. The basic idea of our approach is somehow similar to Damm et al. [9], who presents a particular realization of a system function by the composition of components that are active only in certain modes, and a protocol to transfer the activation between components. Our paper presents a conceptual view on employing component modes for ensuring a safe update at runtime with the support of contracts.

Impact Analysis: Bebawy et al. [3] have developed an impact analysis that allows for an incremental verification of an update. The analysis is used to step through the effects of an update, and ensures that changes will work as intended without causing unwanted side effects. It allows one to determine which other components are affected by an update and to what extent. The procedure described in the paper can be applied iteratively in a bottom-up fashion up to the top-level system. This impact analysis already refers to the update types from [11] and can be used to identify dependencies. However, it refers to the dependencies for an update at the time a system is in downtime. Dependencies during operation are not considered.

Verification: Oertel and Rettberg [26] present an approach to maintain consistency during the change process. Their change management process identifies all required verification and validation activities due to a change. They already mentioned contract-based design for this process, but do not use it explicitly. Bu et al. [7] describe a process for incremental verification of a system after each individual change of one of its components. Cheng and Tisi [8] present an incremental approach for improving a deductive verification based on post-conditions of previously established contracts. The approach takes previous verification results of the conditions and determines whether they can be reused. If not, they are incrementally re-verified.

In summary, the discussed approaches provide a differentiated view on individual update types and their effects in certain aspects, but do not take into account maintenance of consistency conditions of an update process while the system is running. Existing work mainly focuses on on/off approaches in the sense of a before-and-after analysis of the update. The integration and interaction of individual components in the context of the entire system - and how changes affect the system during the update - are not sufficiently addressed to the best of our knowledge. Such a view however is essential to ensure the safe integration of new or modified functionality of the system for updates at runtime.

3   Preliminaries

Our approach to integrate updates at runtime employs contract-based design to formally express and establish the necessary integration conditions of an update process [22]. The underlying concepts are illustrated in Fig. 1. A *system* is the top-level *component* of a set $\mathcal{C}$ of hierarchically nested components. The system in the example is component *ControlUnit*. For sake of brevity, we focus in the following on three of its sub-components: *ObjectDetection* (*OD*), *PathPlanner* (*PP*) and *Controller*. *ControlUnit* receives sensor data *sd* from several sensors. *OD* uses them for detecting objects, which are fed via *fused_objects* into *PP*

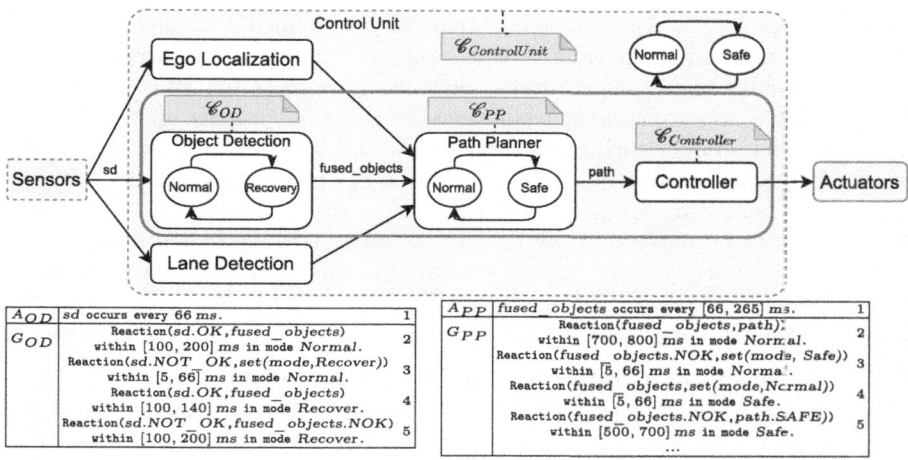

Fig. 1. Example system *ControlUnit*, sub-components, and contract specifications. Component modes and transitions are visualized by transition graphs.

for calculating *path* data to be 'executed' by the *Controller*. Each component has a contract assigned, which specifies the (timing) behavior of the component and its environment. Excerpts of the contracts for *OD* and *PP* are shown at the bottom of Fig. 1. A detailed discussion of the system can be found in [4].

Component Behavior and Specifications: Each component $c \in \mathcal{C}$ is equipped with *ports*, on which the behavior of the component and its environment becomes visible. We differentiate between *event* and *variable* ports. *Event ports* expose the input and output of the component, and are collected in the sets of *input ports* P_c^i and *output ports* P_c^o, respectively. The variable ports are collected in the set P_c^v. Each component must have at least one port, i.e., $P_c := P_c^i \cup P_c^o \cup P_c^v \neq \emptyset$. The set of *system ports* is defined by $\mathcal{P} := \mathcal{P}^i \cup \mathcal{P}^o \cup \mathcal{P}^v$ with $\mathcal{P}^{i/o/v} = \bigcup_{c \in \mathcal{C}} P_c^{i/o/v}$. Input and output ports are collectively referred to as *event ports* $\mathcal{P}^{io} = \mathcal{P}^i \cup \mathcal{P}^o$. In our example, each component is equipped with two ports, an input port and an output port.

The interaction of components $c_1, \ldots, c_n \in \mathcal{C}$ is represented by *signals* $s : \mathcal{P} \rightarrow 2^{\mathcal{P}}$. A signal usually connects an output port $p^o \in \mathcal{P}^o$ with a set of input ports $P^i \subseteq \mathcal{P}^i$. There are two such signals in the example. One signal connects the output port *OD* with the input port of *PP*. The other connects the output port of *PP* with the input port of *Controller*. For connections between two hierarchy levels, signals connect two or more input ports, or two or more output ports. In our example, *ControlUnit* has an input port connected to the input port of *OD*, and an output port connected with the output port of *Controller*.

Behavior observable at an event port $p \in \mathcal{P}^{io}$ is specified over its value domain Σ_p. We assume a special value $\bot \in \Sigma_p$ in every domain, which represents the absence of a value. We define the *dense time* domain $\mathbb{T} = \mathbb{R}_{\geq 0}$ to characterize the occurrence of events. Each event port has non-absent values for a countable set of time points $T \subset \mathbb{T}$. An event e occurring at p is defined as a tuple $e = (\sigma, t)$, which consists of an event value $\sigma \in \Sigma_p$ and the time of its occurrence $t \in T$. A *timed trace* over port p is a infinite sequence $w_p = (\sigma_i, t_i)_{i \in \mathbb{N}}$ of events, where $(t_i)_{i \in \mathbb{N}}$ forms a monotonic sequence of time instances. We require all timed traces to be non-zeno, i.e., for each $t \in T$ exists (σ_i, t_i) such that $t_i \geq t$. We denote the set of timed traces over p by $\Omega_p = \{ w = (\sigma_i, t_i)_{i \in \mathbb{N}} \}$. For port sets $P \subseteq \mathcal{P}^{io}$ we define timed traces $(\boldsymbol{\sigma}_i, t_i)_{i \in \mathbb{N}}$ over P, where $\boldsymbol{\sigma}_i = (\sigma_1, \ldots, \sigma_n) \in \Sigma_{p_1} \times \cdots \times \Sigma_{p_n}$. Denote the set of traces over P by $\Omega_P = \{ w_P = (\boldsymbol{\sigma}_i, t_i)_{i \in \mathbb{N}} \}$. In contrast to event ports, variable ports $p \in \mathcal{P}^v$ have a non-absent value from a value domain V_p at each point in time $t \in \mathbb{T}$. Behavior is defined as functions $v_p : \mathbb{T} \to V_p$. We employ a variable port to specify operating modes of components and systems.

Assume/Guarantee Contracts and Virtual Integration Test: This work follows the contract framework of Assume/Guarantee (A/G) contracts from [5], in which contracts are defined as pairs of an *assumption* A, which specifies behavior of the environment, and a *guarantee* G specifying the behavior of the component. For convenience, we assume a specification language Φ, where each $\varphi \in \Phi$ induces a set $L_\varphi \subseteq \Omega_P$ of timed traces over a port set P. The example in Fig. 1 shows some specification patterns from [22]. The *occurrence* pattern (X occurs every ...) specifies a recurring event with a recurrence rate defined by a time interval. The *reaction* pattern specifies a time delay between different events. For both patterns exist formal mappings to the corresponding trace language. To keep things simple, we assume exactly one contract $\mathscr{C}_c$ assigned to each component $c \in \mathcal{C}$, where $\mathscr{C}_c = (\Phi_c^A, \Phi_c^G)$ such that $\Phi_c^A, \Phi_c^G \subseteq \Phi$. Naturally, each $\varphi \in \Phi_c^A \cup \Phi_c^G$ must refer only to the component ports P_c. For a set $\Phi' \subseteq \Phi$ of specifications, we define $L_{\Phi'} = \bigcap_{\varphi \in \Phi'} L_\varphi$, and the set of timed traces that comply with a given A/G contract as $L_{\mathscr{C}_c} = \Omega_{P_c} \setminus L_{\Phi_c^A} \cup L_{\Phi_c^G}$. In other words, the meaning of a contract complies with the logical implication $\Phi_c^A \implies \Phi_c^G$. This meaning gives reason to the following definition of *contract satisfaction*: If we denote by L_c the possible behavior of component c, we say, c *satisfies* $\mathscr{C}_c$, written $c \models^M \mathscr{C}_c$, if $L_c \cap L_{\Phi_c^A} \subseteq L_{\Phi_c^G}$. In other words, c satisfies its contract if it behaves as specified by the guarantee under all possible behaviors of its environment.

By using contracts, integrity properties are defined for a component, such as consistency and compatibility. A contract is *consistent* if it has at least one implementation $c \in M_{\mathscr{C}}$, i.e. $c \models^M \mathscr{C}$, where $M_{\mathscr{C}}$ denotes the set of implementations of $\mathscr{C}$. A contract is *compatible* if it has at least one valid environment $E \in E_{\mathscr{C}}$, i.e., $E \models^E \mathscr{C}$. There are two main definitions in contract-based design that are relevant in the context of this paper. Any contract theory relies on a *composition* operation that defines how new components are obtained from the composition of other (sub-)components. Along this operation on components, *contract composition* defines how to obtain a contract from the contracts of other lower-level contracts, written $\mathscr{C} = \mathscr{C}_1 \otimes \mathscr{C}_2$. We refer to [5] for the formal definition of composition which is:

$$\mathscr{C}_1 \otimes \mathscr{C}_2 = \min \left\{ \mathscr{C} \; \middle| \; \begin{bmatrix} \forall c_1 \\ \forall c_2 \\ \forall E \end{bmatrix} : \begin{bmatrix} c_1 & \models^M \mathscr{C}_1 \\ \text{and } c_2 & \models^M \mathscr{C}_2 \\ \text{and } E & \models^E \mathscr{C} \end{bmatrix} \implies \begin{bmatrix} c_1 \times c_2 & \models^M \mathscr{C} \\ \text{and } E \times c_2 & \models^E \mathscr{C}_1 \\ \text{and } E \times c_1 & \models^E \mathscr{C}_2 \end{bmatrix} \right\}$$

From this general definition, the parallel composition of A/G contracts can be defined as follows: The composition $\mathscr{C}_1 \otimes \mathscr{C}_2$ of $\mathscr{C}_1 = (A_1, G_1)$ and $\mathscr{C}_2 = (A_2, G_2)$ is the pair (A, G), where $G = G_1 \cap G_2$ and $A = (A_1 \cap A_2) \cup \neg(G_1 \cap G_2)$.

The *refinement* relation defines under which circumstances a component can be replaced by another without violating existing specifications. We say, $\mathscr{C}'$ refines $\mathscr{C}$, written $\mathscr{C}' \preceq \mathscr{C}$, if $E_{\mathscr{C}'} \supseteq E_{\mathscr{C}}$, and $M_{\mathscr{C}'} \subseteq M_{\mathscr{C}}$. It means that component c' allows for more behavior of its environment and has less behavior than c. For our A/G contracts, this translates to $L_{\Phi^{A'}} \supseteq L_{\Phi_c^A}$ and $L_{\Phi_c^{G'}} \subseteq L_{\Phi_c^G}$. Note that $\mathscr{C}_1' \preceq \mathscr{C}_1$ and $\mathscr{C}_2' \preceq \mathscr{C}_2$ implies $\mathscr{C}_1' \otimes \mathscr{C}_2' \preceq \mathscr{C}_1 \otimes \mathscr{C}_2$ (*independent implementability*). For A/G contracts, $\mathscr{C}' \preceq \mathscr{C}$ holds if and only if $A' \supseteq A$ and $G' \subseteq G$. We refer the interested reader to Benveniste et al. [5] for more details. Exploiting contract composition and refinement, we can define what it means for a system (component) S to satisfy a specification. Given that S is specified by a contract $\mathscr{C}_S$, and S is composed by a set of components $\mathcal{C}$, S satisfies its specification, i.e., $S \models \mathscr{C}_S$, if $\otimes_{c \in \mathcal{C}} \mathscr{C}_c \preceq \mathscr{C}_S$.

Checking the condition $\otimes_{c \in \mathcal{C}} \mathscr{C}_c \preceq \mathscr{C}_S$ is also called virtual integration test (VIT). VIT thus can be used to verify that the specification of components in their combination is correct and consistent. For this purpose, the contracts of the individual components are used, which specify the behavior of the component and the expected behavior of its environment. The VIT checks the conditions under which these contracts are consistent in their composition, and whether this composition fulfills the contract of the higher-level component, i.e., whether there is a valid refinement.

For A/G-contracts, the corresponding conditions can be divided into three parts. The first condition checks that the contracts are compatible in their interconnection. To this end, the assumption of each sub-component must be consistent with the guaranteed behavior of the components that provide the input signals for the component. As an example, the output behavior of component OD in Fig. 1 must comply with the assumption about the input behavior of component PP.

Second, the assumptions of all sub-components must be consistent with the assumptions of the higher-level component specified in the contract. In our example, this reduces to checking whether the assumption of *ControlUnit* is a subset of the assumption of component OD: $A_{ControlUnit} \subseteq A_{OD}$.

Finally, a similar condition applies to the guarantee side. More precisely, the guarantees of the sub-components must satisfy the guarantee of the higher-level component. The interested reader is referred to [10] for more details about VIT for A/G contracts.

Operating Modes: Many application scenarios call for specifications that incorporate operational modes. A mode represents an internal state of a component. For example, a driver assistance system may be active only in certain situations. Safety mechanisms typically require distinguishing normal and degraded

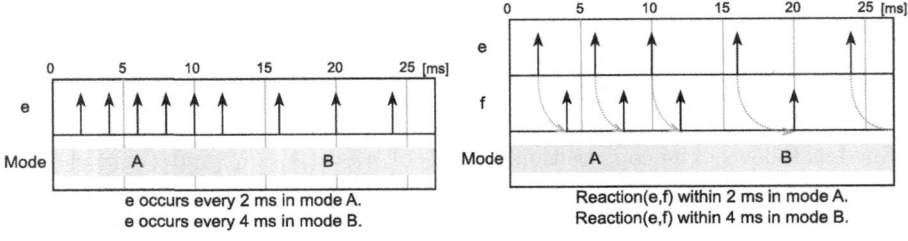

Fig. 2. Example traces of specification pattern.

operation modes of certain components. In our example, $ControlUnit$ and PP both have two operation modes, $Normal$ and $Safe$. If PP does not receive any fused objects (denoted by $fused\_objects.NOK$), it switches to mode $Safe$ within 5–66 ms. In this mode, it tries to bring the vehicle into a safe state within 500–700 ms (e.g. by calculating a path to the hard shoulder of the road). The component switches back to $Normal$ if it receives $fused\_objects$ again. $ObjectDetection$ also has two modes ($Normal$ and $Recovery$), indicating if the received sensor data are valid. $Controller$ has no dedicated modes.

VIT verifies that the specification of a component is consistent with the combined specifications of its sub-components. With modes, this includes that the sub-components are operating in a valid mode combination with respect to the mode of the $ControlUnit$. This of course requires a well-defined mode mapping between the two component levels. In our example, mode mapping is given by $(OD.Normal, PP.Normal) \rightarrow ControlUnit.Normal$. This implies that the combined timing specification of OD and PP in mode $Normal$ has to fulfill the timing specification of $ControlUnit$ in mode $Normal$. All other mode combinations map to $ControlUnit.Safe$, and thus the corresponding timing specifications have to fit, too. The active mode of a component is visible at its interface in the form of a particular variable port $mode$. Modes can be specified in the assumption and in the guarantee of an A/G contract. A mode specified in a guarantee represents the behavior of the component when this mode is active. A mode specified in the assumption represents the expected behavior of the environment, again as long as the component is in the specified mode.

For a better understanding, we want to briefly illustrate the specification patterns used and the traces specified by them. Basically, we are looking at the behavior that becomes visible at event ports of a component. Which mode is active is determined by the port $mode$ at the time an event occurs. The left of Fig. 2 gives an example for the occurrence of event e over modes A and B. The pattern "$Event$ occurs every I ms in mode m" describes the periodic occurrence of $Event$ in a period of interval I when mode m is active. The trace shows a situation where the behavior changes between the patterns when a mode switch between A and B occurs. The pattern "$Reaction(e, f)$ within I ms in mode m" at the right of Fig. 2 describes a time delay in the form of a "reaction" between $Event_1$ and $Event_2$ with the length of the interval I. e precedes f and serves as trigger to check whether mode m is active. More details on these specification patterns and their semantics can be found in [21].

4 Mode View

In this section, we develop a particular *mode view* that enables specifying updates and update processes at the component level. It employs A/G contracts with mode specifications, which allows us to resolve dependencies between components in the update process in a generic way. The basic idea is to consider the operating modes of a component as an internal structure that consists of so-called *mode components*. Suppose a component $c \in \mathcal{C}$ that has modes $\mathcal{M} = \{m_1, m_2, m_3\}$. To establish the mode view, we pretend that each mode m_i of c is realized by a distinct mode component c_{m_i}. Each mode component is specified by a contract $\mathscr{C}_{m_i}$ corresponding to the behavior of component c in mode m_i. With the reasonable assumption that always only one mode component is active at a time, we can define $\mathscr{C}_{m_i}$ such that the integration condition $\mathscr{C}_c \succcurlyeq \mathscr{C}_{m_1} \otimes \mathscr{C}_{m_2} \otimes \mathscr{C}_{m_3}$ holds. We will use this basic idea to update c by replacing the corresponding mode components.

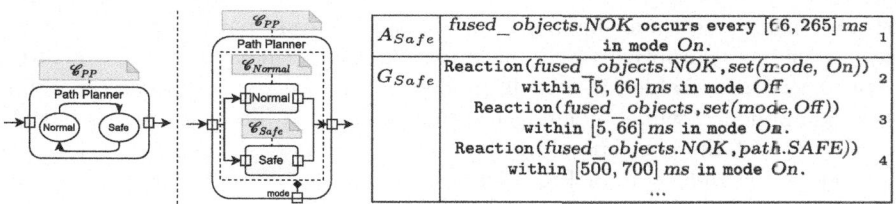

Fig. 3. Mode view of *PathPlanner*, contract $\mathscr{C}_{Safe}$ of mode component *Safe*.

For illustration we consider our example system in Fig. 1. Component *PathPlanner* has the modes $\mathcal{M} = \{Normal, Safe\}$. The behavior of *PathPlanner* is specified by $\mathscr{C}_{PP}$. If we apply the mode view to this component, we obtain a decomposition of the component into two the mode components *Normal* and *Safe*, as depicted at the left side of Fig. 3. The dashed box around the mode components is an abstract representation of a mode mapping.

The component *PathPlanner* in the example is a leaf component, i.e., it does not consist of sub components. If otherwise the considered component is a composite, we can decompose the mode components as well. In this case, the mode components c_{m_i} of component c are constituted by mode components of the sub components of c. The resulting hierarchies of mode components must be of course in accordance with the refinement and composition operations of the CBD. In other words, it must be ensured that contract $\mathscr{C}_{m_i}$ of mode component c_{m_i} again is refined by the composition of it's lower-level mode components. For example, if component *PathPlanner* would be a composite of two sub-components, then mode components *Normal* and *Safe* would also be composed of, say, $Normal_1, Normal_2$ and $Safe_1, Safe_2$, respectively. For mode $Normal$ we would demand $\mathscr{C}_{Normal} \succcurlyeq \mathscr{C}_{Normal_1} \otimes \mathscr{C}_{Normal_2}$, where $\mathscr{C}_{Normal_i}$ is the contract of mode component $Normal_i$ in mode $Normal$.

4.1 On/Off Modes and Contract Transformation

It is a crucial property of the mode view that the newly introduced mode components have exactly two modes, say On and Off, one in which they are active, and one in which they are inactive. It is also fundamental that always only one of the mode components of a component c is in mode On, while all other mode components of c are in mode Off. This of course corresponds with the fact that the original component is always in a certain mode.

The application of the mode view requires that the mode components c_{m_i} are equipped with contracts $\mathscr{C}_{m_i}$ that comply with the specification $\mathscr{C}_c$ of the component c. The required correspondence is the integration condition $\mathscr{C}_c \succcurlyeq \mathscr{C}_{m_1} \otimes ... \otimes \mathscr{C}_{m_n}$. We establish contracts $\mathscr{C}_{m_i}$ in three steps. First, we split the specification of component c with respect to the individual modes, and assign the resulting specifications to the corresponding mode components. Secondly, we take care about mode transitions, and finally about the assumptions.

Generally, splitting a contract into the behavior for individual modes is a complex task. Here come the mode-specific specification patterns from [22] into play, which enable applying a simple transformation scheme. First, specification patterns that are enabled in certain modes are transferred to *all* corresponding mode components, while changing the modes (e.g., m_i and m_j) in the pattern to mode On of the corresponding mode components (e.g., c_{m_i} and c_{m_j}). The contract at the right side of Fig. 3 shows the transfer of the guarantee of component $PathPlanner$ for mode $Safe$ ("Reaction() within ... in mode $Safe$") to the guarantee of mode component $PathPlanner_{Safe}$ ("Reaction() within ... in mode On") for the example.

In case a component does not provide specification of modes like the $Controller$ in our running example, the only viable option is to monolithically replace the entire component while it is inactive. If also no specification exists that guarantees the inactivity of the component sometimes, it cannot be replaced in a safe manner at all, which is of course a prerequisite for updating it. Gracefully deactivating a component is also a necessary condition for performing a hot swap with an additional parallel component. Without this option, it is not possible to deactivate the original component using this procedure without the possibility of introducing issues in the form of at least transient inconsistencies.

A contract is also supposed to specify allowed mode transitions. These transitions define when c changes the mode and how long this change takes. To get a correct specification of mode components, we have to consider these transitions and transform them into the contracts of the mode components. The transformation scheme is as follows: The conditions that lead to the mode change of c, say from mode m_i to m_j, are transformed into a trigger for component c_{m_i} to change from mode On to Off, and for mode component c_{m_j} from mode Off to On at the same time. For example in Fig. 3, we transfer the mode change specification from mode *Safe* to *Normal* ("Reaction(*fused_objects*,*set(mode, Normal)*) within ... in mode *Safe*.") to the guarantee of mode component *PathPlanner$_{Safe}$* ("Reaction(*fused_objects*,*set(mode, Off)*) within ... in mode *On*."). This corresponds to specifying of a mode change from *Off* to *On* for mode component *PathPlanner$_{Normal}$*. As outlined by Kröger et al. [22], there may be pre- and post-phases in the specification to express an interval for obligations between inputs and outputs related to the previous mode. These pre- and post-phases are also transformed to the specifications for the mode components.

Finally, also the contract assumption needs to be transformed. An assumption is translated as an assumption for the corresponding mode component if it is valid for the realized mode. In the example, the assumption of *PathPlanner* has no explicit mode and thus is valid in every mode. That means it becomes an assumption of every mode component of *PathPlanner*. If we transfer the assumption to the mode component *Normal*, it however must be specified only for mode *On*. This ensures that the mode component *Normal* does not make any assumptions about the behavior of the environment in *Off* mode. The exception is the occurrence of a trigger that initiates a mode change from mode *Off* to mode *On*.

4.2 Dependencies

When a component is updated, often also the component's contracts will be adapted. As indicated in Sect. 3, this may lead to the situation where the integration conditions become violated due to the update, because of the dependencies between components regarding their inputs and outputs. As we will see, there are different reasons for a violation of the integration conditions, which have also different impacts on an update with respect to dealing with dependencies. We again consider our example system in Fig. 1, which consists of the components *OD*, *PathPlanner*, and *Controller*, and the corresponding contracts $\mathscr{C}_{OD}$, $\mathscr{C}_{PP}$, $\mathscr{C}_{Controller}$, $\mathscr{C}_{ControlUnit}$. The relevant integration condition thus is given by $\mathscr{C}_{OD} \otimes \mathscr{C}_{PP} \otimes \mathscr{C}_{Controller} \preceq \mathscr{C}_{ControlUnit}$. We want to update the component *PathPlanner* together with an updated contract $\mathscr{C}'_{PP}$. Figure 1 reveals the specific dependencies of component *PathPlanner* in terms of its assumptions on *OD* and its guarantees to *Controller*.

CBD defines a notion of *independent implementability*. It says that a contract $\mathscr{C}$ can be replaced by a contract $\mathscr{C}'$ without any impact on the integration conditions if $\mathscr{C}' \preceq \mathscr{C}$ holds. Applied to A/G-contracts, this means $A' \supseteq A$, and $G' \subseteq G$. In other words the assumption may become weaker and the guarantee may become stronger. These conditions impose dependencies on the updates of individual components. More precisely, the violation of any of the two conditions may require a change of the effected environment component, and determines ordering constraints of these changes. We distinguish the following cases:

Stronger Assumptions: In case that the assumption of the updated component is more restrictive than its original ones (i.e., $A' \subset A$), the environment component providing these inputs may no longer satisfy the new assumption. For consistency, as described in Sect. 3, the guarantee G_{en} of an environment component must be a subset of the successor component, i.e., $G_{en} \subseteq A$. Updating to a more restrictive assumption $A' \subset A$ may lead to the situation where G_{en} is a superset of A', i.e., $G_{en} \supset A'$. As a result, the assumed input cannot be guaranteed, which imposes a violation of the integration conditions. As a consequence, an update of the environment component with respect to its guarantee is necessary to maintain the integration conditions. Moreover, if we want to perform an incremental update, the environment component must be updated first.

In our example, this may be the case if the input for *PathPlanner* is changed to occur every 66–250 ms instead of the original 66–265 ms. This change does not impose an integration issue if the guarantee of the effected component, in our example *OD*, would be consistent to the new assumption. However, the guarantee of *OD* cannot ensure that the input occurs in the new required interval after the update. This means that it would not be a valid environment of *PathPlanner* anymore and results in an update sequence of *OD* before *PathPlanner* to keep the integration condition consistent. Note that an update of *OD* would not violate an integration condition if it tightens the guarantee, i.e., $G'_{OD} \subseteq G_{OD}$.

Weaker Guarantees: In case of a weaker guarantee resulting from an update, namely $G \subset G'$, there is a dependency in the direction of the assumptions of the successor component (A_{sc}). Similarly, as with stronger assumptions, the relation to successive components must be $G \subseteq A_{sc}$. Like a stronger assumption in the other direction, a weaker guarantee may result in G becoming a superset of A_{sc}, i.e., $G \supset A_{sc}$. This again leads to inconsistency in the specification, meaning that the successor component must also be updated. To maintain consistency over the update of all components, the successor component must be updated first.

An example would be the alteration of the reaction time to an input of *PathPlanner* from 500–700 ms to 500–900 ms in mode *Safe*. In this case, also *Controller* must be updated because otherwise the component *Processing* does not provide a valid environment for *Controller* anymore. Consequently, the component *Controller* must be adapted first such that it gets an assumption that reflects consistently with the new behavior of *PathPlanner*.

Stronger Assumptions and Weaker Guarantees: The combination of the previous two impacts requires updates to both environment components and successor components. The update sequence must adhere to the sequence of the previous cases. This results in two valid updates sequences, namely environment component, successor component, original component and successor component, environment component, original component.

4.3   Update Sequences

Establishing the mode view enables replacing individual modes at a time by replacing the associated mode component. If more than one mode must be

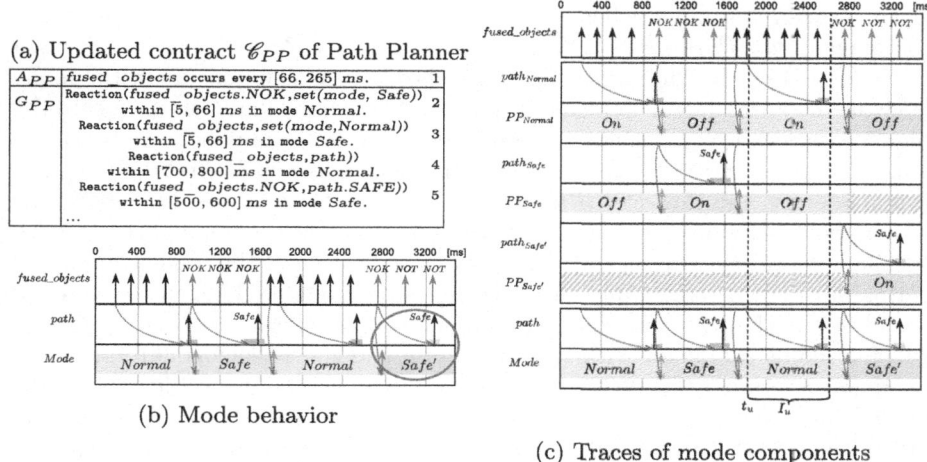

(a) Updated contract $\mathscr{C}_{PP}$ of Path Planner

(b) Mode behavior

(c) Traces of mode components

Fig. 4. Update of component *PathPlanner*.

changed, the change is split into several subsequent updates. In general, we replace mode component c_{m_i} only if it is in mode *Off*. In order to decide when an update could be performed, the specified mode changes in the contract $\mathscr{C}_c$ of component c need to be considered. The conditions under which c is in an updateable state are as following: (1) the mode component that is to be replaced switches into mode *Off*, and (2) it remains there for a amount of time that is needed to perform the update. We denote by t_u a point in time when (1) is fulfilled, e.g., when a certain driving situation occurs. This includes that at time point t_u no obligations between inputs and outputs of the previous mode exist, as they can be specified by the use of pre- and post-phases in the specification patterns introduced in [22]. Meaning that the point in time is after the end of the post-phase. Note that determining this time is out of the scope of this paper. There are approaches to deal with this issue [13,20]. We further denote the time span required to perform an update by I_u. This time depends on the update and the application, so we consider also this value as given.

To illustrate our approach, we refer to our example, and consider an update of component *PathPlanner*. In the following we mark new versions of components by "'". The intended update is shown in Fig. 4, where changes are highlighted with a circle and colored in red. The update affects mode *Safe* of the component, and allows calculating the outputs faster in this mode after the update. Applying the mode view, the update will replace mode component $PathPlanner_{Safe}$.

From contract $\mathscr{C}_{PP}$ we derive when it is in an updatable state, i.e., when mode component $PathPlanner_{Safe}$ is in mode *Off*. For this we consider the timing specification in the contracts. The semantics of the specification patterns define traces that express the behavior regarding input and output as well as mode changes. By analyzing the possible points in time when a mode change may occur, we can determine when $PathPlanner_{Normal}$ is On to replace the mode component $PathPlanner_{Safe}$. A suitable behavior for $PathPlanner$ is shown in the trace of Fig. 4b. The same trace, now showing the components in the mode view during an update is depicted in Fig. 4c. The hatched area shows where the "new" component $Safe'$ is not yet active, and the "old" component $Safe$ can no longer become active. At time point t_u, mode component $PathPlanner_{Normal}$ is in mode On, and thus $PathPlanner$ is in an updateable state. This allows the replacement of mode component $PathPlanner_{Safe}$ which is completed after the specific interval I_u. Subsequently, the new specification of the mode component $PathPlanner_{Safe'}$ will apply the next time the mode is changed to $Safe$. In the example, the new behavior results in a stronger guarantee $G_{Safe'} \subseteq G_{Safe}$, which remains compliant with the integration and consistency conditions.

If we determine (by performing a VIT) that an update would violate the integration conditions of a mode component, it is necessary to keep the affected mode component in mode Off until all necessary adjustments to other components have been made. This of course may result in a degraded functionality over a specific time. If this is not feasible, an option is to utilize hot swapping, which of course requires provisioning of redundant resources. The mode view, however, enables the reduction of those resources to the size of a single mode component. In any case, it is necessary to adapt additional components. Two scenarios to update additional components are described in Sect. 5.

Once one or more mode components have been replaced, we can set the new mode component to On at a valid point in time. In consequence of this modification, the previous component mode is no longer a viable option.

5   Applications in Update Scenarios

The approach described in Sect. 4.3 enables updating components at runtime also in presence of dependencies. It ensures that only inactive parts of the system are updated and in turn no unpredictable behavior occurs. In the following we consider two scenarios for updating multiple components, namely a parallel and a step-wise update. Particularly the latter scenario illustrates the benefit of our approach of maintaining consistency and integration conditions at runtime. It does so by identifying dependencies in the contract specifications to define an ordering of successively updated components, avoiding the need for shutdown of the whole system. As described in Sect. 4.3, we assume values for t_u (time point at which the affected components are in an updateable state) and I_u (time required to complete the update) are known.

We illustrate the scenarios by our running example from Fig. 1. An update shall be performed on the two components $ObjectDetection$ and $PathPlanner$. The update of $ObjectDetection$ results in the fact that a reaction now may require more time (210 instead of 200ms) if the component is in mode $Recover$. In order to compensate for the additional in the even chain, the engineers managed to reduce the maximal time needed to calculate a safe path in $PathPlanner$ by those 10ms. The additional time needed by the $ObjectDetection$ results in a weaker guarantee, which is no more covered by the assumption of *PathPlanner*, and results in a violation of the integration condition if the *PathPlanner* is in mode *Safe*. Consequently, it is necessary to adapt the assumption too. Following our approach, we first transfer both components to the mode view and replace mode component *Recovery* of the *OD* component, and mode component *Safe* of the *PathPlanner* component. The result is shown in Fig. 5a, where the new specifications are depicted at the bottom of the left side, and the mode components at the top of the left side. Now we have two options for the replacement, a parallel update or a step wise update that we describe in the next paragraphs.

Parallel Updates: With a parallel update, all mode components that require adaptation are replaced simultaneously. This implies that all affected components must be in an updateable state at the same time point t_u. In particular, all affected mode components must be in mode *Off* and remain in *Off* for the duration of the update. Obviously, all mode components must be successfully replaced after the scheduled time I_u has elapsed. A significant benefit of a parallel update is the fact that all dependencies can be resolved in one step. Since the affected mode components are replaced simultaneously, no update sequences need to be followed to ensure that the integration conditions are not violated. This leads to a shorter overall update duration. However, the time I_u needed for updating multiple components at once may be a limiting factor. For a parallel update of our example we determine time point t_u where it is possible to replace the mode components *Recovery* and *Safe* together. Since the two mode components are updated simultaneously when they are in the mode *Off*, all consistency and integration conditions remain satisfied.

Step-Wise Updates: For complex systems consisting of many components, update processes can be very time-consuming, especially if an extensive update of many parts is required. Furthermore, in some systems, it is not possible to update several affected components simultaneously due to the mode change behavior, if they are not in an updateable state at the same time. By carrying out the update step by step, i.e., by replacing mode components one after the other, it is possible to update also these systems. This approach indeed may result in a longer overall update duration due to the sequential execution of the individual phases. In order to resolve existing dependencies between the components, an update sequence needs to be determined that ensures the integration condition is not violated across all steps of the update. The time in which a mode component is not usable can be considered individually for each component. This can reduce the time required to replace individual mode components, thereby reducing the individual downtime associated with the update process.

Since a step-wise update is common practice and our given specification allows a step-wise update, based on the different mode changes of OD and PP, we want to illustrate this in more detail. The specified component behavior during the execution of the update with traces is shown in Fig. 5b. In our example, there are in principle different sequences for a step-by-step update, taking into account possible problems due to dependencies, as described in Sect. 4.2. In our example, the PP_{Safe} component is adapted first. We assume that we can replace it at time t_{u_1}. After time I_{u_1} the first update step is completed so that the component PP_{Safe} now expects an input within 66–275 ms instead of 265 ms. In addition, the output is now calculated within 500–690 ms instead of 700 ms. The first step of this update results in weaker assumptions and stronger guarantees of PP_{Safe}, so that it is formally a refinement in CBD. A violation of the integration conditions is thus excluded. In a second step, the mode component *Recover* of *OD* can now be replaced. For this, the time t_{u_2} is assumed. This is after the end of the update of PP to ensure that no inconsistencies occur and thus the integration conditions are not violated. The update is finished after I_{u_2}. After this update, *OD* provides an output in *Recovery* mode within 100–210 ms instead of 200 ms. This update step is an extension of the guarantees. However, due to the previous adaptation of PP, it does not lead to a violation of the integration conditions. The assumptions for the Normal mode remain unaffected, as can be seen in the contract in Fig. 5a. It is conceivable that the update could take place over several mode change cycles, provided that the integration conditions are met. The resulting updated system is the same as in the parallel update shown in Fig. 5a.

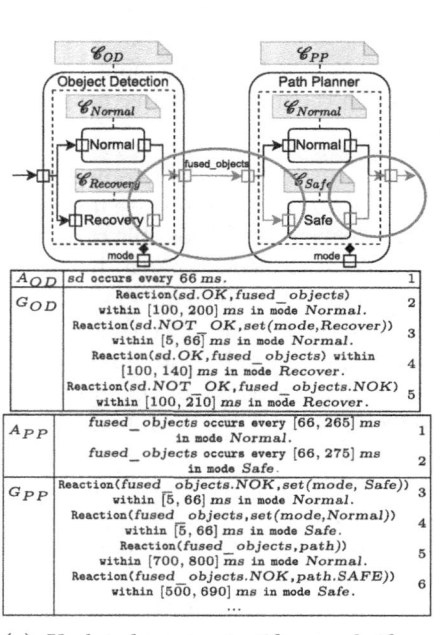
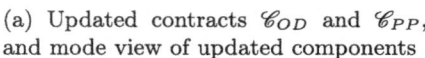
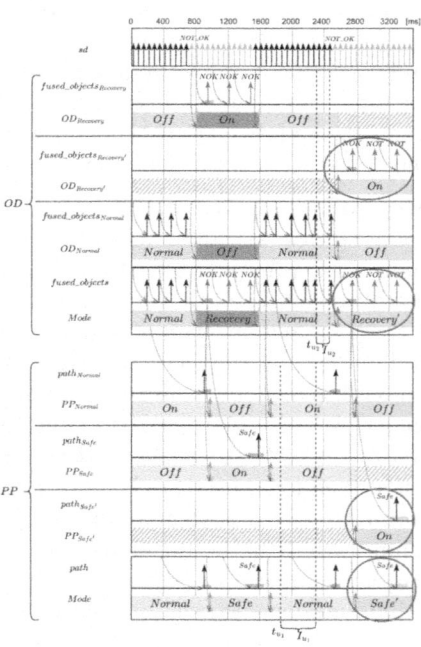

(a) Updated contracts $\mathscr{C}_{OD}$ and $\mathscr{C}_{PP}$, and mode view of updated components

(b) Behavior of *PathPlanning* and *ObjectDetection*

Fig. 5. Step-wise Update with Components *PathPlanning* and *ObjectDetection*.

6   Conclusion

The paper presents an approach of a mode view based on the contract-based design paradigm, in which operation modes of a component are considered as individual mode components, and mode switching translates to turning components on and off. This enables reducing the scope for an update from the system-level down to the component-level. At the same time, the CBD paradigm defines the necessary integration conditions for the update process and thus ensures the consistency of the update process. The approach supports the resolution of dependencies between components with the help of a set of particular specification patterns, combined with impact analysis. We demonstrated the applicability of the approach by two scenarios, showing possible resolutions of dependencies by parallel and step-wise updates, respectively. The presented approach thus closes a gap in continuous DevOps-based design, where systems are continuously developed and updated, based on formal specifications in the contract-based design paradigm. An important next step is to develop tool support, such as automated VIT analysis for the presented specification language. This could be achieved, e.g., by extending the tooling of the MULTIC framework presented in [6].

References

1. AUTOSAR: Guide to mode management (2022). https://www.autosar.org
2. AUTOSAR: Specification of update and configuration management. Technical report, AP R22-11 (2022)
3. Bebawy, Y., et al.: Incremental contract-based verification of software updates for safety-critical cyber-physical systems. In: 2020 International Conference on Computational Science and Computational Intelligence (CSCI). IEEE (2020). https://doi.org/10.1109/CSCI51800.2020.00318
4. Becker, J.S., Koopmann, B., Stierand, I., Westhofen, L.: Providing evidence for correct and timely functioning of software safety mechanisms. In: Software Engineering 2023 Workshops, pp. 66–77. Gesellschaft für Informatik eV (2023)
5. Benveniste, A., et al.: Contracts for System Design. Found. Trends Electron. Des. Autom. $12(2-3)$, 124–400 (2018). https://doi.org/10.1561/1000000053
6. Böde, E., et al.: MULTIC-tooling. In: FAT Series, No. 316, Research Association for Automotive Technology (2019). https://www.vda.de/vda/de/aktuelles/publikationen/publication/fat-schriftenreihe-316
7. Bu, L., Xing, S., Ren, X., Yang, Y., Wang, Q., Li, X.: Incremental online verification of dynamic cyber-physical systems. In: 2019 Design, Automation & Test in Europe Conference & Exhibition (DATE), pp. 782–787. IEEE (2019)
8. Cheng, Z., Tisi, M.: Incremental deductive verification for relational model transformations. In: 2017 IEEE International Conference on Software Testing, Verification and Validation (ICST), pp. 379–389. IEEE (2017)
9. Damm, W., Dierks, H., Oehlerking, J., Pnueli, A.: Towards component based design of hybrid systems: safety and stability. In: Manna, Z., Peled, D.A. (eds.) Time for Verification. LNCS, vol. 6200, pp. 96–143. Springer, Heidelberg (2010). https://doi.org/10.1007/978-3-642-13754-9_6

10. Damm, W., Hungar, H., Josko, B., Peikenkamp, T., Stierand, I.: Using contract-based component specifications for virtual integration testing and architecture design. In: 2011 Design, Automation & Test in Europe, pp. 1023–1028. IEEE (2011). https://doi.org/10.1109/DATE.2011.5763167

11. Geisberger, E., Broy, M.: Cyber-physical systems: visionen, charakteristika und neue fähigkeiten. agendaCPS: Integrierte Forschungsagenda Cyber-Physical Systems, pp. 29–68 (2012)

12. Ghezzi, C., Greenyer, J., Manna, V.P.L.: Synthesizing dynamically updating controllers from changes in scenario-based specifications. In: 2012 7th International Symposium on Software Engineering for Adaptive and Self-Managing Systems (SEAMS), pp. 145–154 (2012). https://doi.org/10.1109/SEAMS.2012.6224401

13. Göttmann, H., Caesar, B., Beers, L., Lochau, M., Schürr, A., Fay, A.: Cost-sensitive precomputation of real-time-aware reconfiguration strategies based on stochastic priced timed games. Softw. Syst. Model. 1–31 (2024)

14. Guissouma, H., Hohl, C.P., Lesniak, F., Schindewolf, M., Becker, J., Sax, E.: Life-cycle management of automotive safety-critical over the air updates: a systems approach. IEEE Access 10, 57696–57717 (2022)

15. Guissouma, H., Klare, H., Sax, E., Burger, E.: An empirical study on the current and future challenges of automotive software release and configuration management. In: 2018 44th Euromicro Conference on Software Engineering and Advanced Applications (SEAA), pp. 298–305. IEEE (2018)

16. Hake, G., Hohl, C.P., Hahn, A.: Continuous contract based verification of updates in maritime shipboard equipment. J. Mar. Sci. Eng. 9(7), 688 (2021)

17. Harel, D.: Statecharts: a visual formalism for complex systems. Sci. Comput. Program. 8(3), 231–274 (1987)

18. Jabbari, R., bin Ali, N., Petersen, K., Tanveer, B.: What is devops? A systematic mapping study on definitions and practices. In: Proceedings of the Scientific Workshop Proceedings of XP2016, pp. 1–11 (2016)

19. Ketfi, A., Belkhatir, N., Cunin, P.Y.: Dynamic updating of component-based applications. In: SERP 2002 (2002)

20. Kröger, J., Fränzle, M.: Updates at runtime for cyber physical systems. A game theoretic approach. In: Software Engineering 2023 Workshops, pp. 54–65. Gesellschaft für Informatik eV (2023)

21. Kröger, J., Fränzle, M.: Mode management in contract-based design. In: SE 2024-Companion, pp. 31–42. Gesellschaft für Informatik eV (2024)

22. Kröger, J., Koopmann, B., Stierand, I., Fränzle, M.: Contract-based specification of mode-dependent timing behavior. Innov. Syst. Softw. Eng. 20(1), 31–47 (2024). https://doi.org/10.1007/s11334-023-00531-4

23. Luz, W.P., Pinto, G., Bonifácio, R.: Adopting devops in the real world: a theory, a model, and a case study. J. Syst. Softw. 157, 110384 (2019)

24. Munk, P., Schweizer, M.: Devops and safety? Safeops! towards ensuring safety in feature-driven development with frequent releases. In: Trapp, M., Schoitsch, E., Guiochet, J., Bitsch, F. (eds.) Computer Safety, Reliability, and Security. SAFE-COMP 2022 Workshops, pp. 145–157. Springer, Cham (2022)

25. Nguyen, T.N.: Component-based software update process in collaborative software development. In: 2008 15th Asia-Pacific Software Engineering Conference, pp. 437–444. IEEE (2008)

26. Oertel, M., Rettberg, A.: Reducing re-verification effort by requirement-based change management. In: International Embedded Systems Symposium, pp. 104–115. Springer, Cham (2013)

27. Panzica La Manna, V.: Dynamic software update for component-based distributed systems. In: Proceedings of the 16th International Workshop on Component-Oriented Programming, pp. 1–8 (2011)
28. Panzica La Manna, V.: Local dynamic update for component-based distributed systems. In: Proceedings of the 15th ACM SIGSOFT Symposium on Component Based Software Engineering, pp. 167–176 (2012)
29. Rakow, A., Kröger, J.: Roles and responsibilities for a predictable update process–a position paper. In: International Conference on Verification and Evaluation of Computer and Communication Systems, pp. 17–26. Springer, Cham (2021)
30. Strathmann, T., et al.: Project overview for step-up! CPS-process, methods and technologies for updating safety-critical cyber-physical systems. In: 2021 Design, Automation & Test in Europe Conference & Exhibition (DATE), pp. 1326–1329. IEEE (2021)
31. Yarza, I., Agirre, I., Mugarza, I., Nitsche, G., Uven, P., Orbegozo, J.M.: Towards a contract-based definition of update-compatibility–modelling safety integration criteria. In: 2023 IEEE 26th International Conference on Intelligent Transportation Systems (ITSC), pp. 710–717. IEEE (2023)
32. Zeller, M.: Towards continuous safety assessment in context of devops. In: Habli, I., Sujan, M., Gerasimou, S., Schoitsch, E., Bitsch, F. (eds.) Computer Safety, Reliability, and Security. SAFECOMP 2021 Workshops, pp. 145–157. Springer, Cham (2021)

Embedded Systems

A Complete Formal Specification and Verification of the BESW Software Control System of the Maeslant Storm Surge Barrier

Adrian Beers[1,2] , Jore Booy[1] , Jan Friso Groote[1]([✉]) ,
Johan van den Bogaard[2] , and Mark Bouwman[2]

[1] Eindhoven University of Technology, Eindhoven, The Netherlands
j.f.groote@tue.nl
[2] Rijkswaterstaat, Utrecht, The Netherlands

Abstract. The Maeslant Barrier is a storm surge barrier that protects Rotterdam and its harbour from storm surges in the North Sea. Its software control consists of three major components, one of which is BesW. BesW is responsible for all the movements of the barrier except for pushing and pulling it. In this document, we report on the complete formal specification of BesW in mCRL2. All its behaviour has been specified, including manual and testing modes. Furthermore, all fault situations have been taken into account. The formalisation allows formal verification of all behavioural properties, formulated in the modal μ-calculus, with the constraints that water levels only have a restricted number of values and not all combinations of failures of pumps and valves are allowed.

Keywords: Formal modelling · Model checking · mCRL2 · Maeslant Barrier · BesW

1 Introduction

The Maeslant Barrier is a storm surge barrier in the Netherlands. It is one of the largest movable structures on earth. It is located at the end of the rivers Maas and Rhine in a human-made canal called the Nieuwe Waterweg, connecting the North Sea with the largest harbour in Europe, namely Rotterdam. In case the sea level rises above a threshold, two huge retaining walls are pushed into the Nieuwe Waterweg and lowered onto a concrete base to almost completely reduce inland water flow.

The software control of the barrier is up for replacement. In order to do this, Rijkswaterstaat, the Dutch governmental body responsible for flood protection,

Research is supported by the Interreg North Sea project STORM_SAFE
www.interregnorthsea.eu/stormsafe

desires to have complete and correct formal descriptions of the prospective software control.

In this paper, we embark upon this wish and ask ourselves whether this control system can be fully modelled, preferably in such a way that correctness properties can be checked. We use the formal specification language and tool mCRL2 for this purpose due to its versatility and its successful use in many comparable large-scale modelling projects [6]. The goal of this case study is to determine to what extent formal modelling and verification can be applied to the software controlling the Maeslant Barrier.

More concretely, we looked into BesW (BesturingsSysteem Nieuwe Waterweg). The software control of the Maeslant Barrier has three main parts. The first part, BOS (Beslis en Ondersteunend Systeem), is the overarching software part responsible for the decisions to close and open the barrier. It instructs the second part, BesW, in terms of the major phases of a closure. BesW is responsible for controlling pumps, valves, doors, locks, a.o., to let the barrier float and sink, flood the dry dock, and open and close the dry dock's door. BesW instructs the third main part, BesL, which is the control system for the locomobile, to move the wall into or out of the river. There are two symmetrical instances for both BesW and BesL for the northern and southern retaining walls.

Our results demonstrate that a complete formal model and property verification of the BESW system is feasible and effective. Not only could the full behaviour of the software control system be modelled, including failing hardware, and Rest- and ITO (testing) modes, but it was also possible to verify or disprove all properties that were formulated on this behaviour. In the model, status and log messages were omitted. In the verification, the water levels were restricted to a representative subset and not all combinations of failing pumps and valves were taken into account.

Unfortunately, for reasons of national security, the precise formal model of the control of the Maeslant Barrier is declared confidential by Rijkswaterstaat. A partial public description of the Maeslant Barrier and the verified properties can be found in [1] on which this article is based. We necessarily have to limit ourselves to describing how the model is constructed and which kind of properties have been verified. But we still believe that reporting on this model is very important as due to its complexity and importance, it can be seen as a landmark in the field of formal methods.

2   Related Work

Dutch water defence works have been the subject of study by formal methods. The decision making system (BOS) of the Maeslant Barrier has been verified using Promela for the communication protocols and Z [13] for system behaviour [14]. Based on the Z specification, an informal C++ implementation was created. Some years later, Madlener et al. [7] studied the code for a specific component, 'Determine Excessive Water Level', and compared the code to the Z specification by translating the C++ code to the PVS theorem prover. Some discrepancies were found between the C++ code and the Z specification.

The control system of the locomobile component of the Maeslant Barrier has been modelled in mCRL2 [16]. In this work, some properties could not be checked as the size of the state space proved to be an issue for verification. Most of the remaining properties were valid, and four properties were found to be false due to errors in the functional description of the system. Sewberath-Misser [12] analysed and improved the mechanical failure probability of a closure based on various storm scenarios. Van der Meulen and Clement [15] verified the decision procedure for closing the barriers of the Eastern Scheldt Barrier (Oosterscheldekering) using HOL90. Wilschut [17] verified safety and liveness properties of the Prinses Marijke Locks in ESL [18], a specification language for system component verification. Reijnen et al. [10] generated PLC code for the Oisterwijksebaan bridge based on a supervisor model. Short of some minor complications due to the interfaces of the supervisor and the sensors, all tests performed were successful.

3 Maeslant Barrier

The Maeslant Barrier is the largest automated storm surge barrier in the Netherlands (Fig. 1). The barrier is open during normal operation to allow for maritime traffic and closes automatically when the water level passes a predetermined threshold.

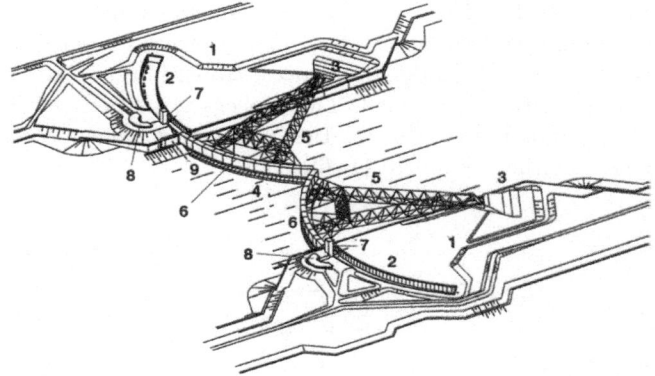

Fig. 1. The Maeslant Barrier

The barrier consists of two symmetric sides, referred to as North and South. They both contain a sector door, which consists of a retaining wall (6), a ball joint (3) and trusses (5) connecting them. Furthermore, there is a parking dock (2) and a locomobile (7). Closing the barrier consists roughly of flooding the docks and opening the docks' doors, after which the locomobiles push the retaining walls into the river, where they sink to the bottom. Opening the barrier follows the reverse sequence with the locomobiles pulling the walls.

The system can be set to the regular operational mode, a mode for waiting for instructions (Rest) or a testing mode (ITO). The operational processes that describe the behavioural steps the system takes to open and close the barrier can be seen in Fig. 2. Most are self-explanatory. 'Equalise Level' and 'Reach Rest Level' are concerned with the difference in water level of the river and the dock.

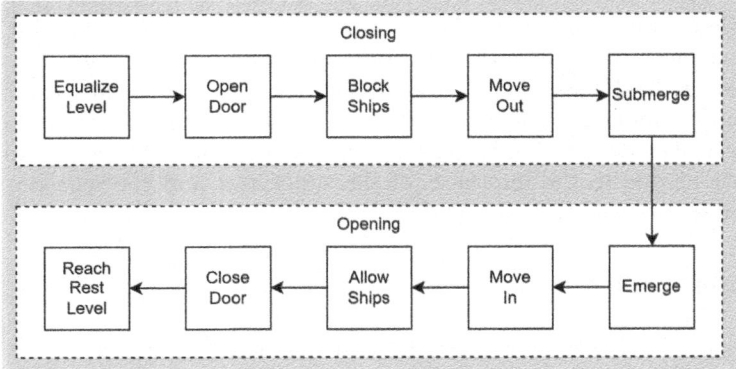

Fig. 2. The operational processes

Processes are activities of an individual system, which may take some time to finish. The current state of a process is the current process 'mode' (see Fig. 3). A process first starts in 'active' mode. The process transitions to the 'finished' state when a finishing condition is reached. The process transitions to the 'stopped' state when a stop command is received. BesW can start a new process when the current processes is either 'stopped' or 'finished'.

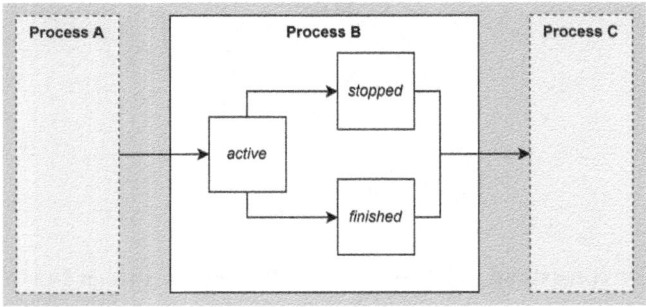

Fig. 3. Process modes

3.1   BesW

BesW (Besturingssysteem Nieuwe Waterweg) is the main control system of the Maeslant Barrier. The system controls the retaining walls, the ball joints, the parking docks and the locomobiles (BesL). BesW for instance instructs BesL with respect to movement, the spring setting and ventilator settings. There is one instance of BesW for each side of the barrier, BesW North and BesW South. Both instances of BesW communicate with each other to exchange statuses and measurements.

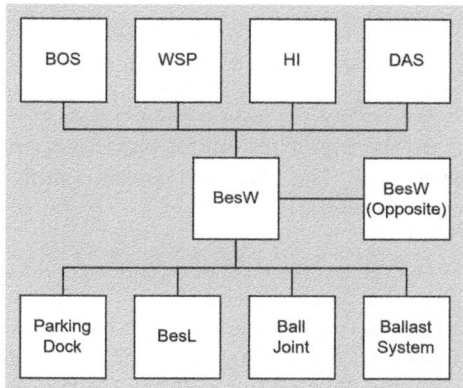

Fig. 4. An overview of the control system of the Maeslant Barrier

BesW receives commands from BOS (Beslis en Ondersteunend Systeem) and WSP (Waterstanden Paneel). BOS is responsible for the decisions to close or open the barrier. HI represents the interface of operators manually controlling the system. DAS (Data Acquisition System) can give commands to BesW in order to perform functional tests during maintenance. BesW North is directly connected to these systems, while BesW South receives the commands from North. See Fig. 4 for an overview.

We explain the subsystems of BesW in further detail. All subsystems can, next to BesW, also be controlled by the Motor Control Center (MCC) if BesW allows for it. Through MCC, more local control of the devices can be taken. Therefore, each process can require slightly different behaviour from each part of the system depending on the source of the instruction, and needs to be modelled separately.

3.2   Parking Dock

Each parking dock has water pumps and a door (see Fig. 5). BesW controls the parking dock devices and takes measurements from it. The most important measurement taken in the parking dock is the water level, which is used to calculate the difference between the water level in the dock and the river. In the opening procedure, the door only opens once the water levels match. The pumps and gates in the dock's door are used to achieve that.

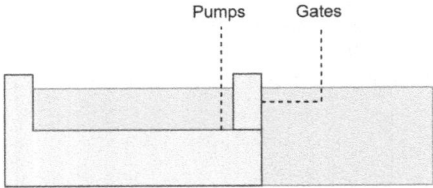

Fig. 5. Parking dock components

The door contains catches, winches, and a pawl to open and close the door. It is powered by a power pack. The door also contains limit switches to indicate whether the door is open or closed.

3.3 BesL

BesL controls the locomobile responsible for the lateral movement of the retaining wall. BesW will instruct BesL on its movement, its spring settings, and its ventilator. It will also inform BesL if the wall has landed on the river bed. BesL in return will inform BesW on its position, its spring setting when enabled, and whether it detects a fire in the locomobile.

3.4 Ball Joint

BesW can instruct the ball joint to be raised to facilitate maintenance and minimise wear and tear on the barrier. It contains six jacks to raise the ball joint, and ventilators to cool the building containing the ball joint.

3.5 Ballast System

The retaining wall contains a ballast system to submerge into and emerge from the river. Valves and pumps transfer water in and out of the door compartments (see Fig. 6). To keep the wall balanced while emerging and submerging, it is vital to coordinate the various pumps to properly distribute the water weight between each compartment. If one or multiple pumps fail (up to some limit), the system should keep working.

Some important measurements the ballast system reports to BesW are the wall slit (the distance between the bottom of the wall and the rived bed), the horizontal tilt of the wall, the water level and volume in each compartment, and the tension exerted by the river on the wall for each side of the wall. More details on the forces on the retaining wall and the data signals of each compartment can be found in [9].

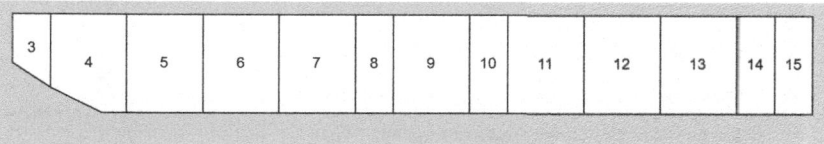

Fig. 6. Ballast compartments

4 mCRL2 Language

mCRL2 [3] is a language and a set of tools to model behaviour of concurrent and distributed systems, based on process algebra theory and abstract data types. We give a minimal example of the modelling capabilities and how one can formulate properties to be verified on the model below. The purpose of this is just to get an impression of the style in which behaviour and properties are described, not to explain all features needed for modelling and verification. The language is described in full in [6].

4.1 Specification

In Fig. 7, a specification describes a traffic light that can be turned red or green. Using the keyword `sort` the colour data sort is defined, giving two options `red` and `green`. With the keyword `act` four actions are defined that define the inputs or outputs of the system. In this case, they specify pressing buttons and setting a traffic light to a certain colour.

By the keyword `proc` a process P is defined that waits for a button press to instruct a light to go to a particular colour, and if not showing that colour, sets the traffic light to it, after which it repeats this behaviour keeping the shown colour in the variable `col`. The dot represents sequential composition, the plus is alternative composition, or a choice between behaviours, and the if-then-else is denoted by `_->_<>_`. mCRL2 supports far more, such as parallel behaviour, a wide range of data types, time, and probabilities.

4.2 Modal Formulae

Properties of a model can be described using modal formulae in the modal μ-calculus. The mCRL2 toolset can then verify these properties against the behavioural model. We give some limited examples to get a feel for modal formulae.

We discern two categories in which most modal formulae fall: safety properties and liveness properties. Safety properties express that nothing bad can ever happen. For instance, the traffic light may never be set to red twice without being set to green in the meantime. This is expressed by `[true*.set_red.!` `set_green*.set_red]false`. It essentially says that after an arbitrary sequence of actions (`true*`) two actions `set_red` cannot follow each other with a sequence not containing the action `set_green` in between, expressed by `(!set_green)*`.

```
sort Colour = struct red | green;
act red_button, green_button, set_red, set_green;
proc P(col: Colour) =
          red_button.(col==green)->set_red.P(red)
                          <> P(col)
       + green_button.(col==red)->set_green.P(green)
                          <> P(col);
init P(red);
```

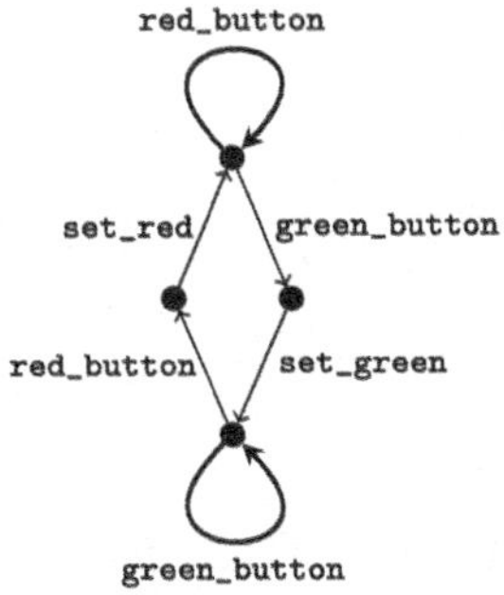

Fig. 7. A process specification recursively setting traffic lights, and its LTS

Liveness properties say that something good will eventually happen. One example is that after pressing the red button, the light will be set to red, formalised for instance by [true*.red_button.!set_red*]<true*.set_red>true.

The modal μ-calculus allows for explicit minimal and maximal fixed points that, when used in a nested way, even allows fairness properties to be formulated. In the minimal and maximal fixed point operators, parameters can be used which makes the language the most expressive modal language currently in existence, more than sufficient to formalise all the properties we encountered. For instance, it allows for linearly expressing LTL properties [4].

5   Model BesW

The specification of the main control system of the Maeslant Barrier is described internally at Rijkswaterstaat in the Detail Software Ontwerp (DSO) document [11]. The document contains a very detailed description of the specified behaviour of BesW in the form of 15.000 lines of low-level code inspired by Siemens PLC programming languages (see Fig. 8). In addition to that, several control tables describe the pump and valve settings of each compartment in the retaining wall, depending on the water levels, the tilt of the wall, and the phase of closure. The DSO is viewed within Rijkswaterstaat as the authoritative document, although it is quite inaccessible and has never been formally checked. The modelling in mCRL2 revealed that the DSO contains at least one issue where, when pumps malfunction, more pumps can be on than the electricity budget allows.

Our model is an interpretation of the DSO and the control tables into an mCRL2 specification. The mCRL2 description is around 5.000 lines, including empty lines. The size of the state space is $4.98*10^{14}$ as calculated using lpsreach.

Besides mended system behaviour, the mCRL2 model deviates from the DSO in the following aspects:

– We separated control instructions from 'coupled' control into two new levels: one for instructions from BOS and one for instructions from human interfaces.

```
FOR   MW_BAL_KOM := 5 TO 13
DO
    IF MX_BAL_OPD_POMP1 [ MW_BAL_KOM ] OR MX_BAL_OPD_POMP2 [ MW_BAL_KOM ]
    THEN
        MW_BAL_OPD_KOM_IN := MW_BAL_OPD_KOM_IN + 1;
    END_IF;
END_FOR;
```

Fig. 8. Snippet of PLC code from the DSO

```
proc Process_HI_OpenDoor(processMode: ProcessMode, system: MainSystem) =
        (processMode == active) -> (
            (system == dock) -> (
                Dock_Door_ChooseWinchOpen_InOrder(requireCatchTimer=false).
                Dock_Door_Open(requireDevicesReady=true).
                Dock_Door_CheckOpened
            ) +
            (system == besl) -> (
            skip
            ) +
            (system == joint) -> (
                Joint_Jack_Control
            ) +
            (system == ballast) -> (
                Ballast_Comps_DrainWithPumps_General.
                Ballast_Comps_DrainWithRestPumps
            )
        ) +
        (processMode == finished) -> (
            (system == dock) -> (
                skip
            ) +
            (system == besl) -> (
                skip
            ) +
            (system == joint) -> (
                Joint_Jack_Control
            ) +
            (system == ballast) -> (
                Ballast_Comps_DrainWithPumps_General.
                Ballast_Comps_DrainWithRestPumps
            )
        ) +
        (processMode == stopped) -> (
            (system == dock) -> (
                Dock_Door_OpenStop
            ) +
            (system == besl) -> (
                skip
            ) +
            (system == joint) -> (
                Joint_Jack_Control
            ) +
            (system == ballast) -> (
                Ballast_Comps_DrainWithPumps_General.
                Ballast_Comps_DrainWithRestPumps
            )
        );
```

Fig. 9. A fragment of mCRL2 specification of BesW

- Actions corresponding to notifications to human operators are omitted to achieve a smaller state space and focus on the control flow itself.
- Sensor measurements are abstracted to single relevant values. For instance, water level sensor data and ballast system data often follow some complex equations based on many sensors, so we only consider the values that might result from such a computation.
- The control of devices is modelled with single actions, instead of using precise control, where, for instance, an output voltage must be high for a certain amount of time for which the DSO uses explicit timers.
- Measurements such as water levels are also discretised to aid in verification.
- The data protocol used for communication with BOS is not modelled.

The model follows the PLC structure where every major process can be in one of the following modes: active, stopped, or finished (see Figs. 2 and 4). It is important to explain the difference between 'processes' in the DSO and 'processes' in mCRL2. In the DSO processes are variables on the basis of which the PLC code decides to set internal or output variables. Meanwhile, processes in mCRL2 are behavioural entities that describe how each subsystem behaves.

In order to keep the state space small, we only allow BOS to let BESw execute conceivable sequences of processes. For example, the retaining wall cannot be instructed to move out, when the door of the dry dock is not open but it is allowed to start closing the door while it is not yet fully opened. In reality BOS can send any sequence of instructions to BESw and our verification does not say anything when this would happen.

In order to give an idea of how the specification looks like, we give a small fragment in Fig. 9 which is exemplary for the whole specification. Influenced by the structure of the DSO – and one can discuss whether this is optimal – the specification repeats itself in cycles, where in each cycle each system performs its tasks. The currently active system is indicated by the process parameter `system`. The shown process opens the door of the dry dock started from HI. For instance, when the process is in the active mode, the `dock` executes three subprocesses to choose the winches, open the door and check the door successfully opened, indicated by processes described elsewhere in the specification. In the same mode, the `joint` system should run the `Joint_Jack_Control` process also described at another spot in the specification. The `besl` system does not perform any task, indicated by the explicit action `skip`. All processes have access to a set of global data variables maintained in a parallel thread.

6   Checking Behavioural Properties

To guarantee that formal specifications are of the required quality, it is necessary to verify behavioural properties [2,8]. We checked 40 properties. These properties were inferred from the DSO, our understanding of the desired behaviour, and from conversations with top experts on storm surge barriers and the top experts on the Maeslant Barrier. We provide a number of examples of these properties. Most of them turned out to be valid immediately, some that required some improvements in the model or the requirement, and one turned out to be actually fundamentally incorrect. All formal properties are public and can be found in [1].

6.1 Properties that Were Immediately Valid

We give some examples of the 36 formulas that were immediately valid. We also give the modal formulas, and give a short explanation of the encoding of the modal μ-calculus.

Open Door: Finishing Condition. The process Open Door will finish if and only if at least two limit switches indicate the door is opened. The formula says that whenever the process Open Door is started and not ended, represented by (!internal_controlEnd)*, and a list of lists of boolean doorOpenedSensors is received from the dock door, then the processMode is equal to finished exactly if at least two different booleans in doorOpenedSensors are set to true, indicating that at least two switches indicate that the door is open.

```
[ true*.
  internal_controlStart(operational, processOpenDoor, active).
  (!internal_controlEnd)*
]
(forall doorOpenedSensors: List(List(Bool)). val(#doorOpenedSensors == 3 &&
    (forall i: Nat. i < 3 => #(doorOpenedSensors.i) == 2)) =>
  [
    input_dockDoorOpened(doorOpenedSensors) .
    (!internal_controlEnd)* .
    internal_controlEnd .
    (!internal_controlEnd)*
  ]
  (forall processMode: ProcessMode.
  [internal_controlStart(operational, processOpenDoor, processMode)]
  val(
    (processMode == finished)
    ==
    (exists i,j,i',j': Nat. (i < 3 && j < 2 && i' < 3 && j' < 2 && i != i'
          && doorOpenedSensors.i.j && doorOpenedSensors.i'.j'))
) ) ) )
```

Move Out: Trimming. During the active mode of process Move Out, trimming will not be active. The encoding is straightforward and says that when the process Move Out is started, and not finished, the action indicating that triming is active cannot happen.

```
[
  true* .
  internal_controlStart(operational, processMoveOut, active) .
  (!internal_controlEnd)* .
  internal_trimmingActive
]
false
```

Submerge: Spring Setting to K2. During the active mode of process Submerge, the spring setting of BesL will be changed to K2 when the wall slit is below 3.5 m. The encoding says that when the process Submerge is active, and when it sets a spring setting, then this spring setting is K2 when the wall slit was measured to be smaller than 3.5 m, which slightly diverges from the informal requirement, but is defensible as the spring setting is changed anyhow.

```
[
   true* .
   internal_controlStart(operational, processSubmerge, active) .
   (!internal_controlEnd)*
]
(forall wallSlitIndex: Nat. val(wallSlitIndex < #wallSlitList) =>
   [
      input_wallSlit(wallSlitList.wallSlitIndex) .
      (!internal_controlEnd)*
   ]
   (forall springSetting: SpringSetting.
      [output_beslSpringSetting(springSetting)]
      val(wallSlitList.wallSlitIndex < 350/100 => (springSetting == K2))
) )
```

6.2 Properties that Became Valid After Refinement

Here we report on some properties we were asked to check but which had to be rephrased to become valid.

Reach Rest Level, Active: Opening Gates. The first property says that the gates will be opened when the dock level is under −2.4 m. After analysing counter examples, we refined the requirement to the following: During the active mode of process Reach Rest Level in the Operational phase, the gates will be opened if the dock level is under −2.4 m, the ball joint is lowered, and the gates are not opened yet, formulated in the modal formula below.

```
[ true* .
   internal_controlStart(operational, processReachRestLevel, active) .
   (!internal_controlEnd)*
]
(forall gatesOpened: List(Bool). val(#gatesOpened == 4) =>
   [
      input_dockGatesOpened(gatesOpened) .
      (!internal_controlEnd)*
   ]
   (forall dockLevelIndex: Nat. val(dockLevelIndex < #dockLevelList) =>
      [
         input_dockLevel(dockLevelList.dockLevelIndex) .
         (!internal_controlEnd)*
      ]
      (forall jackZero: Bool.
         [
            input_jointJackZero(jackZero) .
            (!internal_controlEnd)*
         ]
         (forall gatesOpen: List(Bool). val(#gatesOpen == 4) =>
         [output_dockGatesOpen(gatesOpen)]
         val(dockLevelList.dockLevelIndex <= -240/100 => (forall g: Nat. g < 4
            => (jackZero && !(gatesOpened.g) => gatesOpen.g)
) ) ) ) )
```

Equalise Level, Active: Finishing Condition. We were asked to check the property that the process Equalise Level will finish, if at least two gates are opened. The property had to be rephrased to: The process Equalise Level will finish if and only if the timer for equalising has expired or the dock level is equalised with the river, as formalised by the following formula.

```
[
  true* .
  internal_controlStart(operational, processEqualiseLevel, active) .
  (!internal_controlEnd)*
]
(forall riverLevelIndex: Nat. val(riverLevelIndex < #riverLevelList) =>
  [
    internal_riverLevel(riverLevelList.riverLevelIndex) .
    (!internal_controlEnd)*
  ]
  (forall dockLevelIndex: Nat. val(dockLevelIndex < #dockLevelList) =>
    [
      input_dockLevel(dockLevelList.dockLevelIndex) .
      (!internal_controlEnd)*
    ]
    (forall stateTimerEqualiseLevel: TimerState.
      [
        state''(timer_equalise, stateTimerEqualiseLevel) .
        (!internal_controlEnd)* .
        internal_controlEnd .
        (!internal_controlEnd)*
      ]
      (forall processMode: ProcessMode.
        [internal_controlStart(operational, processEqualiseLevel, processMode
            )]
        val(
          (processMode == finished)
          ==
          (stateTimerEqualiseLevel == expired || dockLevelEqualised(
              dockLevelList.dockLevelIndex, riverLevelList.riverLevelIndex))
) ) ) ) )
```

Parking Dock Devices: Catch. This property stated that during processes where the dock door is closed, the catch will be fastened when positive head, i.e., the water level in the dock, is too low. Also, the catch will be loosened when positive head in the dock is sufficiently high.

This property was purposefully described to be false by subject matter experts to check if formal verification could detect it. The condition that was missing was that fastening the catch also requires that the limit switches indicate the door is closed. This is formalised below.

```
[true*]
(forall process: Process, processMode: ProcessMode.
  [
    internal_controlStart(operational, process, processMode) .
    (!internal_controlEnd)*
  ]
  (forall riverLevelIndex: Nat. val(riverLevelIndex < #riverLevelList) =>
    [
      internal_riverLevel(riverLevelList.riverLevelIndex) .
      (!internal_controlEnd)*
    ]
    (forall dc: List(Bool). val(#dc == 2) =>
```

```
        [
          input_dockDoorClosed(dc) .
          (!internal_controlEnd)*
        ]
        (forall dockLevelIndex: Nat. val(dockLevelIndex < #dockLevelList) =>
          [
            input_dockLevel(dockLevelList.dockLevelIndex) .
            (!internal_controlEnd)*
          ]
          (forall catchFasten: Bool.
            [output_dockCatchFasten(catchFasten)]
            val(
              (
                process == processEqualiseLevel ||
                process == processReachRestLevel ||
                (process == processCloseDoor && processMode == finished)
              )
              =>
              (
                (dc.0 || dc.1)
                &&
                (riverLevelList.riverLevelIndex - dockLevelList.dockLevelIndex
                    < 70/100)
                =>
                catchFasten
              )
              &&
              (
                (riverLevelList.riverLevelIndex - dockLevelList.dockLevelIndex
                    > 100/100)
                =>
                !catchFasten
) ) ) ) ) ) )
```

6.3 An Invalid Property

We were asked to check one property that we were unable to reformulate into
a valid variant. The property states that during the Operational phase, if BesL
indicates that the retaining wall is not well positioned, then the pumps of the
parking dock will not be enabled. It is encoded below. After some discussion, it
turned out that this functionality was deprecated and part of an earlier specification document.

```
[true*]
(forall process: Process, processMode: ProcessMode.
  [
    internal_controlStart(operational, process, processMode) .
    (!internal_controlEnd)* .
    input_beslFinePositioned(false) .
    (!internal_controlEnd)*
  ]
  (forall p: Nat. val(p < 3) =>
    [output_dockPumpEnable(p, true)] false
  )
)
```

6.4 Tools

We verified the properties against the model by first transforming the mCRL2
specification into a Linear Process Specification (LPS). Tools are then applied

to reduce the LPS. Next, the LPS is combined with a modal formula into a Parameterised Boolean Equation System (PBES). After applying tools to reduce the PBES, we solve it. The following commands were used where the specification is given as besw.mcrl2 and the property as property.mcf.

```
mcrl22lps -vn -QO besw.mcrl2 | lpsconstelm | lpssumelm | lpsrewr | lpsparelm
    | lpsstategraph - spec.lps
lps2pbes -m -f property.mcf spec.lps | pbesconstelm | pbesparelm |
    pbesstategraph -QO | pbessolve -QO -rjittyc --threads=4
```

Verification was performed on a system belonging to Rijkswaterstaat. mCRL2 version 202407.1 was used. The system has two AMD EPYC 9254 24-Core processors. Each CPU has 12 DDR5 DIMMs of 64GB for a total of 1.5 TB of memory. We were able to verify each property within forty minutes.

7 Conclusions

We have shown that we can fully model BesW and that verification of various behavioural properties can be carried out effectively. Although detailed and precise, the specification is of limited length and can therefore neatly serve as the specification of any BesW software controller to be made. This provides an overwhelming positive answer to the primary research question whether such systems can be modelled and verified. Without any hesitation, we can state that in the hands of qualified specifiers, guided by domain experts, formal methods are more than capable of precisely modelling the software of systems of the complexity of storm surge barriers and prove that these specifications are of quality. It is important to find the right level of modelling to grasp only the key behaviour [5]. Here, this means primarily avoiding parallel behaviour, abstractly describing the essence of the interactions of BesW with the outside world, and avoiding specifying log messages.

We based the specification on the DSO. This was truly helpful, as – despite its relative inaccessible nature – it provided many behavioural details that we otherwise only could have guessed. This also had a disadvantage in that our mCRL2 specification still resembles the DSO by using a super-loop as most PLC systems do. Removing the loop could make the specification even more compact and accessible. Also, the language mCRL2 would benefit from some adaptations to improve the conciseness and readability of the specification.

The biggest hurdle left for further adoption of formal verification within Rijkswaterstaat in general is education, acceptance, and integration. The concept of modelling and verification is still relatively unknown, but due to this work, it is recognised as a viable option. The advantages of formal models are very much appreciated, but the integration into standard work processes is currently the topic of discussion and investigation.

References

1. Beers, A.: Specification and verification of the main control system of the Maeslant barrier. Master's thesis, Eindhoven University of Technology, Eindhoven (2024)
2. van den Brand, M., Groote, J.: Software engineering: redundancy is key. Sci. Comput. Program. **97**, 75–81 (2015). https://doi.org/10.1016/J.SCICO.2013.11.020
3. Bunte, O., et al.: The mCRL2 toolset for analysing concurrent systems. In: Vojnar, T., Zhang, L. (eds.) TACAS 2019. LNCS, vol. 11428, pp. 21–39. Springer, Cham (2019). https://doi.org/10.1007/978-3-030-17465-1_2
4. Cranen, S., Groote, J., Reniers, M.: A linear translation from CTL* to the first-order modal μ -calculus. Theor. Comput. Sci. **412**(28), 3129–3139 (2011). https://doi.org/10.1016/J.TCS.2011.02.034
5. Groote, J.F., Kouters, T.W.D.M., Osaiweran, A.: Specification guidelines to avoid the state space explosion problem. Softw. Test. Verif. Reliab. **25**(1), 4–33 (2015). https://doi.org/10.1002/STVR.1536
6. Groote, J.F., Mousavi, M.R.: Modeling and Analysis of Communicating Systems. MIT Press (2014)
7. Madlener, K., Smetsers, S., van Eekelen, M.: A formal verification study on the Rotterdam storm surge barrier. In: Dong, J.S., Zhu, H. (eds.) ICFEM 2010. LNCS, vol. 6447, pp. 287–302. Springer, Heidelberg (2010). https://doi.org/10.1007/978-3-642-16901-4_20
8. Osaiweran, A., Schuts, M., Hooman, J., Groote, J., van Rijnsoever, B.: Evaluating the effect of a lightweight formal technique in industry. Int. J. Softw. Tools Technol. Transf. **18**(1), 93–108 (2016). https://doi.org/10.1007/S10009-015-0374-1
9. Ponsioen, L.A.: Investigation and development of a digital twin for the Maeslant barrier. Technical report, Delft (2023)
10. Reijnen, F., van de Mortel - Fronczak, A., Rooda, K., van Dinther, J.: Synthesis and implementation of supervisory control for infrastructural systems. In: 38th Benelux Meeting on Systems and Control 2019, p. 92 (2019)
11. Rijkswaterstaat: Detail Software Ontwerp, Version K 0.9.0 (2021)
12. Sewberath-Misser, V.V.: Improving the reliability of the Maeslant barrier in the delta21 configuration. Master's thesis, Delft (2022)
13. Spivey, J.M., Abrial, J.R.: The Z Notation, vol. 29. Prentice Hall Hemel Hempstead (1992)
14. Tretmans, J., Wijbrans, K., Chaudron, M.: Software engineering with formal methods: the development of a storm surge barrier control system revisiting seven myths of formal methods. Formal Methods Syst. Design **19**(2), 195–215 (2001). https://doi.org/10.1023/A:1011236117591
15. van der Meulen, M., Clement, T.: Formal methods in the specification of the emergency closing system of the eastern Scheldt storm surge barrier. In: Hutter, D., Stephan, W., Traverso, P., Ullmann, M. (eds.) FM-Trends 1998. LNCS, vol. 1641, pp. 296–301. Springer, Heidelberg (1999). https://doi.org/10.1007/3-540-48257-1_19
16. Visscher, M.: Formal modelling and verification of the maeslant barrier locomobile system. Master's thesis, Eindhoven University of Technology, Eindhoven (2023)
17. Wilschut, T.: System specification and design structuring methods for a lock product platform. Ph.D. thesis 1 (Research TU/e / Graduation TU/e), Technische Universiteit Eindhoven, Eindhoven (2018)
18. Wilschut, T., Hofkamp, A.T., Schuijbroek, T.J.L., Etman, L.F.P., Rooda, J.E.: Bridging the gap between requirements engineering and systems architecting: the elephant specification language. Design Sci. **10**, e25 (2024). https://doi.org/10.1017/dsj.2024.30

End-to-End Formal Methods Integrated Development with SysMLv2 Using HAMR

John Hatcliff[(✉)], Jason Belt, Robby, Clint McKenzie, and Catalina Liang

Kansas State University, Manhattan, KS 66506, USA
{hatcliff,belt}@ksu.edu

Abstract. The SAE-standardized AADL modeling language has been a significant enabler for academic and industry research on model-based development with integrated formal methods. However, several factors including industry preference for other modeling languages such as SysML, have hampered adoption of AADL and its associated formal methods technologies. The Object Management Group (OMG) is currently working on the next SysML generation (SysMLv2) that embraces several attractive characteristics of AADL and has chartered the Real-Time Embedded Safety-Critical (RTESC) working group to consider how AADL concepts, semantics, and formal specifications can be brought into the SysMLv2 ecosystem. In this paper, we report on our development of a SysMLv2 front-end for the HAMR formal-methods-integrated model-based development framework. We provide the first illustration of how the RTESC SysMLv2 libraries for AADL concepts can be used in an end-to-end tool for code generation with integrated formal methods at multiple levels. We describe how the GUMBO formal component contract language can be integrated into the SysMLv2 AADL profile to provide: (a) SMT-based integration checking at the model level, and (b) automated testing and verification of component application to architecture contracts. We present a tool architecture that enables HAMR code generation targeting the formally verified seL4 microkernel as well as other formal methods tools being applied to SysMLv2 models in the context of the Collins Aerospace DARPA PROVERS INSPECTA project.

1 Introduction

The SAE-standardized AADL modeling language has been used in both Europe and the US to develop industry critical systems [3,4,6,10,25,35,38]. Moreover, it has been a significant enabler for academic and industry research on model-based development with integrated formal methods. Several projects, often in critical domains such as space and national defense, have used AADL to investigate requirements and design engineering, formal contract-based specifications, and

This work is supported in part by U.S. Defense Advanced Research Projects Agency (DARPA) as part of the Collins Aerospace INSPECTA project.

automated code generation for high-assurance platforms. However, several factors including industry preference for other modeling languages such as SysML and the lack of commercial tooling have hampered adoption of AADL. In turn, this has hampered the ability to transition successful formal methods from the AADL ecosystem into industrial use.

The Object Management Group (OMG) is currently working on the next SysML generation (SysMLv2) that embraces several attractive features of AADL. For example, SysMLv2 is defined using linked graphical and textual views of system models – a feature that AADL has had for at least two decades. Advocates argue that "a textual syntax provides a more precise way to define system models by reducing ambiguity compared to graphical representations." We believe that the presence of a textual view has made it easier to incorporate integrated text-based formal methods specifications such as contract languages into AADL. SysMLv2 also aims to provide a more solid semantic foundation compared to its predecessor. Instead of being derived from UML, it is based on KerML – a new meta-modeling language developed in conjunction with SysMLv2. OMG groups are working on a semantics for KerML based on mathematics and first-order logic, and the overall aim is to have a modernized metamodel that enhances precision, extensibility, and usability.

OMG has established a number of working groups to address SysMLv2 auxiliary topics including a semantics working group and a formal methods working group. It has chartered the Real-Time Embedded Safety-Critical (RTESC) working group to consider how concepts from AADL (and other modeling languages for real-time embedded systems), including semantics and formal specifications, can be brought into the SysMLv2 ecosystem. The primary output of the RTESC working group thus far has been a collection of SysMLv2 library definitions for AADL concepts (e.g., component types, property definitions, etc.). SysMLv2 model elements can inherit from these definitions to specify an AADL-oriented interpretation of each element. Accompanying modeling guidelines indicate how existing SysMLv2 features like `parts`, `interfaces`, and `connections` should be used to realize AADL elements. To validate the correspondence between AADL and this new "embedding" of concepts in SysMLv2, engineers from the Software Engineering Institute (SEI) have developed translators between the two.

Our primary contribution to the RTESC working group has been the vetting of the proposed SysMLv2/AADL libraries in tools and applications as part of the Collins Aerospace DARPA *Pipelined Reasoning of Verifiers Enabling Robust Systems* (PROVERS) research program. As part of a Collins Aerospace team on the earlier DARPA *Cyber-Assured Systems Engineering* (CASE) program, and in collaboration with engineers from Galois, we developed the High-Assurance Modeling and Rapid engineering (HAMR) tool chain [3,17] for multiple platform code generation for AADL. HAMR generates system deployments for the JVM, Linux, and the seL4 verified microkernel platform. In conjunction, we developed the GUMBO component contract language [21], which supports AADL model-level specification and reasoning about component constraints. HAMR translates GUMBO specifications down to code-level contracts for Slang [32] (a safety-critical subset of Scala) and Rust (for verification with the Verus contract checking tool). The HAMR GUMBOX framework translates model-level GUMBO contracts to code-level *executable* contracts (realized as collections of boolean functions) that are used in property-based testing [19], system testing [18], and run-time monitoring.

Collins Aerospace have developed multiple AADL formal methods tools including the AGREE [7] contract language and model-checking framework and the Resolute [11] architecture constraint and assurance case framework. Our tasking on the current Collins Aerospace DARPA PROVERS project includes investigating how these AADL-originated formal methods technologies can be transitioned into the SysMLv2 ecosystem. It is important to understand that scope of this *initial effort* is not to support the entire SysMLv2 language. Rather, it is to support the subset of SysMLv2 that enables representation of AADL modeling concepts and associated formal methods. We refer to this subset as SysMLv2/AADL. This provides a foundation for expanding the scope to address other features of SysMLv2 as well as other specification and analysis capabilities that are currently under development within the SysMLv2 community.

To support this broader investigation, this paper reports our development and application of a SysMLv2/AADL front-end for the HAMR formal-methods-integrated model-based development framework. The contributions of this work are as follows:

- We implement in HAMR a tool architecture that enables code generation and formal methods techniques to be applied to both AADL and SysMLv2/AADL models. This allows previous AADL capabilities that supported industrial use of formal methods to be more easily migrated to SysMLv2 or to support joint AADL and SysMLv2 use.
- We provide SysMLv2 IDE support for HAMR built on top of the VSCode SysIDE extension, which includes using the SysMLv2/AADL libraries being developed by the OMG RTESC working group. We describe how we have implemented SysMLv2/AADL well-formedness validators within the IDE.
- As an example of formal methods migration from the AADL ecosystem into SysMLv2/AADL, we describe how we have migrated the GUMBO component contract language into SysMLv2/AADL and implemented SMT-based verification for GUMBO integration constraints (a subset of the GUMBO contract language for specifying inter-component communication constraints).
- We describe how previous HAMR code generation capabilities, translation of GUMBO contracts to code contracts, verification and property-based testing of code to contracts, and system deployment (e.g., on the verified seL4 microkernel) are now provided for SysMLv2/AADL model-based development.
- We provide an open repository that illustrates the approach on several systems being used in industrial research projects.

This work provides the first illustration of how the emerging OMG RTESC SysMLv2/AADL libraries can be used in an end-to-end tool chain for code generation with integrated formal methods at multiple levels (models, code, deployments on a formally verified microkernel). This represents a key element of the

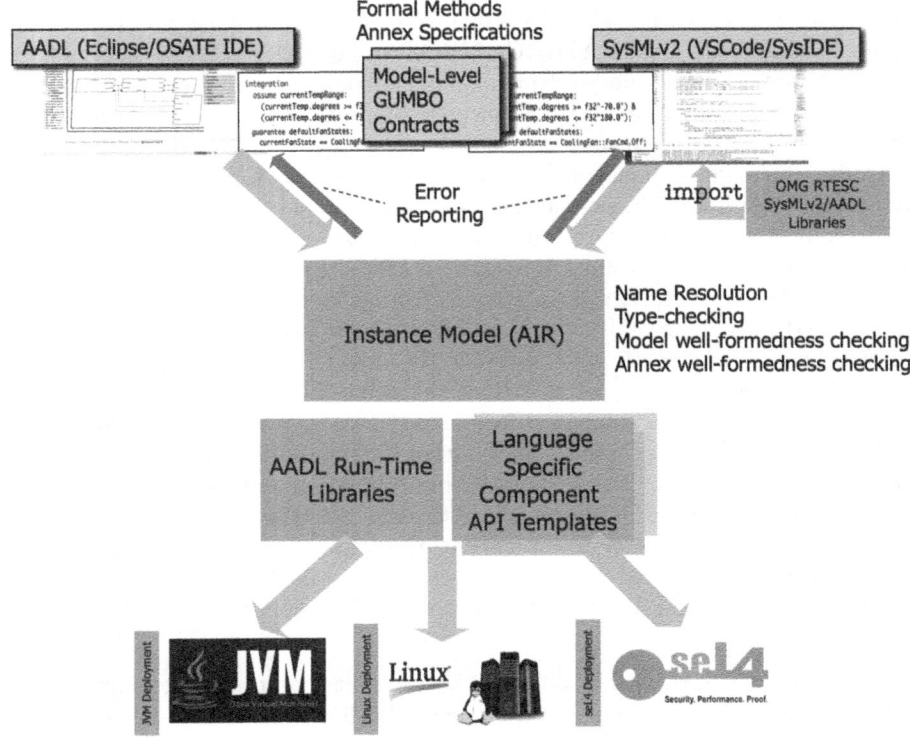

Fig. 1. HAMR Tool Chain – Architecture Concepts.

Collins Aerospace INSPECTA project approach in the DARPA PROVERS program (which aims to illustrate how pipelines of formal methods can be developed to support engineering of critical systems in the defense industry). As part of the INSPECTA project demonstration activities, industry engineers are applying this tool chain to develop experimental versions of unmanned air vehicle mission control systems associated with Collins Aerospace *Launched Effects*[1] product line. As we participate in the RTESC workgroup, these application experiences are providing inputs to the RTESC working group to drive further evolution of the SysMLv2/AADL libraries. The HAMR tool chain [13] and examples described in this paper [14] are available under an open source license.

2   Tool Chain Architecture

In this section, we provide an overview of the HAMR tool chain architecture (illustrated in Fig. 1) and the strategy for integrating SysMLv2-based modeling

---

[1] https://www.collinsaerospace.com/what-we-do/industries/military-and-defense/launched-effects.

of AADL concepts. We first summarize the existing HAMR capabilities, and then describe how support for SysMLv2/AADL concepts are introduced.

SAE International standard AS5506C defines the AADL core language for expressing the structure of embedded real-time systems via definitions of software and hardware components, their interfaces, and their communication. AADL provides a precise, tool-independent, and standardized modeling vocabulary of common embedded software and hardware elements using a component-based approach [9]. The AADL standard defines an *annex* extensibility mechanism that allows additional modeling sublanguages to be defined and used in conjunction with the AADL base language. AGREE, BLESS, and GUMBO are examples of formal contract and behavior languages specified as annexes. The AADL standard also describes run-time services (RTS) – a collection of run-time libraries that implement key aspects of threading and communication pattern behavior. A major subset of the RTS has been formalized and a reference implementation has been developed [20] and mechanized in the Isabelle theorem prover [12]. We have designed our contract language and associated translation to code-level contracts to align with these semantic concepts.

Much of the research community has extended the open source Eclipse-based OSATE AADL modeling tool (top left of Fig. 1) to obtain formal methods oriented analysis and verification for AADL annexes. OSATE has a plug-in architecture (inherited from Eclipse) that allows tool providers to define parsing and other language processing capabilities for AADL annex languages. HAMR uses this plug-in capability to implement language processing for the GUMBO contract language [21]. OSATE also implements an AADL model instantiation by which an AADL *declarative model* (which defines collections of component types and possibly multiple component implementation structures) is instantiated to an *instance model*. This instance model is not typically viewed by the developer. Intuitively, it represents a flattened version of the declarative model (e.g., all component inheritance is flattened, and connections that step through system hierarchy are replaced with connections that directly realize thread-to-thread communication), and it reflects choices of specific implementations of components. Almost all AADL code generation and analysis tools work on this simplified instance model representation.

To decouple its analysis and code generation from a specific IDE and front-end, HAMR defines an *architecture intermediate representation* (AIR) with XML, JSON, and in-memory representations. HAMR translates OSATE's Eclipse Ecore-based representation of an AADL instance model (along with some additional declarative model information) into AIR. Most of the conventional model "semantic analysis" phases (using compiler terminology) such as name resolution, type-checking, etc., are performed on this representation. AIR includes structures for GUMBO specifications (and other HAMR-relevant AADL annex information). It is important to understand that HAMR *does not* generate all the code necessary for a deployable system. It generates threading, port communication, and scheduling infrastructure code that conforms to AADL RTS semantics, as well as application *code skeletons* that engineers fill in to complete the behavior of the system. These code skeletons also include code-level behavior contracts automatically derived from GUMBO model-level contracts as illustrated in Sects. 5 and 6 – enabling code level verification tools to prove that developer-supplied component application code conforms to model-level component contracts. These aspects are reflected in the middle of Fig. 1. HAMR utilizes a Slang-based implementation of the AADL RTS and other run-time libraries. For the JVM platform, HAMR generates all code in Slang – since it is a (high-integrity) subset of Scala, a developer's component implementations can utilize support code written in Scala and Java. Slang can be transpiled to C and Rust. When HAMR targets Linux and the seL4 micro-kernel, the Slang reference implementations of the AADL RTS are transpiled to the chosen target language. HAMR also uses standard templating technology to provide skeletons for threads, data types definitions for model-declared types, etc. for the target programming language the developer has selected for component implementations. Finally, in addition to generating runtime library implementations, HAMR also generates some specific platform configurations and infrastructure (e.g., the kernel partitioning information for the seL4 microkernel), with an accompanying SMT-based formal architecture refinement evidence.

There are multiple workflows and programming language choices supported by HAMR. Using the Logika verification framework [33] for Slang, Slang code can be verified with a high-degree of automation. This provides a basis for developing high-assurance AADL-based systems using Slang directly or via translation of Slang to C (without garbage collection runtime overhead). C code transpiled from Slang can be compiled using standard C compilers, as well as the CompCert Verified C compiler [28]. Recently, along with Rust component support, we have added automatic generation of Rust contracts for Verus [26], which enables Rust component application code to be proved to conform to GUMBO contracts.

Referring to the top right of Fig. 1, the OMG RTESC SysMLv2/AADL libraries can be used in any IDE that supports SysMLv2. We originally used the Eclipse-based SysMLv2 *pilot implementation* sanctioned by the OMG, but changed our approach for several reasons: (1) poor performance, (2) lack of support for Eclipse in Collins Aerospace product groups (whereas there is some use of VSCode), (3) desire to integrate with other VSCode hosted formal methods tools on the INSPECTA project, including the Verus VSCode extension. Therefore, we implemented a HAMR VSCode extension by leveraging the existing SysIDE [37] VSCode extension for SysMLv2 for syntax highlighting and editor support, while directly building an ANTLR-based parser for SysMLv2 using a grammar extracted from the pilot implementation Xtext grammar. The HAMR infrastructure traverses the ANTLR-built nodes, translates AADL concepts into AIR, and back-propagates errors reported by HAMR AIR-based semantic processing to the expected VSCode error markers. We also implement substantial functionality to enforce a variety of AADL well-formedness constraints and also a notion of instantiation similar to OSATE's translation of AADL declarative models to instance models.

A big challenge in migrating AADL Annex-based formal method tools is that SysMLv2 does not include an annex framework like AADL's. Instead of being able to define a custom syntax/grammar, SysMLv2 aims to support inclusion of additional modeling concepts by inheritance and extension of KerML elements. It is unclear at present how all the rich features of AADL's different annexes would be captured in KerML or SysMLv2, and the RTESC committee roadmap delays consideration of this challenge for an indefinite period of time. SysMLv2 does provide some very basic notions of assertions, pre/post-conditions, and architecture constraints, but these are far from sufficient to support even the features of the GUMBO contract language. Since our industry research projects need to immediately transition AADL-annex-based specification languages, we have developed an approach by which SysMLv2's **language** constructs (which allow arbitrary strings to be included in models) can be used to include chunks of AADL annex syntax. We modified a few key points in SysIDE to intercept processing of **language** and re-direct to HAMR plugins for the AADL annex languages that we wish to support. We then implement full syntax highlighting, name resolution, type checking, etc., with functionality distributed across Langium and AIR processing.

This substantial tool engineering effort gives the industry engineers on INSPECTA the ability to immediately build out SysMLv2 models, apply our transitioned formal methods to meet DARPA PROVERS goals, and provide feedback to drive further RTESC work.

3   AADL Libraries for SysMLv2

In this section, we summarize the strategy adopted by the OMG RTESC working group for representing AADL concepts in SysMLv2. Several research groups involved in the work (including our own) developed initial approaches, but the primary inputs to the working group group are based on work by Hugues [22] and Roger and Dissaux [34].

To use AADL concepts in a SysMLv2 package, the developer includes the RTESC-developed SysMLv2/AADL library packages. These include SysMLv2 definitions with names, attributes, structures etc., that indicate AADL concepts. For example, Listing 1.1 provides examples of how AADL component categories are modeled. A top-level abstract SysMLv2 **part** named **Component** is defined, which becomes the top element of an inheritance hierarchy of parts where the part name corresponds to an AADL component category. Listing 1.1 shows how **Thread** and **Data** component categories are represented as **parts** derived from **Component**. The definition of **Thread** illustrates how AADL standard properties like **Period** and **Dispatch_Protocol** are defined as SysMLv2 **part** attributes, which developers will supply values for as they are used in SysMLv2 models.

```
1   abstract part def Component {
2     attribute category : ComponentCategory;}
3
4   part def Thread :> Component {
5     attribute :>> category = ComponentCategory::Thread;
```

```
6    attribute Compute_Execution_Time: Timing_Properties::Compute_Execution_Time;
7    attribute Period: Timing_Properties::Period;
8    attribute Dispatch_Protocol: Thread_Properties::Dispatch_Protocol;
9    attribute Priority: Thread_Properties::Priority; }
10
11   enum def Supported_Dispatch_Protocols {
12     enum Periodic;
13     enum Sporadic;
14     enum Aperiodic;
15     enum Timed;
16     enum Hybrid;
17     enum Background; }
18
19   // Used for AADL Data Modeling
20   part def Data :> Component {
21     attribute :>> category = ComponentCategory::Data;
22     attribute value: Base::DataValue; }
```

Listing 1.1. AADL Library for SysMLv2: Component Categories (excerpts)

Listing 1.2 illustrates how a similar inheritance strategy is used to model AADL interface features like AADL ports.

```
1    abstract port def Feature;
2    port def AbstractFeature :> Feature { inout item type : Component; }
3    port def DataPort :> Feature { inout item type : Component; }
4    port def EventDataPort :> Feature { inout item type : Component; }
5    port def EventPort :> Feature;
```

Listing 1.2. AADL Library for SysMLv2: Port Declarations (excerpts)

When these definitions are used in SysMLv2/AADL models, HAMR implements a variety of checks that enforce AADL's well-formed rules. A simple example is the enforcement of AADL's component category containment rules. For instance, **Thread** components must be contained in **Thread_Group** or **Process** components, **Process** components must be contained in **System** components, etc. In addition, HAMR checks for conditions required by the INSPECTA tool chain, e.g., all **Periodic** thread components have declared **Periods**.

4   Component and System Models

We use the Isolette system US Federal Aviation Administration (FAA) Requirements Engineering Management Handbook (REMH) [27] as a running example. This enables a cross comparison between HAMR SysMLv2 artifacts and AADL Isolette artifacts from our previous work [16,19]. An Isolette is an infant incubator medical device, and the REMH presentation focuses on a heat (infant warming) control subsystem and a safety monitoring subsystem. The REMH uses the example to illustrate best practices in requirements engineering for critical embedded systems, and it presents detailed requirements at multiple levels of abstractions.

We previously constructed an AADL model from Isolette design information in the REMH, and used HAMR to develop Slang implementations of the two subsystems. The architecture (directed by the REMH description) emphasizes periodic threads and data ports. The control system and the safety monitoring system include three periodic threads each. An additional periodic thread is used to implement/simulate the operator interface. Slang extensions were used to simulate the temperature sensor and heater components. HAMR generates the JVM deployment of the system (Scala and Java are used to develop the simulated hardware elements and the GUI for the operator interface). There are 11 thread components, 49 component ports, and 27 connections between the ports, with 10612 non-comment/space source lines of Slang/Scala code (NCSLOC) in the infrastructure code and 184 NCSLOC in the application logic. HAMR can also translate the Slang-based application and AADL RTS code for this example (with the exception of the GUI for the operator interface) to C and deploy the final system to Linux and seL4.

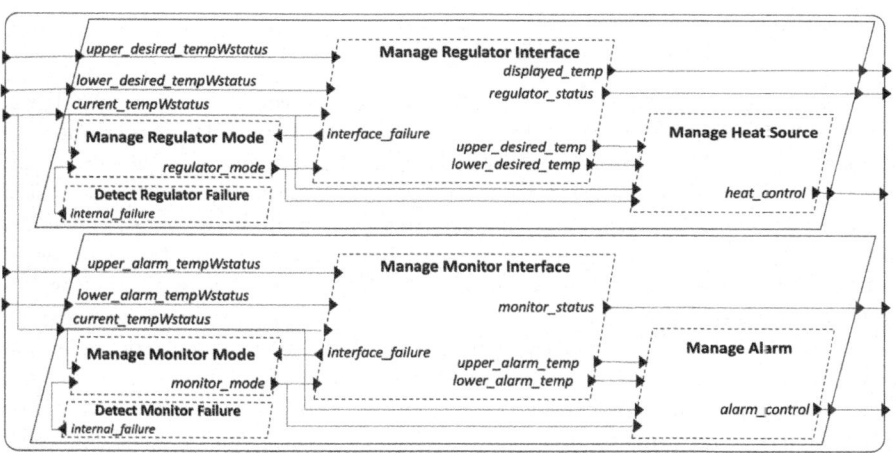

Fig. 2. Isolette - AADL Graphical View of Regulate and Monitor Subsystems.

Figure 2 presents the AADL graphical view of the thread components in the Regulate (controller) and Monitor (safety) subsystems.

```
1   thread Manage_Heat_Source
2     features
3       current_tempWstatus: in data port TempWstatus.impl;
4       lower_desired_temp: in data port Temp.impl;
5       upper_desired_temp: in data port Temp.impl;
6       regulator_mode: in data port Regulator_Mode;
7       heat_control: out data port On_Off;
8     properties
9       Dispatch_Protocol => Periodic;
10      Period => 1000ms;
```

Listing 1.3. Manage Heat Source (MHS) AADL

Listing 1.3 provides the AADL textual definition of the Manage Heat Source (MHS) thread interface, including component ports (lines 2–7) and thread properties (lines 8–10).

```
1    part def Manage_Heat_Source :> Thread {
2        // ======== INPUTS =======
3        in port current_tempWstatus : DataPort { in :> type : TempWstatus; }
4        in port lower_desired_temp : DataPort { in :> type : Temp; }
5        in port upper_desired_temp : DataPort { in :> type : Temp; }
6        in port regulator_mode : DataPort { in :> type : Regulator_Mode; }
7
8        // ======== OUTPUTS =======
9        out port heat_control : DataPort { out :> type : On_Off; }
10
11       // ======== PROPERTIES ======
12       attribute :>> Dispatch_Protocol = Supported_Dispatch_Protocols::Periodic;
13       attribute :>> Period = 1000 [millisecond];
14
15       language "GUMBO" /*{
16           // (in separate figure -- see Figure 3)
17       }*/
18   }
```

Listing 1.4. Manage Heat Source (MHS) SysMLv2

Now we illustrate how these AADL concepts are represented in SysMLv2.[2] Listing 1.4 provides the SysMLv2 textual definition of the MHS thread interface analogous to the AADL definitions in Listing 1.3. Line 1 illustrates how SysMLv2 inheritance is used to indicate that the SysMLv2 **part** represents an AADL thread component. Note that the inheritance for the "thread" framework concept does not preclude inheritance designed as part of the application—SysMLv2 multiple inheritance allows any application inheritance to be realized as well.

Lines 3–9 illustrate how SysMLv2 port declarations are used to represent AADL port declarations. SysMLv2 primitives **in/out port** declare ports, similar to AADL. However, SysMLv2 doesn't have the ability to indicate AADL's **event**, **data**, and **event data** port categories. Instead, these categories are indicated by associating the port to a SysMLv2 type (e.g., **DataPort**) declared in the SysMLv2/AADL library (line 3 of Listing 1.2). The AADL type of the data communicated on the port is then indicated by specializing a **type** attribute value in the associated library declaration with a SysMLv2/AADL element (e.g., **TempWstatus** at line 3) that models an AADL **Data** component, which are used to define types following the standardized AADL Data Model annex.

5   Model-Level Contracts

To illustrate one approach that incorporates AADL annex-based formal methods into SysMLv2, we summarize how we have migrated the GUMBO component contract language and associated tooling. GUMBO includes a variety of contract forms including data invariants, several styles of pre/post-conditions tailored to periodic thread components or sporadic thread components (which tend to emphasize event-based communication), and these can be attached to a variety of model elements. At the bottom of Listing 1.4 at line 16, we indicated the placement of GUMBO contract for the MHS thread component using the SysMLv2 **language** construct. Figure 3 provides excerpts of the contract in the

---

[2] See [14] for a short video demo of the Isolette model in HAMR VSCode extension.

```
1   state
2     lastCmd: On_Off;
3
4   //======= I n i t i a l i z e   Entry  Point Behavior Constraints  ======
5   initialize
6     guarantee
7       initlastCmd: lastCmd == On_Off.Off;
8     guarantee REQ_MHS_1 "If the Regulator Mode is INIT, the Heat Control shall be set to Off"
9         heat_control == On_Off.Off;
10
11  //====== C o m p u t e   Entry  Point Behavior Constraints =====
12    compute
13      assume lower_is_lower_temp:
14        lower_desired_temp.degrees <= upper_desired_temp.degrees;
15
16      guarantee lastCmd "Set lastCmd to value of output Cmd port":
17        lastCmd == heat_control;
18
19    compute_cases
20      case REQ_MHS_1 "If the Regulator Mode is INIT, the Heat Control shall be
21                     |set to Off.":
22        assume regulator_mode == Regulator_Mode.Init_Regulator_Mode;
23        guarantee heat_control == On_Off.Off;
24
25      case REQ_MHS_2 "If the Regulator Mode is NORMAL and the Current Temperature is less than
26                     |the Lower Desired Temperature, the Heat Control shall be set to On.":
27        assume (regulator_mode == Regulator_Mode.Normal_Regulator_Mode)
28            & (current_tempWstatus.degrees < lower_desired_temp.degrees);
29        guarantee heat_control == On_Off.Onn;
30
31    // Contract clauses for REQ_MHS_3,  REQ_MHS_4,  REQ_MHS_5 omitted
```

Fig. 3. SysMLv2 MHS Thread GUMBO Contract (excerpts).

language construct. Like other contract languages (e.g., the state declarations in SPARK Ada), GUMBO contracts include declarations of local state that are relevant to the contract-specified behavior (line 2). The AADL standard dictates that thread code should be structured as "entry point" methods that will be invoked by the underlying scheduling framework. GUMBO provides dedicated contracts for the thread (a) *initialize* entry point that is executed once in the system's initialization phase, and (b) the *compute* entry point that is executed repeatedly (either event-triggered for sporadic components or time-triggered for periodic components) during system execution. Compute entry point contracts can take multiple forms. For sporadic components, contracts clauses can be organized in sections that specify component behavior on arrival of specific events. For periodic components (as in the MHS thread), lines 13–17 provide general pre-conditions (assume clauses) and post-conditions (guarantee clauses) which apply to every dispatch, and these can be extended with contract cases (e.g., as in JML [5]). A contract case applies when its assume clause is satisfied in the pre-state, and the associated guarantee clause must hold in the post-state. Section 6 will illustrate how these contracts are translated by HAMR to code-level contracts. As indicated in Sect. 2, the HAMR SysIDE-based extension supports full syntax highlighting, type-checking, etc. for these contracts.

GUMBO also supports specification of *integration* constraints. These can be attached to a component port to constrain the values flowing in or out of the port. When components are integrated (connected), HAMR model-level verification uses the Logika SMT-based verifier to automatically check that the constraints on an output port imply the constraints on any connected input port (where "connected" can apply to both ports that are directly connected or ports that end up being connected as a result of the flattening achieved by the declarative model instantiation process). As an example, we consider integration constraints on either side of a connection between an Operator Interface (OI) component (omitted in Fig. 2) and the Thermostat subsystem of Fig. 2. Listing 1.5 shows the integration constraints for the Operator Interface (OI) output port upper_alarm_tempWstatus and the input port of the same name on the Manage Monitor Interface (MMI) thread.

```
1   part def Operator_Interface_Thread :> Thread {
2     // (port declarations omitted)
3     // Sender's integeration constraints on its outgoing ports
4     language "GUMBO" /*{
5       integration
6         guarantee Table_A_12_LowerAlarmTemp "Range [96..101]" :
7           96.0 [f32] <= lower_alarm_tempWstatus.degrees and
8             lower_alarm_tempWstatus.degrees <= 101.0 [f32];
9         guarantee Table_A_12_UpperAlarmTemp "Range [97..102]" :
10          97.0 [f32] <= upper_alarm_tempWstatus.degrees and
11            upper_alarm_tempWstatus.degrees <= 102.0 [f32];
12    ...}
13
14  part def Manage_Monitor_Interface :> Thread {
15    // (port declarations omitted)
16    // Receiver's integration constraints on its incoming ports
17    language "GUMBO" /*{
18      integration
19        assume Table_A_12_LowerAlarmTemp "Range [96..101]" :
20          96.0 [f32] <= lower_alarm_tempWstatus.degrees and
21            lower_alarm_tempWstatus.degrees <= 101.0 [f32];
22        assume Table_A_12_UpperAlarmTemp "Range [97..102]" :
23          97.0 [f32] <= upper_alarm_tempWstatus.degrees and
24            upper_alarm_tempWstatus.degrees <= 102.0 [f32];
25    ...}
```

Listing 1.5. Integration Constraints

HAMR's model-level verification will confirm that any temperature value satisfying the guarantee constraint on the OI component will satisfy the assume constraint on the MMI component. Consider a scenario in which we seed a bug by having the lower bound on the OI component (in Table_A_12_LowerAlarmTemp) set to 94.0. Figure 4 shows how HAMR's model-level contract checking detects and reports this bug. The lightning bolts in the left gutter indicate that a verification condition (VC) was generated at that location, and purple highlighting indicates the contract coverage of the VC. Any VC that cannot be discharged is underlined with a red squiggle (lines 96 and 97), and an explanation of the failure is added to the Problems view as seen at the bottom of the figure. Hovering over a VC with the mouse displays the SMT2 script that was generated for it.[3]

As with the entry point contracts, integration constraints are also translated down to the code level. HAMR generates a code API object for each thread, providing getter and setter methods that developers can use to interact with

---

[3] See [14] for a short video demo of the checking of these integration constraints.

the thread's ports. Integration constraints are added by HAMR as Slang/Rust contracts to the API methods, and Logika/Verus can check, for example, that values placed on an outgoing port satisfy the port's guarantee clauses.

6 Code and Auto-Generated Code-Level Contracts

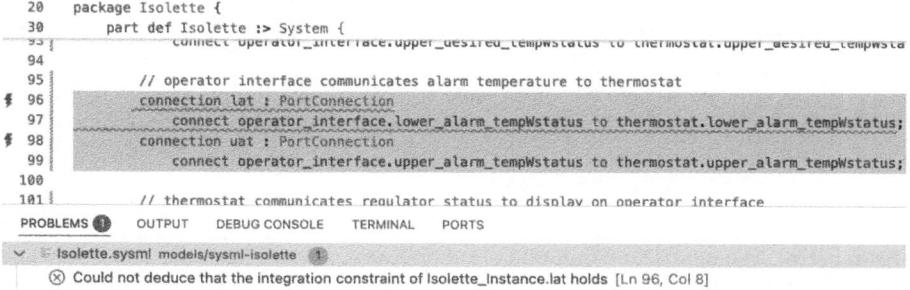

Fig. 4. Violation of an integration constraint.

Following the architecture in Fig. 1, after SysMLv2/AADL models are translated into AIR, the middle- and back-ends of the previous AADL pipeline can be reused. This includes code generation for (a) threading, port communication, and scheduling infrastructure code that conforms to AADL run-time semantics as well as (b) application code skeletons that engineers fill in to complete the system behavior.

In this section, we sketch how our previous application code skeletons and contract generation for AADL Isolette [16] are aligned with features in the SysMLv2 Isolette.

```
1    def timeTriggered(api: Manage_Heat_Source_impl_Operational_Api): Unit = {
2      // -------- Auto-generated contract (excerpts) -----------
3      Contract(
4        Requires(
5          // BEGIN COMPUTE REQUIRES timeTriggered
6          // assume lower_is_less_than_upper_temp
7          api.lower_desired_temp.value < api.upper_desired_temp.value
8          // END COMPUTE REQUIRES timeTriggered
9        Modifies(api,lastCmd),
10       Ensures(
11         // BEGIN COMPUTE ENSURES timeTriggered
12         // guarantee lastCmd
13         //   Set lastCmd to value of output port
14         lastCmd == api.heat_control,
15         // (...other aspect elided...)
16         // case REQ_MHS_2
17         //   If the Regulator Mode is NORMAL and the Current Temperature is less than the
18         //   Lower Desired Temperature, the Heat Control shall be set to On.
19         (api.regulator_mode == Regulator_Mode.Normal_Regulator_Mode &
20           api.current_tempWstatus.value < api.lower_desired_temp.value)
21           -->: (api.heat_control == On_Off.Onn),
```

```
22        // (...other aspects elided)
23        // END COMPUTE ENSURES timeTriggered
24        ))
25     // -------- Developer-supplied application code -----------
26     val lower = api.get_lower_desired_temp().get
27     val upper = api.get_upper_desired_temp().get
28     val regulator_mode = api.get_regulator_mode().get
29     val currentTemp = api.get_current_tempWstatus().get
30
31     var currentCmd = lastCmd
32     regulator_mode match {
33       case Regulator_Mode.Init_Regulator_Mode =>
34         currentCmd = On_Off.Off
35       case Regulator_Mode.Normal_Regulator_Mode =>
36         if (currentTemp.value > upper.value) {
37           currentCmd = On_Off.Off
38         } else if (currentTemp.value < lower.value) {
39           currentCmd = On_Off.Onn }
40       case Regulator_Mode.Failed_Regulator_Mode =>
41         currentCmd = On_Off.Off }
42     api.put_heat_control(currentCmd)
43     lastCmd = currentCmd }
44
```

Listing 1.6. Manage Heat Source Slang Application Code Skeleton, Contract, and Completed User Code

For example, for the MHS thread interface (Listing 1.4) and contracts (Fig. 3), HAMR will generate the Slang method declaration and Logika contract shown in Listing 1.6 up through the end of the contract at line 24. When coding the application logic for the thread, the developer will supply code for the **timeTriggered()** method (lines 26–43), which will be invoked periodically (according to the model-declared **Period** property) by the underlying scheduling framework. Lines 3–24 show excerpts the HAMR auto-generated code-level contract derived from the model-level contract in Fig. 3. The general **assume** clause in the GUMBO **compute** block (Fig. 3, line 13) is translated to a pre-condition in the code-level **Requires(..)** clause (line 7), and the general **guarantee** clause (Listing 3, line 16) is translated to a post-condition in the code-level **Ensures(..)** clause (line 14). HAMR includes delimiters such as those at lines 11 and 23 to mark the beginning and ending of auto-generated contracts. If GUMBO contracts are updated in the SysMLv2 model, HAMR can regenerate updated contracts into the same position in the code (by parsing the file to locate the delimiters), and thus can keep the code-level contracts in sync with the model contracts without clobbering the developer's application code.

Formal verification of the Slang code is performed using Logika. The developer can add additional contracts for local methods and data types not associated with model interfaces. Logika verification of code conformance to contracts is performed compositionally and employs multiple back-end solvers in parallel, including Alt-Ergo [8], CVC4 [2], CVC5 [1], and Z3 [31]. Logika scalability is enhanced using incremental and parallel (distributable) verification algorithms (for details see [33]).

Figure 5 shows how the developer uses the Sireum Integrated Verification Environment (IVE) to develop, debug, and to verify that the code conforms to

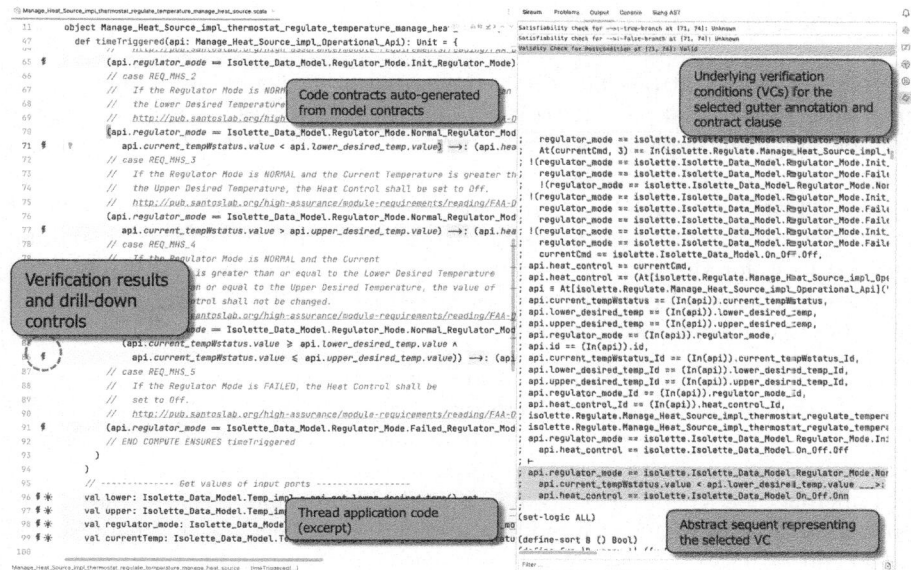

Fig. 5. Logika verification of Manage Heat Source code-level contracts.

the model-derived contract (in Listing 1.6) using Logika.[4] AADL's semantics for threading and port-manipulation ensure that thread implementations can be verified compositionally; abstractly, a thread's behavior is a function from its input port state and local variables to its output port state, with possibly updated local variables (see [12,20]). Logika can be applied interactively (with many features supporting industrial usability and explanation of verification results) or in batch mode as part of a server-based continuous integration process. Logika verifies absence of run-time exceptions and code conformance to contracts in around 15 s for the MHS thread initialize and compute entry points. Smart incremental verification, SMT-query caching, and other optimizations gives substantially faster performance to support on-the-fly re-checking during code editing. In addition, to this formal verification of code to contracts, we have also extended HAMR SysMLv2 to support the GUMBOX property-based testing framework [19]. GUMBOX provides a variety of capabilities for auto-generated property-guided random values for component port inputs and then checking that thread component input/output behavior conforms to executable versions of the component contract.

---

[4] See [14] for a short video demo of this Logika verification, along with automated property-based testing.

7   Capability Demonstrations

Our main objective at this point is to demonstrate to our industry and government stakeholders that the SysMLv2/AADL HAMR tool chain can provide the same development capabilities as using AADL with HAMR – for the types of systems that are needed in the defense domain. A secondary objective is helping the RTESC accumulate example uses of the RTESC libraries to support committee work and to convey progress to the broader OMG SysMLv2 community. Artifacts for the following systems are publicly available [14] to illustrate the end-to-end application of HAMR's SysMLv2/AADL support along with a collection of demonstration videos. ·

Isolette: The Isolette system is useful for supporting the objectives above because we have developed artifacts illustrating end-to-end development [16] – including concept of operations, requirements, models, code, testing, verification, all the way down to system deployments, including a deployment on the seL4 microkernel. The metrics given in Sect. 4 indicate that this is a system concept that can be easily understood by experienced engineers, with the associated end-to-end artifacts browseable within a reasonable amount of time.

Temperature Control: This is a "hello world" example used in our HAMR tutorial that includes 4 thread components, 9 thread component ports, and 5 connections between thread ports, with 6410 NCSLOC in the infrastructure code and 97 NCSLOC in the application logic. One limitation of the Isolette example for exercising the SysMLv2/AADL libraries is that it contains only periodic components and data ports; it does not illustrate event, event data, sporadic components and associated GUMBO contract forms. The temperature control example is useful because it covers these features.

Nuclear Reactor Safety Subsystem: The HARDENS system artifacts [15] were originally developed on a Galois project that aimed to demonstrate end-to-end model-based development technologies and formal methods for the US Nuclear Regulatory Commission. The artifacts included requirements developed according to a rigorous methodology, SysMLv2 system models, application logic written in Galois' Cryptol domain-specific language, and executables derived from the Cryptol tooling (as well as many other artifacts such as assurance cases not relevant to this paper). In the Galois project, the system generation from the SysMLv2 was done by hand. Aiming to demonstrate the applicability of HAMR, we considered the *actuation logic subsystem* (trip signal voting logic) and originally developed a corresponding AADL model (the Galois SysMLv2 modeling and our AADL model are structurally very similar), contracts in GUMBO, and component implementations in Slang. In fact, it was this original exploration that inspired us to support SysMLv2 for HAMR. Since then, we have refactored the original Galois SysMLv2 actuation subsystem models so they can now be used with HAMR. From these updated SysMLv2 models, we have developed deployments for the JVM, Linux, and seL4 microkernel. In the actuation subsystem, there are 15 thread components, 76 thread component ports, and 38 connections between thread ports, with 8847 non-comment/space source lines of Slang/Scala code (NCSLOC) in the infrastructure code and 156 NCSLOC in the application logic.

8   Related Work

The efforts of the OMG RTESC working group (led by Jerome Hugues and Gene Shreve) to produce the SysMLv2/AADL libraries has been a significant enabler for our work. The early investigation of the library concept by Roger and Dissaux [34] and Hugues [22] are resources for more details and rationale.

Other tooling is helping facilitate the combined use of AADL and SysMLv2 and the transition from AADL to SysMLv2. Litwin et al. [29] developed initial suggestions for translating AADL to SysMLv2, and engineers from the Software Engineering Institute have developed bi-directional translations between AADL and SysMLv2. Ellidiss is extending their AADL Inspector tool to support SysMLv2 with real-time synchronous of AADL and SysMLv2/AADL models, allow engineers to more easily integrate both modeling languages into workflows[5].

Molnár et al. [30] reports on the efforts of the OMG Systems Modeling Community Formal Methods Working Group. The paper provides a high-level summary of SysMLv2 semantic concepts and summaries of formal methods tool capabilities being developed by working group members. These include requirements tools, state machine analysis, and test case generation. A work flow integrating the tools is illustrated on a simple example. Kausch et al. [23] provide a semantics for a subset of SysMLv2 by mapping it into a data-flow formalism encoded in the Isabelle theorem prover. This enables proofs of liveness properties of event-driven and state-based SysMLv2 specifications.

9   Conclusion

We have presented an extension of HAMR to support formal-methods-integrated model-based development using the emerging SysMLv2 modeling language. This enables exploration of SysMLv2-based development for realistic embedded systems using model-level verification, formal behavior contracts integrated across models and code, property-based testing and SMT-based verification of code to contracts, with deployment to the formally verified seL4 micro-kernel and associated services. While our primary aim is supporting ongoing research for Collins Aerospace and other teams in the DARPA PROVERS project, we believe that the tool chain can be useful in the broader research community.

Additional AADL Concepts: We have focused on transitioning AADL concepts into SysMLv2 since this provides a very important technology transition pathway for impactful formal methods developed over the last two decades in the

---

[5] AADL Inspector website https://www.ellidiss.com/products/aadl-inspector/.

AADL community. Regarding AADL annex-based formal methods, we are now moving beyond GUMBO to support Resolute's [11] concepts for architecture constraints and assurance cases, as well as concepts from the AGREE [7] contract language. In previous work [36], we developed scalable model-based information flow analysis and visualization tools that utilized AADL's `flow` annotations. SysMLv2 does not have analogous annotations[6], and we are working with the OMG RTESC to develop a proposal for these. More broadly, finding a systematic way to migrate AADL annex concepts is a challenging topic worth exploring.

Extending Beyond AADL Concepts: We are also broadening our scope to address other facets of SysMLv2. For verification and testing, this includes utilizing SysMLv2's native pre/post-conditions and assertions. Our collaborators have previously developed SysMLv2 prototypes for AADL's state machine notations (based on the AADL Behavior Annex) [24], and these could be supported by HAMR verification and code generation.

Exercising New Back-Ends: Having recently added support for (a) Rust code and contract generation and (b) seL4's microkit kernel configuration and programming abstractions (which includes dedicated Rust support), our ongoing case study work includes using HAMR with SysMLv2 to prototype experimental versions of Collins Aerospace UAV mission control software using these technologies.

References

1. Barbosa, H., et al.: CVC5: a versatile and industrial-strength SMT solver. In: International Conference on Tools and Algorithms for the Construction and Analysis of Systems, pp. 415–442. Springer (2022)
2. Barrett, C., et al.: CVC4. In: Gopalakrishnan, G., Qadeer, S. (eds.) CAV 2011. LNCS, vol. 6806, pp. 171–177. Springer, Heidelberg (2011). https://doi.org/10.1007/978-3-642-22110-1_14
3. Belt, J., et al.: Model-driven development for the seL4 microkernel using the HAMR framework. J. Syst. Archit. (2022)
4. Borde, E., Rahmoun, S., Cadoret, F., Pautet, L., Singhoff, F., Dissaux, P.: Architecture models refinement for fine grain timing analysis of embedded systems. In: 2014 25nd IEEE International Symposium on Rapid System Prototyping, pp. 44–50 (2014)
5. Burdy, L., et al.: An overview of JML tools and applications. Int. J. Softw. Tools Technol. Transf. **7**(3), 212–232 (2005)
6. Cofer, D.D., et al.: Cyberassured systems engineering at scale. IEEE Secur. Priv. **20**(3), 52–64 (2022)
7. Cofer, D., Gacek, A., Miller, S., Whalen, M.W., LaValley, B., Sha, L.: Compositional verification of architectural models. In: Goodloe, A.E., Person, S. (eds.) NFM 2012. LNCS, vol. 7226, pp. 126–140. Springer, Heidelberg (2012). https://doi.org/10.1007/978-3-642-28891-3_13

---

[6] SysMLv2 does have a construct called `flow`, but it is used to specify sequential ordering between actions or steps – thus, the semantics is different than AADL flows.

8. Conchon, S., Coquereau, A., Iguernlala, M., Mebsout, A.: Alt-ergo 2.2. In: SMT Workshop: International Workshop on Satisfiability Modulo Theories (2018)

9. Feiler, P.H., Gluch, D.P.: Model-Based Engineering with AADL: An Introduction to the SAE Architecture Analysis & Design Language. Addison-Wesley (2013)

10. Fisher, K., Launchbury, J., Richards, R.: The HACMS program: using formal methods to eliminate exploitable bugs. Philos. Trans. Roy. Soc. A: Math. Phys. Eng. Sci. **375**(2104) (2017)

11. Gacek, A., Backes, J., Cofer, D., Slind, K., Whalen, M.: Resolute: an assurance case language for architecture models. In: Proceedings of the ACM SIGAda Annual International Conference on High Integrity Language Technology (HILT 2014), pp. 19–27. Association for Computing Machinery (2014)

12. Hallerstede, S., Hatcliff, J.: A mechanized semantics for component-based systems in the HAMR AADL runtime. In: Proceedings of the 19th International Conference on Formal Aspects of Component Software (FACS 2023) (2023)

13. HAMR project website (2022). https://hamr.sireum.org

14. SysMLv2 models repository (2022). https://github.com/santoslab/sysmlv2-models

15. HARDENS: high assurance rigorous digital engineering for nuclear safety (artifacts repository). https://github.com/GaloisInc/HARDENS

16. Hatcliff, J., Belt, J.: The Isolette system: illustrating end-to-end artifacts for rigorous model-based engineering. In: Hinchey, M., Steffen, B. (eds.) The Combined Power of Research, Education, and Dissemination. Lecture Notes in Computer Science, vol. 15240, pp. 93–117. Springer, Cham (2025). https://doi.org/10.1007/978-3-031-73887-6_9

17. Hatcliff, J., Belt, J., Robby, Carpenter, T.: HAMR: an AADL multi-platform code generation toolset. In: Margaria, T., Steffen, B. (eds.) ISoLA 2021. LNCS, vol. 13036, pp. 274–295. Springer, Cham (2021). https://doi.org/10.1007/978-3-030-89159-6_18

18. Hatcliff, J., Belt, J., Robby, Hardin, D.: Integrated contract-based unit and system testing for component-based systems. In: Benz, N., Gopinath, D., Shi, N. (eds.) Proceedings of the 16th NASA Formal Methods Symposium (NFM 2024) (2024)

19. Hatcliff, J., Belt, J., Robby, Legg, J., Stewart, D., Carpenter, T.: Automated property-based testing from AADL component contracts. In: Cimatti, A., Titolo, L. (eds.) Formal Methods for Industrial Critical Systems (2023)

20. Hatcliff, J., Hugues, J., Stewart, D., Wrage, L.: Formalization of the AADL runtime services. In: Leveraging Applications of Formal Methods, Verification and Validation - 11th International Symposium on Leveraging Applications of Formal Methods, ISoLA 2022, Rhodes, Greece (2022)

21. Hatcliff, J., Stewart, D., Belt, J., Robby, Schwerdfeger, A.: An AADL contract language supporting integrated model- and code-level verification. In: Proceedings of the 2022 ACM Workshop on High Integrity Language Technology (2022)

22. Hugues, J.: AADLv2 library for SysMLv2. Technical report, CMU/SEI-2023-TN-001, Software Engineering Institute, Carnegie Mellon University (2023). https://apps.dtic.mil/sti/trecms/pdf/AD1207053.pdf. Approved for public release and unlimited distribution

23. Kausch, H., Pfeiffer, M., Raco, D., Rumpe, B., Schweiger, A.: Correct and sustainable development using model-based engineering and formal methods. In: 2022 IEEE/AIAA 41st Digital Avionics Systems Conference (DASC), pp. 1–8. IEEE (2022)

24. Larson, B.R., Chalin, P., Hatcliff, J.: BLESS: formal specification and verification of behaviors for embedded systems with software. In: Brat, G., Rungta, N., Venet, A. (eds.) NFM 2013. LNCS, vol. 7871, pp. 276–290. Springer, Heidelberg (2013). https://doi.org/10.1007/978-3-642-38088-4_19

25. Lasnier, G., Zalila, B., Pautet, L., Hugues, J.: OCARINA: an environment for aadl models analysis and automatic code generation for high integrity applications. In: Kordon, F., Kermarrec, Y. (eds.) Ada-Europe 2009. LNCS, vol. 5570, pp. 237–250. Springer, Heidelberg (2009). https://doi.org/10.1007/978-3-642-01924-1_17

26. Lattuada, A., et al.: Verus: verifying rust programs using linear ghost types. Proc. ACM Program. Lang. **7**(OOPSLA1) (2023)

27. Lempia, D., Miller, S.: DOT/FAA/AR-08/32. Requirements engineering management handbook. Federal Aviation Administration (2009)

28. Leroy, X., Blazy, S., Kästner, D., Schommer, B., Pister, M., Ferdinand, C.: Compcert-a formally verified optimizing compiler. In: ERTS 2016: Embedded Real Time Software and Systems, 8th European Congress (2016)

29. Litwin, K., Amundson, I., Verma, D., McDermott, T.: Transforming AADL models into SysML 2.0: insights and recommendations. SAE Technical Paper 2024-01-1947, SAE International (2024). https://doi.org/10.4271/2024-01-1947

30. Molnár, V., et al.: Towards the formal verification of SysML v2 models. In: Proceedings of the ACM/IEEE 27th International Conference on Model Driven Engineering Languages and Systems, MODELS Companion 2024, pp. 1086–1095. Association for Computing Machinery, New York (2024)

31. Moura, L.d., Bjørner, N.: Z3: an efficient SMT solver. In: International conference on Tools and Algorithms for the Construction and Analysis of Systems, pp. 337–340. Springer (2008)

32. Robby, Hatcliff, J.: Slang: The Sireum programming language. In: International Symposium on Leveraging Applications of Formal Methods, pp. 253–273 (2021)

33. Robby, Hatcliff, J., Belt, J.: Logika: the Sireum verification framework. In: Proceedings of the International Conference on Formal Methods for Industrial Critical Systems (FMICS), pp. 97–116 (2024)

34. Roger, J.C., Dissaux, P.: AADL modelling with SysML v2. ACM SIGAda Ada Lett. **43**(2), 22–28 (2023). https://doi.org/10.1145/3631483.3631486

35. Stewart, D., Liu, J.J., Cofer, D., Heimdahl, M., Whalen, M.W., Peterson, M.: AADL-based safety analysis using formal methods applied to aircraft digital systems. Reliabil. Eng. Syst. Saf. **213**, 107649 (2021)

36. Thiagarajan, H., Hatcliff, J., Robby: Awas: AADL information flow and error propagation analysis framework. Innov. Syst. Softw. Eng. (ISSE) (2021)

37. Vaicenavičius, J., Wiklund, T., Kavolis, D., Draukšas, S., Kalkauskas, A., Vaicenavičius, R.: SysIDE: SysML v2 textual editing & analysis system – overview and applications. In: Proceedings of the International Systems Engineering Symposium (IS2024). Sensmetry (2024). https://sensmetry.com/

38. Ward, D.T., Helton, S.B.: Estimating return on investment for SAVI (a model-based virtual integration process. In: SAE International Nournal of Aerospace (2011)

A Specification-Driven Approach to Embedded FDIR Code Generation

Federico Bonafini[1], Roberto Cavada[2], Alessandro Cimatti[2], Guillermo Gomez[2], and Stefano Tonetta[2(✉)]

[1] Innova Engineering, Tione, Italy
[2] Fondazione Bruno Kessler, Trento, Italy
federico.bonafini@innovaenergie.com,
{cavada,cimatti,ggomezarnedo,tonettas}@fbk.eu

Abstract. Fault Detection, Isolation, and Recovery (FDIR) components are essential for managing faults and ensuring safety and reliability in safety-critical applications. This paper presents a specification-driven approach to the automatic generation of embedded FDIR code. Our method leverages formal specifications of fault conditions and recovery procedures to synthesize fault detection and recovery mechanisms, reducing manual coding and the potential for human error. The proposed toolchain translates high-level specifications into platform-specific embedded code, while model checking can be used to validate and verify the FDIR logic. We detail the underlying architecture, the specification language, and the code generation process, highlighting the flexibility and scalability of the approach. Through a case study in the energy domain, we demonstrate the tool's ability to handle complex fault scenarios, improve development efficiency, and enhance system reliability.

1 Introduction

Embedded software-based systems have enabled the implementation of complex control functionalities, ensuring energy-efficient and adaptive operations, and a high degree of parameterization. Among these capabilities, *fault management* is particularly crucial, especially in safety-critical systems, as it ensures continued operation even in degraded, non-nominal conditions. At design time, hazard analysis and safety assessments are conducted, with fault prevention and recovery strategies implemented through monitoring and reconfiguration procedures, as well as redundant equipment. These safety mechanisms are often then handled by control software, which provides high degree of parametrization and reuse.

The concept of FDIR encompasses a set of functions for fault management that include detecting the occurrence of a fault, identifying it, and applying the appropriate recovery actions. FDIR interacts with the plant to read input data

---

The work is financed by the Autonomous Province of Trento in scope of L.P. No. 6/1999 with determination. No. 592 of 09/08/2021. – Ref.: 2021-AG12-00783. - project NPDCR (New residential heat pump).

A. Remke and B. Steffen (Eds.): FMICS 2025, LNCS 16040, pp. 261–279, 2025.
https://doi.org/10.1007/978-3-032-00942-5_14

and with the controller to command reconfiguration of redundant components or other recovery procedures. FDIR can be conceptually divided into two main components (see Fig. 1): Fault Detection and Isolation (FDI), which focuses on detecting and identifying faults, and Fault Recovery (FR), which applies the most suitable response based on the detected fault.

Designing FDIR modules presents significant challenges. On one hand, FDI often requires to monitor complex temporal extended conditions. On the other, defining appropriate recovery actions requires covering all possible fault combinations and arranging them based on their priorities. In fact, faults can occur even during the execution of a recovery procedure intended to address a different issue with lower criticality. While model-based safety analysis techniques have been proposed to design FDIR components with formal methods,

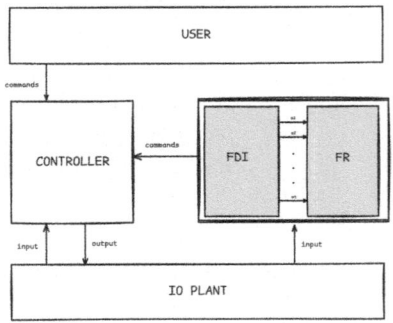

Fig. 1. FDIR function overview

they neglect the complexity of software interfaces and the need of the FDIR software to interact with procedures and data structures provided by the platform.

In this paper, we propose a novel end-to-end approach to the development of FDIR software. The idea is to start from a high-level specification and automatically generate platform-specific code suitable for deployment on embedded controllers with real-time constraints, thereby reducing manual effort and minimizing human error. The advantages of the approach are manifold: first, it can handle many fault conditions avoiding entangled solutions, by separating monitoring from recovery, and defining a clear priority on the concurrent recovery actions; second, it can be adapted to different platforms; third, it allows for the application of formal verification techniques to check the FDIR logic.

The approach has been devised in the context of a long-term collaboration between Innova Engineering (IE) and FBK, and was driven by the goal of defining a structured software development process customized for the portfolio of IE products. We discuss its application to a real-world case study, a heat pump controller that is representative of the most recent products of the company.

The key contributions of this work are as follows:

- A specification-driven methodology for defining fault conditions, detection mechanisms, and recovery procedures in a structured and formalized manner.
- An automated toolchain that translates high-level specifications into platform-specific embedded code.
- A principled integration of formal verification through model checking techniques, enabling rigorous validation of FDIR logic before deployment.
- A case study in the energy domain, demonstrating the effectiveness of our approach in handling complex fault scenarios while enhancing reliability.

2   Related Works

A wide literature studied model-based fault detection and diagnosis, which leverage mathematical models of system dynamics. There are two primary approaches: one rooted in control theory and the other based on logic and artificial intelligence (AI) (see [CDL+04]). The control-theoretic approach [MP71, Ise84, CP99] [Ise05, HKKS10, Ger15, GCD15] relies on dynamic system models (e.g., system of differential equations), and use methods such as state observers, Kalman filters, and parity relations to detect and isolate faults.

The logic and AI-based approach, in contrast, leverages formal methods, expert systems, and machine learning techniques for fault detection and diagnosis. Model-based diagnosis [Rei87, dKMR90] approaches use logic satisfiability to check consistency between expected and observed behavior. Model-Based Safety Analysis (MBSA) uses model checking techniques to analyze the design of safety mechanisms [BV03], including FDIR components. It starts from a component-based model with high level view of the component behaviors, and inject faults in these models to validate the reaction of the FDIR. This process has been integrated in standard aerospace development process [BBC+14] and in a ESA toolchain [BBC+22]. Recent work has also applied model checking to assess and improve fault tolerance of satellite systems [KGK23], focusing on verifying existing logic at system level rather than synthesizing embedded-level components from formal specifications. Logic based specification of FDIR has been formalized in [BCGT14, BCGT15], dealing with the inherent epistemic problem of diagnosability. Finally, the monitoring of properties specified in temporal logic can be solved with runtime verification techniques [BLS11].

In the above mentioned works, recovery mechanisms are also divided between control-theoretic strategies, such as adaptive and fault-tolerant control, and logic or AI-based strategies, such as planning or reinforcement learning. However, in both cases, most of the academic works are not adopted at industrial level [Zol18]. One of the reasons is that they neglect the complexity of managing software procedures for recovery and handling the logic of switching between them, which is the main contribution of this paper. In general, there is a lack of guidance and tool support for implementing complex FDIR components at software level. An example of such efforts is the development of an FDIR software fault tree library for onboard computers [MHSG20], which focuses on reuse and structuring of fault handling logic, though without formal specification or automatic synthesis. In the direction of closing this gap, this paper proposes a specification-based methodology and a tool support applied to a real-world scenario.

3   Preliminary Notions

3.1   Temporal Logics and Formal Verification

We adopt temporal logic [Pnu77] as a formalism for the specification of properties of execution traces. Temporal logics are common in formal verification [CGK+18, BCGT24] to represent different kinds of requirements. Properties over the states (e.g., "temperature>threshold") constitute the basic elements of formulas. Temporal operators such as "always in the future" (G) and "sometimes in the future" (F) can be nested to express complex temporal properties. For example, it is possible express FDIR properties, like requiring that an alarm is triggered whenever the temperature is too high ("`G ((temperature>threshold) implies alarm-high-temp)`"), or that a suitable response is eventually delivered ("`G ((temperature>threshold) implies F recovery-high-temp)`"). In addition to future time operators, it is often convenient to adopt past operators, such as "historically" (H) or "once" (O) in the past and that allow to express properties over past states. Finally, metric operators like in the last n steps (`H [0,n]`) are used to constrain an interval of time. In the following, we use LTL (with all operators mentioned above) for model checking, while runtime verification is applied to PastLTL, the fragment that uses only the past operators.

Model checking is a technique to verify whether the model of a system satisfies a property, i.e. all its traces satisfy the property. The model is typically described as a symbolic transition system and symbolic verification of temporal properties is performed with algorithms combining deduction and reachability through logic-based operations (see [BCGT24] for a survey).

Runtime verification [BLS11] is a lightweight verification technique intended to analyze the observable signals of a running system. The idea is to evaluate a temporal logic specification of the property on the actual execution of the system. Then, the automata-theoretic approach produces an observer that is put in synchronous product to the system under observation and raises a flag then the current trace is violated. Runtime verification is considered to be appealing since it is logically well founded, does not alter the nominal behavior of the system under analysis, and supports various implementation patterns.

3.2   SDL, ASN.1 and OpenGeode

For code generation, we rely internally on SDL and ASN.1, and the OPEN-GEODE tool support. SDL (Specification and Description Language) is an established standard formal language to describe both networks of communicating state machines at system level, and the specification of the behavior of Finite State Machine (FSM). SDL comes with both a graphical and textual notation for the specification of the system, the communication ports and connections, functional blocks definition, and behavior specification in FSM. Transitions are triggered by events such as reception of a queued message, or certain observed condition becoming true, or a timer expiring. Operations admitted in transitions include setting variables and timers, and sending events to other blocks through ports and connections among them. Conditions and operation can be organized in functions and procedures. State machines can be hierarchical, meaning that a given high level state of the machine can contain an inner state machine.

SDL is supported by various commercial and open source editors and compilers. OPENGEODE is an open source graphical editor which features also automatic code generation in Ada and C. OPENGEODE presents both some limitations and extensions to the SDL language. In particular it removes the support for the data type system of SDL, and provides instead support for the ASN.1 specification. ASN.1 is a formal specification used to describe data types with constraints, and constant values. The ASN.1 specification is compiled by ASN1SCC, an open source compiler for ASN.1 for data structures and encoding/decoding code, with multiple target languages like Ada, C and Scala.

The main advantage of using SDL + ASN.1 and OPENGEODE + ASN1SCC over other widespread languages and code generators (e.g. the common pair Stateflow/Matlab) is the well-described and clear formal semantics of SDL which greatly simplified the automatic translation of the FDIR specifications into a FSM based representation in SDL. Using SDL and ASN.1 as standard intermediate languages allowed us to rely on OPENGEODE and ASN1SCC to generate automatically the code, which proved to be easily integrated into both the host and target embedded platforms. However, SDL was not considered for the frontend specification language. Instead, we preferred a tabular format for the specification of the fault modes, in a form very similar to the FMEA tables (Failure Mode and Effects Analysis) which the domain experts are familiar with. For the same reasons, for the specification of the recovery procedures we preferred a syntactically limited language to describe the corresponding procedural steps.

4   Specification-Driven FDIR Code Generation

In this section, we describe the methodology that we propose to generate the FDIR code from a high-level specification. We start from giving an overview of the approach (Sect. 4.1). We then detail the specification in terms of failure conditions (Sect. 4.2), recovery procedures (Sect. 4.3), and failure mode management (Sect. 4.4). In Sect. 4.5 and 4.6, we detail the process of generating respectively the code and the model for formal verification.

4.1   Overview of the Specification-Based Methodology

In this section, we describe the methodology that we propose to generate the FDIR code from a high-level specification and the tool called FDIRGEN that supports it. The tools is publicly available at https://fm.fbk.eu/tools/fdirgen/. We start from giving an overview of workflow of the approach, depicted in Fig. 2. The inputs are the artifacts provided by the user, i.e. the *controller interface* and the *FDIR specification*.

The controller interface consists of a set of declarations to define the signals and the primitives that will be available for the generated FDIR code. These include user-defined data types (e.g., structs, ranged integers), input and output variables, functions to perform calculations over the inputs, and functions representing commands writing on the outputs.

The FDIR specification is given by a table, defining monitoring conditions, recovery procedures and a Finite-State Machine (FSM) defining the operational modes of the FDIR. The specification is therefore hierarchical: the FSM defines

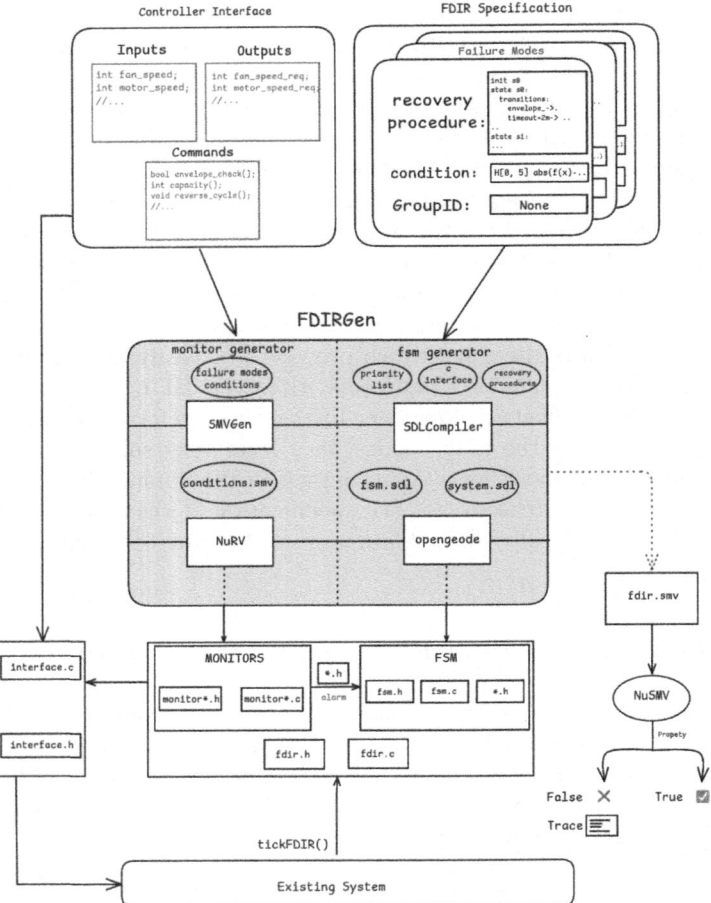

Fig. 2. Workflow of the Specification-Based Approach.

the top-level modes and the transitions to switch between modes; each mode is then associated to a monitoring condition and to a recovery procedure. As shown in Fig. 3, the FDIR specification table is composed of three main parts:

fault detection and isolation conditions defined in PastLTL and specified over input variables and input functions; (detailed in Sect. 4.2)

recovery procedures defined as state machines extended with timeout constraints specified in a domain specific language; the procedures call the output functions to write on output variables; (Sect. 4.3)

priorities and threshold groups determining the mode transitions (Sect. 4.4).

FDIR mode	Fault Detection Condition	Fault Isolation Condition	Priority	Threshold Group	Fault Recovery Procedure
Mode 1		Condition X	High	Group 1	Restart System
Mode 2	Condition A	Condition Y	Medium	Group 2	Switch to Backup
Mode 3		Condition Z	Low	Group 3	Alert Operator

Fig. 3. FDIR Specification Table structure.

The specification is given to the FDIRGEN software, which generates the *FDIR code* that interacts with the system controller. The resulting FDIR code is composed by a *monitor module* and an *FSM module* (Detailed in Sect. 4.5).

The FDIRGEN software can also generate a model specified in SMV, the input language of the nuXmv model checker. The model represents the same FDIR logic that is encoded in the generated code. Thus, the SMV model can be used to validate and verify the FDIR logic with model checking techniques (Detailed in Sect. 4.6).

Running Example. We illustrate the approach through a running example. This is based on a simple specification, with two sources of power, the main one and the secondary that is activated in case of main failure. We want an FDIR system to be able to detect cases where we have been relying on the secondary pump for too long, and cases where both of the power supplies are failing.

Starting from the specification table, for the running example, we can define the following table to express the mentioned properties (we removed group id and isolation condition for space constraints):

FDIR mode	Fault Detection Condition	Priority	Fault Recovery Procedure

Mode 1	$H[0s, 10s] \wedge \neg main$ $\wedge\ H[0s, 20s] \wedge \neg secondary$	1	`init restarted [ restart_power(); ]`
			`state restarted:`
			`  transitions:`
			`    timeout = 75s -> fail`
			`    main -> ok`

Mode 2	$secondary$ $S[10s, 10s]!main$	2	Switch to Backup

Fig. 4. Running example FDIR specification.

As far as interface is concerned, we need both attributes used on the properties and the recovery procedures (these procedures are the ones on the existing system, we just have to specify the header).

Input attributes:

```
bool main;
bool secondary;
```

Commands for the controller:

```
void  recovery();
void  restart_power();
```

4.2 Monitoring Conditions

The monitoring conditions are specified in an extended version of PastLTL over the input variables, where:

- in the atomic conditions, we can specify arithmetic constraints combining input variables with calls to the input functions (e.g., "abs(expect ed_flow()-flow)>delta", where abs is a macro for the absolute value;
- the time bounds of interval in the metric operators are expressed in time units that may be milliseconds (ms), seconds (s), or minutes (m).

The PastLTL operators allow to specify temporally extended conditions. Typical patterns of conditions that we use for monitoring are $H_I(\alpha_1)$ and $\alpha_1 \wedge O_I(\alpha_2)$ where α_1 and α_2 are atomic conditions. The first one identifies the situation in which a condition α_1 lasts continuously in the interval I. The second one identifies the situation in which we detect α_2 and in a previous moment, within the interval I, α_1 was true. Examples of these patters are:

```
H  [0s,  30s]  abs(expected_flow()-flow)>delta
```

which is true in the moment in which, for the last 30 s, the expected flow differed from the actual one more than a certain delta constant;

```
flow=0 & O [0ms, 20ms] flow>high_value
```

which is true in the moment in which the flow drops to zero from a high value that was read in the previous 20 ms.

In order to ease and organize better the specification of the conditions, they are divided into two columns of the specification table. The first column, called *fault detection condition*, should contain the conditions that identify the detection of a fault and trigger the alarm. The second column, called *fault isolation condition*, should contain the conditions that try to discriminate the cause of the problem and used to differentiate between one mode and another. Multiple isolation conditions can be associated to one fault detection condition. For example, to detect a fault we may check if the temperature is different from the set value and does not change. This may be caused by potentially different causes, which can be distinguished by checking if the fan is working and if there is power.

4.3 Recovery Procedures

The recovery procedures are specified in a domain-specific modeling language. This is a textual specification of states, transitions, and timeouts. The purpose is to provide a simple high-level specification of the procedures avoiding cumbersome code for input/output, timers or complex data structures. For example, in order to update an output variable x increasing its value by another input variable y, we would simply write x += y; in SDL external variables cannot be used directly, so we would have to write a getter on each variable access, and a setter on every update; in our example, this would look like the following sequence: get_x(x); get_y(y); set_x(x + y).

Thus, each recovery procedure provides a list of states, and for each state, a list of outgoing transitions that write on the output variables of the controller through the output functions specified in the controller interface and change the state of the procedure. An init statement represents the initial state of the procedure. Optionally, an effects section can follow, specifying initial conditions or setup actions. The procedure may define a set of local variables, followed by the declaration of states utilized within the procedure.

Each program has two implicit terminating states:

- ok: it indicates successful recovery and leads to a nominal system mode.
- fail: it denotes an unrecoverable error, leading to a stophold system mode.

The program terminates whenever one of these two states is entered.

For each state, the program lists a sequence of possible transitions. Each transition has a guard and an effect. The first transition with the guard that evaluates to true is taken, the effect is executed, which include to go to a new state or remain in the current one. Transitions between states are prioritized, with priority determined by the order in which transitions are declared. Each state may optionally specify an invariant condition that must hold upon entry. If the condition is violated, execution transitions immediately to the fail state.

States are equipped with local timeouts, which reset each time the state is re-entered and can be used in the guards of transitions. Additionally, timeouts can be defined over a set of states, resetting whenever execution enters this set from an external state. This feature is useful when modeling loops involving one or more states, allowing explicit control over their execution duration. As for the monitoring conditions, time constraints use time units.

The following listing gives a simple example of recovery procedure.

```
init check_velocity [ req_speed := 0; ]

timeout checking_loop : timeout=3m on
                         {check_velocity , check_temperature};

state check_velocity:
  invar: req_velocity > 0
  transitions:
    checking_loop -> fail
    timeout=2s -> check_velocity
    [velocity > req_velocity \ req_velocity += 2;]
                                -> check_temperature
```

```
state check_temperature:
  transitions:
    checking_loop -> fail
    timeout=420ms -> check_temperature
    [temp > avg_temp \ req_temp += 0.2;]
                                      -> check_temperature
    // if the velocity went down again, keep speeding up
    velocity < req_velocity -> check_velocity
```

4.4   Specification of the **FDIR FSM**

The FDIR FSM consists of a list of modes and a list of mode transitions. The modes are implicitly defined by the rows of the FDIR specification table. Two additional modes are predefined and added to the list: the nominal mode, which is also the initial one; the stophold mode, which is entered when a recovery procedure fails and cannot be exited (at the moment no reset of the FDIR is considered). Figure 5 shows a pictorial view of an example FDIR FSM.

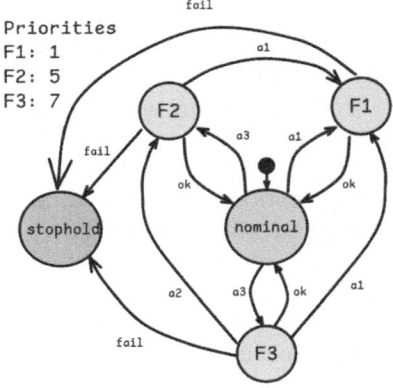

Fig. 5. Top Level FSM example.

The specification table assigns a priority to every mode. The nominal mode is given priority 0, while the stophold mode is given a priority higher than any other.

The specification table assigns also a group and to each group a threshold. The FSM maintains a counter for each group, which is increased whenever the FSM enters a mode of that group. Whenever the threshold is reached, the FSM goes to stophold mode. The purpose is to avoid continuous spurious recoveries, which happens when the procedure brings the FDIR to nominal mode, but the problem is not really solved and the same mode is entered again and again.

Overall, the FSM mode transitions are defined as follows. When the FSM receives an alarm from the monitor the next mode is determined by the following rules:

- if the current mode has higher or equal priority than the new one, then the next mode is determined by the current recovery procedure: it remains the current one if not completed, it becomes nominal if completed, or stophold if aborted;
- if the current mode has lower priority of the new one, then the counter associated to the new mode group is increased, and if it did not reached the threshold, the next mode is set to the new mode; otherwise it is set to stophold. If the mode is changed, the counter of the current mode (if the group is different from the new one) is reset.

4.5   Code Generation Process

The code generation is organized into three main parts, reflecting the three different components of the generated code: *monitor generation*, *FSM generation* and *interface generation*.

The *monitor generation* relies on standard runtime verification techniques to generate a deterministic finite-state automaton to monitor a temporal formula (see, e.g., [BLS11]). In our implementation, we use the NuRV runtime verifier [CTT19] to generate the single monitor code for each property, and then a MonitorHandler is configured to handle these monitors and connect their output to the alarms accepted by the FDIR FSM.

More specifically, the generation of the monitors proceed as follows:

- Preprocess the monitoring conditions to
  - remove time units converting the time constraints into bounds on number of FDIR ticks, and
  - replace functions with fresh variables with the same type of the function return value.
- Generate C monitors with NuRV.
- Generate the MonitorHandler with the glue code to connect the input/output of the monitor with the system controller and the FDIR FSM.

For the *FSM generator*, the code generation relies on OPENGEODE which takes in input an SDL description of the FSM. For this reason, the internal representation of the FDIR FSM is created from the table specification and then dumped into a file with the SDL syntax. OPENGEODE is then called to generate the corresponding C code.

The final step is to generate the code that provides the interface with the controller. This contains, on one side, all the setters/getters and commands accessible from the FDIR component, and on the other side, the implementation of the *tick* function, which performs the duty cycle of reading inputs, calling the monitor, calling the FDIR FSM to update the FDIR mode, update the state of the recovery procedure in the updated mode and writing outputs.

Running Example. The code generation for the interface in our example, could be as follows:

```
// Variables and procedures living in the existing system
extern void restart_power();
extern unsigned char main_power_supply;
// Generated functions ...
void fsm_RI_getsecondary_power_supply(asn1SccTBoolean* value){
    (*value)=secondary_power_supply;
}
//...
```

For the Monitor Handler we follow a clean approach, where we separate the reading of inputs and the checking of the properties (we import a*.h which source files contain the explicit automata for the properties):

```
#include "MonitorHandler.h"
int a3loc = 1; // initial location(state) of the automata.
a3_input_t input_a3;
// ...
void tick_monitors() {
  RV_value val;
  read_inputs(); // Update C monitors with current values.
  val = a3_scalar(&input_a3, NULL, 2, &a3loc);
  if(val == RV_TRUE) fsm_PI_a3(); // send alarm to FSM
  // ...
}
```

The SDL FSM can be viewed from OPENGEODE:

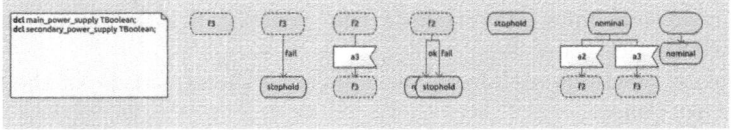

Fig. 6. SDL FSM components of the running example.

4.6 Formal Verification

The generation of the SMV model for formal verification follows a similar approach. The SMV model is modular and reflects the hierarchical structure of the FDIR specification. The top level FSM is represented by the main module, while each FDIR mode is represented by a separate module whose behavior represents the corresponding recovery procedure. For lack of space, we omit the details, but the translation follows the semantics specified in the previous sections in a straightforward way.

The generic structure of the SMV model is reported in the following snippet:

```
MODULE main
-- nominal is lowest priority, and stophold highest.
DEFINE priority := [0, ...];
VAR
    current: 0 .. N+1;
    alarm: 0 .. N+1;
    input_fun0: boolean;
    input_fun1: boolean;
    ...
    input0: ...;
    input1: ...;
    ...
    f1: F1(current, alarm, priority, ...);
    f2: F2(current, alarm, priority, ...);
    ...
TRANS -- stophold as trap state.
    current = 1 -> next(current) = 1
-- higher priorities will get to that state, or ok/fail.
TRANS
    priority[current] < priority[alarm] ->
            (next(current) = alarm | next(current) = 1)
-- lower priorities will keep in the same state, or ok/fail.
TRANS
    priority[current] >= priority[alarm] ->
            (next(current) = current | next(current) = 0
            | next(current) = 1 )

MODULE F1(...)
...
```

The **current** variable represents the current mode. The value "0" represents the nominal mode, the value "1" represents the stophold mode, while the other values represent the user-defined modes.

If an alarm is received and the corresponding mode has a priority higher than the current one, the next mode will be set to the new one or to nominal or to failure. If the alarm corresponds to a mode with lower priority is discarded and the next mode is determined by the module implementing the recovery procedure of the current mode.

Finally, each recovery procedure is translated into an SMV module. The transition follows the definition of transition in a straightforward way.

Running Example. In the development process, tuning the priorities might not be trivial and could lead to inconsistent definitions. One of the possible errors could be that we set up a priority that never triggers because there is a higher priority failure mode that implies the other property. We can leverage model checking to automate this property: "There is no higher priority failure condition that implies a lower priority failure condition". We might have:

Property 1: $H[0\,s, 10\,s] \wedge \neg\text{main} \wedge H[0\,s, 20\,s] \wedge \neg\text{secondary}$

Property 2: $secondary\_supply\,S[10, 10]\neg main\_power\_supply$

If we mistakenly give more priority to Property 2, we find the following warning:

```
-- specification
(((secondary\_power\_supply) S [10,10] (!main_power_supply))
-> ( H [0,10] !main_power_supply &
H [0,20] !secondary_power_supply)) is true
```

Which, in the development process would mean that we can either strengthen the property, remove it, or swap priorities.

5   Heat Pump Controller Case Study

5.1   Description of the System

Innova Engineering is setting up a structured development process for the control software of Innova heat pump systems for heating and air conditioning. As part of this process, the integration of FDIR represents an important asset for reliable control. To avoid entering in proprietary designs of heat pumps, we here use an example that is representative of the most recent products of the company. The example is a cooling/heating system powered by pumps with an exchanger in between, and multiple sensors to monitor the physical dynamics. In order to understand the monitoring properties and recovery procedures, we give a brief introduction to the system.

Figure 7 gives a pictorial view of the case study with detail of the various components' inputs and outputs. The circuit has two pumps, the master pump which works on nominal conditions, and the redundancy pump, for faulty situations. These pumps make the fluid flow into the cooling/heating module (exchanger). The exchanger modifies the liquid's temperature depending on the requested power, its density and a few more variables. The fluid with the desired temperature will be directed to the hot/cold load, and if no problems were detected, start the cycle again. Later, it will be directed in-between components through pipes with flow sensors, measuring the volume of liquid we transfer per second.

5.2   FDIR Specification

All the information about failure modes is listed in Table 1, apart from the group thresholds that are omitted for lack of space (note that empty isolation conditions are interpreted as always true). We briefly discuss here some of the most important monitoring conditions and related recovery:

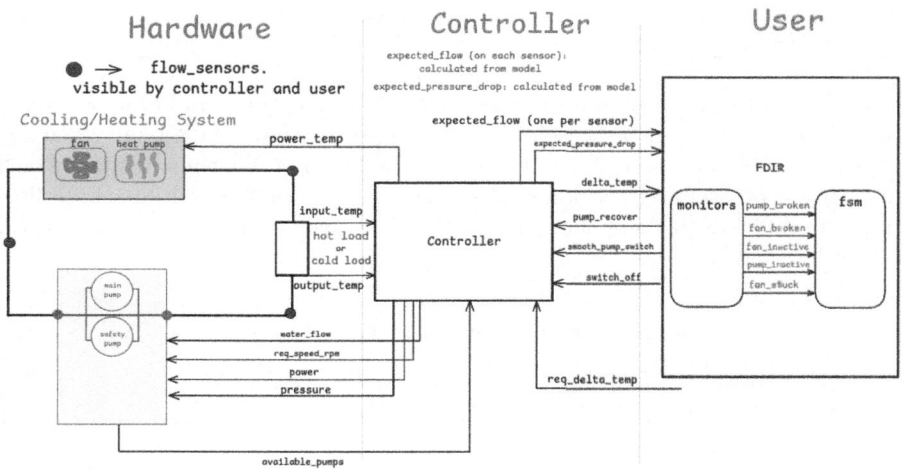

Fig. 7. Heat Pump case study architecture.

- The sum over differences of pressures is not 0, which could mean that the pump is blocked, or there is a leakage in the pipe system. In this particular example, we experience a rise in pressure (for simplicity, we assume that the pressure drop on the cold load is 0):
  - The pump: we will model the pressure rise with:

$$\Delta P\,[\text{kPa}] = 5.62 \times 10^{-6} \times \text{pump\_speed}\,[\text{rpm}]^2 - 4.46 \times \text{flow}\,[\text{m}^3/\text{h}]^2$$

  - The exchanger: $\Delta P = \left(\frac{\text{flow}}{K_v}\right)^2$, where K_v is a coefficient that takes into account exchanger geometry and fluid type.

To check this condition, we define the following formula:

```
H[0s, 45s] (pressure_diff_pump()+pressure_diff_exchanger()) =0
```

where the functions are provided by the controller interface to compute the above expressions. Furthermore, to isolate the problem we could check, for every flow sensor if $flow\_sensor_i$ is far from the expected, and handle the possible leakage. Otherwise, we can assume that there is a blockage in the pump, and try to unstuck it by repeatedly powering on-off.

- The average flow is too far from the expected value. Possible causes are: the primary pipe has experienced a decrease in flow because of a pump obstruction; or, the channel after the exchanger is not letting the fluid keep the natural flow. One full monitoring property could be the following:

```
H [0s, 30s] abs(expected_avgflow()-avgflow)>2 &
O[0s, 30s] abs(expected_flow(2) - flow_sensor_2) > 1
```

- The redundancy pump has to work since the primary pump broke, at least in a span of 10 s.

```
available_pumps[1] S [0s, 10s] !available_pumps[0]
```

Finally, note the combination of detection and isolation conditions with priorities. For example, in the case of the flow sensors, we detect a fault when the average flow diff has been greater than 2 for the last 30 s. We then identify which sensor has a problem by checking each sensor in the last 30 s, but since are flow sensors in different parts of the circuits, they are given different priorities, based on their criticality.

Table 1. FDIR specification of the case study

fault detection condition	isolation condition	prio	recovery procedure
H[0s, 38s] ! available_pumps[0]	H[0s, 10s] !available_pumps[1]	400	init fail [switch_off();]

		100	init wait_recover [fix_pump(0);]
			state wait_recover:
			    transitions:
			    timeout=2s -> ok

available_pumps[1] S[0s, 10s] !available_pumps[0]		300	init fail [switch_off();]

H[0s, 45s] (pressure_diff_pump +
pressure_diff_exchanger) != 0
		300	init power_off
			fix_timeout: timeout=2m on {power_off,
			                        power_on;}
			state power_off:
			    transitions:
			    flow_sensor_0 < 1 -> ok
			    fix_timeout -> fail
			    [timeout=15s \off_pump();] -> power_on
			state power_on:
			    transitions:
			    flow_sensor_0 < 1 -> ok
			    fix_timeout -> fail
			    [timeout=15s \on_pump();] -> power_off

H[0ms, 150ms] (temp_diff ≤ 0 ⟺ hot_load)		220	init ok [req_temp_diff := 0;]

H[0s, 30s]
abs(expected_avgflow()
- avgflow()) > 2
	O[0s, 30s] abs(expected_flow(2)
	- flow_sensor_2) > 1
		185	init pump_stucked [unstuck_pump();]
			state pump_stucked:
			    transitions:
			    [abs(expected_avgflow() - avgflow()) < 1 \
			restart_flow();] -> ok
			    [timeout=1m switch_off();] -> fail

	O[0s, 30s] abs(expected_flow(1) - flow_sensor_1) > 2	190	init fail [switch_off();]

	O[0s, 30s]
	abs(expected_flow(0)
	- flow_sensor_0) > 1
		180	init fixing_exchanger [restart_exchaner();]
			state fixing_exchanger:
			    transitions:
			    exch_power() > 2.3 -> ok
			    timeout=2m -> fail

H[0ms, 350ms]
calculate_fluid(fluid)
= fluid_type_table(fluid)
		250	init switch_fluid [smooth_switch(fluid);]
			state switch_fluid:
			    timeout=3s -> fail
			    calculate_fluid(fluid)
			    = fluid_type_table(fluid) -> ok

H [0s, 2m] req_temp_diff -
temp_diff < temp_diff_thresh
	H[0m, 2m] (fan_req_speed > 0
	& fan_speed > 0
	& abs(fan_req_speed - fan_speed)
	> fan_thresh)
		160	init recover_fan [
			    initial_req := fan_req_speed;
			    fan_req_speed := 0;
			]
			state recover_fan:
			    [timeout 1m \fan_req_speed
			+= fan_rate] -> recover_fan
			    abs(fan_req_speed - fan_speed) < 3 -> ok

	H[0m, 4m] (fan_speed = 0 & fan_req_speed != 0)	160	init fail [switch_off();]
	H[0m, 2m] power_temp_req > MAX_power	200	init ok [power_temp_req := MAX_power;]

5.3   Verification Results

The specification table described in the previous section is used to generate the code of the heat pump controller. The code of the hierarchical FSM combining the FDIR modes and recovery procedures results in C file with 2277 lines of code, without counting the monitors and the controller interface.

In order to check the correctness of this FDIR, we used nuXmv for model checking the generated SMV model, and various tests to verify the generated code. These two verifying techniques are complementary, as the model checking of SMV formally validates that what we wrote in the table specification is what we had in mind, while the testing verifies the actual program execution.

For testing, we set up a simple testing framework where input values as expected output are specified in csv files, with the possibility to inject faults. Tests in C are automatically generated to execute the tests.

We tested each FDIR mode in the presence of no other alarm to verify the correct flow of the state machine in each FDIR mode in isolation. Complementary, we also wrote tests, where higher and lower priority alarms are triggered, and we ignore/react to these information. Since we implemented 12 different properties, we covered a total of 36 different scenarios.

As for model checking, we checked 1) each failure mode transition 2) mode transitions with alarms of different priorities, 3) absence of infinite loops, and 4) reachability of group thresholds.

These kinds of checks are particularly useful for early verification and validation, to find issues in the table specification. An example of issues in an earlier version of the table was found checking a recovery procedure in isolation. The property was $G(alarm = 4) \rightarrow F(current = 0 \,|\, current = 1)$. A counterexample showed that there was an infinite loop moving between power_off and power_on. These problems are solved by introduction timeout groups. We also noticed possible infinite loops when we have a self loop with a condition, and the timeout that keeps track of this loop is in the lowest priority (since the higher priority may always be true, and always keep looping).

6 Conclusions and Future Works

In this paper, we presented a specification-driven approach to the automatic generation of embedded code for fault detection, isolation, and recovery. The proposed approach translates high-level formal specification of monitoring conditions and recovery procedures into platform-specific embedded code. Additionally, model checking techniques provide a means to validate and verify the specified FDIR logic, strengthening its reliability. We demonstrated the approach through a case study in the energy domain.

While the proposed approach significantly reduces manual coding effort by automating the generation of FDIR code from high-level specifications, it still requires to define fault detection conditions and recovery logic in formal notations. Future work will aim to further streamline this process through increased automation. Other directions for future work include optimizing the generated code to meet requirements on timing and memory bounds of specific target platforms, and connecting the proposed methodology to preliminary hazard analysis phases and to system-level analysis of failure modes and effects.

References

[BBC+14] Bittner, B., Bozzano, M., Cimatti, A., De Ferluc, R., Gario, M., Guiotto, A., Yushtein, Y.: An integrated process for FDIR design in aerospace. In: Ortmeier, F., Rauzy, A. (eds.) IMBSA 2014. LNCS, vol. 8822, pp. 82–95. Springer, Cham (2014). https://doi.org/10.1007/978-3-319-12214-4_7

[BBC+22] Bombardelli, A., et al.: COMPASTA: extending TASTE with formal design and verification functionality. In: Seguin, C., Zeller, M., Prosvirnova, T. (eds.) IMBSA 2022. LNCS, vol. 13525, pp. 21–27. Springer, Cham (2022). https://doi.org/10.1007/978-3-031-15842-1_2

[BCGT14] Bozzano, M., Cimatti, A., Gario, M., Tonetta, S.: Formal design of fault detection and identification components using temporal epistemic logic. In: Ábrahám, E., Havelund, K. (eds.) TACAS 2014. LNCS, vol. 8413, pp. 326–340. Springer, Heidelberg (2014). https://doi.org/10.1007/978-3-642-54862-8_22

[BCGT15] Bozzano, M., Cimatti, A., Gario, M., Tonetta, S.: Formal design of asynchronous fault detection and identification components using temporal epistemic logic. Log. Methods Comput. Sci. **11**(4) (2015)

[BCGT24] Bombardelli, A., Cimatti, A., Griggio, A., Tonetta, S.: Another look at LTL modulo theory over finite and infinite traces. In: Jansen, N., et al. (eds.) Principles of Verification: Cycling the Probabilistic Landscape. LNCS, vol. 15260, pp. 419–443. Springer, Cham (2024). https://doi.org/10.1007/978-3-031-75783-9_17

[BLS11] Bauer, A., Leucker, M., Schallhart, C.: Runtime verification for LTL and TLTL. ACM Trans. Softw. Eng. Methodol. **20**(4):14:1–14:64 (2011)

[BV03] Bozzano, M., Villafiorita, A.: Improving system reliability via model checking: the FSAP/NuSMV-SA safety analysis platform. In: Anderson, S., Felici, M., Littlewood, B. (eds.) SAFECOMP 2003. LNCS, vol. 2788, pp. 49–62. Springer, Heidelberg (2003). https://doi.org/10.1007/978-3-540-39878-3_5

[CDL+04] Cordier, M.-O., Dague, P., Lévy, F., Montmain, J., Staroswiecki, M., Travé-Massuyès, L.: Conflicts versus analytical redundancy relations: a comparative analysis of the model based diagnosis approach from the artificial intelligence and automatic control perspectives. IEEE Trans. Syst. Man Cybern. Part B **34**(5), 2163–2177 (2004)

[CGK+18] Clarke, E.M., Grumberg, O., Kroening, D., Peled, D.A., Veith, H.: Model Checking, 2nd ed. MIT Press (2018)

[CP99] Chen, J., Patton, R.J.: Robust Model-Based Fault Diagnosis for Dynamic Systems. The International Series on Asian Studies in Computer and Information Science, vol. 3. Kluwer (1999)

[CTT19] Cimatti, A., Tian, C., Tonetta, S.: NuRV: a nuXmv extension for runtime verification. In: Finkbeiner, B., Mariani, L. (eds.) RV 2019. LNCS, vol. 11757, pp. 382–392. Springer, Cham (2019). https://doi.org/10.1007/978-3-030-32079-9_23

[dKMR90] de Kleer, J., Mackworth, A.K., Reiter, R.: Characterizing Diagnoses. In: AAAI, pp. 324–330. AAAI Press/The MIT Press (1990)

[GCD15] Gao, Z., Cecati, C., Ding, S.X.: A survey of fault diagnosis and fault-tolerant techniques-part I: fault diagnosis with model-based and signal-based approaches. IEEE Trans. Industr. Electron. **62**(6), 3757–3767 (2015)

[Ger15] Gertler, J.: Fault Detection and Diagnosis. In: Baillieul, J., Samad, T. (eds) Encyclopedia of Systems and Control, pp. 764–749. Springer, Cham (2015). https://doi.org/10.1007/978-3-030-44184-5_223

[HKKS10] Hwang, I., Kim, S., Kim, Y., Seah, C.E.: A survey of fault detection, isolation, and reconfiguration methods. IEEE Trans. Control. Syst. Technol. **18**(3), 636–653 (2010)

[Ise84] Isermann, R.: Process fault detection based on modeling and estimation methods - a survey. Autom. **20**(4), 387–404 (1984)

[Ise05] Isermann, R.: Model-based fault-detection and diagnosis - status and applications. Annu. Rev. Control. **29**(1), 71–85 (2005)

[KGK23] Kiesbye, J., Grover, K., Ketínský, J.: Model checking for proving and improving fault tolerance of satellites. In: 2023 IEEE Aerospace Conference, pp. 1–9 (2023)

[MHSG20] Müller, S., Höflinger, K., Smisek, M., Gerndt, A.: Towards an FDIR software fault tree library for onboard computers. In: 2020 IEEE Aerospace Conference, pp. 1–10 (2020)

[MP71] Mehra, R.K., Peschon, J.: An innovations approach to fault detection and diagnosis in dynamic systems. Automatica **7**(5), 637–640 (1971)

[Pnu77] Pnueli, A.: The temporal logic of programs. In: FOCS, pp. 46–57. IEEE Computer Society (1977)

[Rei87] Reiter, R.: A theory of diagnosis from first principles. Artif. Intell. **32**(1), 57–95 (1987)

[Zol18] Zolghadri, A.: The challenge of advanced model-based FDIR for real-world flight-critical applications. Eng. Appl. Artif. Intell. **68**, 249–259 (2018)

Building a Modular Platform for Model Checking Glitch Attacks in RISC-V Programs

Andreas Kjeldgaard Brandhøj[(✉)], Tobias Worm Bøgedal,
René Rydhof Hansen, Kim Guldstrand Larsen, and Danny Bøgsted Poulsen

Department of Computer Science, Aalborg University, Aalborg, Denmark
{akbr,tobiaswb,rrh,kgl,dannybpoulsen}@cs.aau.dk

Abstract. Glitch attacks may change the behaviour of applications by inducing bit-flips in the underlying hardware. Through this, the attacker can bypass security measures of an application. Though most prevalent in systems where an attacker has physical access, recent research has shown that attacks may be performed through software alone [1,10]. It is difficult to understand the impact of glitch attacks on a given application due to an explosion of potential execution paths. In this paper, we present a modular platform for model-checking various types of glitch attacks in RISC-V code. Developers can load a RISC-V program into a configurable virtual machine modelled in UPPAAL with several attacker models available to analyse the impact of glitch attacks. The model is designed to support UPPAAL Classic, SMC, and timed games with TIGA, enabling both symbolic, statistical, and game theoretical analysis. This can provide developers a valuable insight into the impact of glitch attacks on their code. Using FISSC [6], we show how all three methods complement each other.

1 Introduction

Introducing faults into the execution of a running program is called *fault injection* or a *glitch attack* if the fault is caused by abusing/manipulating the hardware. An attacker with sufficient knowledge of a system may perform such an attack, e.g., to bypass access control or force a leak of sensitive information [13]. The effect of a glitch attack is typically to "flip" bits in either in the memory or registers of the underlying hardware, thereby changing data values or the control flow of the program, e.g., by skipping an instruction or jumping to a wrong address. Historically, an attacker has needed physical access to the system in order to perform a glitch attack and flip bits, making industrial control systems (ICS), operational technology (OT), and IoT applications obvious targets. However, this has changed due to Rowhammer attacks where an attacker can semi-deterministically flip a large number of bits in DRAM through software alone [10]. Recently, it has been shown how Rowhammer can be used to successfully attack widely used security critical software components, such as SSH and SUDO authentication [1]. This significantly widens the spectrum of systems that may be targeted by glitch attacks.

For a developer making mission critical applications, e.g., industrial control systems or critical security software like SSH and SUDO, it is almost impossible to understand and take into account all the possible bit-flips a glitch attack may cause and their effects. In this paper, we present a modular and flexible model checking platform for modelling, exploring, and analysing glitch attacks on RISC-V assembly code. Model checking was chosen because this approach provides a high degree of automation and a gentle learning curve. We hope this will entice developers to adopt the platform for verification of their own systems. The platform uses UPPAAL [3] as the underlying model checking engine and combines standard model checking, statistical model checking, and timed-game controller synthesis, making the platform versatile and able to explore many different aspects of glitch attacks, e.g., attack efficacy, generate exhaustive attack strategies, and formally verify attacks and mitigation. These metrics enable developers to reason about their programs and assess the risk of attack or facilitate the creation of attack mitigation in the source code. Furthermore, the platform allows for easy exploration and generation of new glitch attacks by employing a modular approach to attacker modelling. We illustrate the capabilities of the platform using the FISSC [6] benchmarks.

We consider the following to be the main contributions of the paper:

1. Creation of a platform for model checking glitch attacks.
2. Creation of a formal approach to modelling RISC-V programs.
3. Showing different ways of analysing glitch attacks using standard and statistical model checking.
4. Showing the potential for modelling glitch attacks as games.
5. Validation of our platform using FISSC as an example.

2   Model Checking Glitch Attacks

To illustrate the problem of glitch attacks, consider the program snippet in Listing 1.1 (written in C), showing the critical function of a PIN code checker. The code[1] compares the PIN input by the user with the correct (stored) PIN. If the two PINs are identical, the function returns BOOL_TRUE and otherwise it returns BOOL_FALSE. The goal for an attacker would then be to bypass the PIN checker, i.e., enter a *wrong* PIN and still have the checker return BOOL_TRUE.

Even for this small code fragment, there are numerous places and ways to perform a glitch attack, e.g., flipping one bit in the value of the status variable to change it from BOOL_FALSE to BOOL_TRUE, flipping a bit in the size variable to reduce the number of digits checked to zero (essentially checking an empty PIN), or flipping the result of a conditional. It turns out that most of these attacks are

---

[1] The snippet is an excerpt taken from the VerifyPIN_5 program of the FISSC glitch attack benchmark programs [6].

```
BOOL byteArrayCompare(UBYTE* a1, UBYTE* a2, UBYTE size)
{
    int i;
    BOOL status = BOOL_FALSE;
    BOOL diff = BOOL_FALSE;
    for(i = 0; i < size; i++) {
        if(a1[i] != a2[i]) {
            diff = BOOL_TRUE;
        }
    }
    if(i != size) {
        countermeasure();
    }
    if (diff == BOOL_FALSE) {
        status = BOOL_TRUE;
    } else {
        status = BOOL_FALSE;
    }
    return status;
}
```

Listing 1.1. Excerpt of `verifyPIN_5` from the FISSC benchmarks.

not possible, because the code has been *hardened*, e.g., by using non-standard values for BOOL_FALSE (0x55) and BOOL_TRUE (0xAA) that differ in all bits in their binary representation making it harder to flip from one value to the other, and by explicitly verifying that the correct number of PIN digits have been checked.

As the example shows, even for a small code fragment, it can be difficult, time consuming, and require knowledge of the underlying platform to manually determine whether a glitch attack is possible. Instead, we turn to model checking: we first make a model of the program, capturing how data flows in and out of the memory locations that are susceptible to glitch attacks. This model is then combined with a model of an attacker's behaviour in terms of, e.g., which locations can be attacked and how many attacks can be performed within a given time frame. The combined model can now be used to check whether a glitch attack is possible. For our example program, model checking verifies that none of the attacks mentioned above would be successful for an attacker that is only allowed to perform one bit-flip. However, an attacker that is allowed to make two (or more) bit-flips (in the value of a variable) can make a successful attack. The same goes for an attacker that is allowed to skip an instruction, e.g., by flipping bits in the program counter. These attacks will be covered in more detail in later sections.

Model checking can easily be used to find individual attacks with a single attack strategy or to validate that attack strategies cannot be successful. However, to our knowledge, there is no efficient way of retrieving a comprehensive and potentially exhaustive list of all possible successful attacks using a single symbolic model checking query. Lastly, an attacker may not only flip register values. They could also skip instructions, change memory values, etc. An attacker could even do a combination of several attacks to reach their goal.

These concerns show how we need to employ more than standard model checking to get desirable results. We propose that by combining standard model checking with statistical model checking and game semantics, we can overcome the shown weaknesses to get more interesting and useful results when analysing the effects of glitch attacks.

3   Modular Platform

In the following we describe a modular modelling framework for the UPPAAL model checker. The framework allows for modelling a program (in the form of RISC-V assembly code) in parallel with an attacker that may use one or several different kinds of "attack strategies", e.g., to flip register values, skip instructions, or corrupt memory addresses. This allows for in-depth analysis of the impact of certain attacks on the provided code.

The model is generated automatically from a RISC-V program along with parameters such as the allowed number of attacks per run, cooldown, memory size, and which strategies an attacker can use.

UPPAAL was chosen for three main reasons. Firstly, the built-in support for time both in the tool and the underlying theory as this simplifies modelling in a number of cases, including attacks that have to be performed within a narrow timing window; models with variable execution time for instructions and/or attacks (efficiently handled by UPPAAL zone abstraction); and, finally, modelling multi bit-flip attacks with a "cooldown period" between individual attacks, e.g., for simulating attacks with a laser that cannot fire continuously. Secondly, UPPAAL has an extensive and expressive modelling formalism that allows users to write C-like code which is useful for large models, such as a VM. Finally, UPPAAL comprises a number of different model checking engines that can be used on a single model (as long as it fulfils the requirements of each engine). This enables us to analyze a given program in multiple interesting ways without requiring more models.

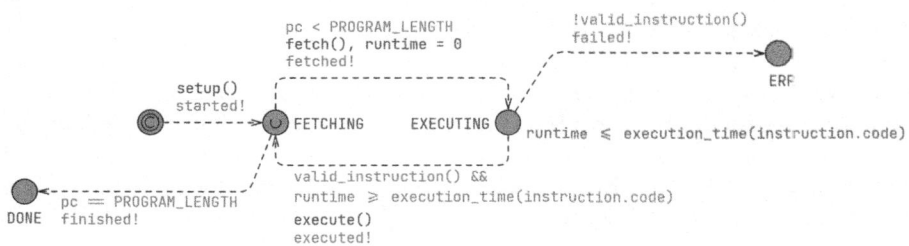

Fig. 1. The VM template.

3.1   The VM Template

The UPPAAL model consists of a template that mimics a Virtual Machine (VM), modelling execution of RISC-V assembly code, along with an attacker template and several attacker strategies. The VM, seen in Fig. 1, works by performing setup which loads the RISC-V program, places the global values of the program into memory, and finally set the stack pointer and program counter. The setup must be done as the immediate first step of every execution of the model thus we make the initial location committed. Once the setup is complete the VM runs a loop where the current instruction is fetched (placed into a global variable) during the transition from FETCHING to EXECUTING and then executed during the transition back to FETCHING. This loop ends when the program is finished (the DONE location) or if an invalid instruction is about to be executed, signifying a VM crash (the ERR location). Invalid instructions occur if an attacker flips a value into another such that executing the current instruction would yield an error in UPPAAL during verification. Examples could be loading/storing values to locations outside allocated memory.

Each transition synchronizes over a specific broadcast channel (fetched!, executed!, failed!, finished!, started!) such that other template may react to what is currently happening in the VM. This can be useful for creating optimised attacker strategies (cf. Subsect. 3.4) or sending other information about the current execution between templates.

All of the edges in the VM template is marked as uncontrollable. Dividing the transitions into controllable and uncontrollable in this way allows us to represent the relationship between the execution of a program (opponent) through the VM and an attacker (proponent) as a game.

Remark 1. UPPAAL divides edges into controllable and uncontrollable edges. This division is used by UPPAAL's strategy synthesis engine to synthesise a controller that guarantee meeting certain requirements, when an opponent actively works against the controller. Here the controller can change the system state by moving along controllable edges while the opponent can move along the uncontrollable edges.

Each instruction executed by the VM takes a certain amount of time as described by the function execution_time(). This function takes the current instruction and computes an approximated execution time, based on changeable durations for register and memory reads and writes performed by the instruction. Using a clock called runtime we have the invariant runtime <= execution_time(instruction.code) on the EXECUTING along with the guard runtime >= execution_time(instruction.code) on the outgoing transition control that the execution of a single instruction takes the correct amount of time. The FETCHING location is made urgent so that time does not pass while the template is in this location.

```
// Writes an int16_t to memory starting at "address".
void w_mem_i16(address_t address, int32_t value) {
    memory[address + 0] = (value >> 8) & 255;
    memory[address + 1] = (value >> 0) & 255;
}
```

Listing 1.2. Function for writing a 16-bit int to memory.

3.2 Modelling Memory

Most of the complexity of the model lies in the implemented C code. When modelling memory, we distinguish between registers and memory. Here memory refers to globals, heap, and stack. The provided program is not stored in memory but in a separate array. Registers are contained in an array called registers with each individual register corresponding to an index in the array. As an example, the value of register a4 is found at registers[a4] with a4 being a constant set to 14. This indirection allows an easy implementation of instructions, etc.

Memory is modelled as an array. However, to more accurately capture how different values are stored compared to others, each index in the array is an 8-bit unsigned integer. This way, we can correctly model values in byte-wise resolution which is useful when including attackers that can perform glitch attacks that affect multiple values in memory. Modelling memory in this way requires us to have functions for reading and writing different integer types to memory. The code for how to write a 16-bit integer to memory can be seen in Listing 1.2, with the code for reading being the reverse operations. In memory, globals are placed at the start of the array. The stack starts at the end of the array and "grows" towards the start, with the stack pointer (the sp register) being used as a reference for exactly which address to use at any given time.

3.3 Modelling Instructions

A program in the model is an array of instructions called program with each line of the program being one index of the array. During execution of a program the program counter (pc in the model) keeps track of which instruction to execute. Each instruction is stored in a struct which can be seen in Listing 1.3.

This structure mirrors the structure of actual RISC-V instructions with different naming for each field. Furthermore, op2 and op3 can be left unused if the translated RISC-V instruction does not use them. The following is an example of how the addi instruction is translated: instruction ex = {ADDI_CODE, a5, a5, 1}. This instruction adds the immediate value 1 to the value stored in register a5 and stores it in register a5. ADDI_CODE is a constant that translates into an integer value. This is used in the function execute() in the VM template to perform the actions corresponding to that instruction with each different instruction having its own code. Currently, we only support the instructions necessary to execute the FISSC programs (cf. [6]). However, new instructions can easily be added to model if needed.

```
typedef struct {
    int32_t code;
    // Mostly always the "rd" register.
    int32_t op1;
    int32_t op2;
    // Mostly always an offset.
    int32_t op3;
} instruction_t;
```

Listing 1.3. The instruction struct.

3.4   The Attacker Model

The attacker in our model consists of an **Attacker** template, seen in Fig. 2, and a number of different templates representing "attack strategies" each of which is a specific attack model that can be performed by the attacker. One of the key features of the platform is how the attack strategies may be mixed and matched as needed. They do not rely on specifics in the provided code but rather operate on the underlying model. Therefore, it is easy to plug any of the provided strategies into the model or create new ones if they follow the same overall structure.

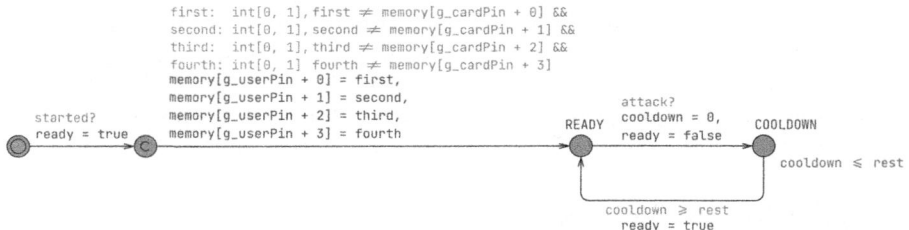

Fig. 2. The Attacker template.

The **Attacker** is used to keep track of a boolean variable called **ready** which is used as a mutex lock. This lock ensures that if an attack strategy is used, no other strategy can be initiated before the prior one finishes. The lock is "grabbed" by one of the attack strategies by synchronizing with the attacker via the **attack** broadcast channel. Furthermore, the **Attacker** template also keeps track of an optional "cooldown" period between attacks if multiple attacks are allowed during a single run of the program. This is beneficial as the cooldown can remove some unrealistic attacks from the results provided by the model. The process for using the platform can be seen in Fig. 3. For our FISSC examples, the attacker also chooses a PIN code to input.

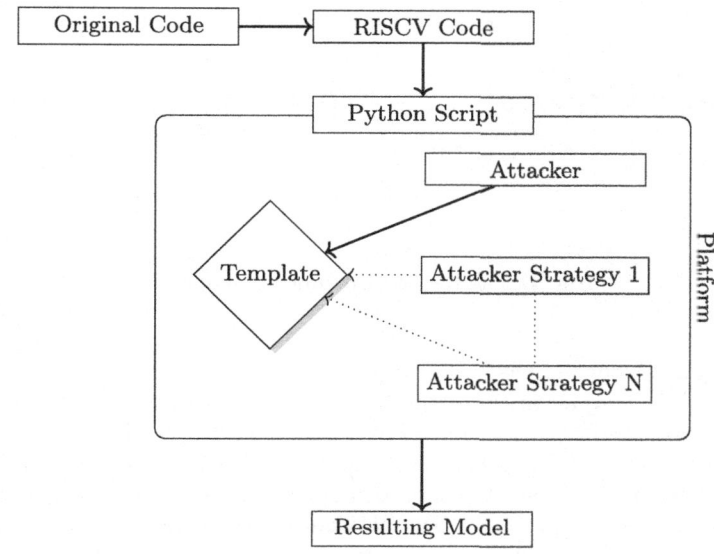

Fig. 3. The process for using the platform.

Table 1. Attacker Strategies supported by the modelling framework.

`RegisterCorruption`	Changes the value in a random register with a bit-flip
`OptimisedRegisterCorruption`	Changes the value in a in-use register with a bit-flip
`PCCorruption`	Performs a bit-flip on the program counter
`InstructionSkip`	Increments the program counter by one
`MemoryCorruption`	Changes data in memory with a bit-flip
`StackCorruption`	Changes data on the stack with a bit-flip
`GlobalsCorruption`	Changes global values in memory with a bit-flip

In the provided model we have include several attack strategies that can be used either directly or as inspiration for new strategies. See Table 1 for an overview.

The strategies show how commonly used fault models are supported. Bit-flips in registers are covered, and can be extended to bit-set and bit-clear. The program counter can both be bit-flipped and instructions can be skipped modeling a double PC increment. Memory can be targeted, including the stack and global variables specifically. The available strategies do not represent all possible fault models but can easily be extended. The included strategies are based on known attacks presented in the literature [1,10,12] and have been chosen to illustrate how strategies may be modelled and used in the tool.

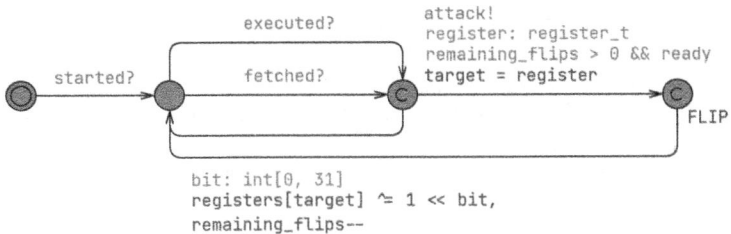

Fig. 4. The RegisterCorruption template.

One thing to note is that RegisterCorruption has two variants. This is to show how optimising an attack strategy may help with program analysis. RegisterCorruption XOR's a random register value with a randomly chosen value used for left shifting. This is very inefficient as there is a high probability that the flip will have no impact. OptimisedRegisterCorruption flips registers before they are read or after they have been written to, reducing the choices available to the attacker. Using it leads to a reduced state space when performing symbolic queries and more successful attacks when performing SMC queries. Later OptimisedRegisterCorruption is referred to as ORC. An example of one of the attack strategy templates can be seen in listing Fig. 4.

Most of the included attack strategies react to broadcast synchronizations from the VM template. This is not strictly necessary, but for use with UPPAAL SMC [5] it does eliminate the need for rates of exponential on the locations that only have outgoing transitions that synchronize over the channels.

4   Using the Platform on FISSC

In this section we use our platform to analyse the FISSC collection of "PIN-checker" programs which compare a user entered PIN against a card PIN. These programs have been specifically designed to be resilient against timing side channels, branch inversions, among other potential attacks on a high and low level [6]. Therefore, the programs serve as an excellent use case for our platform to highlight the strength of combining attack models, scaling to multiple attacks, and learning the strategies of attackers. VerifyPIN_5 is one of the programs found in FISSC with the countermeasures: Hardened booleans, Decrement PTC[2] first, Double calls, and Fixed time loop. Hardened booleans extend booleans to be able to express the values true, false, and tampered - where a single bit flip is insufficient to convert from true to false and vice versa. Double calls refer to checking the user PIN against the card PIN twice and with reversed order of parameters. We consider all FISSC examples but highlight VerifyPIN_5 with inlined calls to the `byteArrayCompare` function. A `countermeasure` function

---

[2] `g_ptc` is a variable determining the amount of tries a user has to input the correct password.

sets a global `g_countermeasure` variable to 1 to signal that some attack has occurred[3].

All FISSC programs are compiled with gcc 14.2.0 to RISC-V (32-bits), and inlined `byteArrayCompare`. In the collection, the PIN codes are statically set as `g_cardPin={1, 2, 3, 4}` and `g_userPin={0, 0, 0, 0}` with `PIN_SIZE=4`. In our model we allow the attacker to choose a value for `g_userPin` before execution of the programs start. To minimize state-space explosion the PIN digits have been abstracted to 0 and 1 where 1 is a correct digit and 0 is an incorrect digit in a PIN such that, `g_cardPin={1, 1, 1, 1}` and the `g_userPin` can be anything other than the `g_cardPin`. In Fig. 2 the attacker choosing a PIN, checking it against the card PIN, and writing it to memory can be seen.

The results presented in the following sections are all gathered using a VM with 64 bytes of memory, an attacker with 100 time units of cooldown, register read/write taking 1 time unit, memory read/write taking 10 time units, and the SC attack has an exponential rate of 1. The scripts for automatically constructing the models and running the experiments can be found on GitHub with a description of how to reproduce the results[4].

4.1   Results

As discussed, for the FISSC programs there are several interesting attack angles that could be analysed. In the following we show how symbolic queries can provide guarantees on resiliency between a wide range of glitch attacks. Furthermore, we show how stochastic analysis can be used to mitigate the state-space explosion that the symbolic queries are susceptible to. E.g. we use stochastic analysis for when the attacker can perform many different attacks during a single execution, which greatly increases the state space of the model. Stochastic analysis can also be used to analyse the behaviour of systems under attack along with the attacker itself. Lastly, we show how strategy synthesis, through the use of game semantics, can provide an understanding of all possible attacks that an attacker can perform to gain undetected access. We also show how strategies can be used to impose restrictions on how an attacker achieves their goal.

Symbolic Verification. Using symbolic queries we found that an attacker can force undetected authentication with an incorrect PIN in all versions of VerifyPIN. However, the number of required attacks vary depending on the different attacks utilised by the attacker.

```
E<> vm.DONE && mem_u8(g_countermeasure) == 0 &&
    mem_u8(g_authenticated) == 170 && remaining_flips == 0
```

---

[3] In the case of VerifyPIN_7 it can also mean that the PIN entered by the user was incorrect.

[4] https://github.com/Brandhoej/uppaal-riscv-vm.

Table 2. All VerifyPIN examples from FISSC under an attacker which can either perform Optimised Register Corruption (ORC), Instruction Skip (IS), or Stack Corruption (SC). The numbers in the cells represents the number of attacks of the specific attack model required to gain undetected access.

VerifyPIN	0	1	2	3	4	5	6	7
ORC	1	1	1	1	1	1	1	1
IS	1	1	1	1	1	2	>3	>3
SC	1	1	1	1	>2	>2	1	>1

The verification of the existence of a glitch attack granting the attacker undetected access is done by checking if it is possible to reach a state where the attacker is undetected, authenticated, and used all attacks available - we are comparing with 170 as that is the hardened boolean value for true.

The query specifically searches for paths where all available number of attacks are used. However, if the precise number of attacks is irrelevant, the last part of the query can be removed. Running the query on all examples, as presented in Table 2, we found they are all vulnerable to a single bit-flip in a some chosen register. It is a bit surprising that a single bit-flip in VerifyPIN_7 grants undetected access because in the example the countermeasure flag is also set if the PIN is incorrect. One could think, because of this, that there are two underlying mitigations that must be bypassed. Running VerifyPIN_7 with an initially triggered countermeasure is insufficient to block the attacker. Performing a single IS attacker would be enough to grant undetected access to all programs except VerifyPIN 5, 6, and 7. VerifyPIN_5 requires two skips, whereas we know that 6 and 7 requires more than three when considering a strategy where an attacker can only perform IS attacks. We found similar results when the attacker performed SC attacks. All except VerifyPIN 0, 1, 2, 3, and 6 only require a single bit-flip in active stack memory at a given time of execution - It is unknown how many flips the rest requires or if any number would be sufficient. Considering VerifyPIN_5 we later show how two IS attacks skips the double call mitigation (found in lines 49–50 of the C-code).

One of the strengthens of the approach is the modularity of the platform. If the attacker is unable to modify the `zero` register it is unable to gain undetected access in VerifyPIN_5 with a single bit-flip in a register. However, if both IS and ORC can be performed then the attacker can, by performing two attacks, gain undetected access.

Stochastic Analysis. The effects of a single bit flip has the potential to make the state space of the model explode to a point where symbolic analysis or strategy synthesis is no longer an option. This obviously only gets worse the more attacks are allowed throughout a single execution of a given program. Using stochastic analysis with UPPAAL SMC we can still analyse programs at the cost of hard guarantees. This allows us to get an understanding of the impact of attacks on larger programs but also the effect of multiple attacks during a single execution.

In Table 3 four million simulations of an attacker using ORC with the ability to do one to five attacks are presented. The results were found with the following query:

```
Pr[<=10000; 4000000] (<> vm.DONE && mem_u8(g_countermeasure) == 0
&& mem_u8(g_authenticated) == 170 && remaining_flips < MAX_FLIPS)
```

The attacker is allowed to perform a specific number of attacks during each simulation with MAX_FLIPS signifying the maximum. The last part of the query (remaining_flips < MAX_FLIPS) ensures at least one attack is performed. As each attack may impact the total runtime of the program, we set the cut-off time for each simulation to be well above the normal execution time (10000 in the query). The results show gaining undetected access is quite rare in some versions of VerifyPIN. Generally, increasing the number of allowed attacks increases the chance of gaining undetected access up to a point. After this point, further attacks may actually decrease the probability of gaining undetected access. This may be due to new attacks counteracting the effects of previous attacks. Additionally, we can observe that the simulations for some versions very rarely results in an undetected access which is the case of VerifyPIN 3, 4, 6, and 7. This highlights the idea that these attacks may be rare in real scenarios.

Using SMC we may also learn about the efficacy of an attacker given certain attack strategies. Figure 5 shows the percentage of crashes given ORC attacks for each VerifyPIN version using the following query:

```
Pr[<=10000; 4000000] (<> vm.ERR && remaining_flips < MAX_FLIPS)
```

The results provide insight into the attacker's influence on the running machine and program. A high probability of a crash can discourage an attacker from performing an attack. In the case of VerifyPIN a crash may indicate an unrecoverable situation where the attacker will never be able to gain undetected access. In general we observe that a single flip across all versions has the same probability of crashing the VM, and multiple flips increase this probability, but may stagnate at three and more flips. This may show that an attacker should aim at flipping one bit in a register, which we also found sufficient to provide undetected access.

Strategy Synthesis. From symbolically verifying VerifyPIN_5 we learned that two IS attacks are sufficient to gain undetected access. One could look at the provided example trace to figure out the point at which the attacks are performed and one-by-one refine the program to be able to withstand the attacks. This approach, if possible, would yield a program that is guaranteed to withstand the attack. However, it is tiresome to mitigate each potential attack one by one as there is no good way of knowing how many there are in total. Furthermore, allowing the attacker to input different PINs adds a layer of complexity if the attacker can attack the global variables of the VM.

Table 3. Total simulated Optimised Register Corruption (ORC) attacks granting the attacker undetected access. Each cell represents an independent test, allowing the attacker to execute up to a maximum number of (optional) attacks, based on a total of 4 million simulations.

Max Attacks #	VerifyPIN							
	0	1	2	3	4	5	6	7
1	152	5	5	0	0	0	0	0
2	247105	229732	1625	0	0	410	0	0
3	257148	228053	553	0	0	179	0	0
4	257521	226712	515	0	34	33	0	0
5	256593	225884	531	6	33	10	1	0

One way to get around these issues is to utilise UPPAAL TIGA [2] to synthesis control strategies for the attacker. The strategies describe what actions the attacker must take in a given state to be guaranteed to win the game - if such a strategy exists. The strategy query would depend on the attacker's objective, which could be to get more future attempts, to get undetected access, or simply not to crash the VM. Synthesizing strategies and storing them under an identifier allows for using them in future queries. The main benefits of them are two-fold: First, They can be used to control the attacker to only perform actions suitable under the strategy, thereby reducing the future explored states and act as a way of tackling the imposed path-explosion problem inherent to model-checking glitch attacks. Second, the strategies can be stored as a file and inspected. This would reveal the underlying actions the attacker performs to reach its goal. In the context of glitch attacks where the goal is to gain undetected access, the synthesized controller reveals how such access can be gained.

A synthesized controller can also be applied to queries to constrain the behaviour of the attacker. A desirable property for an attacker could be that they can increase the number of allowed input attempts if no undetected access can be achieved with a wrong PIN. The strategy could then be to stay undetected while trying to increase the value of the g_ptc variable (which is used to track remaining input attempts). If possible, the attacker could exhaustively exercise all possible PINs and never be detected (In all cases other than VerifyPIN_7, where an incorrect user-defined PIN triggers the countermeasure). The following controller and query describe this scenario:

```
strategy Undetected = control: A<> !mem_u8(g_countermeasure) &&
                    remaining_flips < MAX_FLIPS

E<> mem_u8(g_ptc) > 3 under Undetected
```

In addition to reducing the complexity of querying subsequently under a synthesized controller, saving the controller provides a text file which can be analysed to understand attacker behaviour. From the file it is possible to figure

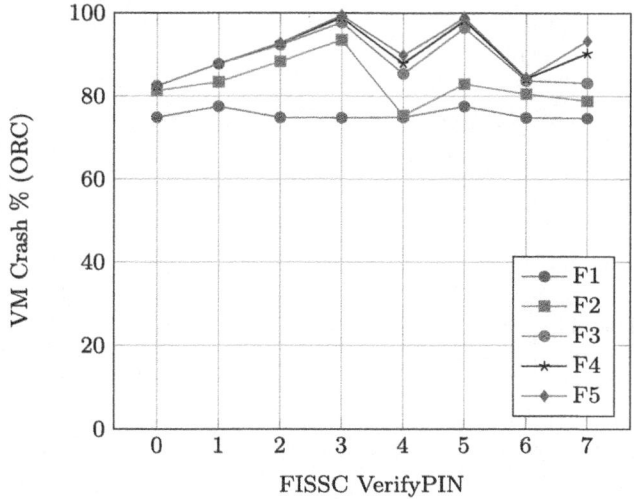

Fig. 5. Percentage of simulated Optimised Register Corruption (ORC) attacks which crashes the VM. Each coordinate is an independent test with 4 a million simulations testing whether the attacker crashed the VM with a maximum number of (optional) ORC attacks.

out what an attacker does with the full state available such as current PC, number of executed instructions, and an attack history. With it, we can take an exhaustive look at what the attacker does when successfully gaining undetected access in VerifyPIN_5.

Figure 6 shows a condensed version of the synthesized controller for the attacker leading to an undetected "win" when performing two IS attacks. Each node in the figure contains the current value for PC along with the number of executed instructions, with each separate tree signifying different attacks that lead to the attacker winning. E.g., the top-left tree shows that if the attacker performs an instruction skip at `pc = 67` after 114 executed instructions, then they have two possible instruction skips that lead to them winning (at `pc = 118` after 211 executed instructions and at `pc = 120` after 213 executed instructions). The sum of all unique strategies is 12 meaning that an attack can perform 12 different attacks which grants undetected authentication with an incorrect PIN.

5 Related Work

To our knowledge, applying formal methods to model and analyse programs for vulnerabilities in regards to glitch attacks is not well explored. Some work [8, 9,16] is focused on simulation of hardware failures by modification of binary code. This approach is used to show that the program, under these conditions, no longer produces the expected result. This work is not validated by model checking and no bit-flips induced at runtime are accounted for. [4] uses UPPAAL

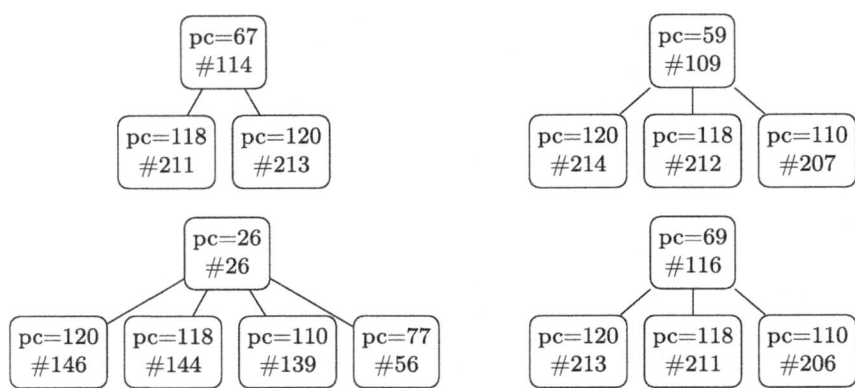

Fig. 6. Visualization of Instruction Skip attacks leading to undetected access when performed just after PC and after # instructions have been executed.

SMC to look at vulnerabilities in SUDO and OpenSSH but the developed models are at the level of basic blocks and the model only allows for the analysis of bit-flips in data flow.

Spensky et al. [15] has created the GlitchResistor tool for creating mitigations against glitch attacks in provided code during compilation. In this work they also remark that glitch attacks rarely succeed outside of controlled environments and require physical access to the targeted device. However, as shown in [1], Rowhammer attacks may be performed through software alone (even targeting stack and register values). Furthermore, this work shows a higher success rate than proposed in [15] when targeting real applications such as SUDO or OpenSSH.

Analysis of the FISSC programs has been done with the tools LAZART [14] and CELTIC [7]. These tools check robustness against high-level multiple transient hardware fault injections focusing on control flow modifications (E.g. inverting conditional checks). They utilise the symbolic execution engine KLEE to generate tests for each fault acting as counterexamples for undetected access. CELTIC performs instruction replacement where a single byte of code is replaced at runtime.

In [11], a Frama-C plugin is developed that integrates KLEE with LAZART. Security properties are specified as assertions within Frama-C, while faults are introduced by mutating the source code. A static dependency analysis is performed using Frama-C to identify relevant fault injection points. This analysis helps narrow down the faults to those that may impact the assertions. Once potential vulnerabilities are identified, attack strategies are generated and evaluated using KLEE.

6   Conclusion

In this paper we have created a platform that is useful for analysing the effects of glitch attacks on RISC-V code. This platform uses the UPPAAL tool suite to perform standard symbolic model checking queries, statistical queries, and synthesisation of controllers for attackers by modelling glitch attacks as timed games. Furthermore, the platform allows for the implementation of different kinds of attack strategies which is useful in bespoke scenarios or to optimise the exploration of vulnerabilities. We believe this shows the potential of formal verification as a tool for reasoning about glitch attacks, which can otherwise be difficult for developers to assess. This is strengthened by our nearly fully automatic platform that does not require special hardware and minimal model checking experience to use.

While standard model checking and statistical model checking can be used to ascertain interesting information about a given model, we also believe that modelling glitch attacks as games shows excellent promise and should be explored further. Our results highlight how different model checking approaches complement each other by tackling different aspects of the problem. For smaller problems, exhaustive model checking is feasible under some attack strategies, for larger programs SMC can be applied to manage the size of the problem. Furthermore, timed games can provide a comprehensive view of vulnerabilities and be used to create controllers that guide an attacker's actions in subsequent queries.

Acknowledgments. This work has been partially supported by the VILLUM Investigator grant S4OS (Scalable analysis and Synthesis of Safe, Secure and Optimal Strategies for Cyber-Physical Systems); the Digital Research Centre Denmark (DIREC) and Innovation Fund Denmark through the bridge project *Secure Internet of Things* (SIoT); and the *Full Stack Cybersecurity* project funded by Nationalt Forsvarsteknologisk Center (NFC).

References

1. Adiletta, A.J., Tol, M.C., Doröz, Y., Sunar, B.: Mayhem: targeted corruption of register and stack variables. In: Proceedings of the 19th ACM Asia Conference on Computer and Communications Security (ASIA CCS) (2024). https://doi.org/10.1145/3634737.3637638
2. Behrmann, G., Cougnard, A., David, A., Fleury, E., Larsen, K.G., Lime, D.: UPPAAL-Tiga: time for playing games! In: Damm, W., Hermanns, H (eds.) CAV 2007. LNCS, vol. 4590, pp. 121–125. Springer, Heidelberg (2007). https://doi.org/10.1007/978-3-540-73368-3_14
3. Behrmann, G., David, A., Larsen, K.G.: A tutorial on UPPAAL. In: Bernardo, M., Corradini, F. (eds.) SFM-RT 2004. LNCS, vol. 3185, pp. 200–236. Springer, Heidelberg (2004). https://doi.org/10.1007/978-3-540-30080-9_7
4. Bøgedal, T.W., Hansen, R.R., Larsen, K.G., Legay, A., Poulsen, D.B.: Statistical analysis of the impact of bit-flips in security critical code. In: Steffen, B. (ed.) AISoLA 2024. LNCS, vol. 15217, pp. 379–397. Springer, Cham (2024). https://doi.org/10.1007/978-3-031-75434-0_25

5. Bulychev, P.E., et al.: UPPAAL-SMC: statistical model checking for priced timed automata. In: Wiklicky, H., Massink, M. (eds.) Proceedings 10th Workshop on Quantitative Aspects of Programming Languages and Systems, QAPL 2012, Tallinn, Estonia, 31 March and 1 April 2012. EPTCS, vol. 85, pp. 1–16 (2012). https://doi.org/10.4204/EPTCS.85.1

6. Dureuil, L., Petiot, G., Potet, M.-L., Le, T.-H., Crohen, A., de Choudens, P.: FISSC: a fault injection and simulation secure collection. In: Skavhaug, A., Guiochet, J., Bitsch, F. (eds.) SAFECOMP 2016. LNCS, vol. 9922, pp. 3–11. Springer, Cham (2016). https://doi.org/10.1007/978-3-319-45477-1_1

7. Dureuil, L., Potet, M.-L., de Choudens, P., Dumas, C., Clédière, J.: From code review to fault injection attacks: filling the gap using fault model inference. In: Homma, N., Medwed, M. (eds.) CARDIS 2015. LNCS, vol. 9514, pp. 107–124. Springer, Cham (2016). https://doi.org/10.1007/978-3-319-31271-2_7

8. Given-Wilson, T., Jafri, N., Legay, A.: Combined software and hardware fault injection vulnerability detection. Innov. Syst. Softw. Eng. 16(2), 101–120 (2020). https://doi.org/10.1007/S11334-020-00364-5

9. Given-Wilson, T., Legay, A.: Formalising fault injection and countermeasures. In: Volkamer, M., Wressnegger, C. (eds.) ARES 2020: The 15th International Conference on Availability, Reliability and Security, Virtual Event, Ireland, 25–28 August 2020, pp. 22:1–22:11. ACM (2020). https://doi.org/10.1145/3407023.3407049

10. Kim, Y., et al.: Flipping bits in memory without accessing them: an experimental study of DRAM disturbance errors. In: Proceedings of the 41st ACM/IEEE International Symposium on Computer Architecture (ISCA 2014), pp. 361–372 (2014). https://doi.org/10.1109/ISCA.2014.6853210

11. Lacombe, G., Féliot, D., Boespflug, E., Potet, M.: Combining static analysis and dynamic symbolic execution in a toolchain to detect fault injection vulnerabilities. J. Cryptogr. Eng. 14(1), 147–164 (2024). https://doi.org/10.1007/S13389-023-00310-8

12. Moro, N., Heydemann, K., Encrenaz, E., Robisson, B.: Formal verification of a software countermeasure against instruction skip attacks. J. Cryptogr. Eng. 4(3), 145–156 (2014). https://doi.org/10.1007/S13389-014-0077-7

13. Murdock, K., Oswald, D.F., Garcia, F.D., Bulck, J.V., Gruss, D., Piessens, F.: Plundervolt: Software-based fault injection attacks against intel SGX. In: 2020 IEEE Symposium on Security and Privacy, SP 2020, San Francisco, CA, USA, 18–21 May 2020, pp. 1466–1482. IEEE (2020). https://doi.org/10.1109/SP40000.2020.00057

14. Potet, M., Mounier, L., Puys, M., Dureuil, L.: Lazart: a symbolic approach for evaluation the robustness of secured codes against control flow injections. In: Seventh IEEE International Conference on Software Testing, Verification and Validation, ICST 2014, 31 March–4 April 2014, Cleveland, Ohio, USA, pp. 213–222. IEEE Computer Society (2014). https://doi.org/10.1109/ICST.2014.34

15. Spensky, C., et al.: Glitching demystified: analyzing control-flow-based glitching attacks and defenses. In: 2021 51st Annual IEEE/IFIP International Conference on Dependable Systems and Networks (DSN), pp. 400–412 (2021). https://doi.org/10.1109/DSN48987.2021.00051

16. Zavalyshyn, I., Given-Wilson, T., Legay, A., Sadre, R.: Brief announcement: effectiveness of code hardening for fault-tolerant IoT software. In: Devismes, S., Mittal, N. (eds.) SSS 2020. LNCS, vol. 12514, pp. 317–322. Springer, Cham (2020). https://doi.org/10.1007/978-3-030-64348-5_25

Author Index

© The Editor(s) (if applicable) and The Author(s), under exclusive license
to Springer Nature Switzerland AG 2026
A. Remke and B. Steffen (Eds.): FMICS 2025, LNCS 16040, p. 297, 2026.
https://doi.org/10.1007/978-3-032-00942-5

The manufacturer's authorised representative in the EU is Springer
Nature Customer Service Centre GmbH, Europaplatz 3, 69115 Heidelberg,
Germany. If you have any concerns regarding our products, please
contact ProductSafety@springernature.com

Printed and bound by CPI Group (UK) Ltd, Croydon, CR0 4YY
28/04/2026
02098529-0001